ECCE ROMANI III

A LATIN READING PROGRAM

FROM REPUBLIC TO EMPIRE

FOURTH EDITION

This North American edition of *Ecce Romani* is based on *Ecce Romani: A Latin Reading Course,* originally prepared by The Scottish Classics Group © copyright The Scottish Classics Group 1971, 1982, and published in the United Kingdom by Oliver and Boyd, a division of Longman Group. This edition has been prepared by American educators and authors:

Ronald B. Palma, Holland School, Tulsa, Oklahoma
David J. Perry, Rye High School, Rye, New York
Revision Editor: Gilbert Lawall, University of Massachusetts, Amherst, Massachusetts

Acknowledgments: Grateful acknowledgment is made to the following for copyrighted material:
New Directions Publishing Corporation
"Landscape With The Fall of Icarus" by William Carlos Williams from *Collected Poems 1939–1962, Volume II.* Copyright © 1962 by William Carlos Williams. Reprinted by permission of New Directions Publishing Corp.
"Institutio Oratoria VIII.6.62–63" by Quintillian from INSTITUTIO ORATORIA translated by John Selby Watson.

Note: Every effort has been made to locate the copyright owner of material reproduced in this component. Omissions brought to our attention will be corrected in subsequent editions.

David J. Perry, for preparing the text on computer and for creating the initial arrangement of the text and graphics
Professor Gilbert Lawall, who improved the presentation of several items and helped make Book III consistent with other parts of the ECCE ROMANI program
Professor Richard A. LaFleur, who helped refine many of the exercises

Cover image: (*top left*): © SuperStock, Inc./SuperStock; (*top right*): © SEF/Art Resource, NY; (*bottom*): © **Araldo De Luca**

Maps: John Burgoyne

Savvas Learning Company LLC, 15 East Midland Avenue, Paramus, NJ 07652

Attributions of third party content appear on pages 356–358, which constitute an extension of this copyright page.

ISBN-13: 978-0-13-361090-1
ISBN-10: 0-13-361090-X
24 22

Authors

Ronald B. Palma
Holland Hall School
Tulsa, Oklahoma

David J. Perry
Rye High School
Rye, New York

Series Editor

Gilbert Lawall
Professor Emeritus of Classics
University of Massachusetts, Amherst, Massachusetts

Consultants

Timothy S. Abney
Marquette High School
Chesterfield, Missouri

Jim Bigger
McLean High School
McLean, Virginia

Melissa Schons Bishop
Windermere, Florida

Peter C. Brush
Deerfield Academy
Deerfield, Massachusetts

Gail A. Cooper
Academy of the New Church
Bryn Athyn, Pennsylvania

Dennis De Young
Montgomery Bell Academy
Nashville, Tennessee

Sally Hatcher
Winsor School
Boston, Massachusetts

Anthony L.C. Hollingsworth
Roger Williams University
Bristol, Rhode Island

Dexter Hoyos
Sydney University
Sydney, Australia

Joan C. Jahnige
Kentucky Educational Television
Lexington, Kentucky

Caroline Switzer Kelly
Covenant Day School
Charlotte, North Carolina

Richard A. LaFleur
University of Georgia
Athens, Georgia

Donald H. Mills
Syracuse University
Syracuse, New York

Andrew Schacht
St. Luke's School
New Canaan, Connecticut

The Scottish Classics Group
Edinburgh, Scotland

Judith Lynn Sebesta
University of South Dakota
Vermillion, South Dakota

David M. Tafe
Rye Country Day School
Rye, New York

Contents

VI: Two Authors of the Early Empire 285

LXXV: The Millionaire 289

LXXVI: The Death of Pliny the Elder 297

Reference Materials

Maps and Plans

INTRODUCTION

You are about to begin Book III, the final book in the *Ecce Romani* series. This book marks an important point in your study of Latin, for you can now begin to read extensively in the works of ancient Roman authors.

Ecce Romani was designed to give you contact with Roman authors from the beginning of the course. In Book I, this took the form of short Latin items such as graffiti and inscriptions. In Book II you read some short poems of Catullus and Martial. You also read some material that was taken from ancient sources and adapted (that is, changed to use only grammar and vocabulary that you had learned), such as the stories of Pyramus and Thisbe and Androcles and the Lion. You may also have read the unadapted extracts from Roman authors such as Ovid, Cicero, Pliny, and Aulus Gellius that appear in Language Activity Book II.

As you move into Book III, you will be dealing only with unadapted Latin; none of the readings has been simplified, although many of them are extracts from longer works. You will also be studying Roman history and politics in greater depth than you have before. Book III begins with selections from a short account (*Breviarium*) of Roman history by the historian Eutropius. It continues with selections from some of the most important authors who lived at the end of the Republic and during the early Empire, including Cicero, Caesar, the emperor Augustus, Suetonius, and Pliny. You will also be introduced to Latin poetry through the writings of Catullus, Ovid, Vergil, and Horace—some of the finest poets in Western civilization.

Reading authentic Latin is rewarding, since you are communicating directly with people who lived in a time and culture very different from your own. It can also be challenging. We have carefully designed Book III as a transitional reader that will give you as much help as possible as you develop your reading skills. This volume is different in some ways from Books I and II of *Ecce Romani*; the new features, such as the readings with facing vocabulary, are described in detail on page 6. Before beginning the reading selections, it is very important to take time to study the reading process described on pages 7–11; you will find that it builds on the skills you have developed in the course of Books I and II. If you practice these strategies consistently, you will become much more skillful at reading authentic Latin texts. **Bonam fortūnam!**

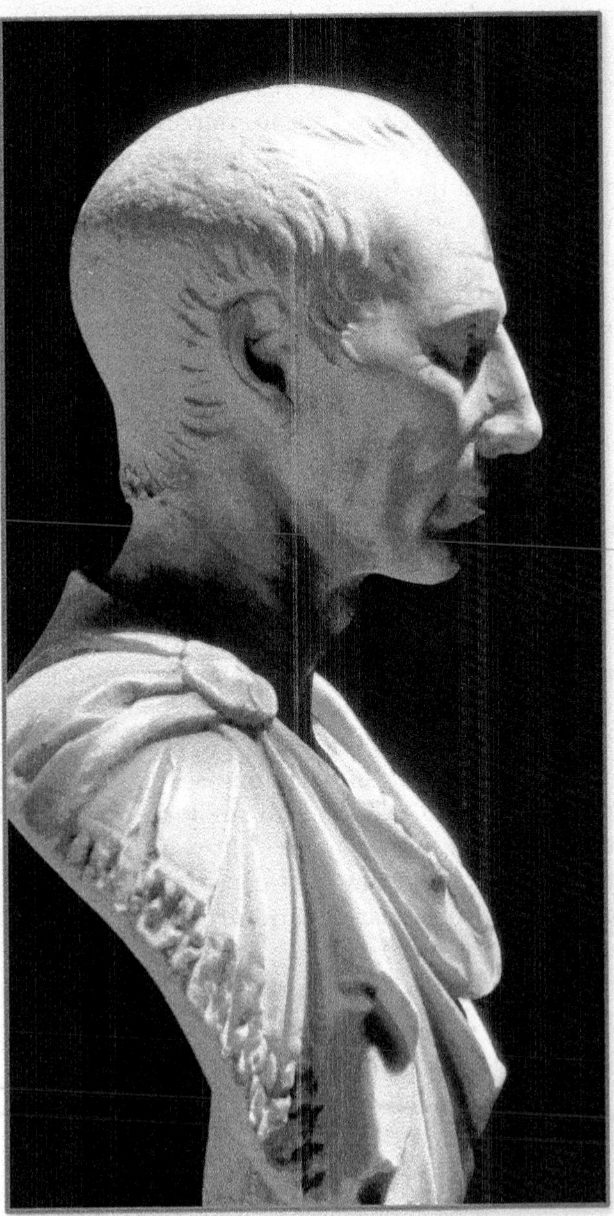

A statue of Julius Caesar, one of the pivotal figures in Roman history and the focus of the Latin readings in Chapter 55
Bust, Julius Caesar

THE END OF THE REPUBLIC AND THE ESTABLISHMENT OF THE PRINCIPATE

Book III is divided into six Parts, each of which focuses on a particular period of Roman history or on certain authors. Part I contains selections from a short handbook of Roman history, the *Breviarium* of Eutropius, and has the following objectives:

- to provide an overview of Roman history between 63 B.C. (Cicero's consulship) and A.D. 14 (death of Augustus)
- to make the transition from reading stories about the Cornelian family to the reading of authentic Latin; see How to Read Latin on pages 6–11 as well as the Reading Notes and Building the Meaning sections throughout Part I
- to review some important grammatical topics first presented in Book II

Background on Roman History and Politics

The Roman Political System

According to tradition, Rome was founded in 753 B.C. by Romulus, who was its first king. Six kings ruled after him; the last one, Tarquinius Superbus, was expelled in 509 B.C. A form of government now referred to as the Republic was then established. Under this government, laws were passed by the assembly of the people and approved by the Senate; the executive branch was headed by two officials known as consuls, who were elected annually for one-year terms. As time went on, additional offices were created: praetors, who served as judges; aediles, who supervised roads, sewers, water supplies, and food supplies; tribunes, who protected the common people against oppression by the nobility; and quaestors, who handled government finances.

An ambitious young politician would often serve as an army officer; he would then return to Rome and run for quaestor. He would advance as far as he could through the sequence of offices (quaestor, tribune, aedile, praetor, and consul), which was known as the **cursus honōrum**. These offices were for a term of one year, with no re-election.

By the mid-second century B.C., Rome was a major power with a large empire, and her system of government was no longer adequate. Why did the system fail? It is hard to give a simple answer to this question, but we can say that this failure resulted from two factors: the nature of Roman politics itself and changes in the values of the Roman upper class.

The Romans did not have political parties in the sense that most modern states do; rather, each individual strove to advance himself by acquiring as much prestige (**dignitās**) and influence (**auctōritās**) as he could. The individual achieved this prestige and influence by being elected to higher and higher offices in the **cursus honōrum**, by becoming a member of the Senate, and by serving the state in other ways, such as governing a province. The individual aristocrat was helped in his quest for **dignitās** by his **amīcī**, people who did favors for him and whom he helped in return, and by his **clientēs**, people of lower social standing who depended on him and who supported him in his political campaigns. Roman politics was—to put it simplistically—the maneuvering by various groups of **amīcī** to advance their own cause. Eventually this maneuvering got out of hand and led to civil war.

The second factor was the value system of the Roman aristocracy. In early Rome, the nobles did not flaunt their wealth in luxurious living but rather considered self-sacrificing service to the state the highest activity. As time went on, Rome became a major power and was no longer threatened with destruction from external enemies; at the same time, the upper classes became richer and richer. Although they still kept service to the state as an ideal, in reality they devoted more and more effort to gratifying themselves. However, this gratification came not only from wealth, but from prestige. By the first century B.C., some ambitious Romans were no longer willing to work within the traditional political system if it denied them the prestige and power they sought; instead, they seized power by force. The result was a gradual breakdown in law and order, leading ultimately to a series of civil wars and a reform of the government.

From Marius to the Death of Caesar

Gaius Marius was a military hero who held the consulship seven times between 107 and 86 B.C. He also introduced the idea of a professional army, with soldiering as a career. Over time, this change caused soldiers to shift their allegiance from the state as a whole to their own general, who paid them and saw to it that they were well looked after. In 88 B.C., Marius became embroiled in a bitter quarrel with Cornelius Sulla about who would command a war in the East. This quarrel turned into a civil war in which Sulla, acting on behalf of the Senate, killed hundreds of Marius' supporters and reorganized the government so that the Senate would be more firmly in control (83–79 B.C.). The next sign of unrest came in 63 B.C. when an ambitious aristocrat named Catiline formed a conspiracy to seize control of Rome; this was exposed and suppressed by the consul Cicero.

Not long after, the general Gnaeus Pompeius (Pompey) returned victorious from the East. He asked the Senate to make permanent his arrangements for the government of several provinces and to grant land to his veterans. The Senate refused. Pompey therefore formed a private arrangement with Marcus Crassus, the wealthiest man in Rome, and Julius Caesar, an ambitious man who was not popular with the Senate and therefore stood little chance of becoming consul. This arrangement is known as the *First Triumvirate*. The three men together were influential enough to secure the election of Caesar as consul for 59 B.C. When the Senate continued to balk at fulfilling Pompey's demands, the triumvirs used armed gangs to keep their opponents away from the voting. Milo and Clodius were two leaders of such gangs.

Caesar manipulated the system of assignments so that he would become governor of the province of Gaul (**Gallia**) after his year as consul. At this time the Romans controlled only a part of the Alps and the southern coast of France; the rest of France, Switzerland, and Belgium (all of which were included in the area called **Gallia**) were outside the Roman sphere. During his nine years as governor, Caesar conquered all the rest of Gaul. He obtained not only a reputation as a skillful general, but also a large amount of money from the sale of slaves and other loot.

The Triumvirate continued to function while Caesar was in Gaul. Crassus became governor of Syria in 54 B.C. but he was soon killed in battle against the Parthians. Pompey remained in Rome, where disorder reigned due to the activities of such political hooligans as the rivals Milo and Clodius. The Senate finally gave Pompey extraordinary powers to end the political violence, which he did; Milo's bodyguards had murdered Clodius in January of 52 B.C., and Pompey had Milo tried for the murder and exiled. (You will read more about this trial in Chapters 64 and 65.)

Caesar was now approaching the end of his governorship of Gaul. You will read in the Latin texts in Chapter 55 how Caesar became sole ruler of the Roman world and how he died. You will then read how his grandnephew, Gaius Octavius, took over leadership of Caesar's followers and himself became sole ruler, under the title Augustus, from 27 B.C. onward.

Augustus Establishes the Principate

Augustus recognized that there had to be a fundamental change in the structure of Roman government. Rule by one man seemed the only way to avoid the factional strife that had plagued Rome for the previous hundred years. Augustus set himself up as this one ruler under the title **prīnceps**, *first citizen*; this form of government is known as the Principate or the Empire. In Part IV of this book, you will read part of Augustus' own account of his principate, the *Res gestae*, and you will look more closely at Augustus and how he managed to make his one-man rule acceptable to the majority of citizens.

Under the Principate, the Senate and the old republican offices (consul, praetor, aedile, and the rest) continued seemingly unchanged, but the real power was concentrated in the hands of the **prīnceps**. Some emperors got along well with the Senate and gave it a large share in the government; others distrusted it and ruled almost entirely through their own agents, who were often freedmen. But, for better or worse, it was under this form of government that the Roman world continued until the last emperor was deposed by the advancing barbarians in A.D. 476.

Eutropius the Historian

We know very little about Eutropius, the historian whose work appears in Part I. He was born sometime around A.D. 340 and later took part in the Persian campaign of the Emperor Julian in 363. He wrote a short handbook of Roman history in ten chapters, entitled *Breviarium ab urbe condita*. It covered Roman history from the foundation of the city by Romulus in 753 B.C. to the death of the Emperor Jovian in A.D. 364, and it was completed by 380. The *Breviarium* has been admired ever since its completion as a straightforward, evenhanded account of Roman history.

How to Read Latin

Helps Provided in This Book

We have included many features designed to help you make the transition into authentic readings and become more skillful at comprehending Latin.

- Because the readings in this volume are unadapted, many new words occur in them. We have therefore arranged the readings on right-hand pages only, with running vocabulary lists and notes on the facing left-hand pages.
- The texts are punctuated and capitalized as English texts would be; punctuation in particular is helpful when reading long, complicated sentences. But remember that the Romans did not use such devices; modern editors put them in.
- After each reading selection there are comprehension questions in English.
- There are a number of Reading Notes and Building the Meaning sections. Some of these review important grammatical topics from Books I and II, some introduce new grammar, and others—the most important ones—provide help in improving your reading skills, building on the reading strategies you learned in Books I and II.

The running vocabulary lists contain all words that were not presented for mastery in Books I and II. (A few mastery words from Books I and II that were not used frequently in the earlier books are also included in the lists.) Words new in Book III that should be learned for mastery are marked with an asterisk (*), as are any repeated mastery words from Books I and II. Such asterisked words should be thoroughly learned, since they are normally not given again in the running vocabularies.

In the vocabulary entries, the most literal or most basic meanings of a word are given first. These are the meanings you should commit to memory as you build up your vocabulary. Any special meanings required by the context appear last.

Italics are used for all translations in the vocabularies and notes; information in regular type is an explanation, not a translation. Observe this distinction carefully.

Steps to Effective Reading

1. Read through the entire sentence, paying careful attention to its structure.
   1a. Notice what information the ending on each word *as you meet it* gives about its form and its use in the sentence.
   1b. Think about what you may expect to find later in the sentence, given what you already have.
   1c. Observe whether the sentence is divided into smaller units, such as clauses or phrases. If so, where do these units begin and end? Do not mix words from one unit with those of another.
   1d. Unless the sentence is very simple, you will probably need to reread it; do so as many times as you need to until you have a good idea how the sentence is structured.
2. After you have completed Step 1, look at the vocabulary and notes given on the left-hand page.
   2a. You will find the meanings of words that are new. You may look up any other words whose meaning you do not know in the end vocabulary at this point.
   2b. The vocabulary entry may help you resolve any uncertainty about forms; the genitive clearly shows to which declension a noun belongs and the infinitive indicates the conjugation of a verb.
   2c. Some of the notes help you with grammar or sentence structure.
   2d. Other notes give you background information that will help you understand the sentence.
3. Now reread the Latin sentence, keeping in mind what you learned from the vocabulary and notes. Reread again if necessary. Even experienced readers of Latin often reread sentences (or parts of sentences) several times, so do not hesitate to do this.
4. On the basis of what you understand so far, answer the comprehension questions.
5. If you feel comfortable answering the comprehension questions, you may translate the sentence into English. Do not try to translate until you have worked carefully through the sentence, following the steps suggested here. You must understand the sentence before you can produce an accurate equivalent in English.

> Always consider endings and sentence structure first, then the meanings of words.

Active Reading

The steps given in the preceding section show that reading is an *active* process. You need to think analytically about each word as you meet it to determine what information you know (or what uncertainties remain to be resolved) and what you may expect later in the sentence. You will remember doing this sort of thing if you have used a reading card in earlier chapters. These three questions will help you read actively:

WHAT FORM IS THIS WORD? For instance, the final **-ō** on **cōgitō** indicates first person singular since it is a verb, while the **-ō** on **annō** indicates dative or ablative singular since **annō** is a second declension noun. Some endings such as **-ō** or **-ēs** are ambiguous and must be interpreted in light of other elements in the sentence or clause.

HOW IS THIS WORD BEING USED? Given what you already have in the sentence, what function does the word serve? For instance, an accusative noun is often a direct object, but may also be part of an accusative and infinitive phrase.

WHAT ELSE CAN I EXPECT IN THE SENTENCE? For instance, a preposition will require an object in the accusative or ablative, while a subordinating conjunction such as **ut** will be completed by a verb.

The First Sentence: Modeling the Process

Here is the first sentence that you will meet in Chapter 55, followed by comments that show how to implement the suggested steps.

> M. Tulliō Cicerōne ōrātōre et C. Antōniō cōnsulibus, annō ab urbe conditā sexcentēsimō nōnāgēsimō prīmō, L. Sergius Catilīna, nōbilissimī generis vir sed ingeniī prāvissimī, ad dēlendam patriam coniūrāvit cum quibusdam clārīs quidem sed audācibus virīs.

Step 1. As you read the sentence initially (rereading if necessary) you should notice the following, *even without knowing the meaning of all the words.*

M. Tulliō . . . cōnsulibus: the comma suggests that these words go together to make a phrase; you may not be certain at this point whether all the nouns are dative or ablative.

annō: this word could be dative or ablative, but its meaning suggests that it is probably ablative, expressing time when.

ab urbe conditā: you expect **ab** to be completed by an ablative noun, an expectation fulfilled by **urbe**; **urbe** is feminine so **conditā** clearly modifies **urbe** (not **annō**); you may remember that this phrase is used to express a year.

sexcentēsimō nōnāgēsimō prīmō: these appear to be adjectives in the ablative, modifying **annō**; the comma suggests that the phrase ends after **nōnō.**

L. Sergius Catilīna: a name, in the nominative; probably the subject of a singular verb.

nōbilissimī generis: nōbilissimī could be nominative plural or genitive singular; the fact that it comes next to **generis**, which can only be genitive, suggests that **nōbilissimī** is genitive also; the genitive usually modifies a noun, and the comma after **Catilīna** suggests that this genitive does not describe **Catilīna** but a noun that will come later in the sentence.

vir: here is the noun that **nōbilissimī generis** describes; **vir** is nominative, so it probably refers to or describes **Catilīna.**

ingeniī prāvissimī: another genitive; the word **sed** helps us realize that there are two contrasting phrases that modify **vir**; the comma suggests that the phrase ends after **prāvissimī.**

ad dēlendam patriam: you expect an accusative to complete **ad**, and **dēlendam** clearly modifies **patriam**; you have not yet learned the form **dēlendam**, so you cannot be sure of its meaning at this point.

coniūrāvit: the singular verb that we expect to find based on seeing the nominative singular subject **L. Sergius Catilīna** earlier in the sentence.

cum quibusdam clārīs quidem sed audācibus virīs: the ablatives show that **cum** is the preposition *with* (not the conjunction).

Now check the vocabulary and notes, printed on page 12 (Step 2). In addition to the meanings of new words, you learn that the first phrase (**M. Tulliō . . . cōnsulibus**) is a kind of ablative absolute that tells the year, and you receive help with **dēlendam**, since you have not yet learned this form. Reread the sentence again as often as you need to (Step 3) until the meaning becomes clear. At this point you should be able to answer the comprehension questions (Step 4) and finally translate into English (Step 5).

Dividing Texts into Sense Units

Separating long sentences into shorter segments is one effective way to make comprehension easier, particuarly as you make the transition into reading authentic Latin. Your teacher may provide such texts for you or ask you to do this for yourself in class. As an example, here is the first sentence printed in sense units:

    M. Tulliō Cicerōne ōrātōre et C. Antōniō cōnsulibus,
    annō ab urbe conditā sexcentēsimō nōnāgēsimō prīmō,
L. Sergius Catilīna,
    nōbilissimī generis vir sed ingeniī prāvissimī,
ad dēlendam patriam coniūrāvit
    cum quibusdam clārīs quidem sed audācibus virīs.

- The core elements of the sentence, the subject **L. Sergius Catilīna** and the verb **coniūrāvit**, are at the left.
- Descriptive elements of the sentence, such as the ablative absolute, the ablative of time when, and the prepositional phrase introduced by **cum** are indented. These elements provide additional information but are subordinate to, or less important than, the subject and main verb.
- The word **vir**, which is in apposition to the subject, and its two genitive modifiers are also indented since they are descriptive, subordinate elements.

Review of Latin Sentence Structure

You noticed that the example above consists of one long sentence and that the sentence was broken down into smaller units, each of which contributed something to the meaning of the whole sentence. Comprehension occurs most easily when you break up such long sentences into shorter units. You can grasp the meaning of each short unit and then integrate each one into the sentence as a whole, as you read and reread the sentence. In English, we break sentences into smaller units without thinking about it. Learning to do this in Latin is an essential part of becoming a skillful reader of Latin. In order to do this, you need to know the kinds of subunits that you may find in a sentence.

Basic Sentence Patterns

Since Chapter 4, you have known about the core elements of sentences: the subject, the verb (transitive, intransitive, or linking), the complement, and the direct object. All Latin sentences are built on one of the following five patterns, which were presented in Book I.

1. Subject and intransitive verb: **Mīlitēs pugnant.**
2. Subject, linking verb, and complement: **Mīlitēs sunt dēfessī.**
3. The verb **esse** stating the existence of something: **Sunt multae arborēs in silvā.**
4. Subject, transitive verb, and direct object: **Caesar mūnera dedit.**
   4a. Pattern 4 may be expanded by adding an object in the dative case: **Caesar mūnera populō dedit.**
   4b. Pattern 4 may be modified by being put into the passive voice: **Mūnera ā Caesare data sunt.**
5. Subject, dative, and intransitive verb: **Populus prīncipī favet.**

Expansion of the Basic Pattern

Any of the basic patterns may be expanded by adding modifiers.

- Nouns are modified by adjectives, by other nouns in the genitive, by relative clauses, or by participles.
- Verbs are modified by adverbs, by prepositional phrases, or by nouns in the ablative without prepositions (including ablative absolutes).

Combining Two Sentences into One

Two basic sentences may be combined into one longer sentence. In such cases, a sentence usually has two or more clauses; each clause has its own core elements. Two equal clauses are connected by coordinating conjunctions such as **et**, **-que**, and **sed**.

Māter magnā vōce vocābat. Līberī domum nōn rediērunt.
→ Māter magnā vōce vocābat, sed līberī domum nōn rediērunt.

One clause may be of greater importance (the main clause) and have one or more clauses dependent on it (subordinate clauses). Subordinate clauses are introduced by subordinating conjunctions, such as **cum, dum, postquam**, or **sī** or by a relative pronoun (**quī, quae, quod**).

Māter magnā vōce vocābat. Līberī domum nōn rediērunt.
→ Quamquam māter magnā vōce vocābat, līberī domum nōn rediērunt.

Other ways of combining two simple ideas into one complex one include participles and ablative absolutes.

Līberī, ā mātre vocātī, tandem domum rediērunt.

Mātre vocante, līberī domum rediērunt.

As a reader, one of your most important tasks is to avoid mixing words that belong to one unit with those that belong to another. As explained on page 9, texts may be arranged according to sense units to clarify the structure of the sentences. Sense units printed on separate lines typically include: the main clause(s); subordinate clauses; ablative absolutes; and participial phrases. Other units such as prepositional phrases or noun phrases without prepositions (ablative of means, of time when; accusative of duration of time, etc.) may be printed on a separate line if they are long and complex; when short and simple they are found on the line with the rest of the clause in which they occur.

Here is another example from Chapter 55:

Britannīs mox bellum intulit,	[main clause]
quibus ante eum nē nōmen quidem	[subordinate clause, indented]
Rōmānōrum cognitum erat,	
eōsque victōs,	[another main clause; the **-que** shows that a new clause begins]
obsidibus acceptīs,	[ablative absolute, indented]
stīpendiāriōs fēcit.	[conclusion of the second main clause]

For a while you may work with texts in sense units since they are easier for you to comprehend as you begin to read the works of Roman authors. Your ultimate goal, however, should be to make these divisions in your head as you read, without seeing them on paper.

1 **M. Tulliō . . . cōnsulibus**: ablative absolute, *during the consulship of Marcus Tullius Cicero the orator and Gaius Antonius* (63 B.C.). Since the consuls were elected annually, naming them identified the year. The other way of expressing the year was the **ab urbe conditā** method found in the next clause.

C. Antōniō: this Gaius Antonius was the uncle of the famous Marc Antony. Note that the Romans always abbreviated **praenōmina** in writing. See the Reading Note on page 17 for a list of these abbreviations.

***condō, condere, condidī, conditus**, *to establish, found.*

ab urbe conditā: *from the founding of the city.* Rome was supposedly founded in 753 B.C.

sexcentēsimus, -a, -um, *600th.*

2 **nōnāgēsimus, -a, -um**, *90th.*

Catilīna: note that this cognomen is masculine even though it is in the first declension.

***genus, generis**, n., *race, class, family.*

***ingenium, -ī**, n., *intelligence, ingenuity, character.*

3 **prāvus, -a, -um**, *depraved, corrupt.* The genitive phrase **ingeniī prāvissimī** goes with **vir**.

ad dēlendam: *for the purpose of destroying, to destroy.*

***patria, -ae**, f., *country, fatherland.*

***coniūrō, -āre, -āvī, -ātūrus**, *to plot, make a conspiracy, conspire.* You will read more about this conspiracy in Chapter 59.

***clārus, -a, -um**, *well-known, distinguished.*

4 **urbe**: = **ex urbe**. The preposition is not used because it is already present in the compound verb **expulsus est**. Note that **urbe** does not agree with **Cicerōne**, although both are ablative.

***socius, -ī**, m., *comrade, ally, associate.*

eius: = **Catilīnae**.

dēprehendō, dēprehendere, dēprehendī, dēprehēnsus, *to seize, catch, arrest.*

carcer, carceris, m., *prison.*

5 **victus**: from **vincō**. When you meet this verb, be careful to note whether the form is active or passive, since the meaning of "he defeated (someone else)" is very different from "he was defeated," i.e., he lost.

***proelium, -ī**, n., *battle.*

***interficiō, interficere, interfēcī, interfectus**, *to kill.*

Quō usque tandem abūtēre, Catilīna, patientiā nostrā? *For how long will you abuse our patience, Catiline?* (Cicero, *In Catilinam* I.1)

LV

The Late Republic

A. Cicero and Caesar

M. Tulliō Cicerōne ōrātōre et C. Antōniō cōnsulibus, annō ab urbe conditā sexcentēsimō nōnāgēsimō prīmō, L. Sergius Catilīna, nōbilissimī generis vir sed ingeniī prāvissimī, ad dēlendam patriam coniūrāvit cum quibusdam clārīs quidem sed audācibus virīs. Ā Cicerōne urbe expulsus est. Sociī eius dēprehēnsī in carcere strangulātī sunt. Ab Antōniō, alterō cōnsule, Catilīna ipse victus proeliō est interfectus.

—Eutropius, *Breviarium* VI.15

1. When did these events take place? (1–2)
2. How is Catiline described? (2–3)
3. What kind of people were involved in Catiline's conspiracy? (3–4)
4. How did Cicero deal with Catiline? (4)
5. What happened to Catiline's associates? (4–5)
6. What two things finally happened to Catiline? (5)

This late nineteenth century mural, located in the building that houses the modern Italian Senate, shows Cicero delivering his first speech against Catiline.

Cicero Accusing Catiline of Conspiracy in the Senate (October 21, 63 B.C.) *Fresco, Cesare Maccari*

6 **nōnāgēsimō**: deduce from **octōgēsimō** (2).
*__posteā__, adv., *afterward, later on.*
7 *__imperō, -āre, -āvī, -ātus__, *to order; to rule, hold supreme power.*
quī posteā imperāvit: i.e., as dictator, a title he assumed in 46 B.C.
L. Bibulō: Eutropius has confused Lucius Bibulus with his father, Marcus Calpurnius Bibulus, who was Caesar's colleague as consul.
*__fīō, fierī, factus sum__, *to be made, be done; to happen; to become*; **est factus**: = **factus est.**

dēcernō, dēcernere, dēcrēvī, dēcrētus, *to decide, assign.*
dēcrēta est: after their year in office was over, both consuls and praetors were usually sent to be governors of provinces.
Gallia, -ae, f., *Gaul* (an area including France, Belgium, Switzerland, and northern Italy).
Illyricum, -ī, n., *Illyricum* (a Roman province on the eastern shore of the Adriatic Sea, including the modern countries of Croatia, Bosnia, and Montenegro; see map on page 18).
8 *__legiō, legiōnis__, f., *legion* (military unit of 3,000–5,000 men).

Helvētiī, -ōrum, m. pl., *the Helvetians* (a Gallic tribe living in what is now Switzerland).
*__appellō, -āre, -āvī, -ātus__, *to call by name, name.*
vincendō: *by conquering.*
9 *__bellum, -ī__, n., *war.*
*__usque__, adv., *continuously, as far as, up to.*
Ōceanum Britannicum: the English Channel.

domō, domāre, domuī, domitus, *to tame, subdue, conquer.*
10 *__ferē__, adv., *almost, nearly.*
*__flūmen, flūminis__, n., *river.*
Rhodanus, -ī, m., *the Rhone River* in southern France (see the map on page 23).
Rhēnus, -ī, m., *the Rhine River*, the traditional boundary between Gaul and Germany.
11 *__pateō, patēre, patuī__, *to be open, be accessible.*
(quae) circuitū patet: *which stretches in circumference*; **omnem Galliam** is the antecedent.
*__bis__, adv., *twice.*
bis et triciēs centēna mīlia passuum: *3,200 miles*, literally, 2 (x 100) + 30 (x 100).
mīlia passuum: a Roman mile was 1000 paces; *miles* is expressed by the plural phrase **mīlia passuum**, *thousands of paces.*

12 *__bellum īnferre__, idiom + dat., *to make war upon.*
cognitus, -a, -um + dat., *known (to).*
eōs: = **Britannōs.**
13 **obses, obsidis**, m., *hostage.*
obsidibus acceptīs: ablative absolute. The tribes gave Caesar hostages to guarantee they would abide by the agreement. If they broke the treaty, the Romans could kill the hostages. Such use of hostages was a regular custom among ancient peoples.
stīpendiārius, -a, -um, *tributary, paying tribute, subject to tribute.*

Galliae: dative with **imperāvit**, *he levied on Gaul;* *__imperō, -āre, -āvē, -ātus__ + dat., *to order.*
tribūtum, -ī, n., *tribute, tax.*
tribūtī nōmine: *by way of a tax, as a tax.*
annuus, -a, -um, *annual, yearly.*
14 **stīpendium, -ī**, n., deduce from **stīpendiārius**, above.
quadringentiēs, adv., *400 times* (400 x 100,000 sesterces = 40,000,000 sesterces).

aggredior, aggredī, aggressus sum, *to attack.*
*__immānis, -is, -e__, *huge, immense, extensive.*

Annō urbis conditae sexcentēsimō nōnāgēsimō quīntō C. Iūlius Caesar, quī posteā imperāvit, cum L. Bibulō cōnsul est factus. Dēcrēta est eī Gallia et Illyricum cum legiōnibus decem. Is prīmus vīcit Helvētiōs, quī nunc Sēquanī appellantur, deinde vincendō per bella gravissima usque ad Ōceanum Britannicum prōcessit. Domuit autem annīs novem ferē omnem Galliam, quae inter Alpēs, flūmen Rhodanum, Rhēnum et Ōceanum est et circuitū patet ad bis et triciēs centēna mīlia passuum. Britannīs mox bellum intulit, quibus ante eum nē nōmen quidem Rōmānōrum cognitum erat, eōsque victōs, obsidibus acceptīs, stīpendiāriōs fēcit. Galliae autem tribūtī nōmine annuum imperāvit stīpendium quadringentiēs. Germānōsque trāns Rhēnum aggressus immānissimīs proeliīs vīcit.

—Eutropius, *Breviarium* VI.17

---

7. What did Caesar accomplish in the year 59 B.C.? (6–7)
8. To what area of the Roman Empire was Caesar assigned as governor? (7)
9. What did he do first? (8)
10. How far did he extend his conquests? (9)
11. What did Caesar accomplish within nine years? (9–10)
12. What had the Britons known about the Romans previously? (12)
13. What three things did Caesar do to the Britons? (12–13)
14. What did Caesar impose on Gaul? (13–14)
15. What happened to the Germans who lived across the Rhine? (14–15)

Reading Note

Interpreting et and -que

Recognizing where clauses begin and end is an important part of reading complex Latin. The conjunctions **et** and **-que** require special attention. Compare these two examples:

> Caesar **et** Bibulus cōnsulēs factī sunt.
> *Caesar **and** Bibulus became consuls.*

> Caesar Britanniam aggressus est **et** Britannī eī obsidēs dedērunt.
> *Caesar attacked Britain **and** the British gave him hostages.*

In the first example, **et** joins two nouns inside one main clause. In the second example, **et** joins two clauses in a compound sentence and the **et** marks the beginning of the second clause. Here are two examples using -**que**:

> Caesar vīcit Helvētiōs multōs**que** aliās nātiōnēs.
> *Caesar conquered the Helvetians **and** many other tribes.*

> Britannī ferōciter resistēbant excessit**que** ex īnsulā Caesar.
> *The British resisted fiercely **and** Caesar left the island.*

1 __hinc__, adv., _from here; next._
__succēdō, succēdere, successī, successūrus__, _to follow, succeed._
__exsecrandus, -a, -um__, _accursed, detestable._
__lacrimābilis, -is, -e__, _lamentable._
__quō__: _through which, by means of which_; take with __mūtāta est__ (line 2).
__praeter__, prep. + acc., _beyond, in addition to._

2 *__populus, -ī__, m., _people._
*__fortūna, -ae__, f., _fortune, luck._
*__mūtō, -āre, -āvī, -ātus__, _to change._ Eutropius means that the __calamitātēs__, deaths of individuals and destruction of property, were surpassed by the changed __fortūna__ of the whole state. He may be thinking of the fact that Caesar's assumption of absolute power as dictator paved the way for the development of imperial rule by his successor Octavian Augustus, one of the most important changes in Roman history.

3 __rediēns__: the present participle of __redīre__.
*__victor__: this noun, in apposition to __Caesar__ (2), can be translated _as victor_ or _victorious._
*__coepī, coepisse, coeptus__ (used in perfect, pluperfect, and future perfect only), _to begin._
*__poscō, poscere, poposcī__, _to demand._
*__cōnsulātus, -ūs__, m., _consulship._
__dubietās, dubietātis__, f., _doubt, hesitation._

4 *__aliquī, aliquae, aliquod__, _some, any._
__sine dubietāte aliquā__: i.e., Caesar was insisting on receiving another consulship, even though he knew there would be much opposition from his political opponents.
*__dēferō, dēferre, dētulī, dēlātus__, irreg., _to carry down; to offer, confer._

__Contrādictum est__: an impersonal expression, _It was opposed, There was opposition._

5 __iussusque__: supply __est__, _and he was ordered._ The Senate took this vote on 1 January 49 B.C.
__dīmissīs__: deduce from __dis-__ + __mittō__. It was illegal for Caesar to bring his army out of his own province, the southern boundary of which was the Rubicon River in northern Italy.
*__exercitus, -ūs__, m., _army._

*__iniūria, -ae__, f., _injury, injustice._
__Propter quam iniūriam__: _Because of this injustice._ The "injustice" was from Caesar's point of view; there was no reason that Caesar had to be granted a second consulship.

6 __Arīminum, -ī__, n., _Ariminum_ (a town near the Rubicon River, modern Rimini; see map on page 18).
__adversum__, prep. + acc., _against._
__adversum . . . vēnit__: on 10 January 49, Caesar led his troops across the Rubicon River, thereby making civil war inevitable. He spoke the famous words __Ālea iacta est__, _The die has been cast_, to describe the irrevocable decision he had just made.

7 *__ūniversus, -a, -um__, _all, entire, whole._
*__nōbilitās, nōbilitātis__, f., _nobility, senatorial class._

8 *__trānseō, trānsīre, trānsiī__ or __trānsīvī, trānsitūrus__, irreg., _to go across, cross over._

*__apud__, prep. + acc., _at the house of, near, at, in._
__Ēpīrus, -ī__, f., _Epirus_ (a province in northwestern Greece; see the map on page 18).
__Macedonia, -ae__, f., _Macedonia_ (a province to the north of Greece).
__Achaea, -ae__, f., _Achaea_ (a province in Greece, on the Gulf of Corinth).
*__dux, ducis__, m., _leader, general._
__Pompeiō duce__: _under the leadership of Pompey_, ablative absolute.
*__contrā__, prep. + acc., _opposite, facing, against._

B. Civil War: Caesar vs. Pompey

While Caesar was in Gaul, Pompey remained in Rome, and Crassus was sent in command of an army to fight the Parthians, a powerful empire on the eastern border of the Roman world (see the map on page 23). In 53 B.C., Crassus was killed in battle. His death brought an end to the First Triumvirate and paved the way for a showdown between Caesar and Pompey.

Hinc iam bellum cīvīle successit exsecrandum et lacrimābile, quō praeter calamitātēs, quae in proeliīs accidērunt, etiam populī Rōmānī fortūna mūtāta est. Caesar enim rediēns ex Galliā victor coepit poscere alterum cōnsulātum atque ita, ut sine dubietāte aliquā eī dēferrētur. Contrādictum est ā Marcellō cōnsule, ā Bibulō, ā Pompeiō, ā Catōne, iussusque dīmissīs exercitibus ad urbem redīre. Propter quam iniūriam ab Arīminō, ubi mīlitēs congregātōs habēbat, adversum patriam cum exercitū vēnit. Cōnsulēs cum Pompeiō senātusque omnis atque ūniversa nōbilitās ex urbe fūgit et in Graeciam trānsiit. Apud Ēpīrum, Macedoniam, Achaeam Pompeiō duce senātus contrā Caesarem bellum parāvit.

(continued)

---

1. What happened next? (1) Why was this event particularly important? (1–2)
2. What did Caesar do as he prepared to leave Gaul? (2–4)
3. Who opposed this action? (4–5)
4. What was Caesar ordered to do? (5)
5. What action did Caesar take in response? (5–6)
6. Who fled to Greece? (6–8)
7. What took place in Epirus, Macedonia, and Achaea? (8–9)

Reading Note

Abbreviations for Praenōmina

You learned in Chapter 11, Roman Life VII, about the three-part name of male Roman citizens: **praenōmen, nōmen**, and **cognōmen**. The Romans used only a few **praenōmina** and these were always abbreviated in writing, as you saw in lines A:1–2 and A:7. Here are the common **praenōmina** and their abbreviations.

A. = Aulus	D. = Decimus	M'. = Manius	S. = Sextus
C. = Gāius	L. = Lūcius	P. = Pūblius	T. = Titus
Cn. = Gnaeus	M. = Mārcus	Q. = Quīntus	Ti. = Tiberius

In the earliest Roman alphabet, *C* stood for the sounds of both *c* and *g*. Later on *G* was added but the conservative Romans continued to use *C* in the abbrevations for Gāius and Gnaeus.

10 ***vacuus, -a, -um**, *empty.*
***dictātor, dictātōris**, m., *dictator.* The dictator was originally a special official appointed in emergencies to rule with absolute power for six months.

Hispānia, -ae, f., *Spain.* The plural is used here because Spain was divided into two provinces.
petiit: = **petīvit**. Eutropius prefers this alternate perfect form of **petō**.

11 **validus, -a, -um**, *strong, powerful.*
tribus: ablative of **trēs**.

12 ***inde**, adv., *from there, then.*
in Graeciam trānsiit: in November 49 B.C.
13 ***dīmicō, -āre, -āvī, -ātūrus**, *to fight, struggle.*

Prīmō proeliō: when Caesar first landed in Greece, his troops fought with Pompey's near the town of Dyrrachium.
***fugō, -āre, -āvī, -ātus**, *to put to flight.*
ēvādō, ēvādere, ēvāsī, ēvāsus, *to escape.*
quia, conj., *because.*
interveniō, intervenīre, intervēnī, interventūrus, *to come between, intervene.*
14 **nec**: = **nōn**.
scīre: *to know how* when followed by a complementary infinitive.
***tantum:** remember that the neuter form of **tantus** may be used as an adverb meaning *only*.
15 **sē**: Caesar. Caesar meant that only on that particular day of the battle (**illō tantum diē**) did Pompey have a chance for victory.

Caesar vacuam urbem ingressus dictātōrem sē fēcit. Inde Hispāniās petiit. Ibi Pompeiī exercitūs validissimōs et fortissimōs cum tribus ducibus, L. Afrāniō, M. Petreiō, M. Varrōne, superāvit. Inde regressus in Graeciam trānsiit, adversum Pompeium dīmicāvit. Prīmō proeliō victus est et fugātus, ēvāsit tamen, quia nocte interveniente Pompeius sequī nōluit, dīxitque Caesar nec Pompeium scīre vincere et illō tantum diē sē potuisse superārī.

—Eutropius, *Breviarium* VI.19–20

---

8. What did Caesar do after he entered Rome? (10)
9. What did he do next? (10)
10. Whose armies did Caesar defeat in Spain? How are these armies described? (10–12)
11. Where did Caesar go after leaving Spain? What happened there? (12–13)
12. What was the outcome of the first battle? (13)
13. Why was Caesar able to escape? (13–14)
14. What two comments did Caesar make about Pompey? (14–15)

The medieval illustration above shows Caesar crossing the Rubicon (B:5–6). It combines elements from the accounts of two Roman writers. The poet Lucan described how, on the night before crossing the Rubicon, Caesar dreamed that the spirit of Rome begged his army to remain on the north bank. According to Suetonius, an unearthly being sat on the riverbank playing a reed pipe while Caesar's army drew near. As the army reached the river, this being seized a trumpet from a soldier, blew a loud blast, and then crossed the river. Interpreting this as a favorable omen, Caesar told his men to follow. Notice that the medieval artist made no effort to depict the ancient world accurately; instead, he showed buildings and clothing from his own time.

Julius Caesar Crossing the Rubicon, *from* Musée Condé, Chantilly, France

BUILDING THE MEANING

Participles (Review)

A participle is a verbal adjective—that is, an adjective formed from a verb. You have already learned the three Latin participles: present active, perfect passive, and future active. Use the chart on page 335 to review the formation of participles. You will recall that participles can be translated in many different ways, and that the literal translation is not always the best:

Caesar **rediēns** ex Galliā victor coepit poscere alterum cōnsulātum.
Caesar, ***returning*** *victorious from Gaul, began to demand a second consulship.* (literal)
Caesar, ***who was returning*** *victorious. . . .*
Caesar, ***while/as he was returning*** *victorious. . . .*
Caesar, ***since he was returning*** *victorious. . . .*

As the example above shows, the action of a present participle always takes place at the same time as the action of the main verb. Therefore, **rediēns** is translated as *was returning* or *returned*, because the main verb **coepit** is in a past tense. The conjunctions *while* and *as* can only be used for translating present participles.

Eōs **victōs** stīpendiāriōs fēcit.
He made them, ***having been conquered****, subject to tribute.* (literal)
He made them subject to tribute ***after/when he had conquered*** *them.*
He made those ***whom he had conquered*** *subject to tribute.*
He ***conquered*** *them* ***and*** *made them subject to tribute.*

The action of a perfect passive participle always is thought of as having taken place prior to the action of the main verb. Therefore **victōs** is translated by an English pluperfect *had conquered* in the second and third translations above. The conjunction *after* can only be used for translating perfect participles.

The perfect participle of a deponent verb is active in meaning; like the perfect passive participle, it usually describes an action as having taken place before the action of the main verb:

Caesar vacuam urbem **ingressus** dictātōrem sē fēcit.
Caesar, ***having entered*** *the empty city, made himself dictator.*

The action of a future participle is thought of as taking place after the action of the main verb. It can be translated with the words *about to* or *going to* or *intending to*:

Caesar, contrā Pompeium **pugnātūrus**, cōpiās parāvit.
Caesar, ***about to fight*** *against Pompey, prepared his troops.*
Caesar, ***who was going*** *to fight against Pompey, . . .*
Since Caesar ***was intending*** *to fight against Pompey, he. . . .*

The participle and its modifiers make up a *participial phrase.* It is essential to identify where such phrases begin and end; the participle often comes at the end of the phrase, and the phrase may be set off by commas. Keep the phrase as an intact unit when you read; do not mix words from a participial phrase with the main clause.

Exercise 55a

Reread Readings A and B and find five perfect participles and one present participle. Tell what word each participle modifies; then translate the sentence containing the participle in at least two ways.

Exercise 55b

Read aloud and identify all participial phrases. Then translate, giving at least two translations for the participles:

1. Catilīna, patriam dēlēre volēns, cum aliīs coniūrāvit.
2. Cōnsul Cicerō Catilīnam reī pūblicae nocitūrum urbe expulit.
3. Catilīna, Rōmā expulsus, ad exercitum suum processit.
4. Multī hominēs Cicerōnem contrā Catilīnam in Forō loquentem audīvērunt.
5. C. Iūlius Caesar in Galliam itūrus mīlitēs cōnscrīpsit.
6. Gallōs prō lībertāte pugnantēs vīcit Caesar.
7. Magnus numerus Gallōrum contrā Caesarem pugnantium occīsī sunt.
8. Caesar Gallīs victīs tribūtum annuum imperāvit.
9. Etiam Germānōs trāns Rhēnum habitantēs Caesar aggressus est.
10. Pompeius et multī senātōrēs, contrā Caesarem pugnātūrī, in Graeciam trānsiērunt.

*__rēs pūblica, reī pūblicae__, f., *state, government*
__cōnscrībō, cōnscrībere, cōnscrīpsī, cōnscrīptus__, *to enlist, recruit*
*__prō__, prep. + abl., *for, on behalf of*
__tribūtum, -ī__, n., *tribute, tax*
__annuus, -a, -um__, *yearly*

Ablative Absolutes (Review)

Observe the following examples:

1a. **Galliā omnīnō victā**, Caesar Rōmam rediit.
Gaul having been completely conquered, *Caesar returned to Rome.* (literal)
When Gaul had been completely conquered, *Caesar returned to Rome.*
When/after he had completely conquered Gaul, *Caesar returned to Rome.*

1b. **Catilīnā contrā rem pūblicam coniūrante**, Cicerō senātum convocāvit.
Because Catiline was plotting against the government, *Cicero summoned the Senate.*
When Catiline was plotting*. . .*

2. **Pompeiō duce** senātus bellum contrā Caesarem parāvit.
   ***With Pompey as leader**, the Senate prepared (for) war against Caesar.*
   ***When Pompey was their leader**, the Senate. . . .*
   ***Under the leadership of Pompey**, the Senate. . . .*

3. **Caesare superbō**, senātōrēs coniūrāvērunt.
   ***Caesar being arrogant**, the senators made a conspiracy.*
   ***Because Caesar was arrogant**, the senators. . . .*

An ablative absolute can consist of a noun plus a participle (examples 1a and 1b), two nouns (example 2), or a noun plus an adjective (example 3); in each case, both words are in the ablative case. It is often best to translate the ablative absolute as a subordinate clause in English. The subordinating conjunctions *when/after*, *since/because*, *while*, *if*, and *although* can be used. In types 2 and 3, supply a form of the verb *to be* in English.

Notice that the rules given on page 20 about the time relationships of participles apply also to ablative absolutes. Thus, in example 1a the perfect passive participle **victā** is translated as *had been conquered*, since it expresses time prior to that of the main verb **rediit**. In example 1b, the present participle **coniūrante** is translated as *was plotting*, since it expresses an action going on at the same time as that of the main verb **convocāvit.**

Exercise 55c

Reread Readings 55 A and B and find four ablative absolutes. Decide whether each one is type 1, type 2, or type 3, and translate.

Exercise 55d

Read aloud and translate; give at least two translations for the ablative absolutes:

1. Cicerōne cōnsule, Catilīna victus interfectusque est.
2. Catilīnā mortuō, rēs pūblica tūta esse vidēbātur.
3. Caesare in Galliā bellum gerente, Pompeius Rōmae mānsit.
4. Tōtā Galliā victā, Caesar alterum cōnsulātum cupīvit.
5. Caesare alterum cōnsulātum poscente, bellum cīvīle factum est.
6. Caesar, respōnsō senātūs acceptō, Rōmam cum exercitū profectus est.
7. Caesare in Italiam regressō, senātus ad Graeciam fūgit.
8. Senātōribus cum Pompeiō ad Graeciam fugientibus, Caesar sē dictātōrem fēcit.
9. Senātū absente, Caesar sē dictātōrem fēcit.
10. Exercitū Pompeiī in Hispāniā superātō, Caesar in Graeciam trānsiit.
11. Prīmō proeliō factō, Caesar ēvāsit quod Pompeius nocte sequī nōlēbat.
12. Pompeiō nocte sequī nōlente, Caesar effūgit.
13. Caesare et Pompeiō in Graeciā pugnantibus, cīvēs in urbe nesciēbant quis victor futūrus esset.

***tūtus, -a, -um**, *safe*
***bellum gerere**, *to wage war*

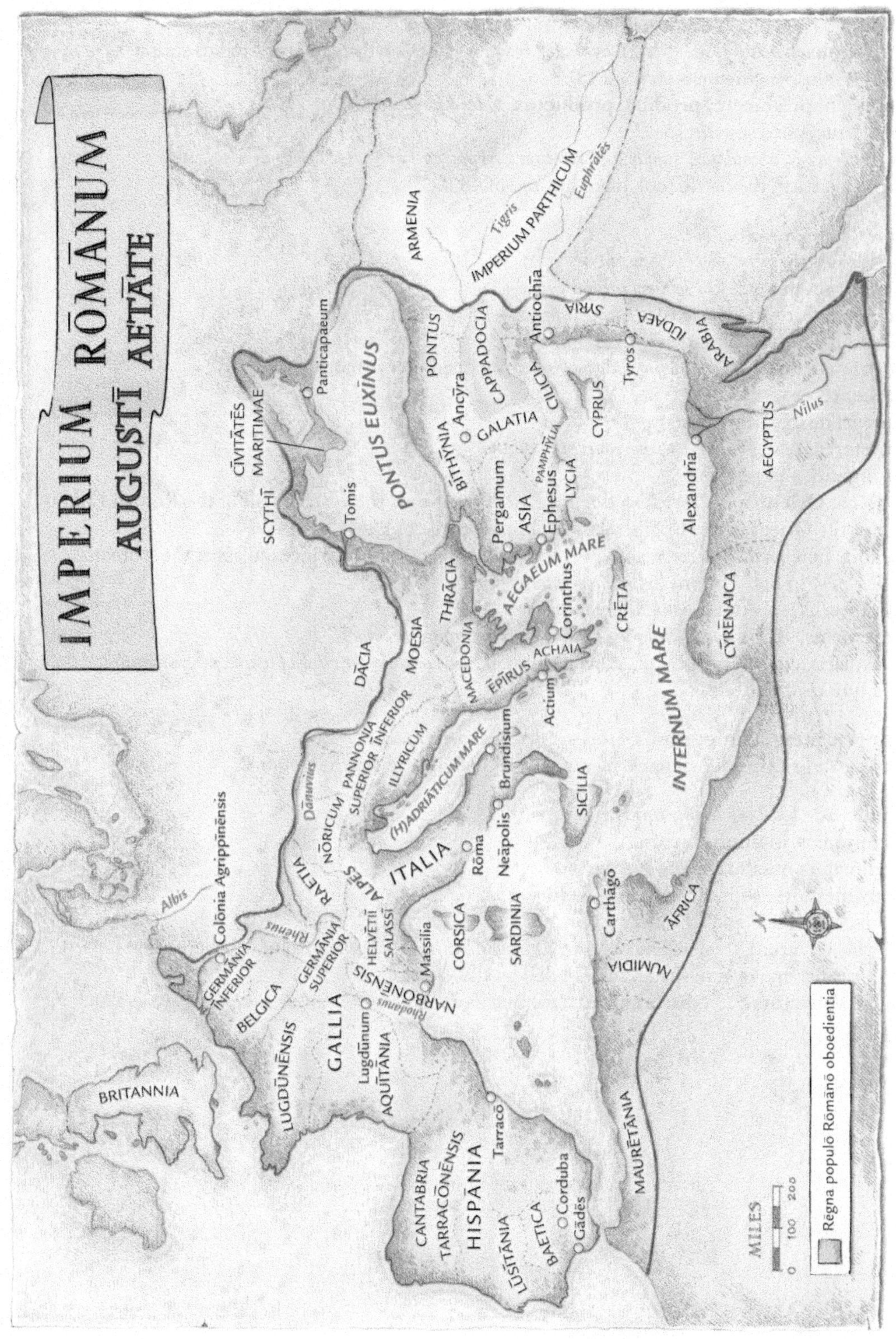

IMPERIUM RŌMĀNUM
AUGUSTĪ AETĀTE
BRITANNIA
LUGDŪNĒNSIS
GALLIA
BELGICA
GERMĀNIA INFERIOR
GERMĀNIA SUPERIOR
Colōnia Agrippīnēnsis
Albis
Rhēnus
RAETIA
NŌRICUM
Dānuvius
PANNONIA SUPERIOR
PANNONIA INFERIOR
DĀCIA
MOESIA
THRĀCIA
SCYTHĪ
CĪVITĀTĒS MARITIMAE
Tomis
Panticapaeum
PONTUS EUXĪNUS
BITHӮNIA
Ancӯra
PONTUS
GALATIA
CAPPADOCIA
ARMENIA
Tigris
IMPERIUM PARTHICUM
Euphrātēs
Antiochīa
SYRIA
Tyros
IŪDAEA
ARABIA
CILICIA
CYPRUS
PAMPHYLIA
LYCIA
ASIA
Pergamum
Ephesus
AEGAEUM MARE
MACEDONIA
EPĪRUS
ACHAIA
Corinthus
CRĒTA
Actium
ILLYRICUM
(H)ADRIĀTICUM MARE
Brundisium
ITALIA
ALPĒS
Rōma
Neāpolis
SICILIA
INTERNUM MARE
CYRĒNAICA
AEGYPTUS
Nīlus
Alexandrīa
HELVĒTIĪ
SALASSĪ
Massilia
CORSICA
SARDINIA
NARBŌNĒNSIS
Rhodanus
Lugdūnum
AQUĪTĀNIA
Tarracō
HISPĀNIA
TARRACŌNĒNSIS
CANTABRIA
LŪSĪTĀNIA
BAETICA
Corduba
Gādēs
MAURETĀNIA
NUMIDIA
Carthāgō
ĀFRICA
N
MILES
0 100 200
Rēgna populō Rōmānō oboedientia

1 **Thessalia, -ae**, f., *Thessaly* (a province in northern Greece).
Palaeopharsālus, -ī, m., *Old Pharsalus* (a town in Thessaly, usually referred to simply as Pharsalus; see the map on page 18).
prōdūcō, prōdūcere, prōdūxī, prōductus, *to lead forward.*
utrimque, adv., *on both sides.*
***cōpia, -ae**, f., *abundance, supply*; pl., *resources, troops.*
2 **dīmicāvērunt**: the battle took place in June of 48 B.C.

aciēs, aciēī, f., *line of battle.*
quadrāgintā, *forty.*
pedes, peditis, m., *foot soldier, infantryman.*
***eques, equitis**, m., *horse soldier, cavalryman.*
sinister, sinistra, sinistrum, *left.*
3 **cornū, cornūs**, n., *horn, wing* (edge of an army lined up for battle).
sexcentī, -ae, -a, *600.*
***dexter, dextra, dextrum**, *right.*
***praetereā**, adv., *besides, too, moreover. in addition.*
quīngentī, -ae, -a, *500.*
Oriēns, Orientis, m., *the rising sun; the East.* This means the eastern half of the Roman Empire, not the Orient in the English sense (China, Japan, etc.).
auxilia: here *auxiliary troops*, soldiers recruited from various provinces to assist the Roman legions. In line 11 it means *reinforcements.*
4 **innumerus, -a, -um**, *countless, innumerable.*
praetōrius, -ī, m., *one holding the rank of praetor, an ex-praetor.*
***cōnsulāris, cōnsulāris**, gen. pl., **cōnsulārium**, m., *one holding the rank of consul, an ex-consul.*
eōs quī: *those who.*

5 ***integer, integra, integrum**, *whole, complete; unhurt, intact.*
nōn integra trīgintā mīlia: *not a complete 30,000*, i.e., fewer than 30,000.

6 ***adhūc**, adv., *still, up to this time.*
in ūnum: = **in ūnum locum**.
meliōribus ducibus: *with better generals.*
7 **convēnerant**: deduce from **con-** + **venīre**.
***orbis, orbis**, gen. pl., **orbium**, m., *circle.*
***orbis terrārum**: *the world*, literally, *circle of lands.* Some Greeks and Romans believed that the world was flat and oval in shape, surrounded by the Ocean.
facile subāctūrae . . . dūcerentur: *(who) would easily subdue the whole world, if they were led. . . .*

C. Pompey's Fate

Deinde in Thessaliā apud Palaeopharsālum prōductīs utrimque ingentibus cōpiīs dīmicāvērunt. Pompeiī aciēs habuit quadrāgintā mīlia peditum, equitēs in sinistrō cornū sexcentōs, in dextrō quīngentōs, praetereā tōtīus Orientis auxilia, tōtam nōbilitātem, innumerōs senātōrēs, praetōriōs, cōnsulārēs et eōs quī magnōrum iam bellōrum victōrēs fuissent. Caesar in aciē suā habuit peditum nōn integra trīgintā mīlia, equitēs mīlle. Numquam adhūc Rōmānae cōpiae in ūnum neque maiōrēs neque meliōribus ducibus convēnerant, tōtum terrārum orbem facile subāctūrae, sī contrā barbarōs dūcerentur.

(continued)

1. What happened at Pharsalus in Thessaly? (1–2)
2. What kinds of soldiers did Pompey's army have? How many of each? (2–3)
3. What other people did Pompey's army include? (3–5)
4. How many foot soldiers and how many cavalry did Caesar have? (5–6)
5. In what way were these armies unique? (6–7)
6. What could they do if they were fighting against foreigners? (7–8)

The French artist Adolphe Yvon depicts the effect of Caesar's seizing power as dictator. Caesar is wearing the laurel wreath and scarlet cloak of a triumphant general. The shrouded figures represent the deaths caused by the civil war. How would you interpret the globe in Caesar's hand and the broken column (note the inscription) at the left?
Caesar, *Oil on canvas, 1875, Adolphe Yvon*

9 ***pugnō, -āre, -āvī, -ātus**, *to fight*.
Pugnātum . . . est: *It was fought, They fought*, an impersonal use of the verb.
contentiō, contentiōnis, f., *strife, struggle*.
victus: = **victus est.**
***postrēmus, -a, -um**, *last, final*.
ad postrēmum: *in the end*.
***castra, castrōrum**, n. pl., *camp*.
10 ***dīripiō, dīripere, dīripuī, dīreptus**, *to plunder, ransack*.

Alexandrīa, -ae, f., *Alexandria* (the capital of Egypt, founded by Alexander the Great; see the map on page 23).
***rēx, rēgis**, m., *king*.
tūtor, tūtōris, m., *guardian, protector*.
11 **datus fuerat**: = **datus erat.**
cui . . . datus fuerat: *to whom he had been assigned as a protector*.
iuvenīlis, -is, -e, *young, youthful*.
***aetās, aetātis**, f., *age*. Do not confuse with **aestās**, *summer*.

12 ***amīcitia, -ae**, f., *friendship*.
ānulus, -ī, m., *ring*.

13 ***fundō, fundere, fūdī, fūsus**, *to pour out, shower, shed*.
***intueor, intuērī, intuitus sum**, *to gaze at, look upon*.
gener, generī, m., *son-in-law*. Pompey was Caesar's son-in-law (even though he was six years older than Caesar) because he had married Caesar's daughter Julia in 59 B.C. to cement the First Triumvirate.
14 ***quondam**, adv., *once, formerly*.

Reading Notes

Linking Quī

A form of the relative pronoun **quī, quae, quod** may be used at the beginning of a sentence to refer back to something mentioned in the previous sentence. This is called a *linking* ***quī*** or a *connecting relative* because it ties the two sentences closely together. There are two examples on page 27:

Quī . . .	*But he* . . . (line 11)
Quō cōnspectō . . .	*When this had been seen* . . . (lines 12–13)

Quī refers back to King Ptolemy and **Quō** refers back to the head of Pompey. A linking **quī** may be translated by a personal pronoun (*he/she/it/they*), with the addition of a conjunction such as *and* or *but* to emphasize the connection with the previous sentence; or it may be translated by a demonstrative (*this, that*). Connecting relatives are easy to identify because they always come at the beginning of a sentence or after a semicolon or colon.

• • •

Asyndeton

In line 12 opposite, we would expect a conjunction such as **et** to link the two main verbs: *But he killed Pompey (and) sent* . . .; but there is no conjunction. Such omission of connecting words is a literary device called *asyndeton*, a Greek word meaning "lack of connection." Another example occurred on page 19. Locate it.

Pugnātum tum est ingentī contentiōne, victusque ad postrēmum Pompeius et castra eius dīrepta sunt. Ipse fugātus Alexandrīam petiit, ut ā rēge Aegyptī, cui tūtor ā senātū datus fuerat propter iuvenīlem eius aetātem, acciperet auxilia. Quī fortūnam magis quam amīcitiam secūtus occīdit Pompeium, caput eius et ānulum Caesarī mīsit. Quō cōnspectō Caesar etiam lacrimās fūdisse dīcitur, tantī virī intuēns caput et generī quondam suī.

—Eutropius, *Breviarium* VI.20–21

---

7. How was the battle fought? (9)
8. What was the outcome of the battle? (9–10)
9. What was Pompey's relationship with the king of Egypt? (10–11)
10. Why did Pompey go to Alexandria? (10–11)
11. What two things did King Ptolemy do? Why? (11–12)
12. How did Caesar react to this event? Why? (12–14)

After defeating Pompey at Pharsalus, Caesar went to Egypt. There he defeated King Ptolemy and installed Ptolemy's older sister, Cleopatra, as queen. He then consolidated his power over the Roman world by defeating an army led by a group of senators in North Africa (46 B.C.) and by defeating the forces led by Pompey's two sons in Spain (45 B.C.).

Reading Note

Figures of Speech

Writers use language in a variety of ways to emphasize a point or express an idea in a fresh, creative fashion. You probably are familiar with similes and metaphors; by comparing one thing to another, an author can clarify the meaning or make the reader think differently about a topic than he or she might otherwise do. Literary devices such as similes and metaphors are called *figures of speech*. Some figures of speech reflect the use of language in creative ways; others involve departures from normal speech patterns, as in the case of asyndeton (opposite); others such as alliteration play with the sound of language. Greek and Roman writers employed many figures of speech, some of which are not often used in English. Each of these figures will be discussed in the notes the first time it appears in this book. If you need to locate the definition of a particular figure later on, refer to Appendix I on page 307. Always ask yourself *why* the author chose to use a particular figure; what does its presence contribute to the text?

The Roman orator and educator Quintilian made the following remark about figures of speech in his *Institutio oratoria (Training of the Orator)*. This passage suggests some of the reasons why the Romans valued the use of figures of speech so highly. Quintilian is speaking about figures of speech in which words that logically go together are separated.

> For speech would often become rough and harsh, lax and nerveless, if words should be ranged exactly in their original order, and if, as each presents itself, it should be placed side by side of the preceding, though it cannot be fairly attached to it. Some words and phrases must, therefore, be kept back, others brought forward, and, as in structures of unhewn stones, each must be put in the place which it will fit. For we cannot hew or polish them, in order that they may close and unite better, but we must use them as they are and find suitable places for them.
>
> —Quintilian, *Institutio oratoria* VIII.6.62–63, translated by J.S. Watson

1 **orbem**: = **orbem terrārum.**

***compōnō, compōnere, composuī, compositus**, *to compose, settle, complete.*

agere: *to act, behave.*

īnsolentius, comparative adverb, *rather arrogantly.*

2 **cōnsuētūdō, cōnsuētūdinis**, f., *custom, practice.*

***ergō**, adv., *therefore.*

***honor, honōris**, m., *honor, mark of honor; position, political office.*

3 **voluntās, voluntātis**, f., *wish, will.*

***praestō, praestāre, praestitī, praestitus**, *to bestow.*

dēferō, dēferre, dētulī, dēlātus, irreg., *to award, grant.*

4 **adsurgō, adsurgere, adsurrēxī, adsurrēctūrus** + dat., *to stand up out of respect for.*

rēgius, -a, -um, *royal, kingly, typical of a king.*

***ac**, conj., *and.*

coniūrātum est: *it was conspired, a conspiracy was made*, an impersonal use of the verb.

in: *against* (as usual when followed by a word referring to a person in the accusative case).

sexāgintā, *sixty.*

5 ***amplius**, adv., *more.*

equitibus: originally this word denoted those who could afford to keep horses and thus serve in the cavalry—citizens of some wealth, though not as wealthy as senators. By the first century B.C., the word came to refer to the wealthy class of businessmen. Their direct involvement in politics was limited, but they exercised considerable influence due to their wealth.

praecipuus, -a, -um, *notable, outstanding.*

coniūrātus, -ī, m., *conspirator.*

duo Brūtī: Marcus Junius Brutus Caepio was a leader of the conspirators; Decimus Junius Brutus Albinus had served under Caesar in Gaul but later joined the conspiracy.

7 **Cūriam**: the original Curia had been burned in 52 B.C. by a mob. The Senate actually met in the Theater of Pompey on this occasion.

8 ***vulnus, vulneris**, n., *wound*

cōnfodiō, cōnfodere, cōnfōdī, cōnfossus, *to dig up; to stab.*

Reading Note

Unexpressed Subjects

The subject of an English sentence is always expressed as a noun or pronoun. This is not always the case in Latin. Compare this Latin sentence and its translation:

Caesarī resistēbant. *They resisted Caesar.*

The Latin sentence has no separate word for the subject, *they*. You have met many such sentences already, but English speakers often do not notice indications that this type of sentence is in operation. You should watch carefully for two things.

a. When you do not see a nominative case word in a sentence or clause, pay particular attention; if there is no indication of a change in subject, the subject established in the previous sentence is probably still in operation. For example, **Caesar**, subject of the first sentence on the opposite page, is also the unexpressed subject of the second sentence (**coepit** = *he began*) and of the **cum** clauses that begin the third sentence.
b. Carefully note all case endings and verb endings that are given. In the example above, the ending **-ī** shows that **Caesarī** is dative and the ending **-nt** shows that the verb is plural. Therefore the sentence cannot mean *Caesar resisted.*

D. The Death of Caesar and the Rise of Octavian

Inde Caesar bellīs cīvīlibus per tōtum orbem compositīs Rōmam rediit. Agere īnsolentius coepit et contrā cōnsuētūdinem Rōmānae lībertātis. Cum ergō et honōrēs ex suā voluntāte praestāret, quī ā populō anteā dēferēbantur, nec senātuī ad sē venientī adsurgeret aliaque rēgia ac paene tyrannica faceret, coniūrātum est in eum ā sexāgintā vel amplius senātōribus equitibusque Rōmānīs. Praecipuī fuērunt inter coniūrātōs duo Brūtī ex eō genere Brūtī, quī prīmus Rōmae cōnsul fuerat et rēgēs expulerat, et C. Cassius et Servīlius Casca. Ergō Caesar, cum senātūs diē inter cēterōs vēnisset ad Cūriam, tribus et vīgintī vulneribus cōnfossus est.

(continued)

---

1. When did Caesar return to Rome? (1)
2. How did Caesar behave after he returned to Rome? (1–2)
3. Give two examples of this behavior. (2–4)
4. Who made a conspiracy against Caesar? (4–5)
5. Who was the ancestor of the two Bruti mentioned in this paragraph? What had he done? (6)
6. Name two leaders of the conspiracy in addition to the two Bruti. (6–7)
7. What happened to Caesar after he entered the Senate meeting? (7–8)

Unlike Eutropius, the Italian artist Camuccini knew that the murder took place in the Theater of Pompey; ironically, Caesar was stabbed at the foot of Pompey's statue, as shown here.
Assassination of Julius Caesar, *Oil on canvas, 1798, Vincenzo Camuccini*

9 **ferē**: Caesar was killed on the Ides of March, 44 B.C. Since Rome was supposedly founded on 21 April 753 B.C., this date was "almost" the 710th year.

reparāta sunt: deduce from **re-** + **parō.**

10 **percussor, percussōris**, m., *assassin.*

cōnsul partium Caesaris: *the consul from Caesar's faction.*

11 **turbō, -āre, -āvī, -ātus,** *to disturb, upset, throw into confusion.*

12 ***hostis, hostis**, gen. pl., **hostium**, m., *enemy.*

***iūdicō, -āre, -āvī, -ātus,** *to judge.*

missī: = **missī sunt**. Eutropius often leaves out forms of **esse.**

***persequor, persequī, persecūtus sum**, *to pursue.*

ad eum persequendum: *to pursue him.*

13 **annōs decem et octō nātus**: *18 years old* (literally, *born for 18 years*).

14 ***nepōs, nepōtis**, m., *nephew, grandson*; Octavian was actually Caesar's grandnephew.

ille: = Julius Caesar.

***testāmentum, -ī**, n., *will.*

***hērēs, hērēdis**, m., *heir.*

hērēdem: *as his heir.*

15 ***potior, potīrī, potītus sum** + abl. or gen., *to get control of, get possession of.*

***rērum potītus (est)**: *got control of affairs*, i.e., became emperor.

profectī: from **proficīscor.**

16 **vīcērunt eum**: at the battle of Mutina in northern Italy, 21 April 43 B.C.

ēvenit, ēvenīre, ēvēnit, *it turns out.*

victōrēs: translate this noun as an adjective, *victorious.*

morerentur: how can you tell that this is from **morior, morī** and not **moror, morārī**?

***quārē**, adv., *for what reason, why; for this reason, therefore.*

Reading Note

Connection Words

On the opposite page, note the words **enim** (10), **ergō** (11), **tamen** (16), and **quārē** (16). All these words show the logical connection between two sentences, and it is typical of Latin to use such words more often than English does. Other such words are **autem, igitur**, and **nam.**

Enim and **nam** (*for*) always explain the reason for what was stated in the previous sentence, while **ergō, igitur**, and **quārē** (*therefore*) show the logical consequence or result of the previous statement. **Tamen** (*however, nevertheless*) expresses a contrast with the preceding statement. **Autem** sometimes indicates a contrast (*but, however*) and sometimes makes a transition to a new idea (*moreover, and now*).

Note that some of these words come first in a sentence (**nam, ergō**, and **quārē**), while others almost always come as the second word (**enim, igitur**, and **autem**). Watch for these very common words as you read.

Annō urbis ferē septingentēsimō decimō, interfectō Caesare, cīvīlia bella reparāta sunt. Percussōribus enim Caesaris senātus favēbat. Antōnius cōnsul partium Caesaris cīvīlibus bellīs opprimere eōs cōnābātur. Ergō turbātā rē pūblicā multa Antōnius scelera committēns ā senātū hostis iūdicātus est. Missī ad eum persequendum duo cōnsulēs, Pānsa et Hirtius, et Octāviānus adulēscēns annōs decem et octō nātus, Caesaris nepōs, quem ille testāmentō hērēdem relīquerat et nōmen suum ferre iusserat. Hic est, quī posteā Augustus est dictus et rērum potītus. Quī profectī contrā Antōnium trēs ducēs vīcērunt eum. Ēvēnit tamen ut victōrēs cōnsulēs ambō morerentur. Quārē trēs exercitūs ūnī Caesarī Augustō pāruērunt.

—Eutropius, *Breviarium* VI.25–VII.1

8. In what year did civil war break out again? (9–10)
9. On whose side was the Senate? (10)
10. What did Antony want to do? (10–11)
11. Why was Antony condemned by the Senate? (11–12)
12. Name the three men sent to crush Antony's army. (13)
13. Give three facts about Octavian. (13–14)
14. What later happened to Octavian? (14–15)
15. What was the outcome of the battle? (15–16)
16. How did Octavian come to command three armies? (16–17)

Locate another example of a linking **quī** (see page 26 for definition) in the selection above.

Reading Note

Dative with Special Intransitive Verbs

In Chapter 27, you learned that some intransitive verbs (those that do not take a direct object in the accusative) can be completed by a word or phrase in the dative case. Two examples are found in the reading above:

> **Percussōribus** enim Caesaris senātus favēbat. (10)
> Quārē trēs exercitūs **ūnī Caesarī Augustō** pāruērunt. (16–17)

The pattern of subject, dative, and intransitive verb is one of the basic Latin sentence patterns (see page 10). In addition to **favēre** and **pārēre**, you have learned the following intransitive verbs that take the dative: **cōnfīdere**, *to trust, have confidence in*; **crēdere**, *to believe, trust*; **imperāre**, *to order*; **nocēre**, *to harm*; **nūbere**, *to marry*; **parcere**, *to spare*; **persuādēre**, *to persuade*; and **placēre**, *to please*.

Infinitives (Review)

You have learned five infinitive forms. Here are all the infinitives of the verb **vidēre**:

	Active	Passive
Present	**vidēre** *to see*	**vidērī** *to be seen*
Perfect	**vīdisse** *to have seen*	**vīsus esse** *to have been seen*
Future	**vīsūrus esse** *to be about to see*	

NOTES

1. The present active infinitive is the second principal part of the verb.
2. The present passive infinitive is usually formed by changing the final -**e** of the present active infinitive to -**ī**. In verbs of the 3rd conjugation, however, the whole -**ere** ending is dropped: **dūcere** becomes **dūcī**, and **cōnspicere** becomes **cōnspicī**.
3. The other infinitives are formed in the the same way for all verbs regardless of the conjugation to which they belong (see the chart on page 329).
4. The future infinitive of **esse** has two forms: **futūrus esse** or **fore**.
5. Deponent verbs have only three infinitives; the infinitives of **loquor** are **loquī**, **locūtus esse**, and **locūtūrus esse**. The present and perfect infinitives of deponents follow the regular rule for such verbs—they have a passive form but are translated actively. The future infinitive of deponents has an active form as well as an active meaning.

Exercise 55e

Form all possible infinitives of the following verbs: **dīmicō, cognōscō, dēleō, aggredior, interficiō, audiō, cōnor,** and **sum**.

Building the Meaning

Indirect Statement (Review)

You have learned that a verb of thinking, saying, or feeling is often followed by a noun in the accusative and verb in the infinitive. This construction is called *indirect statement*:

Caesar est dictātor arrogāns. (direct)
Caesar is an arrogant dictator.

Senātus crēdit **Caesarem esse** dictātōrem arrogantem. (indirect)
The Senate believes (that) ***Caesar is*** *an arrogant dictator.*

The subject of the direct statement (**Caesar**) becomes accusative, and the verb (**est**) becomes an infinitive. Any word that agrees with the "subject accusative" also becomes accusative (**dictātōrem arrogantem**). The word *that* can be left out of the English translation; it is helpful, however, to include it as a signpost that you are dealing with an indirect statement.

In indirect statement, the present infinitive always shows an action going on at the *same time* as the action of the main verb; the perfect infinitive shows an action completed *prior to* the action of the main verb; and the future infinitive shows an action that will take place *after* the action of the main verb. These rules are similar to the rules about the time relationships of participles given on page 20. Notice how the translation of the indirect statements in the following examples changes when the tense of the main verb changes:

Senātus crēdit Caesarem imperāre velle.
The Senate believes that Caesar wants to rule.

Senātus crēdēbat Caesarem imperāre velle.
The Senate believed that Caesar wanted to rule.

Cicerō scit coniūrātiōnem fierī.
Cicero knows that a conspiracy is being made.

Cicerō sciēbat coniūrātiōnem fierī.
Cicero knew that a conspiracy was being made.

Nūntius dīcit exercit***ūs*** Pompeiī superāt***ōs*** esse.
The messenger says that the armies of Pompey have been defeated.

Nūntius dīxit exercit***ūs*** Pompeiī superāt***ōs*** esse.
The messenger said that the armies of Pompey had been defeated.

Caesar scit senātōr***ēs*** sē aggressūr***ōs*** esse.
Caesar knows that the senators will attack him.

Caesar sciēbat senātōr***ēs*** sē aggressūr***ōs*** esse.
Caesar knew that the senators would attack him.

Finally, notice two points:

1. If a perfect passive infinitive or a future infinitive is used, the ending on the participle must agree in gender, number, and case with the subject of the infinitive; the boldface endings in the last two examples show this.
2. The pronoun **sē** in indirect statement refers to the subject of the main verb. See the last pair of examples, where **sē** indicates Caesar, the subject of **scit/sciēbat**, not the senators.

EXERCISE 55f

Read aloud, identify examples of indirect statement, and translate:

1. Caesar alterum cōnsulātum cupiēbat, sed intellēxit Pompeium sē nōn iūtūrum esse.
2. Caesar sciēbat senātum Pompeiō magis quam sibi favēre.
3. Eutropius dīcit exercitūs apud Pharsālum fuisse maximōs.
4. Cīvēs Rōmānī audīvērunt Pompeium fugātum et castra eius dīrepta esse.
5. Pompeius crēdēbat rēgem Ptolemaeum sibi amīcum fore et auxilia datūrum esse; ergō Alexandrīam iit.
6. Cōnstat Caesarem, caput Pompeiī intuentem, lacrimāvisse.
7. Eutropius dīcit Caesarem in Cūriā occīsum esse, sed scīmus rē vērā dictātōrem in theātrō Pompeiī mortuum esse.
8. Dīcitur sexāgintā senātōrēs contrā Caesarem coniūrāvisse.
9. Caesare mortuō, Antōnius nōn crēdēbat adulēscentem Octāvium posse imperāre.
10. Omnēs sciunt Octāvium testāmentō Caesaris adoptātum esse.

***intellegō, intellegere, intellēxī, intellēctus**, *to understand*
***iuvō, iuvāre, iūvī, iūtus**, *to help*
***cōnstat**, *it is agreed*
***rē vērā**, *really, actually*

Praestat enim nēminī imperāre quam alicui servīre: sine illō enim vīvere honestē licet, cum hōc vīvendī nūlla condiciō est. *For it is better to give orders to no one than to be a slave to anyone: for without the former it is possible to live honorably, with the latter there is no way of living.*
(Marcus Junius Brutus, fragment of *De dictatura Pompei*)

The coin on the left was issued by Caesar and clearly shows his autocratic position: CAESAR DICT(ATOR) PERPETVO, *Caesar, Dictator for Life,* a title he assumed in 45 B.C. The coin on the right was issued by the Republican forces in Greece during the civil war to commemorate Caesar's murder. It shows two daggers and the cap that was awarded to slaves when they were given their freedom; it reads EID(IBUS) MAR(TIIS).

BUILDING THE MEANING

Nested Clauses

Sometimes a subordinate clause is located inside the main clause, as in this example:

The book that I wanted was on sale.

Note how the relative clause *that I wanted* interrupts the main clause *The book was on sale.* Such clauses are referred to as *nested clauses.* This type of sentence is much more common in Latin than in English. It is very important to watch where such clauses begin and end. Here are two Latin examples from this chapter:

> . . . quō praeter calamitātēs, quae in proeliīs accidērunt, etiam populī Romanī fortūna mūtāta est. (55B:1–2)

> Ipse (Pompeius) fugātus Alexandrīam petiit, ut ā rēge Aegyptī, cui tūtor ā senātū datus fuerat, . . . acciperet auxilia. (55C:10–11)

How do you know where a subordinate clause starts and stops? It starts with a relative pronoun (**quī, quae, quod**) or a subordinating conjunction (**ut, nē, dum, cum, postquam, ubi, quando, sī**); all these words raise the expectation of a subordinate verb. The clause ends when its meaning is complete. This is very often indicated by a verb, since verbs in Latin tend to come at the end of their clauses. Punctuation often helps.

Ablative absolutes can also be nested inside the main clause:

> Inde Caesar bellīs cīvīlibus per tōtum orbem compositīs Rōmam rediit. (55D:1)

> Remember this important rule: the first clause (the interrupted one) cannot resume until the second clause (the interrupting one) has finished.

EXERCISE 55g

Copy each sentence on a separate sheet. Underline each subordinate clause and each ablative absolute. If one clause is nested inside another, use double underlining for the inner one. Then translate the sentence.

1. Caesar exercitūs Pompeiī in Hispāniā, nē sibi dum contrā Pompeium ipsum pugnābat nocēre possent, superāvit.
2. Caesar in Graeciā, quō ab Hispāniā trānsierat, contrā Pompeium pugnāvit.
3. Pompeius nōluit, nocte interveniente, Caesarem quī vix ā prīmō proeliō effūgerat sequī.
4. Pompeius victus ad mare, quod nōn procul āfuit, recessit et nāvem ut iter ad Aegyptum faceret cōnscendit.
5. Rēx Ptolemaeus in Aegyptō, quamquam amīcus Pompeiī fuerat, tamen eum necāvit.
6. Caesar, cum caput Pompeiī quod sibi ā Ptolemaeō missum erat cōnspexisset, lacrimāvit.
7. Caesar, cum bella cīvīlia quae per tōtum orbem terrārum gesta erant composuit, sē dictātōrem perpetuum fēcit.

1 **Fugātus**: from **fugō, -āre** not **fugiō, fugere.**

***āmittō, āmittere, āmīsī, āmissus,** *to lose.*

cōnfugiō, cōnfugere, cōnfūgī, *to flee for refuge, take refuge.*

cōnfūgit ad Lepidum: in Gallia Narbonensis, on the southern coast of Gaul.

Caesarī: *under (Julius) Caesar.*

magister equitum: a Roman dictator appointed a second-in-command who was known as **magister equitum,** *commander of the cavalry,* although he was not limited to that role by Caesar's time.

2 **suscipiō, suscipere, suscēpī, susceptus,** *to undertake, support, receive* (under one's protection), *protect.*

3 ***opera, -ae,** f., *work, effort.*

operam dare, *to pay attention, make efforts.*

Caesar: this refers to Octavian. Gaius Octavius was Caesar's grandnephew, whom he adopted in his will. The young man's name was then changed to Gaius Julius Caesar Octavianus, and it was as "Caesar" that he was known. When Eutropius uses **Caesar** in the following passages, it usually refers to Octavian (an exception is found in line 8, where it refers to Julius Caesar).

***pāx, pācis,** f., *peace.*

***quasi,** adv., *as if.*

***vindicō, -āre, -āvī, -ātus,** *to avenge, get revenge for.*

4 **fuerat adoptātus**: = **adoptātus erat.**

5 **extorqueō, extorquēre, extorsī, extorsus,** *to wrench, extort, obtain by force.*

vīcēsimus, -a, -um, *twentieth.*

vīcēsimō annō: *in his twentieth year.*

prōscrībō, prōscrībere, prōscripsī, prōscrīptus, *to outlaw.* Proscription was a practice in which the leaders of the winning side in a civil war would post a list of their enemies from the losing side; these men would be killed and their property confiscated. Through such proscriptions the triumvirs both eliminated their political opponents and obtained funds to continue their activities.

cum Antōniō . . . coepit: this is the Second Triumvirate, which lasted from 43 to 33 B.C.

6 **Cicerō ōrātor occīsus est**: on 7 December 43 B.C.

7 **multī aliī nōbilēs**: the proscription lists included about 300 senators and 2,000 equestrians. A number of these men escaped, however, and some were officially restored later on.

THE FALL OF THE REPUBLIC

A. Republicans vs. Caesarians

Fugātus Antōnius, āmissō exercitū, cōnfūgit ad Lepidum, quī Caesarī magister equitum fuerat et tum mīlitum cōpiās grandēs habēbat, ā quō susceptus est. Mox, Lepidō operam dante, Caesar pācem cum Antōniō fēcit et quasi vindicātūrus patris suī mortem, ā quō per testāmentum fuerat adoptātus, Rōmam cum exercitū profectus extorsit ut sibi vīcēsimō annō cōnsulātus darētur. Senātum prōscrīpsit, cum Antōniō ac Lepidō rem pūblicam armīs tenēre coepit. Per hōs etiam Cicerō ōrātor occīsus est multīque aliī nōbilēs.

(continued)

---

1. In what situation did Antony find himself? (1)
2. To whom did Antony flee? (1)
3. What position had this man held?
   What did he control at this time? (1–2)
4. How did Octavian make peace with Antony? (3)
5. What unusual privilege did Octavian extort from the Senate? (4–5)
6. How did he justify this action? (3–4)
7. How was he able to force the Senate to grant him this privilege? (4)
8. What did Octavian do together with Antony and Lepidus? (5–6)
9. Who was killed during the proscriptions? (6–7)

Locate another example of asyndeton (see page 26 for definition) in the selection above.

An aureus issued in 39 B.C. showing the triumvirs Octavian (left) and Antony. They are both designated IMP(erator), victorious general.

8 **interfector, interfectōris**, m., *killer, murderer.*

9 **Macedonia, -ae**, f., *Macedonia* (a province to the north of Greece).
Oriēns, Orientis, m., *the rising sun; the East.*

10 ***igitur**, conj., *therefore.*
remānserat: deduce from **re-** + **manēre.**
ad dēfendendam Italiam: *to defend Italy.*

11 **Philippī, Philippōrum**, m. pl., *Philippi* (a town in Greece; see the map on page 18). The battles at Philippi took place in 42 B.C.

12 ***pereō, perīre, periī** or **perīvī, peritūrus**, irreg., *to die, perish.*
13 **secundō**: = **secundō proeliō.**
cum illīs: = **cum Brūtō et Cassiō.**
victam: this participle refers both to Brutus and to the nobility that fought with him, but is feminine because it is placed closer to **nōbilitātem**, which is feminine.

14 **dīvidō, dīvidere, dīvīsī, dīvīsus,** *to divide.*
15 **Asia, -ae**, f., *Asia* (a Roman province containing what is now the southwestern part of Turkey).
Pontus, -ī, m., *Pontus* (a Roman province containing the northeastern part of Turkey, along the Black Sea).

L. Antōnius: the younger brother of Marc Antony. He opposed Octavian's distribution of land to soldiers, presumably to weaken Octavian's position while strengthening that of his brother. Together with Fulvia, Antony's wife, he raised an army in Italy and was captured after a long siege during the winter of 41–40 B.C. at the town of Perusia.
16 ***commoveō, commovēre, commōvī, commōtus**, *to stir up, start.*

17 **Perusia, -ae**, f., *Perusia* (a town, modern Perugia, north of Rome; see the map on page 18).
Tuscia, -ae, f., *Etruria* (the part of Italy north of Rome).
***cīvitās, cīvitātis**, f., *citizenship; state, government; city* (in this context).

At the battle of Philippi (opposite, 11–14), Octavian vowed to build a temple to Mars if he were victorious. He fulfilled this vow many years later when he made the temple of Mars Ultor (Mars the Avenger) the centerpiece of the new forum he constructed to the north of the original Forum Romanum.
Reconstruction, Forum of Augustus and the Temple of Mars Ultor, first century A.D., I. Gismondi

Intereā Brūtus et Cassius, interfectōrēs Caesaris, ingēns bellum mōvērunt. Erant enim per Macedoniam et Orientem multī exercitūs, quōs occupāverant. Profectī sunt igitur contrā eōs Caesar Octāviānus Augustus et M. Antōnius; remānserat enim ad dēfendendam Italiam Lepidus. Apud Philippōs, Macedoniae urbem, contrā eōs pugnāvērunt. Prīmō proeliō victī sunt Antōnius et Caesar, periit tamen dux nōbilitātis Cassius; secundō Brūtum et īnfīnītam nōbilitātem, quae cum illīs bellum gesserat, victam interfēcērunt. Ac sīc inter eōs dīvīsa est rēs pūblica, ut Augustus Hispāniās, Galliās et Italiam tenēret, Antōnius Asiam, Pontum, Orientem. Sed in Italiā L. Antōnius cōnsul bellum cīvīle commōvit, frāter eius, quī cum Caesare contrā Brūtum et Cassium dīmicāverat. Is apud Perusiam, Tusciae cīvitātem, victus et captus est, neque occīsus.

—Eutropius, *Breviarium* VII.2–3

---

10. What did Brutus and Cassius do? (8–9)
11. Who went to oppose them? Who stayed in Italy? (9–11)
12. Where did the battle take place? (11–12)
13. What two things happened in the first battle? (12–13)
14. What happened in the second battle? (13–14)
15. How was the Roman world divided up after the battle? (14–15)
16. What was Lucius Antonius doing in Italy? (15–16)
17. What eventually happened to Lucius Antonius? (17)

Remains of the Forum of Augustus as they appear today. Compare this photograph with the reconstruction on the opposite page.
Forum of Augustus, Podium of the Temple of Mars, Rome, first century A.D.

1 **M. Agrippa**: Agrippa was one of Octavian's closest friends and one of his generals. In 39–38 B.C., he put down an uprising by the Gauls in Aquitania who had been conquered by Caesar but resented Roman rule.

Aquitānia, -ae, f., *Aquitania* (a province corresponding to southwestern France).

rem . . . gessit: *he managed the situation.* Remember that **gerere** can mean *to do, perform, manage, carry on* as well as *to wear* (clothing).

prosperē, adv., *favorably, successfully.*

2 ***irrumpō, irrumpere, irrūpī, irruptus**, *to burst in, break in.*

Persās: *Persians* really means *Parthians.* The Persians were one of many ethnic groups that made up the Parthian empire on Rome's eastern border (see the map on page 23), but the Romans did not always carefully distinguish the two. Ventidius' victory was in 39 B.C.

Pacorum: notice the accusative case ending on this man's name (and also on **fīlium**).

3 ***ōlim**, adv., *once.*

per ducem Surēnam: King Orodes had not killed Crassus personally, but through an army led by his general Surena. Note that **Surēnam** and **Crassum** are both accusative but refer to different people.

4 **prīmus**: *he was the first to . . .*

***iūstus, -a, -um**, *fair, just, well-deserved.*

***triumphus, -ī**, m., *triumph, victory parade.*

triumphum agere: *to celebrate a triumph.* The victorious general entered Rome and led a parade through the city with his captives to the temple of Jupiter on the Capitoline. Bassus' triumph is described as **iūstissimus** because he was the first Roman general to win a decisive victory over the Parthians.

5 **repudiō, -āre, -āvī, -ātus**, *to reject, divorce.* Antony had married Octavian's sister Octavia to strengthen the alliance between himself and Octavian. See the coin below.

6 **dūxit uxōrem**: *he took as his wife*, a variation on the more common **dūxit in mātrimōnium.** This took place in 37 B.C.

7 ***famēs, famis**, f., *hunger, starvation, famine.* Note the unusual long *e* on the ablative **famē**.

pestilentia, -ae, f., *disease, plague.*

labōrāvit: *suffered from.*

8 ***īnstō, īnstāre, īnstitī** + dat., *to follow, pursue, approach, threaten.*

prō victō: *as the defeated one.*

***recēdō, recēdere, recessī, recessūrus**, *to go back, go away, retreat.*

This coin, issued in 39 B.C., celebrates the reconciliation of Octavian and Antony. It shows Antony on one side and on the reverse Octavia, Octavian's sister, whom Antony married to cement the alliance between the two men. He later divorced her and married Cleopatra (cf. 5–6 opposite).

B. Antony vs. Octavian

Eō tempore M. Agrippa in Aquitāniā rem prosperē gessit et L. Ventidius Bassus irrumpentēs in Syriam Persās tribus proeliīs vīcit. Pacorum, rēgis Orōdis fīlium, interfēcit eō ipsō diē quō ōlim Orōdēs, Persārum rēx, per ducem Surēnam Crassum occīderat. Hic prīmus dē Parthīs iūstissimum triumphum Rōmae ēgit.

Antōnius, quī Asiam et Orientem tenēbat, repudiātā sorōre Caesaris Augustī Octāviānī, Cleopatram, rēgīnam Aegyptī, dūxit uxōrem. Contrā Persās etiam ipse pugnāvit. Prīmīs eōs proeliīs vīcit, regrediēns tamen famē et pestilentiā labōrāvit et, cum īnstārent Parthī fugientī, ipse prō victō recessit.

(continued)

1. Describe Ventidius Bassus' campaign against the Parthians. (1–4)
2. Whom did Antony divorce? Whom did he then marry? (5–6)
3. How did Antony's war against Parthia go at first? (7)
4. What happened to Antony as he was returning from Parthia? (7–8)

Reading Note

Dative with Intransitive Compound Verbs

In Chapter 24, you learned that compound verbs such as **occurrere**, *to run into, meet* and **appropinquāre**, *to approach*, are found with an object in the dative. In line 8 above, you met **īnstāre**, another verb of this type.

This coin shows King Orodes II of Parthia (above: 2–4)

Antony held the king of Armenia partially responsible for his defeat in Parthia (above: 6–8). He therefore seized Armenia in 34 B.C. This coin, depicting Antony, commemorates the event: ANTONI(us) · ARMENIA · DEVICTA, *After the conquest of Armenia*. On the reverse is Cleopatra, with the title REGINA · REGVM, *Queen of Kings*.

9 **Hic**: = Antony (continuing the account from the previous sentence).
***cōgō, cōgere, coēgī, coāctus**, *to compel, force.*
***rēgīna, -ae**, f., *queen.*
10 **cupiditās, cupiditātis**, f., *greed.*
muliebris, -is, -e, *of a woman, womanly.*
***optō, -āre, -āvī, -ātus**, *to wish.*
in urbe: when Romans used **urbs** without specifying any other city, they meant Rome.
rēgnō, -āre, -āvī, -ātus, *to rule.*

Victus est . . . apud Actium: in 31 B.C.
11 **illūstris, -is, -e**, *famous.*
quī locus: = **locus quī**; the relative pronoun here appears in front of its antecedent.
Ēpīrus, -ī, f., *Epirus* (on the western coast of Greece; see the map on page 18).
12 **dēspērō, -āre, -āvī, -ātus**, *to give up hope, despair (of).*
trānseō, trānsīre, trānsiī, trānsitūrus, irreg., *to go across; to desert.*
interimō, interimere, interēmī, interēmptus, *to kill.*

13 **aspis, aspidis**, f., *asp* (a poisonous snake).
admittō, admittere, admīsī, admissus, *to let in, allow to reach.*
venēnum, -ī, n., *poison.*
(Cleopatra) . . . exstīncta est: 30 B.C.

Aegyptus . . . adiecta est: note the feminine gender.
14 ***imperium, -ī**, n., *power; empire.*
***adiciō, adicere, adiēcī, adiectus**, *to add.*
praepōnō, praepōnere, praeposuī, praepositus + dat., *to put in charge of.*
C. Cornēlius Gallus: this man was a long-time associate and friend of Octavian; he had helped defeat Antony's forces in Egypt and was later made the first Roman governor of Egypt.

15 ***iūdex, iūdicis**, m., *judge, magistrate; governor.*

Reading Note

Omission of Words (Gapping)

In line 14, the helping verb **est** is to be supplied with **praepositus** (**est** is already present with **adiecta**). Such omission of words that would be repeated is common in Latin and is called *gapping*. You know that gapping is taking place when you see two clauses that are parallel in structure but only one of which is grammatically complete. In lines 13–14, we have **Aegyptus . . . adiecta est** and in line 14, **praepositus . . . Cornēlius Gallus**; each clause contains a subject and a past participle, with the helping verb **est** stated only the first time. Examples of gapping are also found in 56A:12–13 and 14–15. Review those sentences and analyze how the parallel structure shows which word has to be supplied.

Hic quoque ingēns bellum cīvīle commōvit cōgente uxōre Cleopatrā, rēgīnā Aegyptī, dum cupiditāte muliebrī optat etiam in urbe rēgnāre. Victus est ab Augustō nāvālī pugnā clārā et illūstrī apud Actium, quī locus in Ēpīrō est, ex quā fūgit in Aegyptum et dēspērātīs rēbus, cum omnēs ad Augustum trānsīrent, ipse sē interēmit. Cleopatra sibi aspidem admīsit et venēnō eius exstīncta est. Aegyptus per Octāviānum Augustum imperiō Rōmānō adiecta est praepositusque eī C. Cornēlius Gallus. Hunc prīmum Aegyptus Rōmānum iūdicem habuit.

—Eutropius, *Breviarium* VII.5–7

---

5. Why, according to Eutropius, did Antony engage in a civil war? (10)
6. What does Eutropius claim was Cleopatra's motive? (10)
7. Who defeated Antony? How and where? (10–11)
8. What did Antony do after fleeing to Egypt? Why? (12)
9. What happened to Cleopatra? (13)
10. What arrangements were made for the government of Egypt? (13–15)

The Battle of Actium as imagined by a Dutch artist of the Baroque period. How has the painter conveyed the important elements of the battle, even though some of the details are not historically accurate?
The Battle of Actium, 2 September 31 B.C., *Oil on canvas, 1672, Lorenzo A. Castro*

FORMS

The Subjunctive Mood (Review)

You have learned that Latin has three moods, the indicative, subjunctive, and imperative. Using the charts on pages 329–330, review the formation of the tenses of the subjunctive of regular verbs. Also review the subjunctive of the irregular verbs on pages 333–334.

EXERCISE 56a

Give the requested forms of the following verbs in the present, imperfect, perfect, and pluperfect subjunctive. Use the active voice for numbers 1–7, the passive for 8–12.

1. āmittō *(3rd sing.)*
2. vindicō *(1st pl.)*
3. possum *(3rd pl.)*
4. impediō *(2nd sing.)*
5. commoveō *(1st sing.)*
6. volō *(2nd pl.)*
7. suscipiō *(3rd pl.)*
8. cōnor *(1st sing.)*
9. ferō *(3rd sing.)*
10. cōgō *(1st pl.)*
11. iubeō *(2nd pl.)*
12. regredior *(3rd pl.)*

BUILDING THE MEANING

Sequence of Tenses (Review)

As you learned in Book II, the subjunctive is most often used in various types of subordinate clauses. The tense of the subjunctive used is determined by the sequence of tenses.

SEQUENCE OF TENSES		
	Main Clause Tense of Indicative	**Subordinate Clause** Tense of Subjunctive *Time of action relative to main clause*
Primary Sequence	Present or Future or Future Perfect	Present = *Same time or after* Perfect = *Time before*
Secondary Sequence	Imperfect or Perfect or Pluperfect	Imperfect = *Same time or after* Pluperfect = *Time before*

The following examples illustrate sequence of tenses:

Octāviānus intellegit cūr Antōnius sē **impediat**. *Octavian understands why Antony **is hindering** him.*	(primary sequence, same time)
Octāviānus intellegit cūr Antōnius sē **impedīverit**. *Octavian understands why Antony **hindered** him.*	(primary sequence, time before)
Octāviānus intellegēbat cūr Antōnius sē **impedīret**. *Octavian understood why Antony **was hindering** him.*	(secondary sequence, same time)
Octāviānus intellegēbat cūr Antōnius sē **impedīvisset**. *Octavian understood why Antony **had hindered** him.*	(secondary sequence, time before)

EXERCISE 56b

Read aloud, select the correct form to complete the sentence, and translate:

1. Scīsne quō Antōnius, āmissō exercitū, (īverit, īvisset, īret)?
2. Cum Lepidus operam (det, daret, dederit), Antōnius et Octāviānus inter sē pācem fēcērunt.
3. Omnēs sciunt cūr Antōnius in Aegyptum (fūgisset, fugeret, fūgerit).
4. Antōnius volēbat scīre quot mīlitēs Octāvius (habēret, habeat, habuerit).
5. Cum Antōnius apud Actium (victus sit, victus esset, vincātur), multī ē mīlitibus eius ad Octāvium trānsiērunt.
6. Scīmus quōmodo Cleopatra (mortua sit, mortua esset, morerētur).
7. Magister nōs docuit quis (fuisset, fuerit, sit) prīmus iūdex Rōmānus in Aegyptō.
8. Octāvius, cum Aegyptum imperiō Rōmānō (adiēcisset, adiēcerit, adiciat), Rōmam rediit.
9. Omnēs sciunt ubi Cleopatra sē (interfēcisset, interficeret, interfēcerit).
10. Aegyptum, cum prōvincia Rōmāna (facta sit, facta esset, fiat), C. Cornēlius Gallus administrāvit.

A coin of Augustus, with the legend AEGYPTO CAPTA, *After the capture of Egypt*. The head is that of Augustus; the crocodile symbolizes the Nile and Egypt.

1 ***cōnficiō, cōnficere, cōnfēcī, cōnfectus**, *to accomplish, finish.*
Rōmam rediit: 29 B.C.
duodecimus, -a, -um: deduce from **duo** + **decem.**
2 **quam**: = **postquam**, *after.*
Ex eō: *From that time.*
3 **obtineō, obtinēre, obtinuī, obtentus**, *to hold, possess.*
4 ***initium, -ī**, n., *beginning.*
prīncipātus, -ūs, m., *leadership, principate* (period of an emperor's rule).
***obeō, obīre, obiī** or **obīvī, obitūrus**, irreg., *to die.* Augustus died in A.D. 14.
5 ***commūnis, -is, -e**, *common.*
morte commūnī: i.e., Augustus died a natural death; he was not killed in battle or murdered by political enemies.
oppidum, -ī, n., *town.* The town of Atella was halfway between Naples and Capua.
Campānia, -ae, f., *Campania* (area of southern Italy centering on the Bay of Naples).
in campō Mārtiō: the Campus Martius was a flat area to the northwest of the original city of Rome, first used for military training (hence the name). Later it became the site of many monumental buildings.
6 ***sepeliō, sepelīre, sepelīvī, sepultus**, *to bury.*
immeritō, adv., *unfairly, undeservedly.*
ex maximā parte: *for the greatest part.*
7 **Neque facile ūllus . . . fuit**: *Not easily was anyone*, i.e., it was hard to find anyone who was.
***ūllus, -a, -um**, *any, anyone.*
eō: *than he*, ablative of comparison.
moderātior: Augustus did not take revenge on his opponents in the civil wars.
8 **quibus**: *in which*, ablative of time when.
cīvīlissimē: Augustus did not flaunt his power or exalt himself above other nobles; he was modest in his personal life and preferred not to call attention to his absolute power.
***vīvō, vīvere, vīxī, victus**, *to live.*
9 **līberālis, -is, -e**, *generous.*
***fīdus, -a, -um**, *loyal, faithful.*
ēvehō, ēvehere, ēvexī, ēvectus, *to carry up, raise up.*
honōribus: remember that **honor** may mean *political office.*
aequō, -āre, -āvī, -ātus, *to make equal*; supply **eōs** as direct object of **aequāret**.
10 **fastīgium, -ī**, n., *height, high point; greatness.*
11 **rēs Rōmāna**: *Rome's condition.*
flōreō, flōrēre, flōruī, *to bloom, flourish, prosper.*
12 **invictus**: deduce from **in-** + **vincō.**
13 **penitus**, adv., *thoroughly, completely.*
subigō, subigere, subēgī, subāctus, *tame, conquer, subdue.*
14 **omnēs . . . cīvitātēs**: a group of cities on the Black Sea that had previously been controlled by Mithridates, king of Pontus. **Bosporus** was not a city, as Eutropius states; the name refers rather to the whole kingdom, whose capital was Panticapaeum.
maritimus, -a, -um, *on the shore.*
in hīs: *among them.*
15 **Dācī, -ōrum**, m. pl., *Dacians* (people who lived in what is now Romania).

LVII

The Principate of Augustus

A. Augustus as Emperor

Ita bellīs per tōtum orbem cōnfectīs Octāviānus Augustus Rōmam rediit, duodecimō annō quam cōnsul fuerat. Ex eō rem pūblicam per quadrāgintā et quattuor annōs sōlus obtinuit. Ante enim duodecim annīs cum Antōniō et Lepidō tenuerat. Ita ab initiō prīncipātūs eius ūsque ad fīnem quīnquāgintā et sex annī fuērunt. Obiit autem septuāgēsimō sextō annō morte commūnī in oppidō Campāniae Ātellā. Rōmae in campō Mārtiō sepultus est, vir quī nōn immeritō ex maximā parte deō similis est putātus. Neque enim facile ūllus eō aut in bellīs fēlīcior fuit aut in pāce moderātior. Quadrāgintā et quattuor annīs, quibus sōlus gessit imperium, cīvīlissimē vīxit, in cūnctōs līberālissimus, in amīcōs fīdissimus, quōs tantīs ēvexit honōribus ut paene aequāret fastīgiō suō.

Nūllō tempore ante eum magis rēs Rōmāna flōruit. Nam exceptīs cīvīlibus bellīs, in quibus invictus fuit, Rōmānō adiēcit imperiō Aegyptum, Cantabriam, Dalmatiam saepe ante victam sed penitus tum subāctam, Pannoniam, Aquītāniam, Illyricum, Raetiam, Vindelicōs et Salassōs in Alpibus, omnēs Pontī maritimās cīvitātēs, in hīs nōbilissimās Bosporum et Panticapaeum. Vīcit autem multīs proeliīs Dācōs.

—Eutropius, *Breviarium* VII.8–9

---

1. When did Augustus return to Rome? (1–2)
2. How long did he rule the Roman world alone? How long had he ruled with Antony and Lepidus? (2–3)
3. What was the total length of Augustus' time in power? (3–4)
4. At what age and where did Augustus die? (4–5)
5. To whom was Augustus considered similar? (6)
6. How did Augustus compare with other leaders in his military campaigns? During peacetime? (7)
7. How did Augustus behave toward others during his principate? (8–10)
8. How did the condition of the Roman empire during Augustus' reign compare with earlier times? (11)
9. What did Augustus do with all the places and peoples mentioned in lines 12–15? Locate them on the map on page 23.

1 ***caedō, caedere, cecīdī, caesus**, *to cut down, kill.*
ipsōs: *them*, whole tribes of Germans, as opposed to their soldiers who were killed.
Albis, Albis, m., *the Elbe River.* Augustus' goal (which he did not achieve) was to make the Elbe the eastern border of the Roman empire. See the map on page 23.
fluvius, -ī, m., *river.*
summoveō, summovēre, summōvī, summōtus, *to move out, expel, banish.*
2 **barbaricō**: *foreign territory.*
***ultrā**, prep. + acc., *beyond.*

prīvignus, -ī, m., *stepson.* Drusus and Tiberius were sons of Augustus' second wife, Livia.
3 **administrāvit**: supply this verb in the second clause; review the Reading Note on page 42.
***sīcut**, conj., *just as.*
Pannonicus, -a, -um, *Pannonian* (Pannonia included what is now Austria and Hungary).

4 ***trānstulit**: deduce from **trāns** + **ferō**.
rīpa, -ae, f., *bank* (of a river).
5 **collocō, -āre, -āvī, -ātus**, *to locate, settle.*
***recipiō, recipere, recēpī, receptus**, *to take back, recapture.*

obses, obsidis, m., *hostage.*
quod nūllī anteā: *a thing which (they had done) for no one previously*; **nūllī** is dative singular.
Persae: this means the Parthians (see the note for line 2, page 40).

6 ***signum, -ī**, n., *sign, signal; standard* (a military term). Each legion had its own **signa**, symbols mounted on poles (see the painting on page 25 and the description on page 80). Soldiers knew where to move by following the **signum** of their own regiment. To lose the **signa** to the enemy was an enormous disgrace.
Crassō victō: the dative case with the verb **adimō** expresses *from*. . .

7 **Scythae, -ārum**, m. pl., *Scythians* (a group of people living in what is now Ukraine and southern Russia). See the map on page 23.
Indī, -ōrum, m. pl., *Indians, people of India.*
incognitus, -a, -um, *unknown.*
***mūnus, mūneris**, n., *duty, obligation; gift; gladiatorial show; gift* in this context.

8 **Galatia, -ae**, f., *Galatia* (a province in central Asia Minor; see the map on page 23).
cum: *although.*
9 **prō praetōre**: a praetor or consul often went out as governor of a province after his term of office. His position as governor was referred to as **prō praetōre** or **prō cōnsule**.

***amor, amōris**, m., *love.*
Tantō . . . amōre . . . fuit: *He was so beloved* (literally, *He was of such love*). A noun in the ablative, modified by an adjective, is used to describe a personal quality or characteristic and is called the *ablative of description*.
10 **cīvitātēs**: = **urbēs**.

12 **obsequor, obsequī, obsecūtus sum** + dat., *to obey, yield to; to gratify, honor.*
habitus, -ūs, m., *dress, clothing.*
togātus, -a, -um, *wearing a toga.*
***scīlicet**, adv., *of course, obviously.*

13 ***dīvus, -a, -um**, *divine, deified.* Some Roman emperors were declared to be gods by the Senate after their death as a mark of respect; this had been done for Julius Caesar, who was then known as **Dīvus Iūlius**.

B. More of Augustus' Achievements

Germānōrum ingentēs cōpiās cecīdit, ipsōs quoque trāns Albim fluvium summōvit, quī in barbaricō longē ultrā Rhēnum est. Hoc tamen bellum per Drūsum, prīvignum suum, administrāvit, sīcut per Tiberium, prīvignum alterum, bellum Pannonicum. Quō bellō quadrāgintā captīvōrum mīlia ex Germāniā trānstulit et suprā rīpam Rhēnī in Galliā collocāvit. Armeniam ā Parthīs recēpit. Obsidēs, quod nūllī anteā, Persae eī dedērunt. Reddidērunt etiam signa Rōmāna, quae Crassō victō adēmerant.

Scythae et Indī, quibus anteā Rōmānōrum nōmen incognitum fuerat, mūnera et lēgātōs ad eum mīsērunt. Galatia quoque sub hōc prōvincia facta est, cum anteā rēgnum fuisset, prīmusque eam M. Lollius prō praetōre administrāvit. Tantō autem amōre etiam apud barbarōs fuit ut rēgēs populī Rōmānī amīcī in honōrem eius conderent cīvitātēs, quās Caesarēās nōminārent. Multī autem rēgēs ex rēgnīs suīs vēnērunt ut eī obsequerentur, et habitū Rōmānō, togātī scīlicet, ad vehiculum vel equum ipsīus cucurrērunt. Moriēns Dīvus appellātus est.

—Eutropius, *Breviarium* VII.9–10

---

1. In what two ways did Augustus deal with the Germans? (1–2)
2. How did Augustus run his military campaigns in Germany and Pannonia? (2–3)
3. What was done with the German captives? How many were there? (4–5)
4. What territory did Augustus recover? From whom? (5)
5. Name two things that the Parthians did as signs of respect for Augustus. (5–6)
6. What did the Scythians and Indians do during Augustus' reign? (7–8)
7. What happened to the kingdom of Galatia during Augustus' reign? (8–9)
8. What did friendly foreign kings do to honor Augustus? (9–11)
9. Why did foreign kings come to Rome? What did they do there? (11–13)
10. How did the Senate honor Augustus after his death? (13)

A coin of Augustus showing a kneeling Parthian returning the standards taken from Crassus at the battle of Carrhae (above: 6). The legend (partly missing from this copy of the coin) reads [CAESAR AVGV]STVS SIGN(īs) RECE[PT(īs)].

Denarius, Augustus Mint, Rome

BUILDING THE MEANING

The Subjunctive in Subordinate Clauses (Review)

You have already met in Book II several types of subordinate clauses that use the subjunctive mood:

1. Indirect Questions:

   Senātōrēs rogābant **cūr** Caesar tyrannica **faceret**.
   The senators kept asking ***why*** *Caesar* ***was acting*** *like a tyrant (doing tyrannical things).*

2. Circumstantial Clauses:

   Caesar, **cum** senātūs diē **vēnisset** ad Cūriam, cōnfossus est. (cf. 55D:7–8)
   When *Caesar* ***had arrived*** *at the Senate House on the day of the Senate (meeting), he was stabbed.*

3. Causal Clauses:

   Senātōrēs, **cum** rēgnum Caesaris nōn iam ferre **possent**, coniūrāvērunt.
   The senators made a conspiracy ***because*** *they* ***could*** *no longer endure Caesar's rule.*

4. Result Clauses:

   Tantō amōre apud barbarōs fuit **ut** rēgēs amīcī in honōrem eius **conderent** cīvitātēs. (cf. 57B:9–11)
   He (Augustus) was ***so*** *beloved among foreigners* ***that*** *friendly kings* ***founded*** *cities in his honor.*

5. Indirect Commands:

   Rēgēs barbarī Augustum **ōrābant** **ut** sibi auxilium **daret**.
   Foreign kings ***kept asking*** *Augustus* ***to help*** *them.*

6. Purpose Clauses:

   Multī rēgēs ex rēgnīs suīs vēnērunt **ut** eī **obsequerentur**. (cf. 57B:11–12)
   Many kings came from their realms ***to honor*** *him.*

Key words that indicate result clauses include **adeō, ita, sīc, tālis, tam, tantus**, and **tot**. Indirect commands are introduced by verbs such as **imperāre, monēre, ōrāre, persuādēre**, and **rogāre**. Remember that negative purpose clauses and negative indirect commands are introduced by **nē**, while negative result clauses use **ut . . . nōn**. And, as always when dealing with subordinate clauses, note carefully where clauses begin and end to avoid mixing words that belong in a subordinate clause with the main clause as you read the sentence.

All these constructions follow the rules for sequence of tenses given on pages 44–45. Notice that indirect commands and purpose clauses always use either present or imperfect subjunctive, since the action in such constructions always takes place *after* that of the main verb. The other constructions can use any tense of the subjunctive, as the sense requires. In result clauses, sometimes the perfect subjunctive is found in secondary sequence instead of the imperfect, which seems contrary to the rule. The perfect is used in such clauses to stress the finality or completion (**perfectum** = *completed*) of the action:

> Senātōrēs quīdam Caesarī **adeō** invidēbant **ut** eum **occīderint**.
> *Some senators hated Caesar* ***so much that*** *they* ***killed*** *him.*

Exercise 57a

Read aloud, identify the type of subjunctive clause in each sentence, and translate:

1. Cum Augustus mortuus esset, senātus eum Dīvum appellāvit.
2. Augustus multa bella gessit ut esset pāx per tōtum orbem.
3. Parthī Augustum verēbantur cum esset prīnceps potēns.
4. Tantus prīnceps fuit Augustus ut Eutropius in Breviāriō suō magnopere eum laudāret.
5. Omnēs sciunt cūr populus Rōmānus Augustum amāverit.
6. Augustus Parthīs persuāsit ut signa Rōmāna redderent.
7. Senātus Octāviānō, cum rērum potītus esset, titulum Augustum dedit.
8. Multī rēgēs Rōmam vēnērunt ut Augustō honōrārent.
9. Iūlius Caesar erat tam arrogāns ut senātōrēs eum occīderint.
10. Prīnceps ōrat ut senātus sē iuvet.
11. Nesciō quot bella Augustus gesserit.
12. Augustus ita sē gessit ut nēmō eum occīdere vellet.

Parthī, -ōrum, m. pl., *the Parthians*
*** vereor, verērī, veritus sum,** *to be afraid of, fear*
*** potēns, potentis,** *powerful*
titulus, -ī, m., *title*
sē gerere, *to conduct oneself, behave*

Exercise 57b

Choose the correct form of the subjunctive. Be sure to follow the rules for sequence of tenses (review pages 44–45, if necessary).

1. Antōnius, cum tōtum orbem regere (vellet, velit, volēbat), bellum contrā Octāviānum commōvit.
2. Omnēs sciunt cūr Antōnius bellum (commōvit, commovēret, commōverit).
3. Antōnius contrā Parthōs pugnāvit nē in Syriam iterum (irrumpant, irrūperint, irrumperent).
4. Ībunt ad Actium Cleopatra et Antōnius ut Octāviānum (vincant, vincerent, vincent).
5. Cum (victī sint, victī essent, victī erant), Antōnius et Cleopatra sē interfēcērunt.
6. Aegyptus erat prōvincia tam magna ut Augustus amīcum C. Cornēlium Gallum iūdicem (fēcerit, fēcit, faciat).
7. Cleopatra adeō Antōnium amābat ut cum eō morī (velit, volēbat, vellet).

*** regō, regere, rēxī, rēctus,** *to rule*
*** adeō,** adv., *so much, to such an extent*

Readers in ancient times studied the works of Cicero, Caesar, and other authors from copies written on papyrus scrolls. Shown here is a fragment of papyrus discovered in Hawara, Egypt in 1888. The dry climate of Egypt has preserved many fragments of papyrus and a few entire scrolls. The fibers of the papyrus plant, from which the paper-like writing material was made, are visible as horizontal lines in the photograph. This papyrus fragment was written in the first century A.D., apparently by a student who copied out a line from Vergil's *Aeneid* multiple times. The text (*Aeneid* II.602) reads: *non tibi Tyndaridis facies invisa Lacaenae.*

Hawara papyrus, first century A.D.

Writers of the Late Republic

Overview of Part II

In Part I you received an overview of the political and historical events that took place between 63 B.C. and A.D. 14. In Part II you will read selections from some of the most important writers of the late Republic. Part II has the following objectives:

- to present some of the events of the late Republic in greater depth
- to increase your ability to read Latin prose by working with selections from Cicero and Caesar
- to introduce Latin poetry through the writings of Catullus
- to learn about gerunds and some additional uses of the subjunctive and to review a variety of other grammatical topics

Perhaps the foremost Roman living during the late Republic was Marcus Tullius Cicero (106–43 B.C.). It is appropriate for Cicero to be one of the first Romans whose actual words you read. Not only was he an important political figure, but he was also recognized in his own time and ever since as an outstanding master of Latin prose. Five chapters of this book have been devoted to Cicero's writings because he still has something to say to us. He possessed one of ancient Rome's most versatile minds—brilliant as an orator in the Senate and as a lawyer in the courts, an accomplished letter writer, author of thought-provoking works on philosophy and oratory, and even something of a poet. He was a devoted son, brother, husband, and father, and kept himself and his family alive during perhaps the bloodiest period of civil war in Rome's history. Ever the staunch advocate of the Republic during its final years, Cicero served as a successful public advocate for patriotic causes, quashed a conspiracy against the state while consul, and was the regular proponent of a **concordia ōrdinum** (harmony between the senatorial and equestrian classes).

In Chapter 58, you will read part of a judicial speech of prosecution against a provincial governor, which Cicero gave relatively early in his career. In Chapter 59, you will read selections from his first political speech against the conspirator Catiline, delivered when he was at the height of his consular career. It is hoped that you will come to appreciate Cicero the man, as well as Cicero the writer, as you read the chapters that follow.

1 **vītium, -ī**, n., *fault, weakness, moral defect, vice.*

omnium vītiōrum suōrum: i.e., of Verres, who is the subject of the main verb **cōnstituit.**

***cōnstituō, cōnstituere, cōnstituī, cōnstitūtus**, *to set in place, establish.*

***monumentum, -ī**, n., *memorial; reminder, testimonial.*

indicium, -ī, n., *evidence, proof.*

2 **in prōvinciā Siciliā**: when Verres was governor (**praetor**; see line 3) of the province of Sicily. During the Republic it was common for provincial governors, who were former magistrates from the upper class, to enrich themselves at the expense of the natives.

quam: the antecedent is **Sicilia.**

***iste, ista, istud**, *that.* **Iste** and **ille** both mean *that*, but **iste** almost always expresses contempt or disdain for the person or thing mentioned. Here **iste** refers to Verres.

triennium, -ī, n., *period or interval of three years.*

vexāvit: more powerful than *he annoyed*; *he devastated, ravaged, ruined.*

***perdō, perdere, perdidī, perditus,** *to ruin, ravage, destroy.*

ut . . . possit (3): result clause anticipated by **ita** in the previous line.

ea: = **(prōvincia) Sicilia.**

restituō, restituere, restituī, restitūtus, *to renew, revive, restore.*

restituī: present passive infinitive, rather than 1st person singular of the perfect tense.

***antīquus, -a, -um**, *old, ancient; former.*

3 **status, -ūs**, m., *standing, status, position.*

in antīquum statum: in addition to Egypt and the area around the Black Sea, Sicily was one of the breadbaskets of the ancient world.

***modus, -ī**, m., *way, method.*

***praetor, praetōris**, m., *praetor* (a judicial official); *governor* (since praetors and consuls who had completed their year in office were often assigned as governors of provinces).

Hōc praetōre: *While this man (Verres) was governor*; ablative absolute.

Siculī, -ōrum, m. pl., *Sicilians, people of Sicily.*

lēx, lēgis, f., *law.*

nostra senātūs cōnsulta: = **cōnsulta senātūs Rōmānī**, i.e., the decrees of the Roman Senate. Note how **nostra** agrees with **cōnsulta** but more properly modifies **senātūs.**

4 **iūs, iūris**, n., *right.*

commūnia iūra: *natural rights, the rights common to all.*

tenuērunt: *possessed.*

Tantum: correlates with **quantum** (5): *as much . . . as.*

***quisque, quaeque, quidque**, *each, each person, each one.*

5 **avārus, -a, -um**, *insatiable, acquisitive, greedy.*

libīdinōsus, -a, -um, *intemperate, self-indulgent.*

hominis avārissimī et libīdinōsissimī: this genitive phrase completes the meaning of both **imprūdentiam** and **satietātī.**

imprūdentia, -ae, f., *rashness, indiscretion, impulsiveness.*

subterfugiō, subterfugere, subterfūgī, *to evade, escape the notice of.*

satietās, satietātis, f., *sufficiency, (over) abundance; acquisitiveness, rapacity.*

satietātī: dative with the compound verb **superfuit.**

(*vocabulary and notes continued on opposite page*)

LVIII

A Corrupt Governor

Gaius Verres was a Roman magistrate of the late Republic who was infamous for his misgovernment of the province of Sicily. During his term of office, not only did he disrupt the economy through exorbitant taxation, he also plundered temples, public buildings, and private homes for works of art and disregarded the rights of Roman citizens. When Verres returned to Rome in 70 B.C.*, he was prosecuted for extortion by Cicero, who represented the people of Sicily. Cicero's fierce rival, Quintus Hortensius Hortalus, spoke for the defense.*

A. Greed and Tyranny

Iam vērō omnium vītiōrum suōrum plūrima et maxima cōnstituit monumenta et indicia in prōvinciā Siciliā, quam iste per triennium ita vexāvit ac perdidit ut ea restituī in antīquum statum nūllō modō possit. Hōc praetōre Siculī neque suās lēgēs neque nostra senātūs cōnsulta neque commūnia iūra tenuērunt. Tantum quisque habet in Siciliā quantum hominis avārissimī et libīdinōsissimī aut imprūdentiam subterfūgit aut satietātī superfuit.

(continued)

---

1. What resulted from Verres' presence in Sicily? (1–2)
2. How long was his term of office? (2)
3. What did he do during his tenure? (2)
4. To what extent did Verres' actions affect his province? (2–3)
5. What legal protections for Sicilian citizens did Verres ignore? (3–4)
6. How does Cicero characterize Verres in line 5?
7. Under what conditions could a Sicilian retain possession of what he had? (5–6)

6 **supersum, superesse, superfuī, superfutūrus**, irreg., *to be left over from, survive.*

subterfūgit (5) . . . **superfuit**: i.e., a Sicilian possessed only so much as might have escaped the greedy clutches of Verres. Note the sibilation (use of s-sounds) in these lines, which suggests that Cicero is hissing in revulsion at Verres.

7 **Innumerābilēs pecūniae**: *countless monies, untold (sums of) money.*
arātor, arātōris, m., *plowman, farmer.*
bona, -ōrum, n. pl., *goods, possessions, holdings*; substantive.
nefārius, -a, -um, *unspeakable, abominable, shameless.*
īnstitūtum, -ī, n., *undertaking, arrangement; ordinance, regulation.*
novō nefāriōque īnstitūtō: how do you render the meaning of this ablative phrase?
coāctae: = **coāctae sunt**: the verb **cōgō** here has the force of both *collect* and *compel*, e.g., exact or extort. As you read, note that the word **sunt** is understood to complete verbs in the perfect tense of the passive throughout this passage.

8 **fidissimī**: there are eight superlative adjectives in this passage. What is their effect?
existimō, -āre, -āvī, -ātus, *to think, regard, consider.*
***servīlis, -is, -e**, *of* or *as a slave, slavish, servile.*
cruciō, -āre, -āvī, -ātus, *to torture.*
servīlem in modum cruciātī: slaves could be tortured to reveal information.

9 **nocēns, nocentis**, *harmful, wicked; guilty, criminal.*
***iūdicium, -ī**, n., *judgment.*
iūdiciō līberātī: *set free by court verdict*, i.e., acquitted.
***honestus, -a, -um**, *honorable, upright, reputable.*
***integer, integra, integrum**, *complete, intact; uncorrupted, principled, upright.*

10 **reus, -ī**, m., *defendant.*
absentēs reī factī: i.e., these men were indicted and tried in their absence.
indictus, -a, -um, *unsaid, undisclosed; without a hearing.*
***causa, -ae**, f., *reason; lawsuit, charge, legal case.*
indictā causā: ablative absolute.
***damnō, -āre, -āvī, -ātus**, *to condemn, find guilty.*
ēiectī (sunt): i.e., banished, exiled.
portus, -ūs, m., *port, harbor.*
portūs . . . urbēs: elsewhere, Cicero alleges that a crony of Verres, directed to capture some pirates, allowed them to enter the harbor of Syracuse and sack the city.
mūnītus, -a, -um, *protected, fortified.*

11 ***tūtus, -a, -um**, *secure, safe.*
nauta, -ae, m., *sailor.*
patefaciō, patefacere, patefēcī, patefactus, *to open, throw or lay open, make accessible to.*

12 ***classis, classis**, gen. pl., **classium**, f., *fleet.*
opportūnus, -a, -um, *suitable; well outfitted, well equipped.*

13 **ignōminia, -ae**, f., *dishonor, shame, disgrace.*
āmissae: from **āmittō**, *to lose.*
āmissae et perditae: Verres had illegally discharged sailors from serving in the fleet, designated them in the record as serving on duty, and pocketed their pay. Thus, in an indirect way, he compromised the security of Rome.

Innumerābilēs pecūniae ex arātōrum bonīs novō nefāriōque īnstitūtō coāctae; sociī fīdissimī in hostium numerō exīstimātī; cīvēs Rōmānī servīlem in modum cruciātī et necātī; hominēs nocentissimī propter pecūniās iūdiciō līberātī, honestissimī atque integerrimī, absentēs reī factī, indictā causā, damnātī et ēiectī; portūs mūnītissimī, maximae tūtissimaeque urbēs, pīrātīs praedōnibusque patefactae; nautae mīlitēsque Siculōrum, sociī nostrī atque amīcī, famē necātī; classēs optimae atque opportūnissimae cum magnā ignōminiā populī Rōmānī āmissae et perditae.

(*continued*)

---

8. What was the result of the new and shameless regulation? (7)
9. How were loyal allies characterized? (7–8)
10. What happened to Roman citizens? (8–9)
11. What happened to criminals? For what reason? (9)
12. How were reputable and principled men treated? (9–10)
13. What became of fortified harbors and secure cities? (10–11)
14. What fate did the men of the Sicilian army and navy suffer? (11–12)
15. What happened to the fleets? (12–13)
16. How did these actions reflect on the Roman people? (12–13)

Reading Note

Correlatives

In lines 4–5 on page 55, you saw two words, **tantum** and **quantum**, that are paired, that is, they depend upon each other for their meanings: **tantum . . . quantum**, *as much . . . as*. Such pairs of words are common in Latin and are known as *correlatives*. You already know the correlatives **et . . . et**, *both . . . and*; **aut . . . aut**, *either . . . or*; and **neque . . . neque**, *neither . . . nor*. Most of these words can be used alone with a slightly different meaning than when they are paired. For instance, **tantus** by itself means *so much*, *so great*, but means *as much* when paired with **quantum**. These words are usually separated within the sentence. When you see a word that can be a correlative, be alert to the possibility that its partner may appear further along, affecting the meaning of the first member of the pair. Other examples include **ibi . . . ubi**, *there . . . where*; **nōn sōlum . . . sed etiam**, *not only . . . but also*; **tālis . . . quālis**, *such . . . as*; and **tot . . . quot**, *so many . . . as (many)*.

Nihil tam mūnītum quod nōn expugnārī pecūniā possit.
No place is so well fortified that it cannot be captured by money. (Cicero, *In Verrem* I.II.4)

---

14 **Īdem iste**: *That very same . . .* ; presumably spoken by Cicero in an outraged tone of voice while pointing at Verres.

monumenta: i.e., artworks, monuments.

partim . . . partim (line 15): *partly . . . partly*, i.e., *some . . . others*. Note how this sentence is divided into two parts, each of which contains a relative clause introduced by **quae**.

locuplēs, locuplētis, *affluent, rich, wealthy*.

rēgum locuplētissimōrum: links with **monumenta antīquissima**, as does **nostrōrum imperātōrum**, below.

quae: the antecedent is **monumenta**, which is neuter plural.

15 **ōrnāmentō urbibus**: literally, *for adornment for the cities; an adornment for the cities.*

nostrōrum: = **Rōmānōrum.**

imperātōrum: during the Republic, **imperātor** always means *military commander* or *general* (cf. the verb **imperāre**); only later does it come to mean *emperor*.

victōrēs: *as victors*. Roman love for Greek art actually began during the First Punic War with the Roman capture of Sicily, which had been colonized by the Greeks.

16 **aut dedērunt aut reddidērunt**: i.e., presented as gifts or as property restored from conquest.

spoliō, -āre, -āvī, -ātus, *to despoil, plunder*.

nūdō, -āre, -āvī, -ātus, *to lay bare, strip away*.

omnia: modifies **monumenta** (14). Cicero puts great stress on this adjective by placing it at the end of the sentence, far away from the noun it modifies.

17 **hoc**: refers to those actions of Verres just described.

in: *with regard to, concerning*.

dēlūbrum, **-ī**, n., *a temple; shrine*.

***sānctus, -a, -um**, *venerated, sacred, holy*.

18 ***religiō, religiōnis**, f., *religion; strict observance of religious ritual*.

cōnsecrō, -āre, -āvī, -ātus, *to devote (to), consecrate (to), make holy* or *sacred (to)*.

dēpecūlor, dēpecūlārī, dēpecūlātus sum, *to rob, plunder, pillage*.

deum . . . nūllum: i.e., the image or statue of a god.

***dēnique**, adv., *finally, at last*.

quī: the antecedent is **deum.** The subjunctive (**vidērētur**) is used when a general, rather than a specific, example is given.

eī: *to him* (Verres).

***paulō**, adv., *a little, slightly*.

19 **affabrē**, adv., *with craftsmanship, skillfully*.

paulō magis affabrē: *in a slightly more skillful manner*; note this sequence of adverbs.

artificium, -ī, n., *skill, craftsmanship;* (**ars** + **faciō**).

antīquō artificiō: ablative of manner.

factus: = **factus esse**, completing the meaning of **vidērētur**.

Īdem iste praetor monumenta antīquissima, partim rēgum locuplētissimōrum, quae illī ōrnāmentō urbibus esse voluērunt, partim etiam nostrōrum imperātōrum, quae victōrēs cīvitātibus Siculīs aut dedērunt aut reddidērunt, spoliāvit nūdāvitque omnia. Neque hoc sōlum in statuīs ōrnāmentīsque pūblicīs fēcit, sed etiam dēlūbra omnia sānctissimīs religiōnibus cōnsecrāta dēpecūlātus est; deum dēnique nūllum Siculīs, quī eī paulō magis affabrē atque antīquō artificiō factus vidērētur, relīquit.

— Cicero, *In Verrem* I.IV.12–14

17. What did Verres do to ancient works of art? (14, 16)
18. From where had some of these antiquities come? (14)
19. What were the intentions of these benefactors? (15)
20. What was another source of such artworks? (15–16)
21. What other places did Verres pillage? How are these characterized? (17–18)
22. What was Verres' final sacrilege? (18–19)
23. On what basis did Verres make his selection of sacred objects? (18–19)

Reading Note

Relative Clauses of Characteristic

You have seen many relative clauses introduced by the relative pronoun **quī** followed by a verb in the indicative mood. In lines 18–19 above, the **quī**-clause is completed by the verb **vidērētur**, which is subjunctive. This relative clause, which is known as a *relative clause of characteristic*, describes a *type* of person or thing, rather than one that is actual or specific. Cicero is describing the type of art object that appealed to Verres, rather than a specific object. Subordinate clauses of this kind usually follow indefinite words or phrases such as **nēmō est quī** (*there is no one who . . .*), **is est quī** (*he is the type* or *kind of person who . . .*), and **sunt quī** (*there are those of the sort who . . .*).

Relative clause with the indicative: **Verrēs erat vir quī deōs nōn verēbātur.**
Verres was a man who (in fact) did not respect the gods.

Relative clause with the subjunctive: **Verrēs erat vir quī deōs nōn verērētur.**
Verres was the type of man who did not respect the gods.

The rostra from which Cicero gave this speech may have looked something like this structure, a 20th-century reconstruction of the rostra begun by Julius Caesar and completed by Octavian in 42 B.C. The earlier rostra was located in front of the Curia (see the plan on page 147); this later one is next to the temple of Saturn.

1 **Herculēs, Herculis**, m., *Hercules* (patron god of Agrigentum). Remains of the temple of Hercules survive today in the sacred area of the town. See the picture on page 63.

Agrigentīnus, -ī, m., *a citizen of Agrigentum* (a city on the southern coast of Sicily, modern *Agrigento*).

apud Agrigentīnōs: i.e., at Agrigentum.

***sānē**, adv., *certainly, of course; exceedingly, extremely*; take with **sānctum** and **religiōsum**.

2 **aes, aeris**, n., *copper, bronze.*

***simulācrum, -ī**, n., *image, likeness, effigy; statue.*

quō: *than which*; ablative of comparison after **pulchrius**, following. Determine the sense of this clause by following the Latin word order.

***quisquam, quisquam, quidquam** or **quicquam**, *anyone, anything.*

3 **vīdisse**: perfect infinitive in indirect statement after **dīxerim** (2), *I could say.*

pulchrius: neuter comparative adjective, modifying **quicquid**, the direct object of **vīdisse.**

usque eō: *as far as, to such a point that.*

***iūdex, iūdicis**, m., *judge, member of the jury*; said with respect, e.g., *gentlemen of the jury.*

rictum, -ī, n., *the open mouth.*

eius: i.e., of Hercules.

mentum, -ī, n., *chin.* It was customary when praying to touch the chin of the god's image.

sit: completes the result clause anticipated by **eō** in line 3.

attrītius: *rather* or *somewhat worn away*; comparative adjective, neuter singular.

4 **prex, precis**, f., *prayer.*

grātulātiō, grātulātiōnis, f., *thanksgiving, gratitude.*

nōn sōlum . . . vērum etiam: a more emphatic variation of **nōn sōlum . . . sed etiam.** Cf. **neque sōlum** in lines 16–17, page 59.

veneror, venerārī, venerātus sum, *to honor, revere, pay respect to.*

venerārī: present infinitive, as is **ōsculārī**, below, dependent upon **solent** in line 5.

ōsculor, ōsculārī, ōsculatus sum, *to kiss.*

5 **iste**: to whom does this pronoun refer?

Agrigentī: *in* or *at Agrigentum*; locative case.

Tīmārchides, Tīmārchidis, m., *Timarchides* (a notorious freedman of Verres).

duce Tīmārchide: ablative absolute.

***repente**, adv., *suddenly, unexpectedly.*

nocte intempestā: *at an inopportune time of night, in the dead of the night.*

6 **armātus, -a, -um**, *armed, equipped with weapons.*

concursus, -ūs, m., *assault, raid.*

***impetus, -ūs**, m., *attack.*

fit concursus atque impetus: note how the subject and main verb of this sentence are postponed in order to build anticipation.

vigil, vigilis, m., *(night) watchman.*

fānum, -ī, n., *holy place, consecrated area, shrine.*

7 ***tollō, tollere, sustulī, sublātus**, irreg., *to raise, lift up.*

cum: *although.*

obsistō, obsistere, obstitī, obstitus, *to stand in the way, make a stand.*

mulcō, -āre, -āvī, -ātus, *to beat, rough up, thrash.*

8 **clāva, -ae**, f., *knotted stick, cudgel.*

fūstis, fūstis, gen. pl., **fūstium**, m., *club, cudgel.*

B. A Herculean Labor

Herculis templum est apud Agrigentīnōs nōn longē ā forō, sānē sānctum apud illōs et religiōsum. Ibi est ex aere simulācrum ipsīus Herculis, quō nōn facile dīxerim quicquam mē vīdisse pulchrius usque eō, iūdicēs, ut rictum eius ac mentum paulō sit attrītius, quod in precibus et grātulātiōnibus nōn sōlum id venerārī vērum etiam ōsculārī solent. Ad hoc templum, cum esset iste Agrigentī, duce Tīmārchide repente nocte intempestā servōrum armātōrum fit concursus atque impetus. Clāmor ā vigilibus fānīque custōdibus tollitur; quī prīmō cum obsistere ac dēfendere cōnārentur, male mulcātī, clāvīs ac fūstibus repelluntur.

(*continued*)

---

1. Where was the temple of Hercules located? (1)
2. How was this place regarded by the people of Agrigentum? (1–2)
3. What of importance was found there? (2)
4. What personal comment does Cicero make about the beauty of this object? (2–3)
5. In what condition was this object? (3–4)
6. What customs of the local people explained the condition of this object? (4–5)
7. What happened at the temple one night? Who was involved? (5–6)
8. Who raised the alarm? (6–7) What did they do at first? With what result? (7)
9. How did the hostilities end? (8)

Reading Notes

Cum Concessive Clauses

In line 7 above, you met a **cum** clause with the subjunctive, **cum . . . cōnārentur**. The best meaning for **cum** in this context is *although*, a use of **cum** known as *concessive*. The word *concessive* indicates that the statement within the **cum** clause is granted or assumed as true by the speaker or writer. A **cum** concessive clause is often (but not always) accompanied by the word **tamen**, *nevertheless*, in the main clause. You have also met the word **quamquam**, *although*, which introduces a concessive clause, usually with the indicative.

• • •

The Vivid or Historic Present

In the passage above, you saw the verbs **fit** (6), **tollitur** (7), and **repelluntur** (8). These verbs are in the present tense even though Cicero is describing events that took place in the past. You learned in Chapter 30 that this use of the present tense is referred to as the *vivid* or *historic present* and is used to make the action more vivid for the listener or reader.

9 ***dēmōlior, dēmōlīrī, dēmōlītus sum**, *to pull down, remove.*

dēmōlīrī . . . cōnantur: statues were usually placed on stone pedestals.

***signum, -ī**, n., *sign, mark, military standard; image, figure, statue*, i.e., of Hercules.

vectis, vectis, gen. pl., **vectium**, m., *lever, crowbar.*

labefactō, -āre, -avī, -ātus, *to shake or shudder, cause to totter.*

***fāma, -ae**, f., *rumor, report.*

tōtā urbe: = **in tōtā urbe.**

10 **percrēbrēscō, percrēbrēscere, percrēbruī, percrēbitus**, *to become frequent* or *well known, spread far and wide.*

expugnō, -āre, -āvī, -ātus, *to capture, take by storm or force.*

***patrius, -a, -um**, *father's, ancestral.*

expugnārī deōs patriōs: indirect statement after **fāma . . . percrēbruit.**

adventus, -ūs, m., *arrival.*

necopīnātus, -a, -um, *unexpected* (**nec** + **opīnor**).

repentīnus, -a, -um, *sudden, unforeseen.* Cf. **repente**, line 5, page 61.

11 **praedōnum**: probably pirates.

ex domō: i.e., of Verres.

ex cohorte praetōriā: *from the governor's staff.* The **cohors praetōria**, or praetorian cohort, attended the provincial governor (**praetor**). Note the contrast between where the brigands might have come from (10–11) and where they did come from (11), in Cicero's opinion.

manum: **manus** can mean *band of men*, as well as *hand*; **manum** is the subject of **vēnisse.**

12 ***īnstruō, īnstruere, īnstrūxī, īnstructus**, *prepare, arrange, draw up for battle.*

vēnisse: perfect infinitive in indirect statement after **fāma . . . percrēbruit**, lines 9–10. How is the perfect tense of **vēnisse** expressed, given the perfect tense of the main verb **percrēbruit**?

afficiō, afficere, affēcī, affectus, *to influence;* of the body, *weaken, impair, deplete.*

aetāte tam affectā: *because of such weakened age, so weakened with age*, i.e., so old. Parallels **vīribus tam īnfirmīs** later in the line.

***vīribus**: from **vīs**, *strength.*

13 **quī**: the antecedent is **Nēmo**, line 12. What type of clause is this? See page 59.

eō nūntiō: i.e., the news of the attempted theft of the statue (lines 9–10).

excitātus: *awakened* (from sleep); remember that it was the middle of the night (lines 5–6).

surrēxerit: perfect subjunctive of **surgō**; note also **arripuerit** in line 14.

***tēlum, -ī**, n., *weapon.*

14 ***fors**, abl. **forte** (only in nom. and abl. sing.), *chance, luck, fortune.*

***itaque**, adv., *and so.*

fānum, -ī, n., *consecrated area, shrine.*

***concurrō, concurrere, concurrī, concursūrus**, *to rush together, assemble quickly.*

concurritur: literally, *it is rushed together (by them), they rush together.*

Posteā dēmōlīrī signum ac vectibus labefactāre cōnantur. Intereā ex clāmōre fāma tōtā urbe percrēbruit expugnārī deōs patriōs, nōn hostium adventū necopīnātō neque repentīnō praedōnum impetū, sed ex domō atque ex cohorte praetōriā manum fugitīvōrum īnstructam armātamque vēnisse. Nēmō Agrigentī neque aetāte tam affectā neque vīribus tam īnfirmīs fuit quī nōn illā nocte eō nuntiō excitātus surrēxerit, tēlumque quod cuique fors offerēbat arripuerit. Itaque brevī tempore ad fānum ex urbe tōtā concurritur.

(*continued*)

---

10. By what means did the thieves attempt to procure the statue? (9)
11. Of what were the townspeople informed? By what means? (9–10)
12. Who were not attempting the theft? (10–11)
13. From where did the bandits come? (11) What kind of men were they? (11–12)
14. Who answered the call for help? (12–13)
15. What had these individuals been doing? (13)
16. What did they use as weapons? (13–14)
17. Summarize the response of the townsfolk. (14)

Reading Note

Passive Verbs Used Impersonally

In line 14 above, you will note that there is no nominative subject of the verb **concurritur** and that the literal sense requires that the unexpressed subject be *it*, i.e., *it is rushed together*. The context makes it clear that the townspeople of Agrigentum are coming together, so a better translation of **concurritur** would be *there is a rush* or *they rush together*, *they flock*. We say that such verbs (usually intransitive) are used *impersonally* because no personal subject is expressed. Verbs are used impersonally when the writer wishes to emphasize the *action*, rather than the person or persons performing the action. In Book II, you met this example of an impersonal passive:

> Complūrēs hōrās ācriter **pugnābātur**. (48:18)
> ***The fighting went on** fiercely for several hours*, literally, ***It was fought*** . . .

You also met this example in Chapter 55:

> **Coniuratum est** in eum . . . (55D:4)
> ***A conspiracy was made** against him*, literally, ***It was conspired*** . . .

An impersonal passive can often be translated by an English abstract noun (*the fighting*); another option is to use an English active verb (*they were fighting*).

The city of Agrigentum had several temples in the Doric style. These are the remains of the temple of Hercules mentioned in Reading B.
Temple of Hercules, Agrigento, Sicily

15 **Hōram amplius**: = **Amplius quam hōram; hōram** is accusative expressing extent of time.
in dēmōliendō signō: *in taking down the statue*. For **dēmōlior**, see line 9.
mōlior, mōlīrī, mōlītus sum, *to labor at, exert oneself, struggle.*
mōliēbantur: *had been struggling.*
illud: **signum**, the statue.
16 **labō, -āre, -āvī, -ātus**, *to be about to fall, waver, totter.*
nūllā labābat ex parte: literally, *it tottered from no direction*; *it did not totter in any direction.*
cum: *although*, another example of **cum** concessive (see the Reading Note on page 61).
subiciō, subicere, subiēcī, subiectus, *to set* or *place under.*
dēligo, -āre, -āvī, -ātus, *to fasten, tie up.*
dēligātum: supply **signum**.
17 ***membrum, -ī**, n., *limb of the body.*
omnibus membrīs: *with respect to all its (the statue's) limbs.*
rapere: dependent upon **cōnārentur** in a condensed version of the previous **cum** clause.
rapere ad sē: *to drag toward themselves.*
fūnis, fūnis, gen. pl., **fūnium**, m., *cable, rope.*

18 **lapidātiō, lapidātiōnis**, f., *stone-throwing* (cf. **lapis, lapidis**).
dant: the subject is **nocturnī mīlitēs**, following.
***sēsē**, alternate form of **sē** (no difference in meaning).
***fuga, -ae**, f., *flight, escape.*
dare sēsē in fugam: literally, *to give oneself into flight; to flee.*
praeclārī imperātōris: sarcasm.

19 **sigillum, -ī**, n., *small figurine or statuette*. **Sigillum** is a diminutive of **signum**.
perparvulus, -a, -um, *very little, tiny.*
nē . . . revertantur: negative purpose clause.
inānis, -is, -e, *empty; empty handed.*
ad istum praedōnem religiōnum: Cicero refers to Verres in a way that highlights one of his most outrageous traits, his willingness to steal from sacred places.
revertor, revertī, reversus sum, *to come back, return.*

20 **Numquam tam male est**: literally, *It is never so badly*; *Things are never so bad.*
***quīn**, conj. + subjunctive, *that . . . not.*
***aliquis, aliquis, aliquid**, *someone, something, anyone, anything.*
facētē et commodē: *appropriately humorous.*
***velut**, conj., *just as, as.*
in hāc rē: *on this occasion.*
21 ***aiō**: *to affirm, say*. A defective verb found only in the pres. and imperf. tenses.
nōn minus . . . quam: *no less . . . than.*
verrēs, verris, m., *hog; boar*. Cicero makes a joke out of the fact that the **cognōmen** of the thieving governor literally means *boar.*
aper, aprī, m., *male hog, boar.*
22 **Erymanthius, -a, -um**, *Erymanthian*, of the Erymanthus mountains of Arcadia, in Greece. The fourth labor of Hercules was to bring the vicious Erymanthian boar back to King Eurystheus.
***referō, referre, retulī, relātus**, irreg., *to bring back; to count among.*
referre: *assign (to), count (among);* take with **in labōrēs** (21).
***oportet, oportēre, oportuit**, *it is fitting, ought, should.*
oportēre: infinitive in indirect statement after **aiēbant** in the preceding line.

Hōram amplius iam in dēmōliendō signō permultī hominēs mōliēbantur; illud intereā nullā labābat ex parte, cum aliī vectibus subiectīs cōnārentur commovēre, aliī dēligātum omnibus membrīs rapere ad sē fūnibus. Ac repentē Agrigentīnī concurrunt; fit magna lapidātiō; dant sēsē in fugam istīus praeclārī imperātōris nocturnī mīlitēs. Duo tamen sigilla perparvula tollunt, nē omnīnō inānēs ad istum praedōnem religiōnum revertantur. Numquam tam male est Siculīs quīn aliquid facētē et commodē dīcant, velut in hāc rē aiēbant in labōrēs Herculis nōn minus hunc immānissimum verrem quam illum aprum Erymanthium referre oportēre.

— Cicero, *In Verrem* II.IV.94–95

---

18. For how long did the bandits try to remove the statue? (15)
19. What were their various attempts to dislodge it? (16–17)
20. What was the result of these efforts? (15–16)
21. What did the townspeople suddenly do? (17–18)
22. What resulted from this? (18)
23. What booty did the bandits carry off? (18–19)
24. Why did they take these objects? (19–20)
25. What general observation does Cicero make about the Sicilians in line 20?
26. What humor did they express regarding their experience with Verres? (21–22)

Cicero was so successful in his opening speech against Verres that Hortensius recommended that his client go into exile. He fled to the Gallic port city of Massilia (modern Marseilles), where he remained until 43 B.C., when he was marked for death by Antony, who had developed a fancy for some of Verres' stolen art treasures.

Questions for Thought and Discussion

1. How does Cicero use his oratorical skills to demonstrate to the jury his distaste for Verres, as a man and as a fellow Roman?
2. Does Verres remind you of any specific individual, or type of individual, in your experience?

King Eurystheus ordered Hercules to capture the Erymanthian boar, a ferocious, powerful beast, and bring it to him. When Hercules returned with the boar, Eurystheus was so terrified that he hid in a large storage jar.
Vase, Greece, approx.sixth century B.C.

Catiline Plots to Seize Power

You learned in Chapter 55 that the Roman aristocrat Lucius Sergius Catilina formed a conspiracy to seize control of Rome and that the conspiracy was suppressed by the consuls Cicero and Gaius Antonius. While dealing with the conspiracy, Cicero delivered four speeches against Catiline. In Chapter 59 you will read portions of the first one, in which Cicero publicly revealed the existence of the conspiracy and denounced Catiline to the Senate. This speech is one of the most famous in history, and it demonstrates the oratorical ability that enabled Cicero to rise to Rome's highest office despite the fact that he did not come from a senatorial family.

Catiline was born to an ancient patrician family whose wealth and power had gradually declined over the centuries. After a successful career as an army officer, he worked his way up through the **cursus honōrum** and was elected praetor in 68 B.C. After serving as governor of Africa, he returned to Rome to run for consul. Before he could do so, however, he was brought to trial on charges of mismanagement of his province of Africa. At the trial, he enjoyed the support of many prominent politicians and was acquitted. Many of the same men backed him when he ran for consul in 64. Despite this support, Catiline lost to Marcus Tullius Cicero and Gaius Antonius, partly because many of the aristocrats disliked the economic policies Catiline put forth as a candidate—he advocated the cancellation of debts and other measures to help the urban poor. In 63 Catiline ran again, but by this time he had lost much of the support he had enjoyed during his first campaign. After being defeated a second time, Catiline realized that his only hope of gaining power was through force.

Catiline formed a conspiracy that appealed mainly to those who felt they had nothing to lose. Some of these men were aristocrats who had been cut off from the usual sources of advancement, while others were poor people, including many of Sulla's former soldiers, who saw Catiline as a potential benefactor. Catiline's plan was to raise an army in the countryside and then march on Rome; as the army approached the city, his associates were to create chaos by murdering their political opponents and setting fires; Catiline would then enter the city and seize power. Catiline sent Gaius Manlius, a veteran from Sulla's army, to raise troops in Etruria while he organized his plans in Rome. Rumors came to Rome about Manlius' activities in northern Italy and in late October of 63 the Senate posted night watches throughout the city and passed a decree granting the consuls special powers to deal with the emergency. However, Cicero was still hampered by a lack of legal evidence against Catiline; the information that he had came from informants among the conspirators. Two of the conspirators were supposed to assassinate Cicero in the predawn hours on 7 November, but Cicero had been warned and stationed extra guards outside his house. On 8 November, Cicero held a meeting of the Senate in the temple of Jupiter Stator and placed armed guards around the temple. It was here that he delivered his first speech against Catiline, some of which you will read in Chapter 59.

After being publicly denounced by Cicero, Catiline fled the city and joined Manlius' army. He wanted to bring his army south before the government could raise troops to oppose him. Meanwhile, the remaining conspirators continued their efforts in Rome. They approached a delegation from the Allobroges, a Gallic tribe, who had come to Rome to protest mistreatment by Roman officials. The Allobroges reported this contact to Cicero, who urged them to obtain written proof. Some of the conspirators wrote letters to the

Allobroges; these letters were seized as they were being taken north and provided the evidence that Cicero needed. Five leading conspirators were executed without trial, which effectively put an end to the conspiracy in the city. Cicero's colleague Gaius Antonius then marched north with an army and defeated what was left of Catiline's forces (many of his followers had deserted after hearing the news from Rome). Catiline himself was killed fighting bravely in battle.

It is difficult to evaluate Catiline accurately, since the two sources that we have (Cicero's speeches and Sallust's history, written about 20 years after the conspiracy) are both extremely hostile to Catiline. Although described by Cicero and Sallust as an utterly depraved and vile person, Catiline may well have been no worse than other Roman politicians who seized power by force, such as Sulla, Julius Caesar, and Octavian.

Oratory: A Path to Power in Rome

Skill in public speaking, or rhetoric, was a requirement for political success in Rome, for all public offices required speechmaking and the ability to persuade. By Cicero's time, a Roman youth who had completed literary and linguistic studies with a **grammaticus** would finish his education by studying with a **rhētor**, an instructor in public speaking who taught skills in debate and in advocating a particular course of action. The preparation of a speech included gathering of material and its proper arrangement, selection of appropriate language, memorization, and delivery. A good speech had a certain structure to it, including a beginning (**exōrdium**), designed to win the favorable attention of the audience; the body (consisting of **partītiō**, *outline*; **cōnfirmātiō**, *arguments for the case*; and **refūtātiō**, *rebuttal of opponent's case*); and a conclusion (**perōrātiō**) designed to summarize the arguments and appeal to the jurors' emotions. In *De oratore*, Cicero wrote:

> Eloquence requires many things: a wide knowledge of very many subjects (verbal fluency without this being worthless and even ridiculous), a style, too, carefully formed not merely by selection, but by arrangement of words, and a thorough familiarity with all the feelings which nature has given to men, because the whole force and art of the orator must be put forth in allaying or exciting the emotions of the audience.

The imperial writer Tacitus in his *Dialogus de oratoribus* reflects nostalgically on the "Golden Age" of Roman oratory during the final years of the Republic:

> The more influence a man could wield by his powers of speech, the more readily did he attain to high office, the farther did he, when in office, outstrip his colleagues, the more did he gain favor with the great, authority with the Senate, and name and fame with the common people.

1 **Quō usque**: *Up to what point, How far.*
tandem: *really, in fact*; here **tandem** emphasizes the point and does not mean *finally.*
abūtor, abūtī, abūsus sum + abl., *to abuse.*
abūtēre: the ending **-re** is an alternative to the more common **-ris** for second person singular verbs (passive or deponent). The long **-ē-** marks it as future tense.

***furor, furōris**, m., *madness, frenzy.*
2 **ēlūdō, ēlūdere, ēlūsī, ēlūsus**, *to make fun of; to get the better of, make a mockery of.*

effrēnātus, -a, -um, *uncontrolled, unbridled.*
***iactō, -āre, -āvī, -ātus**, *to toss around*; **sē iactāre**, *to display, show off, flaunt itself.*
audācia, -ae, f., *boldness, recklessness.*

Nihil: used as an emphatic equivalent of **nōn**; it might be translated *not at all* or *not in any way.*
tē: direct object of **mōvērunt** (4).
3 **praesidium, -ī**, n., *protection, defense, garrison, guard.*
Palātium, -ī, n., *the Palatine Hill* (home of Cicero and many other prominent Romans).
vigilia, -ae, f., *wakefulness, watch, night watch*, referring to the night watches that were posted throughout Rome starting in late October.
concursus, -ūs, m., *coming together, assembly.*
bonōrum: *good men.*
4 **mūnītus, -a, -um**, *protected, fortified*, referring to the guards Cicero placed around this meeting of the Senate.
habendī senātūs: *of holding (a meeting of) the Senate.*
hōrum: *of these men*, referring to the assembled senators.
***ōs, ōris**, n., *mouth, face.*
***vultus, -ūs**, m., *face, expression.*
ōra vultūsque: *faces and expressions*; we might say *facial expressions.* Cicero imagines angry looks as the senators learn about the conspiracy.

5 **Patēre . . . vidēs** (6): this sentence consists of two halves, each containing an indirect statement with the head verb placed after the accusative and infinitive phrase.
cōnstringo, cōnstringere, cōnstrīnxī, cōnstrictus, *to bind, tie, restrain.*
scientia, -ae, f., *knowledge.*
tenērī: the verb **tenēre** can have the idea of *hold in check, keep under control.*
6 ***coniūrātiō, coniūrātiōnis**, f., *conspiracy.*

Quid proximā . . . cēperis (7): five indirect questions depending on **ignōrāre** (7); **quem . . . ignōrāre** is another indirect statement, whose head word is **arbitrāris** (7).
***proximus, -a, -um**, *nearest, most recent, last.*
***superior, superior, superius**, gen., **superiōris**, *higher; earlier, previous;* **proximā nocte** refers to the night before Cicero delivered the speech, **superiōre** to the night before that (note how the words **nocte** and **ēgeris** are gapped—see the Reading Note on page 42).
7 ***cōnsilium, -ī**, n., *plan.*
quid cōnsiliī: *what plan.*
nostrum: genitive of **nōs.**
***arbitror, arbitrārī, arbitrātus sum**, *to think, judge.*

LIX

Cicero Denounces Catiline

A. Cicero's Indignation

Quō usque tandem abūtēre, Catilīna, patientiā nostrā? Quam diū etiam furor iste tuus nōs ēlūdet? Quem ad fīnem sēsē effrēnāta iactābit audācia? Nihilne tē nocturnum praesidium Palātī, nihil urbis vigiliae, nihil timor populī, nihil concursus bonōrum omnium, nihil hic mūnītissimus habendī senātūs locus, nihil hōrum ōra vultūsque mōvērunt? Patēre tua cōnsilia nōn sentīs, cōnstrictam iam hōrum omnium scientiā tenērī coniūrātiōnem tuam nōn vidēs? Quid proximā, quid superiōre nocte ēgeris, ubi fueris, quōs convocāveris, quid cōnsiliī cēperis, quem nostrum ignōrāre arbitrāris?

(*continued*)

---

1. Cicero asks three rhetorical questions in order to criticize Catiline. What are they? (1–2)
2. Name six things that Cicero suggests might have caused Catiline to give up his plans. (2–4)
3. Of what should Catiline be aware? (5–6)
4. What five things do all the senators know? (6–7)

Reading Note

Rhetorical Questions

A speaker may ask a question that is designed not to obtain actual information but to make a point with the audience or to influence their thinking in some way. This is called a *rhetorical question.*

Ō flexanima atque omnium rēgīna rērum ōrātiō! *O Eloquence who moves men's minds, queen of all things!* (Marcus Pacuvius, *Hermiona*)

---

8 ***mōs, mōris**, m., *custom, habit*; pl., *character, morals.*

Ō tempora, ō mōrēs: the accusative case is used for exclamations. This famous phrase is often quoted to express disapproval of decline in standards of conduct.

haec: neuter plural substantive, *these things*, referring to Catiline's activities; object of both **intellegit** and **videt**.

cōnsul: note that Cicero is referring to himself in the third person.

hic: Catiline. Imagine Cicero pointing to Catiline as he says this.

vīvit: the implication is that Catiline should already have been executed for his crimes.

Vīvit?: Through this rhetorical question, Cicero expresses outrage that Catiline has not yet been put to death and makes a transition into his next thought.

***immō**, adv., *rather, on the contrary.*

Immō vērō etiam: *Why he even . . . .*

9 **particeps, participis** + gen., *sharing in, participating in; a participant.*

***notō, -āre, -āvī, -ātus**, *to mark, mark out.*

***dēsignō, -āre, -āvī, -ātus**, *to mark, indicate, designate.*

10 ***caedēs, caedis**, gen. pl., **caedium**, f., *slaughter, killing, murder.*

ad caedem: Catiline had plotted to murder several people, including Cicero himself, as Cicero describes later in the speech.

quemque: modified by **ūnum**, *each one.*

nostrum: genitive of **nōs**.

Nōs . . . fortēs virī: referring to Cicero and the other senators.

vidēmur: in the passive the verb **videō** often means *to seem.*

11 **istīus**: genitive of **iste**, referring to Catiline.

vītō, -āre, -āvī, -ātus, *to avoid.*

vītēmus: *we were to avoid.* Cicero is being sarcastic, implying that the senators should be taking action to deal with Catiline rather than worrying about their own safety. Not all the senators believed in Catiline's guilt, while a few such as the praetor Lentulus were active members of the conspiracy; so one of Cicero's goals in this speech was to motivate the Senate to act.

Ad mortem . . . dūcī: i.e., to be executed.

iussū, noun used only in the abl. sing., *by the order.*

iam prīdem, adv., *a long time ago.*

12 **oportēbat**: the two infinitive phrases **tē . . . dūcī** (11) and **cōnferrī pestem** (12) serve as the subjects of this verb: *For you to be led was fitting, It was fitting for you to be led.*

in tē: the preposition **in** means *against* or *upon* when it is followed by a person's name or a personal pronoun in the accusative.

***cōnferō, cōnferre, contulī, collātus**, irreg., *to bring together; to bestow, apply.*

***pestis, pestis**, gen. pl., **pestium**, f., *plague; destruction, death.*

māchinor, -ārī, -ātus, *to design, scheme, plot.*

Ō tempora, ō mōrēs! Senātus haec intellegit, cōnsul videt; hic tamen vīvit. Vīvit? Immō vērō etiam in senātum venit, fit pūblicī cōnsiliī particeps, notat et dēsignat oculīs ad caedem ūnum quemque nostrum. Nōs autem fortēs virī satis facere reī pūblicae vidēmur, sī istīus furōrem ac tēla vītēmus. Ad mortem tē, Catilīna, dūcī iussū cōnsulis iam prīdem oportēbat, in tē cōnferrī pestem, quam tū in nōs omnēs iam diū māchināris.

—Cicero, *In Catilinam* I.1–2

---

5. Why is it surprising that Catiline is still alive? (8)
6. Describe two things that Catiline continues to do, even though the conspiracy has been revealed. (9)
7. What does Cicero claim that Catiline is doing with regard to the senators? (9–10)
8. For whose benefit are the senators doing enough if they stay alive? (10–11)
9. What Latin words express the idea that Catiline is planning to kill the senators? (11)
10. What does Cicero say should have been done to Catiline? By whose authority? (11–12)
11. What should be the manner of Catiline's death? (12)

Reading Note

Anaphora

In lines 2–4 on page 69, the word **nihil** is repeated six times. Such repetition of a word is called *anaphora*. Anaphora emphasizes the idea that is repeated and is often found in a series of parallel phrases or clauses, as in this example. This is one of Cicero's favorite rhetorical devices.

Marcus Tullius Cicero
Marble bust, Florence, Italy, first century B.C.

1 ***gēns, gentis**, gen. pl., **gentium**, f., *family, clan*; pl., *peoples, nations*.
Ubinam gentium: *Where in the world*, literally, *Where of the nations*; the particle **-nam** strengthens **ubi**.

2 **patrēs cōnscrīptī**: *enrolled fathers*, an honorific title for members of the Senate.
3 **cōnsiliō**: *council*.
quī: *(those) who*. **Quī** is the subject of **cōgitent** (4); see the Reading Note on gapping, page 42.
interitus, -ūs, m., *death*.
nostrō omnium interitū: *our death of all* = *the death of us all*.
4 **dē**: note that the genitive phrases **huius urbis** and **orbis terrārum** are placed between the preposition and its object **exitiō** (4), which is gapped.
***adeō**, adv., *so much, to such an extent; moreover, in addition*. This adverb must be distinguished from the verb **adeō, adīre**, *to come to, approach*.
***exitium, -ī**, n., *destruction, ruin*.

cōnsul: *I, the consul*; **cōnsul** is in apposition to **ego**.
5 ***sententia, -ae**, f., *feeling, opinion*.
hōs . . . sententiam rogō: *I ask them for their opinion*; i.e., they are still carrying out the normal business of the Senate, despite being involved in the conspiracy.
quōs . . . oportēbat: this relative clause comes before its antecedent **eōs**.
***ferrum, -ī**, n., *iron, object made of iron, sword*.
trucīdō, -āre, -āvī, -ātus, *to slaughter, kill*.

6 **apud Laecam**: a meeting of conspirators had taken place at the house of Laeca on the evening of 6 November 63 B.C. Cicero learned about the meeting from his informants, who were the source of the details that he reports in the following sentence.
distribuistī partēs Italiae: i.e., Catiline assigned his followers to go to various areas of Italy.
statuō, statuere, statuī, statūtus, *to determine, decide, decree*.
quō . . . placēret: supply **tibi** with **placēret**, *where* (**quō**) *it was pleasing to you* = *where you wanted*.
7 ***dēligō, dēligere, dēlēgī, dēlēctus**, *to choose*.
quōs: *(those) whom*.
dīscrībō, dīscrībere, dīscrīpsī, dīscrīptus, *to distribute, divide; to assign*.
8 **cōnfirmō, -āre, -āvī, -ātus**, *to strengthen; to confirm, assert*.
cōnfirmāstī: a contracted form of **cōnfirmāvistī**.
tibi esse: *there was to you* = *you had*.
paulum, -ī, n., *a small amount, a little*.
9 **mora, -ae**, f., *delay*. (Do not confuse with **mors, mortis**, *death*.)
***paulum, -ī**, n., *a small amount, a little*.
paulum morae: i.e., Catiline had to wait a little before leaving.

Reading Note

Dative of Possession

In lines 8–9 opposite, you saw the phrase **paulum tibi esse . . . morae**, literally, *a little delay was to you*, better English *you had a little delay*. In this construction, called the *dative of possession*, the owner goes in the dative, the thing owned becomes the subject, and the verb is always a form of **esse**. Here is another example:

Catilīnae erant multī sociī. *Catiline had many associates* (lit., *Many associates were to Catiline*).

B. Catiline's Plans

Ō dī immortālēs! Ubinam gentium sumus? In quā urbe vīvimus? Quam rem pūblicam habēmus? Hīc, hīc sunt in nostrō numerō, patrēs cōnscrīptī, in hōc orbis terrae sānctissimō gravissimōque cōnsiliō, quī dē nostrō omnium interitū, quī dē huius urbis atque adeō dē orbis terrārum exitiō cōgitent! Hōs ego videō cōnsul et dē rē pūblicā sententiam rogō et, quōs ferrō trucīdārī oportēbat, eōs nōndum vōce vulnerō! Fuistī igitur apud Laecam illā nocte, Catilīna, distribuistī partēs Italiae, statuistī quō quemque proficīscī placēret, dēlēgistī, quōs Rōmae relinquerēs, quōs tēcum ēdūcerēs, dīscrīpsistī urbis partēs ad incendia, cōnfirmāstī tē ipsum iam esse exitūrum, dīxistī paulum tibi esse etiam nunc morae, quod ego vīverem.

(*continued*)

---

1. Cicero expresses his outrage by asking three rhetorical questions. What are they? (1–2)
2. Where are the people Cicero is describing? (2–3)
3. What are these people thinking about? (3–4)
4. What is Cicero doing about these people that he sees? (4–5)
5. What should happen to these people? (5)
6. What is Cicero actually doing? (5)
7. Where does Cicero claim that Catiline was on the night in question? (5–6)
8. What three decisions did Catiline make in lines 6–7?
9. For what purpose did Catiline assign sections of the city? (7–8)
10. What did Catiline assert would happen? (8)
11. Why could the plans not be carried out immediately? (8–9)

Reading Note

Partitive Genitive

In lines 8–9 above, you met the phrase **paulum morae**, *a little delay*. In English the word *little* is an adjective modifying *delay*; but in Latin **paulum** is a noun and is modified by another noun in the genitive. You have met similar phrases before, such as **nihil malī**, *nothing bad* (21:7), **satis temporis**, *enough time* (23f:14), **aliquid novī**, *something new* (25:12–13), **plūs vīnī**, *more wine*, and **nimis vīnī**, *too much wine* (34:23). This is called the *partitive genitive*, and it is particularly common in phrases that indicate an amount or quantity. For another example see 59A:7, **quid cōnsiliī**, *what plan*.

10 ***reperiō, reperīre, repperī, repertus**, *to find.*
istā cūrā: *from that worry*, an ablative of separation with **līberārent**.
sēsē: subject of the infinitive **interfectūrōs esse**, forming an indirect statement dependent on the verb **pollicērentur** (11).

11 **lectulus, -ī**, m., *little bed.*
***polliceor, pollicērī, pollicitus sum**, *to promise.*

vixdum, adv., *scarcely then, hardly then* (stronger form of **vix**).

12 **etiam**: *even*, modifying **dīmissō**.
coetus, -ūs, m., *assembly, meeting.*
***comperiō, comperīre, comperī, compertus**, *to find out, learn, discover.*
mūniō, -īre, -īvī, -ītus, *to build; to fortify.*

13 **quōs . . . mīserās**: It was customary for **clientēs** or others with business to come to greet a great man early in the morning. Cicero is being ironically humorous here, since this **salūtātiō** would have been fatal had it occurred.
salūtātum: *to greet.*

14 **ego**: subject of the main verb **praedīxeram**, even though it comes after the relative pronoun **quōs**. The same word order works in English: *whom I had predicted would come.*
multīs ac summīs virīs: Latin uses the word *and* (**et / atque / ac**) between two adjectives that modify one noun, but English does not.
id temporis: partitive genitive.

15 **Quae**: how do you know this connecting relative is neuter plural and not feminine singular?
pergō, pergere, perrēxī, perrēctus, *to continue, go ahead, proceed.*
quō coepistī: supply **īre**, reinforcing the idea that Catiline was on the verge of leaving Rome (cf. line 8). Cicero wanted to force Catiline to go by denouncing him in public, since his departure would convince some of those in Rome who were still uncertain about his guilt.
ēgredere: how do you know this is not an infinitive? What form is it?
aliquandō, adv., *at some time, now, finally.*

16 **nimium**, adv., *too much, very much*; **nimium diū**, *for too long.*
imperātōrem: this word originally meant *commander, general*; only later did it come to mean *emperor.*
tē imperātorem: *you (as its) commander.*
Manliānus, -a, -um, *of Manlius, Manlius'*. Manlius was the soldier sent to organize Catiline's army in Etruria.

17 **tuōs**: *your friends, your people*, a masculine substantive.
sī minus, quam plūrimōs: *if (you take) fewer (than all of them), (take) as many as possible.* The verb **ēdūc** (17) is understood with **quam plūrimōs** and implies a form such as **dūcēs** to go with **minus**; also, the word **omnēs** in the first clause shows that **(quam) omnēs** is to be supplied with the comparative **minus**. This is a complex example of gapping (see the Reading Note on page 42).

***metus, -ūs**, m., *fear.*
metū: *from fear*, another ablative of separation.

18 **dummodo**, conj. + subjunctive, *provided that.*
intersit: deduce from **inter** + **sum**.

***versor, -ārī, -ātus sum**, *to stay, be situated; to be involved with, engaged in.*

19 ***sinō, sinere, sīvī, situs**, *to allow.*

Repertī sunt duo equitēs Rōmānī, quī tē istā cūrā līberārent et sēsē illā ipsā nocte paulō ante lūcem mē in meō lectulō interfectūrōs esse pollicērentur. Haec ego omnia vixdum etiam coetū vestrō dīmissō comperī; domum meam maiōribus praesidiīs mūnīvī atque firmāvī; exclūsī eōs, quōs tū ad mē salūtātum māne mīserās, cum illī ipsī vēnissent, quōs ego iam multīs ac summīs virīs ad mē id temporis ventūrōs esse praedīxeram.

Quae cum ita sint, Catilīna, perge, quō coepistī, ēgredere aliquandō ex urbe; patent portae; proficīscere. Nimium diū tē imperātōrem tua illa Manliāna castra dēsīderant. Ēdūc tēcum etiam omnēs tuōs, sī minus, quam plūrimōs; purgā urbem. Magnō mē metū līberābis, dummodo inter mē atque tē mūrus intersit. Nōbīscum versārī iam diūtius nōn potes; nōn feram, nōn patiar, nōn sinam.

—Cicero, *In Catilinam* I.9–10

---

12. What would the two equestrians do? (10)
13. What did they promise that they would do? When? (10–11)
14. When did Cicero learn about these things? (11–12)
15. What action did he take? (12)
16. Whom did he keep out of his house? (13)
17. What prediction had Cicero made about these people, and to whom? (13–14)
18. What does Cicero urge Catiline to do? (15–16)
19. Who has been missing Catiline? What function would Catiline have? (16)
20. Whom should Catiline take with him? How many should he take? (17)
21. Under what conditions will Cicero be freed from fear? (17–18)
22. What will Cicero not permit? (18–19)

Roman mosaic showing an orator
Germany, second to third century A.D.

1 **Magna . . . habenda est . . . grātia** (2): *Great thanks must be given.*
Iovī Statōrī: *Jupiter Stator, Jupiter the Stayer.* According to legend, Romulus vowed a temple to Jupiter if he prevented the Roman army from being routed in a battle against the Sabines, so the description **antīquissimō** is appropriate. The spot (in the Forum on the Via Sacra) was consecrated but the temple was not built until the early 3rd century B.C.
2 **taeter, taetra, taetrum**, *disgusting, foul.*
īnfestus, -a, -um, *hostile.*
3 **totiēns**, adv., *so often.*

4 **perīclitor, -ārī, -ātus sum**, *to be in jeopardy; to risk.*
Nōn est . . . summa salūs perīclitanda: *The ultimate safety must not be risked.*
reī pūblicae: genitive modifying **salūs** (3).

Quam diū: *As long as.*
cōnsulī dēsignātō: Catiline tried to assassinate Cicero after he was elected but before he took office and again during the elections held in 63 to choose consuls for 62.
īnsidior, -ārī, -ātus sum + dat., *to plot against, lay a trap for.*
5 **mē**: object of **dēfendī** later in the clause.
***prīvātus, -a, -um**, *private, personal.*
dīligentia, -ae, f., *diligence, care, attention.*

Cum: *When.* This is not the preposition *with* (even though it is followed by an ablative).
comitia, -ōrum, n. pl., *assembly of the people; election*; **comitia cōnsulāria**, *election of consuls.*
proximīs comitiīs cōnsulāribus: ablative of time when.
6 **campō**: the Campus Martius; see the note for 57A:5, page 46.
***competītor, competītōris**, m., *political rival.*
comprimō, comprimere, compressī, compressus, *to repress, check.*
7 **cōnātus, -ūs**, m., *attempt.*
nefārius, -a, -um, *unspeakable, wicked.*
praesidiō et cōpiīs: ablative of means.
nūllō tumultū . . . concitātō: ablative absolute.
concitō, -āre, -āvī, -ātus, *to stir up.*
8 **quotiēnscumque**, adv., *however often, as often as.*
petīstī: contracted form of **petīvistī.**
per mē: *through my own efforts, on my own.*
obstō, obstāre, obstitī + dat., *to stand in the way of, oppose, hinder.*
perniciēs, perniciēī, f., *ruin, destruction.*
9 ***coniungō, coniungere, coniūnxī, coniūnctus**, *to join together, join closely, link.*

Reading Note

Cum with the Indicative

You already know that the conjunction **cum** is usually completed by a verb in the imperfect or pluperfect subjunctive to express the circumstances or cause of an action. Less frequently, **cum** is completed by an indicative verb that states the precise the time of an action, as in **cum . . . voluistī** (opposite: 5–6). **Cum** with the indicative should always be translated *when* or *after*.

C. Cicero's Personal Danger

Magna dīs immortālibus habenda est atque huic ipsī Iovī Statōrī, antīquissimō custōdī huius urbis, grātia, quod hanc tam taetram, tam horribilem tamque īnfestam reī pūblicae pestem totiēns iam effūgimus. Nōn est saepius in ūnō homine summa salūs perīclitanda reī pūblicae. Quam diū mihi cōnsulī dēsignātō, Catilīna, īnsidiātus es, nōn pūblicō mē praesidiō, sed prīvātā dīligentiā dēfendī. Cum proximīs comitiīs cōnsulāribus mē cōnsulem in campō et competītōrēs tuōs interficere voluistī, compressī cōnātūs tuōs nefāriōs amīcōrum praesidiō et cōpiīs nūllō tumultū pūblicē concitātō; dēnique, quotiēnscumque mē petīstī, per mē tibi obstitī, quamquam vidēbam perniciem meam cum magnā calamitāte reī pūblicae esse coniūnctam.

---

1. To whom must thanks be given ? (1)
2. Why must thanks be given? (2–3)
3. What situation does not arise very often? (3–4)
4. What did Catiline do when Cicero was consul-elect? (4)
5. How did Cicero deal with this situation? (4–5)
6. What did Catiline want to do during the next round of elections? (5–6)
7. How did Cicero prevent this? What did not happen? (6–7)
8. What did Cicero do whenever Catiline attacked him? (8)
9. Why might Cicero have been justified in seeking public support against Catiline? (8–9)

The French government issued a series of medals commemorating events during the reign of the Emperor Napoleon I. The designer of this medal chose Jupiter Stator as a symbol of steadfastness in the face of adversity. The depiction of Jupiter is based on Roman models, which often show him seated with a spear and thunderbolt. Below Jupiter's feet is the legend NAPOLEON A SCHOENBRUNN MDCCCIX, referring to the palace outside Vienna where Napoleon had taken up residence while arranging peace terms with Austria.
Private collection

10 **apertē**, adv., *openly*.
petis: *you attack*.
11 ***tēctum, -ī**, n., *roof*; pl., *house*.
***vīta, -ae**, f., *life*.
exitium, -ī, n., *destruction*.
***vocō, -āre, -āvī, -ātus**, *to call*.
vāstitās, vāstitātis, f., *emptiness, wasteland; devastation*.

12 ***quoniam**, conj., *since, because*.
id: direct object of **facere** (13); two relative clauses that begin with **quod** are nested between **id** and the phrase **facere nōndum audeō** that completes the clause begun with **quoniam**. Translate **id quod** as *that which* or *the thing which*.
prīmum: *primary, fundamental, most important, desirable*.
huius imperiī: *this power (of mine)*, referring to Cicero's position as consul.
disciplīna, -ae, f., *teaching; practice*. Cicero implies that it would be in accordance with traditional strict Roman practices for a traitor to be summarily executed.
proprius, -a, -um, *one's own, special, particular (to), appropriate (to)*, with genitive.
13 ***audeō, audēre, ausus sum**, semi-deponent + infin., *to dare (to)*.
id quod: note the parallel structure between the first half of the sentence (**quoniam . . . audeō**) and the main clause; both have **id** as direct object, modified by relative clauses.
ad: *in reference to, in regard to*.
sevēritās, sevēritātis, f., *severity, strictness*.
lēnis, -is, -e, *soft, gentle, mild*.

14 **interficī**: *to be killed*, present passive infinitive (do not confuse with **interfēcī**, *I killed*).
resideō, residēre, resēdī, *to remain seated; to stay behind, be left, remain*.
***reliquus, -a, -um**, *the rest, the remaining, the other*.
coniūrātī, -ōrum, m. pl., *conspirators*.
15 ***manus, -ūs**, f., *hand; band, group*.
sīn (**sī** + **nē**), conj., *if on the other hand, but if*.
dūdum, adv., *a short time ago; just now; formerly*; **iam dūdum**, *for some time now*.
***hortor, hortārī, hortātus sum**, *to encourage, urge*.
hortor: the present tense with a phrase such as **iam dūdum** shows an action begun in the past and continuing into the present, *I have been encouraging*.
exhauriō, exhaurīre, exhausī, exhaustus, *to drain out*.
***comes, comitis**, m., *companion*.
16 **perniciōsus, -a, -um**, *destructive, ruinous*.
sentīna, -ae, f., *dregs, scum*.

***dubitō, -āre, -āvī, -ātus**, *to doubt, hesitate*.
mē imperante: ablative absolute.
17 ***sponte**, abl. (nom. not used), f., *of one's own accord, voluntarily*.
tuā sponte: note the parallel structure of this phrase with **mē imperante** (16).
faciēbās: *you were beginning to do*. The imperfect can express the idea of starting an action.
cōnsul hostem: the word **hostem** is emphasized by being placed last in the sentence and by standing next to **cōnsul**.

(*vocabulary and notes continued on opposite page*)

D. Catiline Must Leave the City

Nunc iam apertē rem pūblicam ūniversam petis, templa deōrum immortālium, tēcta urbis, vītam omnium cīvium, Italiam tōtam ad exitium et vāstitātem vocās. Quārē, quoniam id, quod est prīmum, et quod huius imperiī disciplīnaeque maiōrum proprium est, facere nōndum audeō, faciam id, quod est ad sevēritātem lēnius et ad commūnem salūtem ūtilius. Nam sī tē interficī iusserō, residēbit in rē pūblicā reliqua coniūrātōrum manus; sīn tū, quod tē iam dūdum hortor, exieris, exhauriētur ex urbe tuōrum comitum magna et perniciōsa sentīna reī pūblicae. Quid est, Catilīna? Num dubitās id mē imperante facere, quod iam tuā sponte faciēbās? Exīre ex urbe iubet cōnsul hostem. Interrogās mē, num in exilium; nōn iubeō, sed, sī mē cōnsulis, suādeō.

—Cicero, *In Catilinam* I.11–13

1. What is Catiline now doing? (10)
2. Name four things that Catiline wants to destroy. (10–11)
3. What does Cicero not dare to do? (12–13)
4. How does Cicero describe the action he will take? (13–14)
5. What will happen if Cicero orders Catiline to be executed? (14–15)
6. What will happen if Catiline leaves the city? (15–16)
7. What should Catiline not hesitate to do under Cicero's orders? (16–17)
8. What is the consul ordering? (17)
9. What question might Catiline ask? What is Cicero's answer? (17–18)

18 **num**, conjunction introducing an indirect question, *whether*; not the same as the question word that implies a negative answer (as in line 16). A verb such as **exeās** is implied from **exīre** in the previous sentence.
cōnsulō, cōnsulere, cōnsuluī, cōnsultus, *to consult, ask for advice.*
suādeō, suādēre, suāsī, suāsūrus, *to propose, suggest, urge.*

Reading Note

The Construction is quī

In lines 12 and 13 above, you met the phrase **id quod**, *that which, the thing which*. It is very common in Latin to find a form of the pronoun **is, ea, id** serving as the antecedent of a relative pronoun. Such phrases may be translated *the one who, the person who, he/she who* or, if neuter, *that which, the thing which*. Here is another example:

Eī quī Catilīnae favent ex urbe discēdere dēbent.
***Those who** support Catiline should leave the city.*

Sometimes the form of **is** is omitted and must be supplied in translation:

. . . dēlēgistī **(eōs) quōs** Rōmae relinquerēs (B:7)
*. . . you chose **(the ones) whom** you would leave in Rome*

Find another example of this construction on page 75, and locate on page 73 an instance where the form of **is** must be supplied.

The Roman War Machine

In no other phase of life did the Romans show their talent for organization more than in the military. The Roman army was organized into units called legions (**legiōnēs**), each of which had a number and a name, such as the **Legiō IX Hispāna**; Caesar's favorite was the 10th. A legion contained approximately 5,000 men organized into ten cohorts (**cohortēs**). Each cohort contained six centuries (**centuriae**), composed of about 80 men. The century was commanded by a centurion (**centuriō**), an experienced veteran who carried a wooden swagger-stick with which to discipline his men.

The historian Tacitus, describing a mutiny that occurred in Germany during the first century A.D., tells this story about a centurion:

> A centurion named Lucilius was killed by his troops at the start of the mutiny. This man had earned their hatred because of the punishments he handed out among his men. They had nicknamed him **Cedo alteram** (*Gimme another*) because every time he broke his vine-stick on a soldier's back he called for another.
>
> —Tacitus, *Annales* I.23

The highest-ranking centurion (**prīmus pīlus**) of each legion headed the senior centurions (**prīmī ōrdinēs**) all of whom served in the First Cohort. By the beginning of the Empire, the Roman armed forces numbered some 390,000 men (10,000 Italian forces, 150,000 Roman legionaries, and 230,000 allied infantry, cavalry, and irregular troops).

The legion and its units were identified by particular standards or insignia (**signa mīlitāria**). The standard (**signum**) of each century was borne by a standard-bearer (**signifer**) and the silver eagle (**aquila**) of each legion by an "eagle-bearer" (**aquilifer**). A legion could be dissolved after losing its standard in battle, as happened when Crassus lost the eagles to the Parthians in 53 B.C. (see 57B:6 and the coin on page 49). Caesar describes the bravery of an **aquilifer** who led a charge during the Roman landing in Britain in 54 B.C.:

> The Romans were hesitant because of the depth of the water when the eagle-bearer of the 10th legion, after praying to the gods that his action might bring them luck, cried: "Jump down, comrades, unless you want to surrender the eagle to the enemy. I at least intend to do my duty to my country and my general." With these words, he jumped from the ship and advanced on the enemy with the eagle in his hands. When the other soldiers saw this, they urged each other not to allow such a disgrace to happen and also jumped while the men in the ships followed them.
>
> —Caesar, *Commentarii de bello Gallico*, V.1

Statuette, Roman legionary, second to first century, B.C.

Legionary footsoldiers (**peditēs**) of the Republic were equipped for both offensive and defensive fighting. The main offensive weapons (**tēla**) for an infantry soldier included a pike or heavy javelin with a long metal shank (**pīlum**), which was thrown from a distance before the charge into the enemy, and a short sword (**gladius**) used for hand-to-hand combat. Each soldier carried two **pīla**, one lighter and shorter than the other. The longer **pīlum** was seven feet in length. The point of the spear was made of soft metal to enable it to bend when it penetrated an enemy shield, making the shield heavy and unwieldly. The **gladius**, from which is derived the word gladiator, was used for cutting and thrusting. The defensive equipment consisted of a bronze and iron helmet (**galea**) and body armor (**lōrīca**) worn over a woolen tunic. Each footsoldier also carried a four-foot, slightly curved shield (**scūtum**) of wood covered with leather and bound with metal. You will learn more about how these and other weapons were used on the battlefield when you read Chapter 60.

Roman soldiers carried with them all equipment (**impedīmenta**) necessary for battle and for life on the march. Their 45-pound packs led to the nickname "Marius' mules." The organization of the Roman army enabled it to make camp (**castra pōnere**) quickly and efficiently while on the march. Each soldier had a specialized task for which he carried the appropriate tools. The camp's perimeter was secured by a ditch (**fossa**) dug by soldiers and by an earthen rampart (**agger**) constructed from the excavated earth and topped by a palisade (**vāllum**) of upright pointed stakes. The fortifications themselves were known as **mūnītiōnēs**. Within the fortress, the soldiers' tents (**tabernācula**), usually made of leather, were then set up in fixed positions. The function of the **castra** was to protect and house occupying Roman troops. A **castra** was constructed every night, even if it were to last for only a single night. These temporary camps, when placed in particularly strategic locations along the frontier, often were turned into permanent stone forts, which became centers of Romanization in the provinces. These centers eventually became towns and cities that modeled themselves on Rome and that could apply for citizenship and other rights. Many modern British place names, such as Manchester, Leicester, and Rochester, take their names from the Roman word **castra**. Other cities of the Roman Empire, such as Colonia Agrippinensis (modern Cologne, in Germany) derived from permanent settlements (**colōniae**) of retired legionaries.

This carving from the Column of Trajan shows Roman soldiers defending a camp.
Plaster mold of the Column of Trajan, commissioned by Napoleon III, 1860

Just as the Romans adopted many customs from the peoples they conquered, so did their enemies adopt weapons and techniques that they then used against the Romans themselves. In the passages in this chapter, you will read about Caesar and the battles that the Romans fought in Gaul. You will learn that the Gauls used Roman-style siege weaponry in attacking a Roman camp. Such siege weapons included the "tortoise" (**testūdō**), a "shell" made of interlocking shields used to protect soldiers while attacking fortifications. This term is also used to describe a shed used to protect a battering ram or sappers who undermined walls. The Gauls also used a wooden tower on wheels (**turris ambulātōria**) from which archers (**sagittāriī**) and slingers (**funditōrēs**) could attack walls from above. Such towers could also house a battering ram that could swing away at a fortification wall. Caesar describes these siege weapons of the Gauls by using their equivalent Roman names. It is almost certain these Gallic weapons, such as the **turris** and **testūdō**, were taken, perhaps literally, from the Romans themselves. The projectiles used by the Gauls in attacking the camp, as described by Caesar in Reading 60A, were **glandēs** (acorn-shaped bullets of lead, stone, or other materials that were shot from a hand-held sling or **funda**) and **iacula** (hand-thrown missiles or javelins). As Caesar takes pains to note, these missiles could be heated or set aflame and were therefore a hazard to Roman stockades. The Gauls also made use of a smaller javelin, called a **verūtum**, that had a throwing thong and was used by light-armed Roman infantry. Apparently the Gauls did not have sophisticated Roman style artillery, such as the **ballista**, a heavy torsion machine that hurled wooden darts or stone spheres. In this chapter, you will read about how two Roman centurions helped save the day when their camp was besieged and nearly taken by a fierce Belgic tribe, the Nervii.

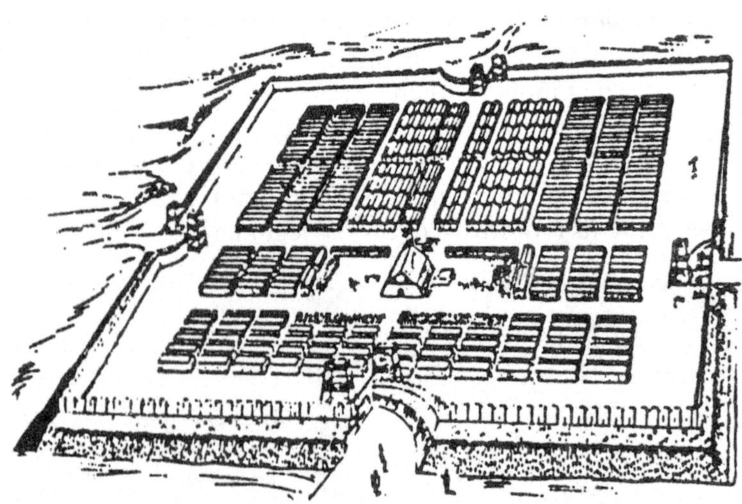

Layout of a Roman army camp
Illustration, Roman army camp plan

Two Rival Centurions

Gaul (**Gallia**) was a loose aggregation of various tribes that inhabited what is now northern Italy, western Switzerland, France, Belgium, and parts of the Netherlands and Germany west of the Rhine river (see the map on page 23). To the Romans, the Gauls, now also known as Celts, were half-civilized "barbarians" who had long hair and wore trousers.

Caesar's war chronicles in seven books, the *Commentarii de bello Gallico* (*Commentaries on the Gallic War*) describe his military campaigns against the Gauls, Britons, and Germans during the years 58–52 B.C. Nearly everyone who studied Latin during the twentieth century can quote the first few words of his "Gallic Wars": **Gallia est omnis dīvīsa in partēs trēs**. Cicero described Caesar's written words as **nūdī, rēctī, et venustī** (*spare, direct, and appealing*). Caesar writes in the third person to provide the Romans back home with the impression that he was personally detached from the events he describes. He also uses the vivid or historic present tense often, as he was not unaware of the value of involving his readers in the action as intensely as possible. Caesar's motives in writing the *Commentaries* were clearly propagandistic. Note how, in this chapter, he emphasizes the ultimate triumph of the Romans, whom the Gauls had hopelessly trapped, by telling the heroic story of the centurions Pullo and Vorenus. His objective was to secure popular support for his military affairs and for his tenuous political position, by presenting a picture of himself as a brave and skillful general whose well-trained soldiers could achieve victory even in difficult situations.

The action of Book V of Caesar's *Commentarii de bello Gallico* takes place in the year 54 B.C. While Caesar was away in Rome, the Belgic tribes of Gaul revolted against the Roman occupation, which had begun four years earlier on the pretext of protecting a Gallic ally of Rome from a migration by the Helvetii, another Gallic tribe, located in what is now Switzerland. The reading passages in this chapter present a close look at one incident during the revolt. Two Roman commanders have been killed, the Germans threaten from the east, and the Nervii have besieged a winter camp in northern Gaul. The Romans in the camp find themselves in imminent danger of being overwhelmed by the enemy.

"Vae victīs!" "*Woe to the conquered!*" Spoken by the Gallic chief Brennus, after Gallic mercenaries had swept down the Italian peninsula and plundered Rome in 390 B.C. That day, 18 July, became thereafter in Roman history a day of ill omens.

---

1 **oppugnātiō, oppugnātiōnis**, f., *attack, assault.*
coortō: from the deponent verb **coorior**.
***ventus, -ī**, m., *wind.*
maximō coortō ventō: look for ablative absolutes throughout the reading passages that follow, as this construction is common in Caesar's writing.
fervēns, ferventis, *boiling, seething; extremely hot.*
fūsilis, -is, -e, *softened.*
argilla, -ae, f., *potter's clay.* The bullets may have been shaped and fired like pottery dishes to harden them, then reheated before use.
fūsilī ex argillā: note that the preposition **ex** is placed between the adjective and the noun of the phrase it governs. The word to be emphasized, here **fūsilī**, is often found first in its phrase or clause.
glāns, glandis, m., *acorn; bullet*, i.e., an acorn-shaped projectile shot from a sling.
2 **funda, -ae**, f., *sling.*
fervefactus, -a, -um, *hot, heated*; cf. **ferventēs** (1).
iaculum, -ī, n., *dart, javelin.*
Gallicus, -a, -um, *of Gaul, Gallic.*
strāmentum, -ī, n., *straw.*
***tegō, tegere, tēxī, tēctus**, *to cover.* The Romans had followed the example of the Gauls in constructing their living quarters with thatched roofs.
3 **coepērunt**: the subject is *they* (the Nervii).

Hae: to what previous noun does this refer?
***ignis, ignis**, gen. pl., **ignium**, m., *fire.*
***comprehendō, comprehendere, comprehendī, comprehēnsus**, *to seize, catch.*
magnitūdine: *because of their size.*
4 **differō, differre, distulī, dīlātus**, irreg., *to carry in different directions, scatter, spread.*

***sīcutī**, conj., *as if, as, just as, just as if.*
***pariō, parere, peperī, partus**, *to give birth to; to acquire, gain.*
explōrō, -āre, -āvī, -ātus, *to investigate; to assure, confirm.*
sīcutī partā . . . victōriā: ablative absolute. Conjunctions are usually not included with ablative absolutes (but we supply them when we translate). Sometimes, however, the Romans did use conjunctions as part of ablative absolutes, as Caesar does here with **sīcutī**. This ablative absolute indicates that the Nervii were overconfident because they believed victory was assured.

5 **turrēs . . . coepērunt**: for the technical military terms used in this sentence, see "The Roman War Machine" on pages 80–82.
scālae, -ārum, f. pl., *ladder(s)* (plural noun with singular or plural meaning).

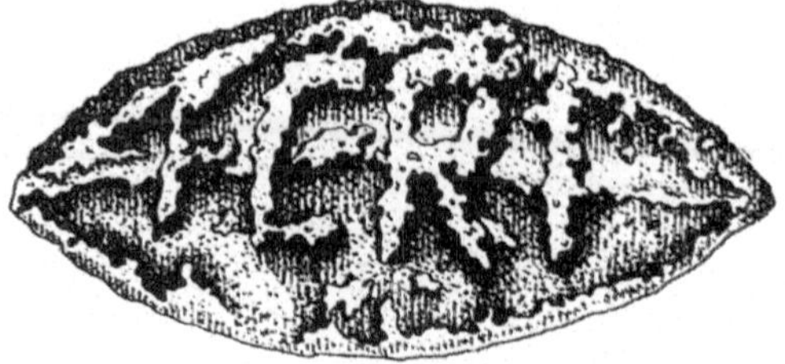

A Roman bullet, discussed on the opposite page
Claudia Karabaic, illustrator

A. Siege of a Roman Camp

Septimō oppugnātiōnis diē, maximō coortō ventō, ferventēs fūsilī ex argillā glandēs fundīs et fervefacta iacula in casās, quae in mōre Gallicō strāmentīs erant tēctae, iacere coepērunt. Hae celeriter ignem comprehendērunt et ventī magnitūdine in omnem locum castrōrum distulērunt. Hostēs maximō clāmōre, sīcutī partā iam atque explōrātā victōriā, turrēs testūdinēsque agere et scālīs vāllum ascendere coepērunt.

(*continued*)

---

1. For how long had the Nervii surrounded the Roman camp? (1)
2. What, of special note, happens on this day? (1)
3. What enemy tactics cause the fire in the Roman camp? (1–2)
4. What about the construction of the Roman huts causes them to burn so easily? (2)
5. What condition spreads the fire throughout the camp? (3)
6. Cite the Latin that indicates the Nervii had already considered themselves victorious. (4–5)
7. By what means do the Nervii attempt to attack the rampart? (5)

Slingers and Bullets

Slingers (**funditōrēs**; see the picture on page 87) were an important part of all ancient armies; the lead, stone, or ceramic projectiles they used had a range and accuracy as great as or greater than ancient bows and arrows, and bullets have been found in many archaeological sites (see the sample on the opposite page). Flavius Vegetius Renatus, author of a handbook on Roman military practice composed during the late Empire, wrote as follows:

> It is indeed appropriate for young people to be trained carefully to throw stones either with their hands or with slings. The inhabitants of the Balearic islands are said both to have been the first to have discovered the use of slings and to have trained so skillfully that mothers allowed their small sons to touch no food, except that which they had struck with a well-aimed stone from a sling. For often against warriors protected by helmets and coats of mail and armor, smooth stones shot from a sling or slingstaff are more serious than all arrows, since they bring a lethal wound onto unharmed bodies and without unpleasantness of bloodshed the enemy perishes through the blow from a stone. Moreover, no one is unaware that slingers fought in all battles of the ancients. This skill therefore must be learned by all recruits through frequent practice, because it is no effort to carry a sling. And sometimes it turns out that a conflict is held in stony places, that some mountain or hill must be defended, that barbarians must be driven off from the siege of forts or cities with stones and slings. (*Epitoma rei militaris*, I.16)

The projectiles used by slingers were pointed ovals that often contained curses directed at the enemy. The bullet shown opposite was found at Asculum, an Italian city that had revolted against Rome and was besieged by Pompeius Strabo, father of Pompey the Great (91 B.C.). The inscription reads: **Ferī** (side 1) **Pompeium** (side 2), *Strike Pompey*. Other bullets found there read **Asculānīs dōnum,** *a gift for the people of Asculum*; **Fugitīvī, perīstis**, *Deserters, you're dead;* and **Em tibi malum malō**, *Here's an evil thing for you, an evil (person).*

6 ***at**, conj., *but.*
mīlitum: the Romans.
***virtūs, virtūtis**, f., *courage, virtue, merit.*
ea: here not *this* or *that*, but *such*.
***praesentia -ae**, f., *presence.*
ut: introducing a three-part result clause completed in lines 8–10 below. The result clauses are set up by **tanta** and **ea** in line 6.
cum: *although.*
torreō, torrēre, torruī, tostus, *to set on fire, scorch, burn.*
torrērentur . . . premerentur (7) . . . **intellegerent** (8): the unstated subject is the (Roman) soldiers, carried over from **mīlitum** in line 6. For unexpressed subjects, see page 28.

7 **-que**: connects the clause **cum . . . torrērentur** (6) with **(cum) . . . premerentur**; the second **-que** connects **(cum) . . . premerentur** with **(cum) . . . intellegerent** (7–8).
***multitūdō, multitūdinis**, f., *large number; crowd, mob.*
***premō, premere, pressī, pressus**, *to harass, press hard.*
***impedīmenta, -ōrum**, n. pl., *supplies, baggage* (plural noun with singular meaning; from **impediō**).
omnia impedīmenta atque fortūnās cōnflāgrāre: indirect statement dependent on **intellegerent** (8). Note that this construction is found within the subjunctive clause introduced by **cum** (6), which itself is embedded in the subjunctive clause introduced by **ut** (6).

8 **cōnflāgrō, -āre, -āvī, -ātus**, *to burn up, be on fire.*
nōn modo: *not only*; correlates with **sed** (9) and **ac tum** (9).
dēmigrandī causā: *for the sake of abandoning.*
***dēcēdō, dēcēdere, dēcessī, dēcessūrus**, *to leave, depart.*
dēcēderet: the verb completing the first part of the result clause introduced by **ut** (6).
nēmō: note that the subject here is postponed until the end of its clause for dramatic effect.

9 ***respiciō, respicere, respexī, respectus**, *to look behind.*
respiceret: the verb completing the second part of the result clause introduced by **ut** (6).
quisquam: refers to the individual Roman soldiers.
sed paene nē respiceret quidem quisquam: *but hardly anyone even looked back.*
***ācer, ācris, ācre**, *sharp, keen, fierce.*
pugnārent: the verb completing the third part of the result clause introduced by **ut** (6).

10 **nostrīs**: *for our men.*
longē, adv., *by far.*
habuit: the subject remains **hic diēs**.
ēventus, -ūs, m., *result, outcome.*
ut . . . vulnerārentur atque interficerētur (11): result clauses introduced by **habuit ēventum** in line 10.

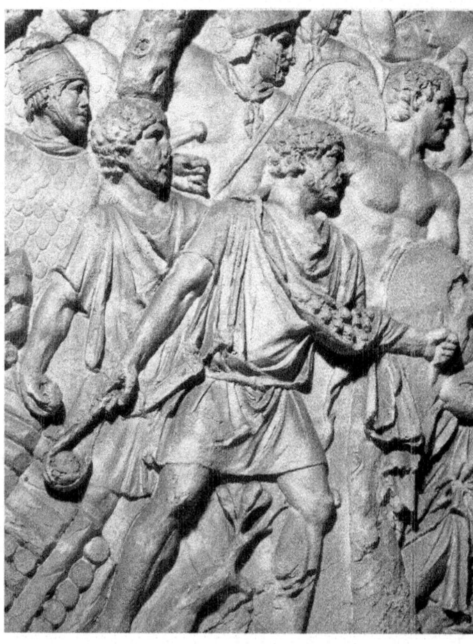

Funditor
Bas-relief frieze encircling Trajan's Column, A.D. 113

At tanta mīlitum virtūs atque ea praesentia animī fuit ut, cum undique torrērentur maximāque tēlōrum multitūdine premerentur suaque omnia impedīmenta atque fortūnās cōnflāgrāre intellegerent, nōn modo dēmigrandī causā dē vāllō dēcēderet nēmō, sed paene nē respiceret quidem quisquam, ac tum omnēs ācerrimē fortissimēque pugnārent. Hic diēs nostrīs longē gravissimus fuit; sed tamen hunc habuit ēventum, ut eō diē maximus numerus hostium vulnerārētur atque interficerētur.

(*continued*)

1. With what Latin words or phrases does Caesar describe his soldiers' spirit? (6)
2. What three things have been happening to his men that forecast disaster? (6–8)
3. How do Caesar's men refrain from showing their fear? How do they demonstrate their courage? (8–10)
4. How is this day characterized by Caesar? (10)
5. What prevents the day from being a total disaster? (11)

Reading Note

Nested Clauses II

In Chapter 55 (page 35), you learned that one clause can be embedded or nested inside another. An important rule is that the first clause, the one that is interrupted, cannot resume until the nested clause is complete. In line 6 above, you met **ut**, which clearly introduces a clause, then immediately you encountered the conjunction **cum**. The conjunctions -**que** and -**que** (7) show that the **cum** clause has three parts to it; once it is complete, the result clause begun by **ut** can resume. Notice how the conjunctions and adverbs (-**que** twice in the **cum** clause and **nōn modo**, **sed paene**, **ac tum**, each introducing one of the three verbs in the result clause) help guide you through this long complex sentence.

12 **Paulum**: take with **intermissā flammā**.
intermittō, intermittere, intermīsī, intermissus, *to discontinue, interrupt.*
quōdam locō: = **in quōdam locō**.
adigō, adigere, adēgī, adāctus, *to drive up* or *toward.*
***contingō, contingere, contigī, contactus**, *to touch, reach, make contact with.*
turrī adāctā et contingente (vāllum): note the different tenses of the participles in this ablative absolute.
13 ***centuriō, centuriōnis**, m., *centurion;* commander of a century, which was nominally 100 men.
ex eō: **eō** refers to **locō** in the same line. Note how the relative clause is embedded within the prepositional phrase.
-que: connects **recessērunt** and **remōvērunt.**
suōs: = **suōs mīlitēs**.
14 **nūtus, -ūs**, m., *nod, gesture.*
hostēs: nominative or accusative? How can you tell?
sī . . . vellent: *if they (the Nervii) wanted.*
introeō, introīre, introiī, introitūrus, irreg., *to go in, enter.*
vocāre coepērunt: the Roman soldiers were "inviting" the enemy soldiers to engage, indicating that they were not discouraged by their desperate situation.
quōrum: the antecedent is **hostēs.**
15 **ausus est**: from the semi-deponent verb **audeō.**
nēmō: note again how **nēmō** terminates its clause, for emphasis; cf. line 8.

***lapis, lapidis**, m. *stone.*
lapidibus coniectīs: given the meaning of **dēturbātī** (15), it appears that the Romans inside the fort were throwing the stones, which was a standard battle tactic for defending against a siege.
dēturbō, -āre, -āvī, -ātus, *to force away, dislodge.*
dēturbātī: = **dēturbātī sunt**. The unexpressed subject of this verb is *they* (the Nervii), since the closest masculine plural reference is to them (**quōrum** in line 14). The sentence contains two clauses, **dēturbātī (sunt)** and **turris succēnsa est**, connected by **-que**.
succendō, succendere, succendī, succēnsus, *to set on fire, burn.*

Reading Note

Adjectives as Substantives

In line 10 on the previous page, you met the sentence **Hic diēs nostrīs longē gravissimus fuit**. The context requires that the adjective **nostrīs**, *our (men)*, be translated with a noun such as **virīs** or **mīlitibus** understood. This use of an adjective as a noun is called a *substantive.* You have met substantives before, e.g., **multa et mīra**, *many wonderful things* (23:12). You can recognize substantives if you always keep in mind the basic patterns of Latin sentences. For example, the sentence **Nostrī Gallōs vīcērunt** fits the pattern subject—direct object—transitive verb. But there is no nominative noun, and **Nostrī** cannot agree with **Gallōs**; therefore **Nostrī** must be a substantive, acting as the subject. Also pay attention to the gender of substantives: **nostrī** (masculine) = *our men*, **nostrae** (feminine) = *our women*, **nostra** (neuter) = *our things*. Locate another example of a substantive in the reading on the opposite page.

Paulum quidem intermissā flammā et quōdam locō turrī adāctā et contingente vāllum, tertiae cohortis centuriōnēs ex eō, quō stābant, locō recessērunt suōsque omnēs remōvērunt, nūtū vōcibusque hostēs, sī introīre vellent, vocāre coepērunt; quōrum prōgredī ausus est nēmō. Tum ex omnī parte lapidibus coniectīs, dēturbātī turrisque succēnsa est.

—Caesar, *Commentarii de bello Gallico,* V.43

6. What happens during a lull in the fire? (12)
7. In what two ways do the Roman centurions respond to this latest attack? (13–14)
8. What do the centurions do next? (14)
9. How do the Nervii respond? (14–15)
10. With what tactic do the Romans respond to the Gallic attack? (15)
11. How, finally, do the Romans take control of the situation? (15–16)

Reading Note

Ellipsis

In the Reading Note on page 42, you learned that words that need to be used twice in a sentence may be expressed only once; the reader relies on the parallel structure as a guide to reusing the word expressed only once. Sometimes, however, Roman authors omitted words that would be used only once in a sentence, a usage called *ellipsis*. This is particularly common with forms of **esse** that would be used with a perfect participle, as with **dēturbātī (sunt)** in line 15 above. In this example Caesar expresses how quickly and easily his soldiers drove the Nervii away by disposing of them in one word.

A relief showing a Roman legionary fighting a barbarian. Note the thatched hut in the background, similar to those described in line 2 (page 85).
Rome, early second century A.D.

1 **in eā legiōne**: i.e., the legion led by Quintus Cicero (brother of the orator) that had been wintering in the territory of the Belgae and was being besieged by the Nervii.
quī . . . appropinquārent: what is the significance of the subjunctive verb in this clause? (See the Reading Note on page 59.)
***ordō, ordinis**, m., *order, class, rank.*
prīmīs ōrdinibus: *the first rank* (of centurions in a legion).
2 **Titus Pullō et Lūcius Vorēnus**: in apposition to **centuriōnēs** (1).

Hī: = Pullo and Vorenus.
perpetuās inter sē contrōversiās: the prepositional phrase is placed between the adjective and the noun it modifies.
quīnam, quaenam, quodnam, *which.*
3 ***anteferō, anteferre, antetulī, antelātus**, irreg., *to put ahead, prefer.*
quīnam anteferrētur: *which of them was to be preferred*, indirect question depending on **contendēbant.**
omnibus annīs: literally, *in all the years* = *in every year*; ablative of time when.
locus, -ī, m., *place; rank.*
dē locō: *about* or *for the rank of first centurion.*
simultās, simultātis, f., *animosity, rivalry.*
summīs simultātibus: *with their very great rivalry.* Make clear the distinctions in meaning among the ablative phrases **omnibus annīs, dē locō**, and **summīs simultātibus.**
contendō, contendere, contendī, contentus, *to contend, struggle, fight.*

4 **ad**: = *at.*
mūnītiō, mūnītiōnis, f., *fortification.*
pugnārētur: *it was being fought*, an impersonal passive (see the Reading Note on page 63). With **ācerrimē**, translate by an English noun, i.e., *fighting was fiercest.*
Quid: *Why?*
5 **locum**: *chance, opportunity*; cf. line 3.
probō, -āre, -āvi, -ātus, *to demonstrate, establish, prove.*
tuae probandae virtūtis: *of proving your courage.*

6 **Haec cum dīxisset**: **Haec** is placed in an emphatic position outside of the clause.
prōcēdit . . . irrumpit (7): Caesar uses the present tense here and in **continet** (7) to draw the reader into the action, as if he were there.
quae pars: *which part.* Note that the relative pronoun **quae** precedes its antecedent **pars.** A clearer expression of what is meant here in lines 6–7 would be . . . **in partem hostium, quae cōnfertissima est vīsa, irrumpit.** The conciseness of the Latin here is typical of Caesar's writing. His description also helps us see things from Pullo's point of view.
cōnfertus, -a, -um, *compressed, closely packed.*
7 **est vīsa**: what is the special meaning of **videō** in the passive voice?

Nē: here equivalent to **Nōn.**
sēsē . . . vallō continet: *keeps himself within the stockade*, i.e., remains inside.
omnium: *of all (people*, i.e., *his fellow soldiers)*; substantive.
8 **veritus**: past participle of **vereor.**
exīstimātiō, exīstimātiōnis, f., *opinion, judgment.*
omnium veritus exīstimātiōnem: i.e., Vorenus was afraid of what his fellow soldiers would think if he did not emulate and try to surpass Pullo.
***subsequor, subsequī, subsecūtūs sum**, *to follow.*

B. Rivalry Between Two Roman Centurions

Erant in eā legiōne fortissimī virī, centuriōnēs, quī prīmīs ōrdinibus appropinquārent, Titus Pullō et Lūcius Vorēnus. Hī perpetuās inter sē contrōversiās habēbant, quīnam anteferrētur, omnibusque annīs dē locō summīs simultātibus contendēbant. Ex hīs Pullō, cum ācerrimē ad mūnītiōnēs pugnārētur, "Quid dubitās," inquit, "Vorēne? Aut quem locum tuae probandae virtūtis exspectās? Hic diēs dē nostrīs contrōversiīs iūdicābit." Haec cum dīxisset, prōcēdit extrā mūnītiōnēs, quaeque pars hostium cōnfertissima est vīsa, irrumpit. Nē Vorēnus quidem sēsē tum vāllō continet, sed omnium veritus exīstimātiōnem subsequitur.

(*continued*)

1. Who were Pullo and Vorenus? (1–2)
2. What was the cause of their rivalry? (2–3)
3. Who instigated the competition between the two centurions during the battle? (4)
4. With what words did Pullo provoke his rival? (4–6) With what action? (6–7)
5. How did Vorenus respond to this challenge? What finally caused him to change his mind? (7–8)

Gaius Julius Caesar
Marble bust, Naples, 100–44 B.C.

9 **mediocris, -is, -e,** *of medium size, fairly small.*
***spatium, -ī,** n., *space,* i.e., between Pullo and the enemy.
relictō: past participle of **relinquō.**
pīlum, -ī, n., *pike, javelin.*
immittit: again, Caesar uses the present tense to bring the reader into the moment.
multitūdine: i.e., of the attacking Gauls.

10 **trāiciō, trāicere, trāiēcī, trāiectus,** *to pierce.*
quō: a linking **quī** (see page 26).
***percutiō, percutere, percussī, percussus,** *to strike.*
percussō et exanimātō: *having been struck and having been knocked unconscious; after this man had been struck senseless.*
scūtum, -ī, n., *shield.*
prōtegō, prōtegere, prōtegī, prōtēctus, *to protect, cover.*
prōtegunt: The understood subject of this verb and those that follow (**coniciunt** and **dant**) is the Nervii. For unexpressed subjects, see page 28.
hunc: also refers to the Gaul whom Pullo had wounded.
in hostem: i.e., Pullo; Caesar continues to speak from the point of view of the Nervii, so here the enemy are the Romans themselves. Be especially careful to identify the subject of each verb in this description of back and forth action.

11 **ūniversus, -a, -um,** *all together.*
***coniciō, conicere, coniēcī, coniectus,** *to hurl or throw together.* Cf. **trāiciō**, line 10.
regrediendī: *of retreating.*
facultās, facultātis, f., *chance, occasion, opportunity.*

trānsfigō, trānsfigere, trānsfixī, trānsfixus, *to pierce through.*
Pullōnī: *with respect to Pullo, of Pullo.*

12 **verūtum, -ī,** n., *a javelin, short spear.*
balteus, -ī, m., *sword belt.*
dēfigō, dēfigere, dēfixī, dēfixus, *to stick firmly.* Cf. **trānsfigō**, above.
āvertō, āvertere, āvertī, āversus, *to turn aside, knock aside.*
***cāsus, -ūs,** m., *misfortune, mishap.*
vāgīna, -ae, f., *the scabbard or sheath of a sword.*
cōnantī: understand **eī**, *with reference to him (Pullo) trying, while he tries.*

13 **morātur**: transitive here, i.e., it takes the direct object **dextram . . . manum.**
impedītum: modifies **Pullōnem,** understood.
circumsistō, circumsistere, *to surround.*

Reading Note

Dative of Reference

Note the word **Pullōnī** in the dative case in line 11. The dative case always indicates a person who is involved in the action in some way, but not as subject or direct object. Sometimes the person in the dative is an indirect object of a verb such as give, tell, or show. At other times the dative indicates the person whom the action affects without the idea of giving or telling, a usage known as the *dative of reference.* This usage, in which the action described affects the person in some way, is known as the *dative of reference.* The word *for* or the phrase *with reference to* may be used as a literal translation, e.g., **trānsfigitur scūtum Pullōnī**, *the shield is pierced through with reference to Pullo.* An English possessive, such as *Pullo's shield is pierced,* may also be used. Another example of the dative of reference is **cōnantī** in line 12.

Mediocrī spatiō relictō, Pullō pīlum in hostēs immittit atque ūnum ex multitūdine prōcurrentem trāicit; quō percussō et exanimātō hunc scūtīs prōtegunt, in hostem tēla ūniversī coniciunt, neque dant regrediendī facultātem. Trānsfīgitur scūtum Pullōnī et verūtum in balteō dēfīgitur. Āvertit hic cāsus vāgīnam et gladium ēdūcere cōnantī dextram morātur manum, impedītumque hostēs circumsistunt.

(*continued*)

---

1. How did Pullo first engage the enemy? With what result? (9–10)
2. How do the Nervii rescue their comrade? (10)
3. What action do they perform, in response to Pullo's attack? To whom does **hostem** refer here? (10–11)
4. What is the general effect of this Gallic counterattack? (11)
5. What two things happen to Pullo as a result? (11–12)
6. To what does the phrase **hic cāsus** (12) refer?
7. What does Pullo attempt to do, and what prevents him? (12–13)
8. How do the enemy react to Pullo's difficulty? (13)

This statue, a Roman copy of a Greek original, depicts a dying Gaul. The mustache, hairstyle, and torque around his neck identify him as a Gaul; compare the photographs on pages 100 and 103.
Marble sculpture, replica of bronze original

14 **succurrō, succurrere, succurrī, succursūrus** + dat., *to give aid to, run to help.*

succurrit: note again how Caesar uses the present tense to dramatize the action.

***inimīcus, -ī**, m., *personal enemy, rival.*

labōrantī: a present participle used as a substantive, *as he struggles*, referring to Pullo.

subveniō, subvenīre, subvēnī, subventūrus + dat., *to relieve, come to the rescue (of).*

hunc: Vorenus. Pay close attention to the use of the forms of **ille** and **hic** in this passage.

sē: referring to **omnis multitūdō** (15).

cōnfestim, adv., *without delay, immediately.*

15 **illum**: = **Pullōnem.**

trānsfixum: = **trānsfixum esse**, perfect passive infinitive of **trānsfigō** in indirect statement; the subject of the infinitive is **illum.** The omission of **esse** is an example of ellipsis, for which, see page 89.

comminus, adv., *in close quarters, in hand-to-hand combat.*

16 **rem gerit**: *carries on the fight.*

ūnō: one of the Gauls.

reliquōs: = **reliquōs virōs**; the adjective **reliquōs** is used substantively here.

cupidius, comparative adverb, *rather/too, even more eagerly.*

17 **locum . . . īnferiōrem**: a dip or depression in the ground.

dēiciō, dēicere, dēiēcī, dēiectus, *to throw down;* in passive, *to fall.*

concidit: the short *i* shows that this is a compound of **cadō** (not **caedō**).

rūrsus: *in turn*; remember that Pullo himself had been surrounded just a short time before.

subsidium, -ī, n., *support, aid, help.*

18 **ambō**: Pullo and Vorenus.

complūribus: i.e., of the enemy.

laus, laudis, f., *praise, applause.*

sēsē: = Pullo and Vorenus, the reflexive object of **recipiunt**.

***sē recipere**, idiom, *to take oneself back, return, withdraw, retreat.* Cf. **dare sē in fugam**, 58B:18.

19 ***uterque, utraque, utrumque**, *each (of two), both.*

fortūna . . . utrumque versāvit: *each suffered a reversal of fortune*; literally, *fortune turned each around.*

certāmen, certāminis, n., *contest, rivalry.*

utrumque: i.e., Pullo and Vorenus, referring to each.

versō, -āre, -āvī, -ātus, *to turn around, influence.* Do not confuse with **vertō** and **versor**.

ut . . . esset neque (19–20) **. . . posset**: what word sets up these result clauses?

alter alterī: *one to/for the other.* **Alter** serves two functions: it goes with **alterī inimīcus** (19–20), *the one hostile to the other*; it also goes with **auxiliō salūtīque esset** (20), *the one was a help and salvation for the other.*

20 **inimīcus, -a, -um** + dat., *unfriendly (to), hostile (to)*; cf. **inimīcus** as a noun in line 14.

dīiūdicō, -āre, -āvī, -ātus, *to determine, judge, decide.*

neque . . . posset: the subject is the passive infinitive **dīiūdicārī**, i.e., *and a decision was not possible*; literally, *and it could not be decided.*

***uter, utra, utrum**, *which, which one (of two).*

uter utrī: *which of the two . . . to which*, i.e., *which of the two . . . to the other.* Cf. **alter alterī** (19).

virtūte: *in* or *with respect to courage.*

anteferendus, -a, -um, *preferable.*

Succurrit inimīcus illī Vorēnus et labōrantī subvenit. Ad hunc sē cōnfestim ā Pullōne omnis multitūdō convertit: illum verūtō trānsfixum arbitrantur. Gladiō comminus rem gerit Vorēnus atque ūnō interfectō reliquōs paulum prōpellit: dum cupidius īnstat, in locum dēiectus īnferiōrem concidit. Huic rūrsus circumventō subsidium fert Pullō, atque ambō incolumēs complūribus interfectīs summā cum laude sēsē intrā mūnītiōnēs recipiunt. Sīc fortūna in contentiōne et certāmine utrumque versāvit, ut alter alterī inimīcus auxiliō salūtīque esset neque dīiūdicārī posset, uter utrī virtūte anteferendus vidērētur.

—Caesar, *Commentarii de bello Gallico* V.44

1. What does Vorenus do? (14)
2. How do the Nervii react to his arrival? In what belief do they do this? (14–15)
3. How does Vorenus engage the enemy? (15–16)
4. What results from his attack? (16)
5. What bad luck does Vorenus experience during the battle? (16–17)
6. In what situation does Vorenus find himself? (17)
7. Who brings him help? (17)
8. What do Pullo and Vorenus do after dispatching some of the enemy? (18–19)
9. How do their fellow soldiers receive them? (18)
10. To whom or what does Caesar give credit for what had happened? (19)
11. What reason does he give for saying this? (19–20)
12. What is the final outcome of the rivalry, according to Caesar? (20–21)

Reading Note

The Double Dative

In lines 19–20 above, the words **alterī . . . auxiliō salūtīque** mean *as help and salvation for the other*. This phrase contains two words in the dative; **alterī** is a dative of reference (see page 92) while **auxiliō salūtīque** expresses purpose or function. This example illustrates what is known as the *double dative*, the combination of a dative of reference and a dative of purpose. The verb in such sentences is usually a form of **esse** (here, **esset**). Here are two more examples:

Exercitus Rōmānus metuī Gallīs fuit. *The Roman army was a cause of fear to the Gauls.*
Haec rēs nōbīs cūrae est. *This situation is a concern to us.*

Double datives may be awkward in English if translated literally, so you may want to find alternative translations.

Questions for Thought and Discussion

1. Why do you think that Vorenus made the decision that he made? Would you have done the same thing?
2. What does his decision tell us about Roman soldiers? Does this comradeship have any analogies in modern America?
3. Why do you think Caesar chooses to tell this particular story in the *De bello Gallico*?
4. In what ways does Caesar dramatize and even exaggerate what happened?

BUILDING THE MEANING

Conditional Sentences

A conditional sentence has two parts:

1. a subordinate clause (*protasis*) introduced by **sī** (negative **nisi**) expressing a condition;
2. a main clause (*apodosis*) describing the situation that results if this condition is fulfilled.

You have already met many *simple* or *factual* conditions such as the following:

Sī tū rem bene **geris, gaudeō.** *If you **are successful**, I **am happy**.*

These conditions present no problems in translation because they are very similar to English. You have also met some factual conditions that refer to the future. In such sentences, the verb in the *if*-clause is in either the future or the future perfect tense but is translated by an English present tense:

Sī tū rem bene **gerēs**, ego **gaudēbō**.
*If you **are** successful (literally, **will be** successful), I **will be happy**.*

Sī tū rem bene **gesseris**, ego **gaudēbō**.
*If you **are** successful (literally, **will have been** successful), I **will be happy**.*

In this type of conditional sentence, when the action in the **sī**-clause takes place at the same time as that in the main clause, the *future* tense is used in the protasis (first example); when the action in the **sī**-clause will have been completed before the action in the main clause takes place, the *future perfect* is used (second example). The verbs in simple or factual conditions are indicative.

In addition to factual conditional sentences, there are ***imaginary*** or ***unreal*** conditions. In such sentences, the speaker is imagining something that might have happened in the past (but didn't), might be happening now (but isn't), or might happen in the future (but isn't likely). The verbs in such conditions always use the subjunctive mood:

a. Imaginary conditions referring to the past use the pluperfect subjunctive; translate *had . . . , would have . . .* :

   Nisi Vorēnus Pullōnī **succurrisset**, Pullō **interfectus esset**.
   *If Vorenus **had** not **run to help** Pullo, Pullo **would have been killed**.*

b. Imaginary conditions referring to the present use the imperfect subjunctive; translate *were . . . , would . . .* :

   Nisi Vorēnus Pullōnī **succurreret**, Pullō **labōrārētur**.
   *If Vorenus **were** not **running to help** Pullo, Pullo **would be in trouble**.*

c. Imaginary conditions referring to the future use the present subjunctive; translate *were to/should . . . , would . . . :*

Nisi Vorēnus Pullōnī **succurrat**, Pullō **interficiātur**.
*If Vorenus **were** not **to run to help** Pullo, Pullo **would be killed**.*

Sometimes you will meet *mixed* conditions, which have different tenses in the protasis and apodosis:

Nisi Vorēnus Pullōnī **succurrisset**, Pullō **mortuus esset**.
*If Vorenus **had** not **run to help** Pullo, Pullo **would be dead**.*

Note that the apodosis in a conditional sentence may precede the *if*-clause or that the *if*-clause may be embedded within the apodosis:

Caesar sollicitus **fuisset**, **sī scīvisset** Gallōs castra obsidēre.
*Caesar **would have been** worried **if he had known** the Gauls were besieging the camp.*
***If he had known** the Gauls were besieging the camp, Caesar **would have been** worried.*

Castra Rōmāna, **sī portae frangantur**, **capiantur.**
*The Roman camp, **if the gates should be broken down**, **would be captured**.*
***If the gates should be broken down**, the Roman camp **would be captured**.*

Conditional sentences provide a good illustration of the basic difference between the indicative and subjunctive moods. The indicative states a fact or asks a simple question; the subjunctive shows that an action is hypothetical or unreal in some way.

Exercise 60a

Read aloud, identify the time (past, present, or future) and type (factual or imaginary) of each condition, and translate. Make clear the distinction in meaning between the sentences in each pair.

1. Sī Caesar in castrīs mānsisset, Gallī impetum nōn fēcissent.
2. Sī Caesar in castrīs maneat, Gallī impetum nōn faciant.
3. Nisi scūtum Pullōnis tēlō trānsfixum esset, gladiō suō ūsus esset.
4. Nisi scūtum Pullōnis tēlō trānsfixum erit, gladiō suō ūtī poterit.
5. Vorēnus, sī prūdēns erit, intrā vallum manēbit.
6. Vorēnus, sī prūdēns fuisset, intrā vallum mānsisset.
7. Casae, nisi fervefacta iacula ā Gallīs iacerentur, ignem nōn comprehenderent.
8. Casae, nisi fervefacta iacula ā Gallīs iacientur, ignem nōn comprehendent.
9. Sī Gallī vāllum castrōrum scālīs ascendere possint, Rōmānōs vincant.
10. Sī Gallī vāllum castrōrum scālīs ascendere potuissent, Rōmānōs vīcissent.
11. Omnēs Nerviī rebelliōnem facient, sī castra Q. Cicerōnis capta erunt.
12. Omnēs Nerviī rebelliōnem fēcissent, sī castra Q. Cicerōnis capta essent.
13. Sī Vorēnus prīmus pīlus fiat, sitne Pullō īrātus?
14. Sī Vorēnus prīmus pīlus fiet, eritne Pullō īrātus?

***ūtor, ūtī, ūsus sum** + abl., *to use.*

1 **nātiō, nātiōnis**, f., *people*; not a nation, in the modern sense.
admodum, adv., *completely*.
dēdō, dēdere, dēdidī, dēditus, *to dedicate* or *devote* (to something + dat.)
***ob**, prep. + acc., *on account of, because of.*
quī: the antecedent **eī** is understood; also before **quīque** in line 2. Review the Reading Note on page 79.

2 **afficiō, afficere, affēcī, affectus**, *to affect, afflict, weaken.*
morbus, -ī, m., *illness.*
in proeliīs perīculīsque: = **in perīculīs proeliōrum.**
victima, -ae, f., *sacrificial animal* (slain to please or placate the gods); *victim.*

3 **immolō, -āre, -āvī, -ātus**, *to slay, sacrifice.*
sē immolātūrōs: = **sē immolātūrōs esse**, *that they will sacrifice . . .* ; ellipsis. Supply **hominēs** as direct object.
voveō, vovēre, vovī, votus, *to pledge, vow.*
administer, administrī, m., *assistant.*

4 **Druidēs, -um**, m. pl., *the Druids*, a class of priests that held authority among the Gauls and Britons.
ūtuntur: note that this verb is used with both **administrīs** and **Druidibus**; in English, supply the word *as* with one of the nouns, i.e., *they make use of the Druids as assistants.*
prō, prep. + abl., here meaning *(in return) for, (in exchange) for*; cf. line 2.
Prō vītā hominis nisi hominis vīta reddātur: this means that those in ill health or physical danger sacrifice someone else so that their own lives may be spared.
nisi: introduces the subordinate clause, but follows the prepositional phrase **prō vītā hominis**, which should be an element within the clause. The conjunction is delayed so that Caesar can create the chiasmus around the word **nisi**.
nōn posse: infinitive in indirect statement, the subject of which is **nūmen** and which is dependent on **arbitrantur** (5).

5 ***nūmen, nūminis**, n., *divinity, divine will.*
plācō, -āre, -āvī, -ātus, *to pacify, appease.*
arbitrantur: the unexpressed subject is *they* (the Gauls).
pūblicē, adv., *publicly, in public*; take with **habent.**
eiusdem generis: regular public sacrifices of the same kind as the private ones (2–4).
īnstitūta: past participle of **īnstituō**, *to establish.*

6 **immānī magnitūdine**: *of enormous size*, modifying **simulācra.**
quōrum: the antecedent is **simulācra.**
contexō, contexere, contexuī, contextus, *to weave together.*
contexta: with **membra.**
vīmen, vīminis, n., *shoot, twig.*

7 **quibus succēnsīs**: this ablative absolute refers to the wicker figures (**contexta vīminibus membra**).
circumveniō, circumvenīre, circumvēnī, circumventus, *to surround, envelop.*
exanimantur: literally, *they are deprived of the breath of life* (**ex** + **anima**), *they die, they expire.*

LXI

Customs of the Gauls

In the following chapters of the Commentaries, *Caesar describes, almost in the fashion of a travelogue, various social customs of the Gauls, including religion, authority over which was held by the priests, called Druids. Because no records of the Gallic Celts have survived, much of what we know about these people comes from Caesar's war chronicles. Note in these passages how Caesar sees the customs of the Gauls through Roman eyes.*

A. Some Gruesome Gallic Rituals

Nātiō est omnis Gallōrum admodum dēdita religiōnibus atque ob eam causam, quī sunt affectī graviōribus morbīs, quīque in proeliīs perīculīsque versantur, aut prō victimīs hominēs immolant aut sē immolātūrōs vovent administrīsque ad ea sacrificia Druidibus ūtuntur. Prō vītā hominis nisi hominis vīta reddātur, nōn posse deōrum immortālium nūmen plācārī arbitrantur pūblicēque eiusdem generis habent īnstitūta sacrificia. Aliī immānī magnitūdine simulācra habent, quōrum contexta vīminibus membra vīvīs hominibus complent; quibus succēnsīs circumventī flammā exanimantur hominēs.

(*continued*)

1. What place does religion hold in the lives of the Gauls? (1)
2. What groups of people particularly feel the need to placate the gods? (2)
3. What rituals do the Gauls perform in connection with these situations? (2–4)
4. Who is responsible for carrying out these rituals? (3–4)
5. If someone dies, how are the gods to be placated? (4)
6. What gruesome sacrifice does Caesar describe in lines 6–8?

Reading Note

Chiasmus

In line 4 above, you met the words **vītā hominis . . . hominis vīta**. This is a figure of speech called *chiasmus*, a name derived from the Greek letter chi (χ) because the words are "crossed" to form a contrastive pattern A-B-B-A. Another example occurred in 60B:11–12; study those lines and explain what words there make the chiasmus. Such an arrangement emphasizes or highlights the words that make up the chiasmus; in line 4, the life of the man who is spared is contrasted with the life of the man who is sacrificed.

9 ***supplicium, -ī**, n., *(capital) punishment, execution.*
supplicia: nominative or accusative?
***fūrtum, -ī**, n., *theft.*
latrōcinium, -ī, n., *robbery.*
noxia, -ae, f., *offense, crime.*
sint comprehensī: perfect passive subjunctive of **comprehendō**. What type of subjunctive clause is **quī . . . sint comprehensī**? See page 59.

10 ***grātus, -a, -um** + dat., *pleasing to, gratifying to.*
dīs: = **deīs**.
arbitrantur: what type of grammatical construction does this word govern?

eius generis: i.e., of the criminals listed in line 9.
***dēficiō, dēficere, dēfēcī, dēfectus**, *to fail, be lacking.*

11 **innocentēs, innocentium**, m. pl., *the innocent*; substantive.
ad . . . supplicia dēscendunt: *they resort to* (literally, *descend to*) *sacrificial offerings of the innocent.* Note the separation of the preposition (**ad**) from its object (**supplicia**) and that the subjects, the Gauls, of both **arbitrantur** (line 10) and **dēscendunt** (line 11) are unexpressed.

Reading Note

Special Deponent Verbs with the Ablative

In line 4 on the previous page, the word **Druidibus** serves as the object of the deponent verb **ūtuntur**, but it is in the ablative case. There are five special deponent verbs that use the ablative case as their object:

fruor, fruī, frūctus sum, *to enjoy, have benefit of*
fungor, fungī, fūnctus sum, *to perform, discharge*
potior, potīrī, potītus sum, *to obtain, get possession of* (**potior** can also take the genitive)
ūtor, ūtī, ūsus sum, *to use, make use of*
vēscor, vēscī, *to eat, feed on*

Compounds of these verbs (e.g., **abūtor**, 59A:1) also take the ablative.

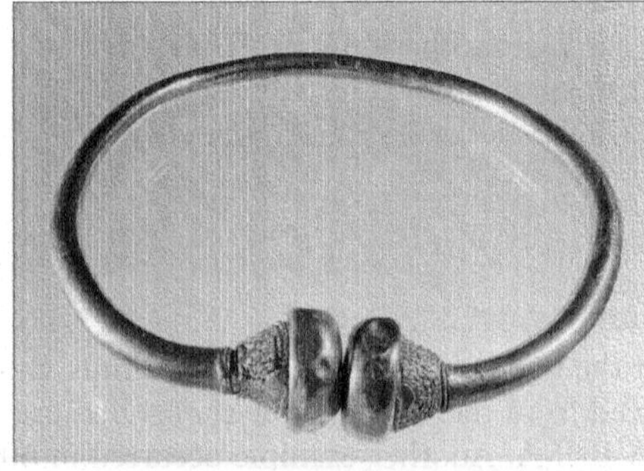

This is a picture of a 1st century B.C. Gallic gold torque, worn around the neck, perhaps as a symbol of nobility or religious leadership. It was made of twisted rods or tubes, usually of bronze or gold. The torque lasted for centuries as a symbol of Gallic identity and has inspired the design of popular modern jewelry. Such finely crafted metalwork and the coinage of the Celts, which consisted almost entirely of gold, may have made up the bulk of the war treasure that Caesar took from Gaul.
Gold torque, first century B.C.–first century A.D.

Supplicia eōrum, quī in fūrtō aut in latrōciniō aut aliquā noxiā sint comprehensī, grātiōra dīs immortālibus esse arbitrantur. Sed cum eius generis cōpia dēfēcit, etiam ad innocentium supplicia dēscendunt.

---

7. For what crimes can a Gaul be executed? (9)
8. What justification is given for executing a criminal? (10; see also 4–5)
9. What shocking observation does Caesar make in lines 10–11?

A Gallic stone relief of Mercury (B:12–14), now in the Carnavalet Museum in Paris, dated to the Gallo-Roman period. There are at least seven Gallic deities associated or combined with the Roman god Mercury, many of them associated with bears, boars, and hunting.
Relief, stone pillar base, Gallo-Roman, Paris, found in 1704

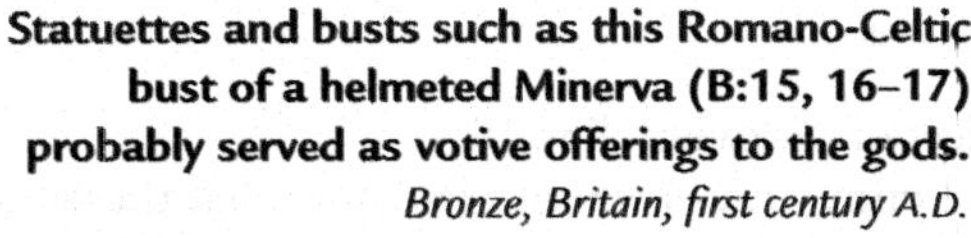

Statuettes and busts such as this Romano-Celtic bust of a helmeted Minerva (B:15, 16–17) probably served as votive offerings to the gods.
Bronze, Britain, first century A.D.

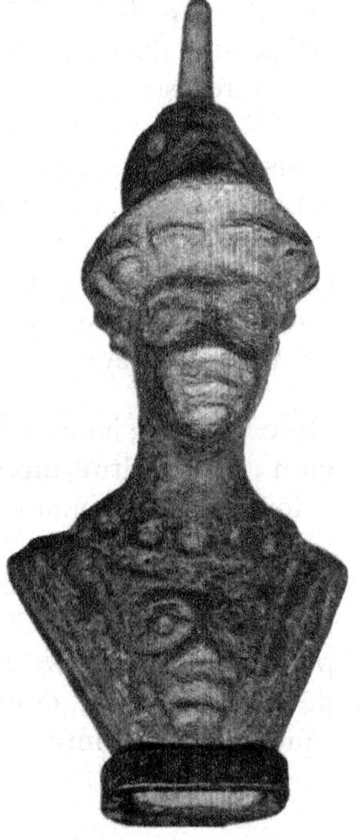

12 ***colō, colere, coluī, cultus**, *to cultivate; to revere, worship.*
colunt: the unexpressed subject is *they* (the Gauls).

Huius: = **Mercurī**. See the picture on the previous page.
13 **ferunt**: here, *they declare* or *say (that).*
hunc (Mercurium) . . . ferunt: note that the infinitive **esse** is missing from this indirect statement and the one in the next line, which also depends upon **ferunt**, understood.
ducem: *guide* in this context.
ad, prep. + acc., *for the purpose of, in regard to, for*; consider the meaning required by the context before making your decision.
quaestus, -ūs, m., *gain, acquisition.*
14 **mercātūra, -ae**, f., *business, trade.*
vim maximam: direct object of **habēre**.
arbitrantur: this verb governs the infinitive **habēre** in indirect statement, paralleling the previous two infinitive phrases, which are governed by **ferunt** (13).

Post hunc: supply **colunt**, from line 12.
Apollinem et Mārtem et Iovem et Minervam: Caesar gives Roman names to these deities. For Minerva, see the picture on the previous page. Note, too, that Latin uses conjunctions in expressing a list, whereas English would use commas and the word *and.*

15 **quam reliquae gentēs**: the verb **habent** is omitted but understood here. For gapping, see page 42. Note Caesar's sparing use of words in these sentences.
opīniō, opīniōnis, f., *idea, belief.*
opīniōnem: serves as the antecedent of the relative pronoun **quam**, which it follows. In this sentence, Caesar makes the observation that Gallic deities are the same as those found elsewhere.
16 **dēpellō, dēpellere, dēpulī, dēpulsus**, *to drive away.*
dēpellere: this infinitive, and those that follow, depend upon **habent opīniōnem** in indirect statement. Note the similarity in structure of the sentences in lines 12–14 and 15–17.
***opus, operis**, n., *work.*
artificium, -ī, n., *craft.* Cf. Mercury as **inventor artium** (13).
initium, -ī, n., *beginning, origin.*
17 **caelestis, -is, -e**, *of heaven, belonging to heaven*; here, as substantive, *the heavenly ones, the gods.*
imperium caelestium: although both words end in **-ium**, they have different functions. What are they?

Huic: = **Mārtī**; indirect object of **dēvovent**, line 18.
cum . . . cōnstituērunt and **cum superāvērunt** (18): note that these **cum** clauses are found with the indicative; how does this affect the meaning? (See the Reading Note on page 76.)
18 **quae bellō cēperint**: does this relative clause describe a specific example or general type of war booty? See page 59.
plērumque, adv., *on most occasions, generally, usually.*
dēvoveō, dēvovēre, dēvōvī, dēvōtus, *to vow, dedicate* (to a deity).
19 **-que**: connecting **immolant** and **cōnferunt**.

B. The Religion of the Gauls

Deōrum maximē Mercurium colunt. Huius sunt plūrima simulācra: hunc omnium inventōrem artium ferunt, hunc viārum atque itinerum ducem, hunc ad quaestūs pecūniae mercātūrāsque habēre vim maximam arbitrantur. Post hunc Apollinem et Mārtem et Iovem et Minervam. Dē hīs eandem ferē quam reliquae gentēs habent opīniōnem: Apollinem morbōs dēpellere, Minervam operum atque artificiōrum initia trādere, Iovem imperium caelestium tenēre, Mārtem bella regere. Huic, cum proeliō dīmicāre cōnstituērunt, ea quae bellō cēperint plērumque dēvovent: cum superāvērunt, animālia capta immolant reliquāsque rēs in ūnum locum cōnferunt.

---

1. Who is the chief deity of the Gauls? (12)
2. What are his three areas of influence? (12–14)
3. What other gods does Caesar mention and what are their spheres of influence? (14–15, 15–17)
4. When the Gauls contemplate a battle, what do they vow (dedicate) to Mars? (18)
5. When the Gauls win a battle, what two customs do they observe? (18–19)

Reading Notes

Interlocked Word Order or Synchysis

Interlocked word order attracts attention by patterning words in a crisscross manner or A-B-A-B pattern, such as **hunc omnium inventōrem artium** in lines 12–13. The intermingling of the adjective-noun combinations **hunc inventōrem** and **omnium artium** emphasizes the close association of the word pairs and gives a closely knit expression.

Two coins minted in Rome in 48 B.C. showing a Gallic man and woman. The figures are depicted in a style very different from that used to depict Romans on coins from the same era; apparently the artist wanted to give a reasonably accurate idea of what Gauls actually looked like. The man is wearing a torque (or perhaps a necklace) and has a shield behind his head.

20 **sē omnēs**: refers to the Gauls and serves as the subject of **prognātōs (esse)** in indirect statement depending on **praedicant**. Note the use of ellipsis here and below, with **prōditum.**

Dīs, Dītis, m., *Dis*, also known as *Dis Pater*, was an alternative name for Pluto, god of the underworld, who was considered the common father of the Gauls. The original Celtic name for this deity is lost.

prōgnātus, -a, -um, *sprung from, born from.*

praedico, -āre, -āvī, -ātus, *to declare, affirm.*

id: *this*, i.e., the fact that Dis is their common father.

***prōdō, prōdere, prōdidī, prōditus,** *to transmit, hand down.*

21 **spatium, -ī,** n., *space, extent, length.*

noctium: = **numerō noctium.**

22 **diēs nātālis**: *birthday.*

initia: take this word with both **mēnsium** and **annōrum. Initia** probably refers to the first day of the month or the year.

sīc: for what kind of subjunctive clause is this word a signpost?

noctem diēs: note that day follows night in the word order!

23 **īnstitūtum, -ī,** n., *institution.* Cf. **īnstituō**, A:5.

hōc: *in this (the following) way, in such a way.* Caesar now goes on to explain how the Gauls differ from other peoples.

ab reliquīs: i.e., of mankind; substantive.

differō, differre, distulī, dīlātus, irreg., *to be different* or *differ from.*

suōs līberōs: serves as the subject of the infinitive **adīre**, in line 24, which is dependent on **patiuntur**.

24 **adolēscō, adolēscere, adolēvī,** *to grow up, reach adulthood.*

ut . . . possint: purpose clause.

mūnus: neuter; is it nominative or accusative here?

***mīlitia, -ae**, f., *military service.*

***sustineō, sustinēre, sustinuī, sustentus**, *to sustain, endure; undertake, undergo.*

***palam**, adv., *openly.*

palam sē adīre nōn patiuntur: i.e., fathers do not allow their sons to approach them in public until they have reached adulthood.

cum adolēvērunt, ut . . . possint: note that these two clauses are nested inside the clause **quod suōs līberōs** (23) **. . . adīre nōn patiuntur**.

25 **fīlium**: this word serves as the subject of the indirect statement **assistere . . . dūcunt**.

puerīlī aetāte: *of youthful age, when still a boy.*

assistō, assistere, asstitī, *to take one's place, stand near* or *in the presence of.*

***turpis, -is, -e**, *improper, disgraceful.*

dūcunt: like **ferunt** (B:13), this verb can mean *they consider.*

C. Some Strange Customs

Gallī sē omnēs ab Dīte patre prōgnātōs praedicant idque ab Druidibus prōditum dīcunt. Ob eam causam spatia omnis temporis nōn numerō diērum sed noctium fīniunt; diēs nātālēs et mēnsium et annōrum initia sīc observant ut noctem diēs subsequātur. In reliquīs vītae īnstitūtīs hōc ferē ab reliquīs differunt quod suōs līberōs, nisi cum adolēvērunt, ut mūnus mīlitiae sustinēre possint, palam sē adīre nōn patiuntur fīliumque puerīlī aetāte in pūblicō in cōnspectū patris assistere turpe dūcunt.

---

1. What tradition handed down by the Druids is mentioned in line 20?
2. How do the Gauls reckon time? (21)
3. When does day follow night? (22)
4. What observation does Caesar make about the similarity of Gallic customs to those of other peoples? (22–23)
5. At what point do Gallic men allow their sons to approach them in public? (23–25)
6. When is a Gallic youth considered to have reached adulthood? (24)
7. What is the Gallic attitude toward those who break this tradition? Cite the Latin word that expresses this. (25)

Reading Note

Ablative of Description

In line 25 above, you find the ablative phrase **puerīlī aetāte**, *of youthful age*. A noun in the ablative case (**aetāte**) with a modifying adjective (**puerīlī**), when used to describe the character, quality, or size of someone or something, is known as the *ablative of description*. Notice that there is no preposition in Latin. This kind of description could also be expressed with the genitive, e.g., **puerīlis aetātis**, *of youthful age*. For other examples of the ablative of description, see 57B:9–10, **Tantō amōre . . . fuit**, *He was so beloved* (literally, *He was of such great love*), and 61A:6, **immānī magnitūdine**, *of enormous size*.

26 **quantās**: correlates with **tantās**, *as much (money) as*.
dōs, dōtis, f., *dowry* (a gift given by the bride's family to the groom).
dōtis nōmine: *by way of a dowry, as a dowry*.
ex suīs bonīs: *from their own goods;* how is the adjective **bonīs** used here?
aestimātiō, aestimātiōnis, f., *assessment, accounting*.
27 ***commūnicō, -āre, -āvī, -ātus**, *to unite, link, join*.

coniūnctim, adv., *in common, jointly*.
***ratiō, ratiōnis**, f., *thinking, reckoning; account*.
28 ***frūctus, -ūs**, m., *profit*.
vītā superāre, idiom, *to survive, live longer*; literally, *to surpass in life*.
pars utrīusque: *the share of each*.
29 **superiōrum temporum**: *of past times, previous years*.

in uxōrēs . . . in līberōs: here, **in** means *toward, over*.
nex, necis, f., *death*.
30 ***potestās, potestātis**, f., *power*.
pater familiae: *head of the family*, a Roman term.
illūstriōre locō nātus: *of distinguished birth*; literally, *born of rather high status or standing*.
dēcessit: *has departed*, i.e., is deceased.
***propinquus, -ī**, m., *relative*.
31 **dē morte sī rēs in suspīciōnem venit**: literally, *if the situation comes under suspicion concerning the death*, i.e., if the death is suspicious.
dē morte: note that this prepositional phrase is found outside the clause to which it belongs.
in servīlem modum: *in (accordance with) the manner of a slave*, i.e., under torture, as was the case in Roman practice. Cf. 58A:8.
32 **quaestiōnem habēre**, idiom, *to hold a trial* or *investigation*, another Roman term.
comperiō, comperīre, comperī, compertus, *to find out, discover*.
sī compertum est: the passive verb in this condition is impersonal (see the Reading Note on page 63), *if it has been discovered, if discovery has been made*, i.e., that foul play was involved in the husband's death.
excruciō, -āre, -āvī, -ātus, *to torment, torture*.
excruciātās: supply **eās**, i.e., wives discovered to have been involved in their husband's death.

33 ***fūnus, fūneris**, n., *funeral*.
***cultus, -ūs**, m., *attention, care; worship; culture*.
prō cultū: *according to the culture*, i.e., standard of living.
sūmptuōsus, -a, -um, *expensive, lavish*.
34 **fuisse arbitrantur**: indirect statement, the subject of which is (**omnia**) **quae**.
***cor, cordis**, n., *the heart; something dear to the heart, beloved*.
vīvīs: *for those being alive, the living*; substantive use of **vīvus, -a, -um**.
vīvīs cordī: literally, *(dear) to the heart for the living*, i.e., dear to their heart while alive. Do you recognize this construction? If not, see page 95.
35 **suprā hanc memoriam**: = **suprā hoc tempus**.
***dīligō, dīligere, dīlēxī, dīlēctus**, *to love, cherish*.
iūstīs fūneribus: this refers to the formalities of the actual funeral service, followed by cremation of the deceased, with the slaves and dependents mentioned previously.
36 ***ūnā**, adv., *together, together with*.
***cremō, -āre, -āvī, -ātus**, *to cremate*.

D. Marriages and Funerals

Virī quantās pecūniās ab uxōribus dōtis nōmine accēpērunt, tantās ex suīs bonīs aestimātiōne factā cum dōtibus commūnicant. Huius omnis pecūniae coniūnctim ratiō habētur frūctūsque servantur: uter eōrum vītā superāvit, ad eum pars utrīusque cum frūctibus superiōrum temporum pervenit. Virī in uxōrēs, sīcutī in līberōs, vītae necisque habent potestātem; cum pater familiae illūstriōre locō nātus dēcessit, eius propinquī conveniunt et, dē morte sī rēs in suspīciōnem venit, dē uxōribus in servīlem modum quaestiōnem habent et, sī compertum est, ignī atque omnibus tormentīs excruciātās interficiunt. Fūnera sunt prō cultū Gallōrum magnifica et sūmptuōsa: omniaque quae vīvīs cordī fuisse arbitrantur in ignem īnferunt, etiam animālia, ac paulō suprā hanc memoriam servī et clientēs, quōs ab eīs dīlēctōs esse cōnstābat, iūstīs fūneribus cōnfectīs ūnā cremābantur.

—Caesar, *Commentarii de bello Gallico* VI.16–19

---

1. How does a newly married Gallic couple establish their financial estate? (26–27)
2. How is the worth of the common property assessed? (27–28)
3. What happens to the common property when one of the spouses dies? (28–29)
4. What powers did men have and over whom? (29–30)
5. When the male partner in a marriage dies, why might an inquiry be held? (30–31)
6. Who conducts the inquiry? (30–31) For what specific reason? (31)
7. What procedure is used to question the wife? (31–32)
8. What results if the wife is found guilty? (32–33)
9. What comment does Caesar make about Gallic funerals? (33)
10. What is cremated with the dead? (34) What about in earlier times? (35–36)

Questions for Thought and Discussion

1. What aspects of Gallic culture might have caused Romans to think of Gauls as "barbarians"?
2. What evidence does Caesar provide regarding Gallic attitudes toward men? Women? Children? Toward religious belief? Social and economic status? Jurisprudence? Marriage?
3. What aspects of Gallic culture perhaps seem more civilized than some Roman attitudes and customs?
4. What evidence do you find in these readings of a blending of Gallic and Roman culture?

A Casualty of War

In A.D. 9, three Roman legions under the command of Quinctilius Varus were annihilated by the Germans. This epitaph commemorates a centurion who fell in this battle. It was inscribed on a *cenotaph* (a tomb with no remains) probably erected shortly after the disaster.

Roman inscriptions make extensive use of abbreviations (you should be able to think of two reasons why). Carefully compare the transcription at the top with the expanded version given below it and then translate.

Rome, 9 A.D.

M CAELIO T F LEM BON
Ɔ LEG XIIX ANN LIII S
CECIDIT BELLO VARIANO OSSA
INFERRE LICEBIT P CAELIVS T F
LEM FRATER FECIT

Mārcō Caeliō Titī fīliō, Lemōniā [tribū], [domō] Bonōniā, centuriōnī Legiōnis XIIX, annōrum LIII sēmissis; cecidit bellō Variānō. Ossa īnferre licēbit. Pūblius Caelius Titī fīlius, Lemōniā [tribū], frāter fēcit.

Lemōnia, one of sixteen tribes into which Roman citizens were divided for voting purposes
tribus, -ūs, f., *tribe*
Bonōnia, -ae, f., *Bononia* (modern Bologna)
Ɔ: an abbreviation for **centuriō**
sēmis, sēmissis, m., *one-half*
Variānus, -a, -um, *of Quinctilius Varus*
ōs, ossis, n., *bone*
īnferō, īnferre, intulī, illātus, irreg., *to put, place in* or *on*

Note that Marcus Caelius is shown holding a vine stick, a mark of his rank (recall the story about the centurion given on page 80) and wearing **phalerae**, the Roman equivalent of medals.

When identifying himself in a formal or legal way, a freeborn Roman included his father's **praenōmen** in the genitive, followed by the letter **F** for **fīlius** (normally placed between the **nōmen** and the **cognōmen**; in this inscription, no **cognōmen** is given) as well as his voting tribe.

A freedman took the **praenōmen** and **nōmen** of his former master and kept his slave name as his **cognōmen**; instead of his father's name, he gave the name of his former master. So the man shown at the left of Caelius is **M(ārcus) Caelius M(ārcī) L(ībertus) Prīvātus**, *Marcus Caelius Privatus, freedman of Marcus.*

CATULLUS

Gaius Valerius Catullus was born into an equestrian family at Verona (northern Italy) about 84 B.C. As a young man, he moved to Rome where he soon established a reputation as a poet. Like many young upper class Romans he served for a year (57 B.C.) on the staff of a provincial governor. This experience was apparently not a pleasant one, and Catullus took no further part in the political career that was traditional for a young man of his social position. Instead he remained in Rome for the rest of his life, writing poetry and spending time with his friends. He apparently died at about age 30 in 54 B.C., but the exact date is uncertain.

Catullus' poems treat many topics. Some poems mock people whose behavior Catullus did not like, including two nasty poems about Julius Caesar; others express his affection for his friends or anger at people who betrayed him; several address the question of what constitutes good poetry, a topic about which Catullus had very strong opinions. Catullus was influenced in particular by the Greek poet Callimachus, who believed that short poems, carefully refined and worked out, were better than the traditional long epics.

The most famous poems of Catullus, however, relate to a passionate love affair. Roman poets normally referred to their lovers by fictitious names in their poems; Catullus calls the woman he loved Lesbia, an allusion to the Greek island of Lesbos. Lesbos was the home of Sappho and Alcaeus, two poets whose work was considered among the most highly refined poetry ever produced. By using this name, Catullus suggests that his lover was an exceptionally elegant and sophisticated woman. Roman tradition says that her real name was Clodia. If so, there were three women named Clodia, sisters of the notorious politician Publius Clodius Pulcher, who could have been Catullus' love. (You will read about the murder of Clodius in Chapters 64 and 65.) Lesbia may have been Clodia Metelli, wife of the politician Metellus Celer, but this is not certain.

Catullus was very much in love with Lesbia, perhaps more so than she was with him. The romance deteriorated and was ultimately broken off. Catullus' poetry reflects all facets of the affair. In some poems he is deliriously happy with Lesbia, while in others he lashes out at her for betraying his love by seeing other men. In this chapter, you will read several of the 'Lesbia' poems, followed by a few that deal with other themes.

Roman poetry was built around various patterns of long and short syllables (see the appendix on meter, pages 308–311; the meter of each poem is identified in the notes). But even without studying meter formally you can begin to appreciate the rhythm that Catullus built into the verses. Practice reading aloud, making sure to hold all the vowels marked with a macron longer than those that are not marked.

Meter: Hendecasyllabic (for information about meter, see Appendix II, page 308)

1 **Vīvāmus, amēmus**: *Let us live, let us love.*
2 **rūmor, rūmōris**, m., *rumor, talk, gossip.*
sevērus, -a, -um, *strict.*
3 **aestimō, -āre, -āvī, -ātus**, *to judge, value something* (acc.) *at a certain amount* (gen.).
aestimēmus: *let us value.*
ās, assis, m., *as*, small Roman coin.

4 ***sōl, sōlis**, m., *sun.*
occidō, occidere, occidī, occāsus, *to fall down;* (of stars, etc.) *to set.*
5 **nōbīs**: this word should be taken both as a dative of reference with **brevis lūx**, *our short light*, and also with the phrase **est . . . dormienda**, *we must sleep.*
***semel**, adv., *once.*

7 ***mī**: = **mihi.**
bāsium, -ī, n., *kiss.*
mīlle, centum: these references to hundreds and thousands may be intended to create an image of someone using an abacus, which had separate columns for tens, hundreds, and thousands, to add up large numbers.
8 ***dein**: shorter form of **deinde.**
9 **usque**, adv., *continually, without stopping.* Notice how the elisions in this line, which connect the first three words together without a break, reinforce the meaning of **usque.**

11 **conturbō, -āre, -āvī, -ātus**, *to throw into confusion, mix up.*
nē sciāmus: *so that we will not know* (how many kisses there are), a negative purpose clause.
12 **nē quis malus**: *so that no evil person.*
***invideō, invidēre, invīdī, invīsus**, *to look askance at; to cast a spell on; to envy, begrudge.*
13 **bāsiōrum**: partitive genitive with **tantum.**

Meter: Elegiac couplet

1 **formōsus, -a, -um**, *beautiful, attractive.*
***candidus, -a, -um**, *white, bright, fair-skinned.*
2 **rēctus, -a, -um**, *straight, upright, with good posture; right, proper.*
***singulī, -ae, -a**, *one at a time, separately, individually.*
cōnfiteor, cōnfitērī, cōnfessus sum, *to admit, acknowledge.*

3 **Tōtum illud**: *All that*, i.e., Quintia's physical beauty. These words are accusative, with **esse** understood in indirect statement dependent on **negō.**
***negō, -āre, -āvī, -ātus**, *to say no, deny.*
venustās, venustātis, f., *a quality given by the goddess Venus; attractiveness, charm, elegance.*
4 **mīca, -ae**, f., *grain, small amount.*
sal, salis, n., *salt; humor, wit.* Humor spices up conversation, as salt brings out the flavor of food.

5 **cum . . . tum . . .**, correlatives, *not only . . . but also . . . .*
6 **omnibus**: dative with **surripuit**, *from all (women).*
ūna: *alone, by herself.*
Venus, Veneris, f., *the goddess Venus*; in plural, *allurements, charms.*

A. Many Kisses

Vīvāmus, mea Lesbia, atque amēmus,
rūmōrēsque senum sevēriōrum
omnēs ūnius aestimēmus assis!
Sōlēs occidere et redīre possunt:
nōbīs cum semel occidit brevis lūx,
nox est perpetua ūna dormienda.
Dā mī bāsia mīlle, deinde centum,
dein mīlle altera, dein secunda centum,
deinde usque altera mīlle, deinde centum.
Dein, cum mīlia multa fēcerīmus,
conturbābimus illa, nē sciāmus,
aut nē quis malus invidēre possit,
cum tantum sciat esse bāsiōrum.

—Catullus 5

---

1. What two things does Catullus suggest that he and Lesbia do? (1)
2. Who is talking about the lovers? (2)
3. How does Catullus suggest that he and Lesbia handle this gossip? (3)
4. What can suns do? (4)
5. How is human life different from that of suns? (5–6)
6. What does Catullus want from Lesbia? (7–9)
7. When will they mix up the kisses? (10)
8. Why will they do this? (11–13)

B. Lesbia's Special Qualities

Quīntia formōsa est multīs. Mihi candida, longa,
    rēcta est: haec ego sīc singula cōnfiteor.
Tōtum illud "formōsa" negō: nam nūlla venustās,
    nūlla in tam magnō est corpore mīca salis.
Lesbia formōsa est, quae cum pulcherrima tōta est,
    tum omnibus ūna omnēs surripuit Venerēs.

—Catullus 86

---

1. How do many people feel about Quintia? (1)
2. How does Catullus feel about her? (1–2)
3. Why is Quintia not attractive to the speaker? (3–4)
4. What qualities make Lesbia attractive? (5–6)

Reading Note

Hyperbole

In lines A:7–9 above, Catullus asks for many thousands of kisses, obviously an impossible amount. Such use of extreme exaggeration is called *hyperbole*.

Meter: Elegiac couplet

1 ***iūcundus, -a, -um**, *pleasant.*
Iūcundum: connected with **perpetuum** (2) by the conjunction **-que**.
prōpōnō, prōpōnere, prōposuī, prōpositum, *to set forth, propose, offer.*
prōpōnis: introduces an indirect statement with **amōrem / hunc nostrum** as subject and **iūcundum . . . perpetuumque** as complement.

2 ***fore**: alternative form for **futūrum esse**.

3 **Dī**: vocative plural of **deus**. Catullus is invoking the gods in a prayer.
***facite**: when followed by an **ut** clause with the subjunctive, **facere** means *see to it that, bring it about that.*

4 **ex animō**: this idiom, literally *from the mind*, would be expressed in English as *from the heart.*

5 **ut liceat**: *so that it may be permitted*, a purpose clause.
tōtā . . . vītā: the ablative, instead of the more common accusative, is used here to express extent of time.
***perdūcō, perdūcere, perdūxī, perductus**, *to extend, prolong.*

6 **aeternum . . . amīcitiae**: explain why this line is an example of synchysis (see the Reading Note on page 103).
***foedus, foederis**, n., *pact, treaty, alliance.*
amīcitia, -ae, f., *friendship.*

Meter: Elegiac couplet

1 ***mulier, mulieris**, f., *woman.*
***tantum . . . quantum**, *as much as.* The neuter forms are used here as adverbs.
amātam: = **amātam esse**.

2 **vērē**: this could modify either **dīcere** or **amātam**; think about which makes better sense.

3 ***fidēs, fideī**, f., *faith, good faith, reliability, trust.*
ūllō . . . foedere: = **in ūllō foedere**; prepositions are frequently omitted in poetry where they would be used in prose.

4 **in amōre tuō**: *in (my) love for you.*
reperiō, reperīre, repperī, repertus, *to find.*

Meter: Elegiac couplet

1 **Nūllī**: dative case, object of **nūbere**.
sē . . . mālle: indirect statement introduced by **mea mulier dīcit**; **nūbere** is a complementary infinitive with **mālle**.
***nūbō, nūbere, nūpsī, nūptūrus** + dat., *to put on a veil for, to marry* (used of a woman marrying a man; the reference is to the orange veil worn by a bride).

2 **sī . . . petat**: *if Jupiter were to seek*; the use of the subjunctive in this clause suggests that it is extremely unlikely that Jupiter would ever ask Lesbia to marry him.
sē: remember that this pronoun is reflexive, i.e, refers back to the subject of the main verb (**mulier**); so what does it mean in this sentence?

3 **mulier cupidō**: these words belong inside the relative clause that begins with **quod**, but are placed to the left of the clause marker; a more common word order would be **sed quod mulier dīcit . . . .**
cupidus, -a, -um , *desirous, eager.*
amantī: the present participle is equivalent to a noun, *lover.*

C. Catullus' Hope for the Future

Iūcundum, mea vīta, mihi prōpōnis amōrem
hunc nostrum inter nōs perpetuumque fore.
Dī magnī, facite ut vērē prōmittere possit,
atque id sincērē dīcat et ex animō,
ut liceat nōbīs tōtā perdūcere vītā
aeternum hoc sānctae foedus amīcitiae.

—Catullus 109

1. What, according to the poet, is Lesbia offering? (1–2)
2. What does the poet want the gods to do? (3–4)
3. How long could their friendship last? (5)
4. How is the friendship described? (6)

D. No Greater Love

Nūlla potest mulier tantum sē dīcere amātam
vērē, quantum ā mē Lesbia amāta mea est.
Nūlla fidēs ūllō fuit umquam foedere tanta,
quanta in amōre tuō ex parte reperta meā est.

—Catullus 87

1. What can no woman say? (1–2)
2. What has never been found in any treaty? (3–4)

E. A Woman's Words

Nūllī sē dīcit mulier mea nūbere mālle
quam mihi, nōn sī sē Iuppiter ipse petat.
Dīcit: sed mulier cupidō quod dīcit amantī,
in ventō et rapidā scrībere oportet aquā.

—Catullus 70

1. What does the poet's lover say? (1–2)
2. What should one do with a woman's words to a lover? (3–4)

Meter: Elegiac couplet

1 **sōlum**: how do you know that this word agrees with **Catullum** and not with **tē**?
*__nōscō, nōscere, nōvī, nōtus__, *to find out, get to know*; in perfect, *to know*.
nōsse: contracted form of **nōvisse**.
2 **prae**, prep. + abl., *before, in front of, in place of.*
Iovem: accusative of **Iuppiter.** All cases of this name except the nominative have the stem **Iov-** (hence the English form *Jove* as well as *Jupiter*).

3 **ut**: *as*, since the verb **dīligit** (4) is indicative, not subjunctive; **dīligit** is gapped.
*__vulgus, -ī__, n., *crowd, mob.* Note the gender.
4 **gnātus, -ī**, m., *son.*
gener, generī, m., *son in law.*

5 **Nunc**: note the forceful placement of this word, which creates a transition in time between the past (lines 1–4) and the present (lines 5–8).
*__quārē__: = **quā rē**, *for this reason, therefore* (**quā** is a linking **quī**).
etsī, conj., *although.*
impēnsus, -a, -um, *strong, earnest.* What form is **impēnsius**?
ūrō, ūrere, ussī, ustus, *to burn*; the word is used here metaphorically, *to set on fire (with love).*
6 **vīlis, -is, -e**, *cheap, worthless.*
*__levis, -is, -e__, *light, insubstantial, fickle, meaningless.*

7 **quī**, older form of **quō**, *how.*
potis, indeclinable, *possible.*
8 **bene velle**, *to wish well, have positive feelings for, regard, esteem.*

Meter: Elegiac couplet

1 *__ōdī, ōdisse__, *to hate*. This verb exists only in the perfect, pluperfect, and future perfect tenses; the perfect has a present meaning, so **ōdī** = *I hate.*
quārē: *for what reason, why*; here **quā** is a question word, introducing the indirect question **quid faciam**, not a linking **quī** as in F:5.
requīrō, requīrere, requīsīvī, requīsītus, *to look for, seek, ask.*
2 **fierī sentiō**: the pronoun **id** is understood from the previous line.
excruciō, -āre, -āvī, -ātus, *to torment, torture.*

A young woman playing the lyre, accompanied by a young man
Relief, Roman altar, first century B.C.

F. Catullus' Love for Lesbia

Dīcēbās quondam sōlum tē nōsse Catullum,
    Lesbia, nec prae mē velle tenēre Iovem.
Dīlexī tum tē nōn tantum ut vulgus amīcam,
    sed pater ut gnātōs dīligit et generōs.
Nunc tē cognōvī: quārē etsī impēnsius ūror,
    multō mī tamen es vīlior et levior.
Quī potis est, inquis? Quod amantem iniūria tālis
    cōgit amāre magis, sed bene velle minus.

—Catullus 72

---

1. What did Lesbia used to say? (1)
2. What did Lesbia not want? (2)
3. In what way did Catullus love Lesbia? (3–4)
4. How does Catullus feel now that he knows Lesbia? (5)
5. How does Lesbia appear to him now? (6)
6. What two things does Catullus feel compelled to do as a result? (7–8)

G. Conflicting Feelings

Ōdī et amō. Quārē id faciam, fortasse requīris.
    Nesciō, sed fierī sentiō et excrucior.

—Catullus 85

---

1. What two feelings is Catullus experiencing? (1)
2. What question might Catullus be asked? (1)
3. How would he answer this question? (2)
4. What does Catullus feel? (2)
5. What word summarizes his feelings? (2)

Reading Note

Metaphor

In line F:5 above, you saw that Catullus used the verb **ūrōr**, *I am on fire*, to describe his passion for Lesbia. The word is not used literally, but instead implies a comparison, such as *I feel as though I am on fire*. The use of a word to suggest a comparison when its literal meaning cannot be true is called a *metaphor*.

Meter: Choliambic

1 ***dēsinō, dēsinere, dēsiī, dēsitus**, *to abandon, stop, cease from.*
dēsinās: the present subjunctive here and in line 2 expresses a mild command.
ineptiō, -īre, *to act like a fool, be foolish.*
2 **pereō, perīre, periī, peritūrus**, irreg., *to die, perish.*
dūcās: here, as sometimes, **dūcere** has a mental sense, *lead (in the mind), consider, regard.*
perditum dūcās: *consider as lost.*
3 **fulgeō, fulgēre, fulsī**, *to gleam, shine.*
fulsēre: = **fulsērunt.**
4 **ventitō, -āre, -āvī, -ātus**, *to come.*
5 **nōbīs**: = **ā mē**; Roman poets often use the first person plural instead of the singular.
quantum, *as much as.*
nūlla: *no (other girl).*
6 **iocōsus, -a, -um**, *full of jokes, playful, fun.*
iocōsa: neuter plural substantive.
9 ***impotēns, impotentis**, *lacking power (over self), lacking self-control.*
nōlī: supply **velle**, based on **nōn vult** in the first half of the line.
10 **quae**: *(the one) who* (review the Reading Note on page 79).
sector, sectārī, sectātus sum, *to keep following, run after.*
sectāre: singular imperative of a deponent verb.
11 **obstinātus, -a, -um**, *resolute, fixed, stubborn.*
***mēns, mentis**, f., *mind.*
perferō, perferre, pertulī, perlātus, irreg., *to carry through, endure to the end, bear patiently.*
obdūrō, -āre, -āvī, -ātus, *to be tough.*
13 **tē**: object of **requīret** and of **rogābit**; with the second verb it agrees with **invītam.**
invītam: *(since) you (are) unwilling.*
14 **nūlla**: a more emphatic way of saying **nōn.**
15 ***scelestus, -a, -um**, *wicked.*
vae tē, *woe to you, so much the worse for you.*
16 ***bellus, -a, -um**, *pretty, attractive.* Do not confuse with the noun **bellum**, *war.*
17 **dīcēris**: the long **-ē-** makes the verb future, *will you be said.*
18 **bāsiō, -āre, -āvī, -ātus**, *to kiss*; cf. **bāsium**, A:7.
labellum, -ī, n., *little lip.*
mordeō, mordēre, momordī, morsus, *to bite.*
19 **dēstinātus, -a, -um**, *fixed, determined.*

Reading Note

The Ending -ēre

In line 3 opposite, you met **fulsēre**, where **-ēre** is an alternate ending for **-ērunt**, the third person plural of the perfect tense. This alternate ending is common in poetry and is sometimes found in prose as well. You can usually tell that such forms are not infinitives because **-ēre** is attached to the perfect stem, not to the present stem: **manēre** = *to remain*, **mānsēre** = *they remained.*

H. Letting Go

Miser Catulle, dēsinās ineptīre,
et quod vidēs perīsse perditum dūcās.
Fulsēre quondam candidi tibī sōlēs,
cum ventitābās quō puella dūcēbat,
amāta nōbīs quantum amābitur nūlla.
Ibi illa multa cum iocōsa fīēbant,
quae tū volēbās nec puella nōlēbat,
fulsēre vērē candidī tibi sōlēs.
Nunc iam illa nōn vult: tū quoque impotēns nōlī,
nec quae fugit sectāre, nec miser vīve,
sed obstinātā mente perfer, obdūrā.
Valē puella, iam Catullus obdūrat,
nec tē requīret nec rogābit invītam.
At tū dolēbis, cum rogāberis nūlla.
Scelesta, vae tē, quae tibi manet vīta?
Quis nunc tē adībit? Cui vidēberis bella?
Quem nunc amābis? Cuius esse dīcēris?
Quem bāsiābis? Cui labella mordēbis?
At tū, Catulle, dēstinātus obdūrā.

—Catullus 8

---

1. What is Catullus urging himself to do? (1–2)
2. What happened when Catullus followed his girl's lead? (3–4) How did he feel then? (5)
3. What things happened in the past? (6) How did Catullus and his girl feel about this? (7)
4. What five things does Catullus encourage himself to do? (9–11)
5. What is Catullus doing now? What will he not do? (12–13)
6. How does he claim the girl will feel? Why? (14)
7. What seven questions does Catullus ask his girl? (15–18)
8. What does he tell himself to do? (19)

BUILDING THE MEANING

The Subjunctive as Main Verb

You know that the subjunctive mood is used in many kinds of subordinate clauses (see Chapter 57, page 50). The *present* subjunctive can also be used in a *main* or *independent* clause to give a command or exhortation. It may be translated *let* . . . . The negative is **nē**.

Vīvāmus, mea Lesbia, atque **amēmus**, (62A:1)
Let us live, *my Lesbia, and* ***let us love***,

Nē verba senum sevēriōrum **audiant**.
Let them not listen *to the words of the rather strict old men.*

When used in the first person plural, such independent subjunctives are called *hortatory* (from **hortor, -ārī,** *to encourage*); when used in the third person, they are referred to as *jussive* (from **iubeō, iubēre,** *to order*). They are found less often in the second person, but may be used to give a command that is more gentle than the imperative, as in lines 1–2 of Catullus 8 on the previous page.

EXERCISE 62a

Read aloud, identify all examples of independent subjunctive, and translate:

1. Dent amantēs inter sē multa bāsia.
2. Nē quis malus amantibus noceat.
3. Dīcāmus omnēs Lesbiam esse pulchriōrem Quīntiā.
4. Sit perpetuus amor Catullī Lesbiaeque.
5. Dī magnī faciant ut Lesbia vērē prōmittat.
6. Liceat amantibus amōrem tōtam vītam perdūcere.
7. Scrībāmus verba amantium in ventō et in aquā.
8. Intellegās, Catulle, Lesbiam tē nōn iam amāre.
9. Nē vīvat miser Catullus.
10. Amōrem Lesbiae et Catullī memoriā semper teneāmus.

quis malus, *any evil person*

EXERCISE 62b

The following is a love charm laid on a woman named Vettia by a man named Felix; it was found in Tunisia, scratched on a lead tablet. Read it aloud, identify nine examples of the jussive subjunctive, and translate it:

Faciat quodcumque dēsīderō Vettia quam peperit Optāta, amōris meī causā, nē dormiat neque cibum accipere possit. Amet mē, Fēlīcem quem peperit Fructa; oblīvīscātur patris et mātris et propinquōrum suōrum et amīcōrum omnium et aliōrum virōrum. Sōlum mē in mente habeat, dormiēns vigilāns ūrātur frīgeat ardeat Vettia amōris et dēsīderī meī causā.

quīcumque, quaecumque, quodcumque, *whoever, whatever*
pariō, parere, peperī, partus, *to give birth, bear*
quam peperit Optāta: *whom Optata bore.* The author of the charm wants to make sure that it is applied to the right Vettia, so he specifies who her mother is.
***oblīvīscor, oblīvīscī, oblītus sum** + gen., *to forget*
dormiēns vigilāns, *(whether) sleeping (or) awake*
frīgeō, frīgēre, *to freeze, be cold*
***ardeō, ardēre, arsī**, *to blaze up, burn*
dēsīderium, -ī, n., *desire*

Caveat ēmptor! Let the buyer beware!

Gaudeāmus igitur, iuvenēs dum sumus.
Then let us rejoice, while we are young. (Medieval student song)

Reading Latin Poetry

You know that separating long sentences into shorter units as you read is very important for comprehension (review pages 6–11) and you have been encouraged to do this, as needed, while studying the prose texts in Chapters 55–61. This principle is true also when reading poetry, but the poet has already organized the text into lines whose form depends on the meter being used. It is worth noting that the lines of verse are often sense units in themselves, which makes it easier for you to understand the Latin. For instance, in Catullus 5 (Reading A), line 1 is a self-contained unit; lines 2–3 together make a unit; line 4 is a complete thought; line 5 is the entire **cum** clause, while line 6 is the main clause. It is certainly possible for the sense to run over from one line into the next; Catullus 12 (Reading I, page 121) has several examples of this. Even so, Latin poetry does not usually feature the long, complex sentences found in the prose of Cicero and many other writers.

Exercise 62c

Review Catullus 8 (Reading H, page 117) and note where the sense units correspond with the lines of verse and where they do not.

The elegiac couplet (Readings B–G) is a special case. In the elegiac meter, the two lines of the couplet usually work together as a unit of thought. Very often the poet will state an idea at the beginning of a couplet and then explain it or modify it. For example, in the first couplet of Catullus 86 (Reading B), Catullus begins by stating how Quintia appears to many, and then contrasts this with his own view of her. The second couplet contains the poet's assertion that all Quintia's qualities do not add up to "beautiful" followed by his explanation of why this is so. It is rare for a unit of meaning to run over from one couplet to the next.

Exercise 62d

Examine Readings D, E, and F and show how the two-line couplets relate to the ideas that Catullus is expressing in these poems.

A Roman curse tablet (*dēfīxiō*), similar to the one presented in Exercise 62b opposite. This tablet was found in Britain near a temple of Mercury and was written between A.D. 150–250. In Britain as in Gaul, Mercury was one of the most important gods (cf. 61B), and many curse tablets ask his aid in carrying out the curse.
©The British Museum and the Centre for the Study of Ancient Documents

Meter: Hendecasyllabic

1 **Marrūcīne Asinī**: the man's name was Asinius Marrucinus; the **cognōmen** is placed first and the **praenōmen** is not given.
sinister, sinistra, sinistrum, *left.*

2 **bellē**, adv., *beautifully, in a nice way.*
in iocō: English would use the plural, *in jokes;* **in iocō atque vīnō**, i.e., at a party.

3 **tollis**: in this context *lift* = *steal.*
linteum, -ī, n., *linen; object made of linen, cloth, napkin.*
neglegentiōrum: a substantive. Remember that the comparative can be translated *too* or *rather* as well as *more.*

4 **salsus, -a, -um**, *salty; witty, funny.*
Fugit tē: *It escapes you*, i.e., you don't get it, you miss the point.
ineptus, -a, -um, *foolish.*

5 **quamvīs**, adv., *however much you want; very, extremely.*
invenustus, -a, -um, *uncharming, unattractive.*

6 **Polliōnī**: Asinius Pollio, brother of Asinius Marrucinus. This is probably Gaius Asinius Pollio, Roman historian, orator, and friend of Julius Caesar.

7 **vel talentō**, *even at (the cost of) a talent.* A talent was a very large sum of money.

8 **mūtārī**: *to be changed*, i.e., to be undone, reversed.
velit: subjunctive in a relative clause of characteristic (see the Reading Note on page 59).
lepōs, lepōris, m., *charm, elegance.*

9 **differtus, -a, -um** + gen., *stuffed full (of).*
facētiae, -ārum, f. pl., *humor, wit.*

10 **hendecasyllabōs**: *hendecasyllables*, lines of verse in the hendecasyllabic meter.
trecentōs: as in Catullus 5 (Reading 62A), the number 300 is used to stand for any large amount. Catullus means that he will write poems attacking Asinius Marrucinus unless he gets his napkin back. In fact, a number of Catullus' surviving poems are nasty attacks on various people he did not like, so this was not an empty threat.

12 **aestimātiō, aestimātiōnis**, f., *value.*
aestimātiōne: *because of its value*, ablative of cause.

13 **vērum**, adv., *but.*
mnēmosynum, -ī, n., *reminder, memento, keepsake.*
sodālis, -is, gen. pl., **sodālium**, m., *comrade, friend.*

14 **sūdārium, -ī**, n., *towel* (literally, *sweat-cloth*); *napkin.*
Saetabus, -a, -um, *Saetaban, from Saetabis* (a town in Spain famous for its flax).
Hibērus, -a, -um, *Iberian, Spanish*; as substantive, *inhabitant of Iberia, Spaniard.*

15 **mūnerī**: *as a gift*, dative of purpose, forming a double dative with **mihi**.
Fabullus: one of Catullus' friends, mentioned in other poems.

16 **Vērānius**: another of Catullus' friends.
haec: neuter plural, referring to the **sūdāria** (14).
amem: *that I love*, subjunctive completing the idea of **necesse est**.

17 **ut**: supply **amō** (based on **amem** from the previous line).
Vērāniolum meum: *my little Veranius, my dear Veranius*, a diminutive expressing affection.

As you learned on page 109, not all of Catullus' poems relate to his affair with Lesbia. The following poems provide a sample of other themes that are typical of Catullus, including friendship and a tendency to mock those of whose behavior he did not approve.

I. Dealing with a Thief

Marrūcīne Asinī, manū sinistrā
nōn bellē ūteris: in iocō atque vīnō
tollis lintea neglegentiōrum.
Hoc salsum esse putās? Fugit tē, inepte:
quamvīs sordida rēs et invenusta est.
Nōn crēdis mihi? Crēde Polliōnī
frātrī, quī tua fūrta vel talentō
mūtārī velit: est enim lepōrum
differtus puer ac facētiārum.
Quārē aut hendecasyllabōs trecentōs
exspectā, aut mihi linteum remitte,
quod mē nōn movet aestimātiōne,
vērum est mnēmosynum meī sodālis.
Nam sūdāria Saetaba ex Hibērīs
mīsērunt mihi mūnerī Fabullus
et Vērānius: haec amem necesse est
ut Vērāniolum meum et Fabullum.

—Catullus 12

A Roman banquet as shown in a Pompeian wall painting
Fresco, Pompeii

1. What general comment does Catullus make about Asinius Marrucinus' behavior? (1–2)
2. What specifically does he do that Catullus finds offensive? (2–3)
3. How might Marrucinus regard this behavior? (4)
4. What does Marrucinus not understand? (4–5)
5. Who besides Catullus finds Marrucinus' behavior offensive? What would this person want to happen? (6–8)
6. How is this person different from Marrucinus? (8–9)
7. What two options does Catullus offer? (10–11)
8. Why is Catullus so concerned about this napkin? (12–13)
9. Where did the napkins come from? (14–16)
10. How does Catullus feel about the napkins and why? (16–17)

Reading Note

Diminutives

A *diminutive* is a word that indicates small size or small amount, such as "doggy" or "droplet." In Latin, diminutives are formed by adding a syllable containing the letter **-l-** to the base word, as in the name **Vērāniolum** (above: 17); **labellum**, *little lip* (H:19); and **sigillum**, *statuette* (59B:19). In both English and Latin, diminutives can convey a variety of feelings, ranging from affection to contempt.

Meter: Hendecasyllabic

2 **antistō, antistāre, antistitī** + dat., *to stand in place of, be equal to, be worth.*
trecentīs: see note on I:10 on page 120. What is the effect of the hyperbole?
3 **penātēs, penātum**, m. pl., *the Penates*, spirits that watched over the household.
4 **ūnanimus, -a, -um**, *of one mind, harmonious, loving.*
anus, -ūs, f., *old woman*; here used as an adjective, *aged.*
5 **nūntiī**: remember that **nūntius** can mean either *messenger* or *message, news* (here the latter).
***beātus, -a, -um**, *happy, joyful.*
6 **vīsō, vīsere, vīsī**, *to see.*
audiam: supply **tē** as direct object, modified by **nārrantem** (7).
Hibēr, Hibēris, m., *inhabitant of Iberia, Spaniard.*
Hibērum: genitive plural modifying **loca, facta, nātiōnēs** in the next line.
7 **loca**: this word is masculine in the singular but may be neuter in the plural.
nātiō, nātiōnis, f., *people, tribe* (not *nation* in the modern sense).
loca, facta, nātiōnēs: asyndeton (see page 26).
8 **applicō, -āre, -āvī, -ātus**, *to apply, bring in contact, hug.*
collum, -ī, n., *neck.*
9 **suāvior, -ārī, -ātus sum**, *to kiss.*
10 **quantum est hominum beātiōrum**: *however many (of) rather happy people there are*; **hominum beātiōrum** is a partitive genitive.
11 **quid**: translate as *who* (the word takes its gender from the neuter phrase **quantum est** in line 10).
mē: ablative of comparison with **laetius . . . beātiusve.**
***-ve**, enclitic conjunction, *or.* (An enclitic, like **-que**, attaches to the previous word.)

Meter: Elegiac couplet

1 **Rūfe**: the identity of this Rufus is not certain. A young man named Marcus Caelius Rufus became one of Clodia's lovers. He was prosecuted in 56 B.C. for **vīs**, *political violence* (the murder of an ambassador) and was defended by Cicero, who claimed that the prosecution had been motivated by Clodia's desire for revenge because Caelius had broken off the affair. As you read, consider what factors might make it likely (or not) that the Rufus in this poem is the same as the one defended by Cicero.
mihi: the dative goes both with **crēdite**, *believed by me*, and with **amīce**, *my friend.*
nēquīquam, adv., *to no point, in vain.*
crēdite: vocative of the perfect participle of **crēdō**.
2 ***pretium, -ī**, n., *price, cost.*
malum, -ī, n., *bad thing, difficulty, trouble*; a substantive.
3 **sīcine**: *is this the way?*, the question word **-ne** added to the adverb **sīc**.
subrēpō, subrēpere, subrēpsī, subreptus + dat., *to crawl under, sneak up on, creep up on.*
subrēpstī: = **subrēpsistī**.
perūrō, perūrere, perussī, perustus, *to burn, set on fire.*
intestīna perūrēns, *burning my insides*, i.e., causing me great anguish.
4 **ei**, interjection expressing dismay; **ei** is pronounced as one syllable.
miserō: supply **mihi**, *from miserable me*, dative of separation with **ēripuistī**.
nostra: = **mea**. Roman poets often use the first person plural when the singular is meant.

(*vocabulary and notes continued on opposite page*)

J. A Friend Returns Home

Verānī, omnibus ē meīs amīcīs
antistāns mihi mīlibus trecentīs,
vēnistīne domum ad tuōs penātēs
frātrēsque ūnanimōs anumque mātrem?
Vēnistī. Ō mihi nūntiī beātī!
Vīsam tē incolumem audiamque Hibērum
nārrantem loca, facta, nātiōnēs,
ut mōs est tuus, applicānsque collum
iūcundum ōs oculōsque suāviābor.
Ō quantum est hominum beātiōrum,
quid mē laetius est beātiusve?

—Catullus 9

---

1. How does Catullus describe Veranius? (1–2)
2. To what places and people does Catullus think Veranius has returned? (3–4)
3. How does Catullus regard this event? (5)
4. In what condition has Veranius arrived? (6)
5. What will Catullus hear Veranius doing? (6–7)
6. How will Catullus demonstrate his joy at Veranius' return? (8–9)
7. What emotion does the exclamation in line 10 express?
8. Catullus asks a rhetorical question (see page 69) to make clear his feelings about Veranius' arrival. What is the question? (11)

K. Betrayed by a Friend

Rūfe, mihī frūstrā ac nēquīquam crēdite amīce
(frūstrā? immō magnō cum pretiō atque malō),
sīcine subrēpstī mī, atque intestīna perūrēns
ei miserō ēripuistī omnia nostra bona?
Ēripuistī, heu heu nostrae crūdēle venēnum
vītae, heu heu nostrae pestis amīcitiae.

—Catullus 77

---

1. How does Catullus describe his belief in Rufus' friendship? (1)
2. How does he alter that description? (2)
3. What has Rufus done? (3–4)
4. What two images does Catullus use to describe the effects of Rufus' betrayal? (5–6)

5 ***ēripiō, ēripere, ēripuī, ēreptus**, *to snatch from*.
Ēripuistī: the answer to the question in line 4. In conversation Romans often answered a question by repeating the key word, with a negative added if needed. So the answer to **Ēripuistī?**, *Did you snatch?*, is **Ēripuistī**, which we could translate as *Yes, you did.*
***heu**: = **ēheu**.
***crūdēlis, -is, -e**, *cruel*.

L. The Best and the Worst

Disertissime Rōmulī nepōtum,
quot sunt quotque fuēre, Mārce Tullī,
quotque post aliīs erunt in annīs,
grātiās tibi maximās Catullus
agit pessimus omnium poēta,
tantō pessimus omnium poēta,
quantō tū optimus omnium patrōnus.

—Catullus 49

---

1. In what flattering way does Catullus address Cicero? (1)
2. How does he continue the flattery? (2–3)
3. What is Catullus doing in regard to Cicero? (4–5)
4. How does Catullus describe himself? (5)
5. How does he carry this description one step further? (6–7)

Meter: Hendecasyllabic

1 **disertus, -a, -um**, *eloquent.*
disertissime: superlative in the vocative case.
nepōs, nepōtis, m., *nephew, grandson, descendant.*
Rōmulī nepōtum: the Romans.
2 **quot sunt**: *as many as there are.*
fuēre: why can this not be an infinitive? Review the Reading Note on page 116.
Mārce Tullī: remember that Cicero's full name was Marcus Tullius Cicero.
3 **post**: the adverb, *afterward, later on* (not the preposition *after*).
4 ***grātiās agere,** *to give thanks (to), to thank.*
5 **poēta**: remember that this first declension noun is masculine.
6 **tantō . . . quantō** (7), *by so much . . . as*; what are such pairs of words called? (See the Reading Note on page 57.)
7 **tū**: supply **es**.
***patrōnus, -ī**, m., *patron.* **Patrōnī** were rich and powerful men who helped those of lesser status in various ways, including defending them in court if necessary. So the word also came to be applied to those who defended others, whether or not they had a traditional patron/client relationship in other ways.

Questions for Thought and Discussion

1. Catullus correlates his description of Cicero as **optimus omnium patrōnus** (7) with a description of himself as **pessimus omnium poēta** (6). It is clear from some of Catullus' other poems that he considered himself better than many poets. How does this fact affect our understanding of Poem 49?
2. What else in the poem might suggest that it is not to be taken literally?

THE VALUE OF FRIENDSHIP

In this chapter, you will meet a different Cicero, Cicero the philosopher. His discourse on friendship, *Laelius de amicitia* (*Laelius on Friendship*), which is written in the manner of a Greek philosophical treatise, takes the form of an imaginary dialogue between prominent figures of the middle Republic: Gaius Laelius, who was surnamed Sapiens, and his sons-in-law, Gaius Fannius Strabo and Quintus Mucius Scaevola. The dialogue is set in the time following the sudden death of Scipio Africanus Minor, who was the adopted grandson of Scipio Africanus, conqueror of Hannibal. Laelius' affection for the now deceased Scipio Minor leads to discussion about the nature of friendship. Cicero admired Scipio Minor as a model statesman and made him the central character in his dialogue *De re publica*.

In ancient Rome, the meaning of **amīcitia** ranged from describing companionship between two individuals, which included goodwill (**benevolentia**) and affection (**cāritās**), to the formal relationship between states. Both senses of the word were dependent upon the concept of **fidēs**, or trust. The idea of **amīcitia** often had a utilitarian meaning as well, which was a practical side that was particularly Roman. In his speech *Pro Roscio Amerino* (*For Roscius Amerinus*) Cicero observed, "We cannot do everything by ourselves. A second party is relatively useful in other things. It is for that reason that friendships (**amīcitiae**) are formed, so that mutual services may be shared for the common good of both (parties)." True friendship was often thought possible only between individuals of the same gender or the same social or economic status.

Here is what the Greek scientist and philosopher Aristotle, pupil of Plato, wrote about friendship in the 4th century B.C.:

> Friendship is a virtue ... to say so much implies that friendship is a noble thing — i.e., that it is worthy to be pursued as an end in itself. Further, friendship is among the most indispensable requirements of life: it is, in fact, valuable not only as an end, but as a necessary means to life .... It is an observed fact that men find friendship indispensable in good fortune, in bad fortune, and at all periods of their life.
>
> —*The Nicomachean Ethics*, Book VIII.1155a3–5

As you read Cicero's thoughts on **amīcitia** in this chapter, consider the similarities between his ideas and those of Aristotle and reflect on your own thoughts and feelings about friendship.

1 **nihil aliud nisi**: literally, *nothing else if not; nothing other than.*
omnium . . . rērum: these genitives complete the meaning of **cōnsēnsiō** (2).
cum: *along with, together with, joined with.*

2 ***benevolentia, -ae**, f., *kindness, goodwill.*
cāritās, cāritātis, f., *affection, esteem, love.*
cōnsēnsiō, cōnsēnsiōnis, f., *agreement, accord, harmony* (**cum** + **sentiō**).
quā: literally, *than which, than this*, a linking **quī** referring to **amīcitia** (1); ablative of comparison dependent upon **melius** (3).
***an**, conj., *whether, or.*
haud sciō an: *I do not know whether*, i.e., I doubt whether. This expression introduces the indirect question **an . . . sit . . . datum** (2–3).
excipiō, excipere, excēpī, exceptus, *to leave out, exclude, omit.*
sapientia, -ae, f., *good sense, wisdom*. Cf. *homo sapiens*.
exceptā sapientiā: how do you translate this grammatical construction?
nīl quicquam . . . sit . . . datum: Laelius says *(I do not know whether) not anything (= nothing) has been given*; English would express this as *(I do not know whether) anything has been given.*

3 **melius**: modifies **nīl** (2).
sit . . . datum: = **datum sit**, perfect passive subjunctive, the subject of which is **nīl**.
dīs: = **deīs**.

***dīvitiae, -ārum**, f. pl., *wealth, riches*. Note the emphatic position of this word.
praepōnō, praepōnere, praeposuī, praepositus, *to place before, prefer.*

4 **valētūdō, valētūdinis**, f., *well being, health.*
honōrēs: *political offices* (as in the phrase **cursus honōrum**).
***voluptās, voluptātis**, f., *amusement, gratification, pleasure.*

Illa . . . superiōra: i.e., those items just mentioned. Supply **sunt**.

5 **cadūcus, -a, -um**, *frail, perishable, fleeting* (from **cadō**).
posita . . . in: *dependent on.*
nōn tam . . . quam: *not so (much) . . . as*; correlatives.

6 **temeritās, temeritātis**, f., *instability, capriciousness, fickleness.*

Sōlem ē mundō tollere videntur quī amīcitiam ē vītā tollunt.
Those who take away friendship from life seem to take away the sun from the world.
(Cicero, *De amicitia* XXIII.47)

Vērum etiam amīcum quī intuētur, tamquam exemplar aliquod intuētur suī.
He who looks upon a true friend looks as if upon a sort of image of himself.
(Cicero, *De amicitia* VII.23)

In the following passages from Cicero's De amicitia, *keep in mind that Laelius is speaking.*

A. What Is Friendship?

Est enim amīcitia nihil aliud nisi omnium dīvīnārum hūmānārumque rērum cum benevolentiā et cāritāte cōnsēnsiō; quā quidem haud sciō an, exceptā sapientiā, nīl quicquam melius hominī sit ā dīs immortālibus datum. Dīvitiās aliī praepōnunt, bonam aliī valētūdinem, aliī potentiam, aliī honōrēs, multī etiam voluptātēs. Illa autem superiōra cadūca et incerta, posita nōn tam in cōnsiliīs nostrīs quam in fortūnae temeritāte.

—Cicero, *De amicitia* VI.19–20

---

1. What is friendship, according to Laelius? What are its characteristic features? (1–2)
2. What other aspect of human life does Laelius consider greater than friendship? (2)
3. From where is friendship obtained? (3)
4. What types of things do others prefer to friendship? (3–4)
5. What are the disadvantages of these? (4–5)
6. For what reason are these to be considered disadvantages? (5–6)

The sarcophagus (stone coffin) of Lucius Cornelius Scipio Barbatus. This sarcophagus was originally one of many in the tombs of the Scipio family on the Via Appia outside Rome.
Rome, circa 200 B.C.

1 **prīncipiō**, adv., *at first, in the first place, first of all.*
quī: *how*; archaic form of the ablative **quō** = **quō modō**, *in what way.*
vītālis, -is, -e, *vital, of or belonging to life; full of vitality.*
vīta vītālis: i.e., a life worth living.
Ennius: Ennius (239–169 B.C.) is considered the father of Roman poetry. He wrote the *Annales*, an epic in praise of Rome, of which only fragments remain. Ennius was buried in the family tomb of the Scipios. Cicero quotes or paraphrases him several times in the *De amicitia*.
quae: introduces the subjunctive verb **conquiēscat** in a relative clause of characteristic (see the Reading Note on page 59). To whom or what does this pronoun refer?
nōn: take with **conquiēscat** (2).
amīcī: nominative plural or genitive singular?
2 **conquiēscō, conquiēscere, conquiēvī, conquiētus**, *to find or be at rest, find repose.*

***dulcis, -is, -e**, *sweet.*
Quid dulcius: supply **est.**
quīcum: *(someone) with whom*; **quīcum** is an archaic form of **quōcum**; cf. **quī** (1).
quīcum . . . audeās: another relative clause of characteristic.
sīc loquī ut tēcum: literally, *to speak in such a way as with yourself*, i.e., *to speak as (if) with yourself.*

3 **Quī esset:** *How would there be?* For this form of **quī**, see line 1.
esset: the conclusion of the conditional **nisi habērēs**, following.
prosperus, -a, -um, *fortunate, successful, prosperous* (**prō** + **spērō**).
nisi habērēs: *unless you had, if you did not have.* Cicero's use of a present imaginary condition here indicates that it could not possibly happen or be true that one could enjoy the fruits of success without a friend with whom to share them.
quī . . . gaudēret: what type of clause? Understand a word such as **eum** as the antecedent of **quī** (see the Reading Note on page 79).
illīs: = **prosperīs rēbus.**
***aequē**, adv., *equally.*
aequē ac: *equally as, just as, the same as.*
tū ipse: supply **gaudērēs**; for gapping, see the Reading Note on page 42.

4 **Adversās**: supply **rēs.**
ferre: *to bear, endure.*
sine eō: refers to the person described in the following relative clause.
illās: = **adversās (rēs).**
gravius, comparative adverb, *more seriously, more painfully.*
tū: supply **ferrēs**; another example of gapping.

B. The Value of Friendship

Prīncipiō quī potest esse vīta "vītālis," ut ait Ennius, quae nōn in amīcī mutuā benevolentiā conquiēscat? Quid dulcius quam habēre, quīcum omnia audeās sīc loquī ut tēcum? Quī esset tantus frūctus in prosperīs rēbus, nisi habērēs, quī illīs aequē ac tū ipse gaudēret? Adversās vērō ferre difficile esset sine eō, quī illās gravius etiam quam tū ferret.

(*continued*)

1. What does the poet Ennius say about friendship? (1–2)
2. What advantage of friendship does Laelius describe in lines 2–3?
3. Of what value is friendship in good times? (3–4) In bad times? (4–5)

A painting from a French manuscript of about 1500 that contains a translation of Cicero's *De amicitia* and *De senectute (On Old Age)*. Cato, seated in the elaborate chair, is the main speaker in *De senectute*; the other two figures represent Scipio and Laelius. At the left is Cicero at work on the *De senectute*.

Parchment, last quarter of the fifteenth century, Fol. 19, illuminated by Martin de Braga

6 ***dēnique**, adv., *finally, then; and then* (introducing a new stage in the argument).
cēterae rēs: Laelius had been discussing the advantages of friendship.
expetō, expetere, expetīvī, expetītus, *to seek out, strive after, desire.*
opportūnus, -a, -um, *convenient, suitable, advantageous, useful.*
singulus, -a, -um, *separate, one at a time, each.*
opportūnae . . . ferē singulīs: *are each generally useful for one purpose only.*
dīvitiae: for this and other things that people prefer to friendship, see Reading A, lines 2–4.

7 **ut ūtāre**: this and the succeeding **ut** clauses are purpose clauses.
ūtāre: = **ūtāris**, present subjunctive of **ūtor**. Note this alternative form of the 2nd person singular (**-re** = **-ris**) here and in the three examples that follow in lines 7–8. Be careful about active and passive meanings here; **ūtāre** and **fungāre** are deponent and so have active meanings, but **colāre** and **laudēre** are not deponent and have passive meanings.
***ops, opis**, f., *power, influence.*

8 ***dolor, dolōris**, m., *pain.*
***careō, carēre, caruī, caritūrus** + abl., *to be without, be free from, lack.*
mūneribus: *functions, tasks.*
fungor, fungī, fūnctus sum + abl., *to carry out, perform.* For deponents with the ablative, see the Reading Note on page 100.

Amīcitia: Laelius now goes on to discuss friendship.
amīcitia . . . continet: note how here in lines 8–10 a general statement is given, followed by illustrative examples, which balances the structure of lines 6–8.
quōquō, adv., *to whatever place, wherever.*

9 **verteris**: *you will have turned, you turn*; future perfect active.
praestō, adv., *present, at hand.*
nūllō locō: = **ē nūllō locō**, picking up the prepositional prefix of **exclūditur.**
intempestīvus, -a, -um, *untimely; present at an incorrect or inappropriate time.*

10 **nōn aquā, nōn ignī**: ablative objects of **ūtimur.** Note the asyndeton.
ut aiunt: *as they say, as the saying goes.*
locīs plūribus: = **in locīs plūribus**; *on more occasions, in more situations.*

11 **secundās rēs**: *favorable times; prosperity.*
splendidus, -a, -um, *brilliant, radiant, bright.*
adversās: = **adversās rēs**; parallels **secundās rēs**, above.
partiō, partīre, *to share, divide* (cf. **pars, partis**).
commūnicō, -āre, -āvī, -ātus, *to allot, share.*

12 **leviōrēs**: understand **facit** from the previous line, paralleling **splendidiōrēs facit.** For gapping, see the Reading Note on page 42.

Dēnique cēterae rēs quae expetuntur opportūnae sunt singulae rēbus ferē singulīs; dīvitiae, ut ūtāre; opēs, ut colāre; honōrēs, ut laudēre; voluptātēs, ut gaudeās; valētūdō, ut dolōre careās et mūneribus fungāre corporis. Amīcitia rēs plūrimās continet: quōquō tē verteris, praestō est, nūllō locō exclūditur, numquam intempestīva, numquam molesta est. Itaque nōn aquā, nōn ignī, ut aiunt, locīs plūribus ūtimur quam amīcitiā. Nam et secundās rēs splendidiōrēs facit amīcitia et adversās partiēns commūnicānsque leviōrēs.

—Cicero, *De amicitia* VI.22

---

4. What does Laelius say about other desires of mankind? (6)
5. What five examples does he use to illustrate such desires? What is the purpose of each of these? (6–8)
6. What do we learn about friendship in line 8, in contrast to other things in lines 6–8?
7. What are some specific advantages of friendship? (8–10)
8. What is the meaning of the proverb in line 10?
9. In what way does friendship enhance success? In what way does it reduce the burden of adversity? (11–12)

Vetus est enim lēx illa iūstae amīcitiae idem amīcī semper velint.

For that is a timeless law of impartial friendship that friends should always want the same thing.

(Cicero, *Pro Plancio* II.5)

---

1 **cadūcae**: see Reading A, line 5.
aliquī: *some (persons or individuals)*.
anquīrō, anquīrere, anquīsīvī, anquīsītus, *to seek out, search for* (from **quaerō**).
anquīrendi sunt: *must be searched for*.
2 **quōs dīligāmus et ā quibus dīligāmur**: relative clauses of characteristic (see the Reading Note on page 59). There are several additional clauses of this type in the lines that follow.
cāritāte . . . benevolentiāque sublātā: ablative absolutes.
sublātā: past participle of **tollō**, *to raise up, take away*.
omnis: modifies **iūcunditās** (3).
3 **est . . . sublāta**: = **sublāta est**.
iūcunditās, iūcunditātis, f., *pleasure, joy*.

Mihi: *With respect to me*, i.e., Laelius; dative of reference; see the Reading Note on page 92.
vīvit . . . vīvet: emphatic, as is the alliteration with **virtūtem**.

4 ***equidem**, adv., *indeed, truly, for my part*.
5 **ex omnibus rēbus**: here, **rēbus** means *benefits, gifts, blessings*.
***tribuō, tribuere, tribuī, tribūtus**, *to allot, bestow, grant*.
quod . . . possim: relative clause of characteristic.
6 **Scīpiōnis**: Remember that, in the setting of the *De amicitia*, Scipio Minor had recently died. Interestingly, Cicero's own beloved daughter Tullia had died in the year previous to the year in which he wrote *De amicitia* (44 B.C.). His grief at her loss may have triggered his interest in philosophy.

In hāc: = **In amīcitiā**.
cōnsēnsus, -ūs, m., *harmony, concord, agreement*.
in hāc: note the emphasis provided by the anaphora and the balance of the phrases.
7 **oblectātiō, oblectātiōnis**, f., *delight, amusement, enjoyment*.

***nē . . . quidem**: *not even*.
8 **minimā . . . rē**: *on the smallest point, in the slightest way*.
quod . . . sēnserim: *(the kind of thing) which I would have felt*, i.e., as far as I was aware.
ipse quod nōllem: supply **audīvisse**.
nōllem: imperfect subjunctive of **nōlō**. What type of clause is this? (See the Reading Note on page 59.)
9 **Ūna domus erat**: supply **nōbīs**; literally, *There was one home to us, We had one home*. This probably means that each felt at home in the house of the other. Understand **nōbīs** and **erat** in the remaining phrases of this sentence. Review the Reading Note on page 72 for the dative of possession.
victus, -ūs, m., *victuals, food*.
commūnis: *shared*.
peregrīnātiō, peregrīnātiōnis, f., *foreign travel*.
10 **rūsticātiō, rūsticātiōnis**, f., *life in the country*.

C. Laelius' Friendship with Scipio

Sed quoniam rēs hūmānae fragilēs cadūcaeque sunt, semper aliquī anquīrendī sunt quōs dīligāmus et ā quibus dīligāmur; cāritāte enim benevolentiāque sublātā omnis est ē vītā sublāta iūcunditās. Mihi quidem Scīpiō, quamquam est subitō ēreptus, vīvit tamen semperque vīvet; virtūtem enim amāvī illius virī quae exstīncta nōn est. Equidem ex omnibus rēbus quās mihi aut fortūna aut nātūra tribuit, nihil habeō quod cum amīcitiā Scīpiōnis possim comparāre. In hāc mihi dē rē pūblicā cōnsēnsus, in hāc rērum prīvātārum cōnsilium, in eādem requiēs plēna oblectātiōnis fuit. Numquam illum nē minimā quidem rē offendī, quod quidem sēnserim, nihil audīvī ex eō ipse quod nōllem. Ūna domus erat, īdem victus, isque commūnis, neque sōlum mīlitia, sed etiam peregrīnātiōnēs rūsticātiōnēsque commūnēs.

—Cicero, *De amicitia* XXVII.102–103

---

1. How does Laelius characterize human affairs? (1)
2. For what must we search because of this? (1–2)
3. What happens if goodwill and affection are taken away? (2–3)
4. How does Laelius describe Scipio's death? (3)
5. What does he mean by the words **vīvit . . . vīvet**? (3–4)
6. What aspect of Scipio's character did Laelius admire? What does he say about this? (4)
7. How does Laelius describe his friendship with Scipio? (5–6)
8. In what three specific ways did Scipio express his friendship? (6–7)
9. What does Laelius say in lines 7–8 about their friendship?
10. What things did Laelius and Scipio share? (9–10)

Reading Note

Hyperbaton

In lines 2–3 above, the word **omnis** modifies **iūcunditās** but is separated from it by four intervening words. Such wide separation of words that logically belong together is called *hyperbaton*. Hyperbaton generally serves to emphasize the words that are separated. In this example, the hyperbaton is reinforced by the placement of **iūcunditās** at the end of the sentence.

Questions for Thought and Discussion

1. Compare Cicero's idea of friendship with that described by Aristotle (page 125). (Be aware that these descriptions are three hundred years apart in time.)
2. Has the concept of friendship changed much since Cicero's time? If so, how?
3. Were Lesbia and Catullus friends, according to Cicero's description of friendship? What about Pullo and Vorenus? What does friendship mean to you?
4. Are people more or less friendly now than previously, in your opinion? In either case, why do you think this is so?

BUILDING THE MEANING

The Gerund or Verbal Noun

In Book II you met the following:

Mārcus fīnem **recitandī** fēcit. (39:1)
*Marcus made an end **of reciting**, i.e., finished reciting.*

You found a similar form in Chapter 59B:7:

Nōn modo **dēmigrandī** causā, . . . *Not only for the sake **of abandoning** . . .*

Both examples contain a *gerund* or *verbal noun*, corresponding to the English verbal noun ending in *-ing*. The Latin gerund is active in meaning, *abandoning*, and is formed by adding **-nd-** to the present stem of the verb, plus a 2nd declension neuter singular ending. (Note the spelling of the word geru**nd**.) There are no plurals and there is no nominative case. Here are the forms:

	1st	2nd	3rd	3rd -iō	4th
Gen.	parandī	habendī	mittendī	iaciendī	audiendī
Dat.	parandō	habendō	mittendō	iaciendō	audiendō
Acc.	parandum	habendum	mittendum	iaciendum	audiendum
Abl.	parandō	habendō	mittendō	iaciendō	audiendō

Note: the gerunds of **īre** are **eundī, eundō, eundum, eundō.**

The gerund can function in any of the usual constructions of nouns in the various cases.

1a. In the genitive case the gerund is used with **causā** or **grātiā** to express purpose:

Cicerō saepe scrībēbat bene **scrībendī causā.**
*Cicero wrote often **for the sake of writing (in order to write, to write)** well.*

1b. The gerund in the genitive case is also used with special adjectives:

Cicerō **cupidus** bene **scrībendī** erat.
*Cicero was **desirous of writing** well.*

2a. The dative case of the gerund is used when the gerund serves as the indirect object:

Cicerō multum temporis **scrībendō** dabat.
*Cicero was giving much time **to writing**.*

2b. The gerund in the dative case is also used with special adjectives:

Cicerō scrīpsit multa **idōnea legendō.**
Cicero wrote many things ***suitable for reading.***

3. In the accusative case, the gerund is found with **ad**, to show purpose (*in order to, to*):

Cicerō multa legēbat **ad** bene **scrībendum.**
Cicero read much ***for the purpose of writing (in order to write, to write)*** *well.*

4a. The gerund in the ablative case is used in prepositional phrases with **dē**, **ex**, and **in**:

Cicerō multa lēgerat **dē scrībendō.**
Cicero had read many things ***about writing.***

4b. The gerund in the ablative case may also serve as an ablative of means:

Cicerō nōtissimus factus est bene **scrībendō.**
Cicero became very well known ***by writing*** *well.*

Exercise 63a

Read aloud, locate the gerund, and note its case. Then translate the entire sentence.

1. Amīcī eundem modum vīvendī saepe habent.
2. Necesse est nōbīs amīcōs habēre ad bene vīvendum.
3. Cicerō dē amīcitiā scrībendi causā multa Aristotelis lēgerat.
4. Cicerō propter modum scrībendī factus est praeclārus.
5. Cōgitāvitne Cicerō Scīpiōnem idōneum gubernandō esse?
6. Quid dulcius est quam habēre amīcum colloquendī causā?
7. Cicerō scrīpsit hominem ad duās rēs esse nātum, ad intellegendum et agendum.
8. Multa inter nōs commūnicandō, bonī amīcī factī sumus.

*__idōneus -a, -um__ + dat., *fit, suitable*

Latin Gerunds in English

These Latin phrases used in English all contain gerunds.

modus operandi, *method of operation*
modus vivendi, *way of living*
onus probandi, *burden of proof*

The Gerundive or Verbal Adjective

In Chapter 60B:5, you met this sentence:

> Aut quem locum tuae **probandae virtūtis** exspectās?
> *Or what opportunity **of proving** your **courage** do you foresee?*

The form **probandae** has the marker **-nd-**, but it cannot be a gerund because it is clearly feminine. This is a *gerundive* and it serves as a *verbal adjective* modifying the noun **virtūtis**. The gerundive is also referred to as the *future passive participle.* It is formed in the same manner as the gerund except it has all the endings of 1st and 2nd declension adjectives, i.e., those of **magnus, -a, -um**. Here are the forms of the gerundive:

1st	2nd	3rd	3rd-iō	4th
para***ndus, -a, -um***	habe***ndus, -a, -um***	mitte***ndus, -a, -um***	iacie***ndus, -a, -um***	audie***ndus, -a, -um***

As with the gerund, the gerundive and the noun it modifies can function in any of the usual constructions of nouns in the various cases. The example above, **probandae virtūtis**, is found in a genitive phrase. Remember that, in form and function, *the gerundive is an adjective*, which means that it will modify a noun or pronoun.

The Romans preferred a gerundive to a gerund when the thought required a direct object. For example, the sentence, "Did Cicero write about friendship for the sake of having friends?" could be translated with a gerund in the genitive case ("of having"), dependent on **causā**, and a direct object ("friends") of the verbal idea contained in the gerund:

> Scrīpsitne Cicerō dē amīcitiā **amīcōs habendī** causā?
> *Did Cicero write about friendship for the sake **of having friends*** (better English, *to have friends)?*

The Romans, however, preferred both to put the direct object of the gerund (i.e., **amīcōs**) into the genitive case, dependent upon **causā**, and to modify it with a gerundive (an adjective).

> Scrīpsitne Cicerō dē amīcitiā **amīcōrum habendōrum** causā?
> *Did Cicero write about friendship **for the sake of having friends*** (better English, *to have friends)?*

Study the comparative chart on page 137 and be sure that you understand the differences between the gerund and gerundive.

The Gerund	**The Gerundive**
is a verbal noun;	is a verbal adjective;
is equivalent to the English verbal noun in *-ing*;	agrees with a noun or pronoun;
is present and active in meaning;	is future and passive in meaning;
and has only the neuter singular gen., dat., acc., and abl. cases.	and has all the case forms of the adjective **magnus, -a, -um**.

EXERCISE 63b

Read aloud and tell whether each sentence contains a gerund or a gerundive; for gerundives, identify the word modified. Then translate the entire sentence.

1. Amīcus ad amīcum offendendum nihil agit.
2. Plūrēs amīcī audiendō quam loquendō obtinērī possunt.
3. Necesse est omnibus amīcōs et sociōs expetere, vītae vītālis habendae causā.
4. Num Cicerō crēdit aliquōs dīvitiīs ūtendō amīcitiam obtinēre?
5. Rēbus hūmānīs fragilibus, amīcō dīligendō vītam iūcundē agere possumus.
6. Fīēmusne fēlīciōrēs cum amīcīs colloquendō?
7. Laelius dē amīcitiā loquēbātur memoriā Scīpiōnis tenendī causā.
8. Dantne omnēs philosophī operam amīcīs habendīs?

vītālis, -is, -e, *worth living*
vītam agere, *to live one's life*
iūcundē, adv., *with pleasure, agreeably*
operam dare + dat., *to give attention to, work at*

EXERCISE 63c

Complete each of the following sentences with the correct form of the gerund or gerundive; use the context to determine the proper case ending. Then translate the entire sentence.

1. Cicerō sē rogābat, "Quid scrībam ad __________ dē amīcitiā? (docēre)
2. Scrīpsitne Cicerō *Dē amīcitiā* Scīpiōnis __________ causā? (laudāre)
3. Nēmō nōn idōneus est amīcīs ___________. (habēre)
4. Amīcī conservantur maximē __________. (dīligere)
5. Quī erat modus ___________ Cicerōnis? (cōgitāre)
6. Possumus habēre plūrēs amīcōs __________ quam __________. (audīre, dīcere)
7. ___________ plūrima discēmus. (legere)
8. Crēscit __________. (īre) (Motto of the State of New Mexico)

***cōnservō, -āre, āvī, -atus**, *to keep*
***crēsco, crēscere, crēvī, crētus**, *to grow, increase*

Warships such as the ones shown in this Pompeian wall painting played an important role in the wars, both foreign and civil, of the late Republic. Octavian used them to win the battle of Actium and become sole ruler of the Roman world. Note the rams (rostra) attached to the bows of the ships and the decks bristling with armed soldiers.
Fresco, Pompeii, first century A.D.

VIOLENCE AND CIVIL WAR IN THE LATE REPUBLIC

Overview of Part III

In Parts I and II, you learned that the last century B.C. was a time of political turmoil. It was characterized by the ascendancy of certain individuals who used military power and political intrigue to challenge control of the government by the senatorial class, which had ruled Rome since 509 B.C. In this Part, you will explore this time of turmoil in greater detail. Part III has the following objectives:

- to show the connection between violence and politics during the late Republic
- to continue to help you develop your ability to read Latin prose by reading selections from Asconius, Cicero, and an oration in praise of a senator's wife
- to continue your introduction to Latin poetry through a poem of Horace
- to present some new grammatical topics, including additional uses of the gerundive, indefinite pronouns, and several new uses of the subjunctive

Background for Chapters 64–66

The events of 53–52 B.C. serve to illustrate the political forces and public personalities of the late Republic. Throughout the decade of the 50s, political gangs, led by Publius Clodius Pulcher, agent of Caesar, and by Titus Annius Milo, henchman of the senatorial faction, opposed each other and disrupted the normal constitutional processes of state. Milo and Clodius themselves became political candidates for the elections of 53, Milo as a candidate for consul and Clodius for praetor. The subsequent postponement of these elections due to violence eventually led to the murder of Clodius by Milo. In 52, Cicero delivered a courtroom speech of defense on behalf of his friend Milo, a speech that has been preserved and is titled *Pro Milone* (*For Milo*). The commentary on this speech by Quintus Asconius Pedianus, a scholar of the first century A.D. who consulted official records of the trial, gives a very different perspective on the murder from that presented by Cicero.

As champion of the Senate and a political idealist, Cicero was often confused by the perplexities of politics and became caught between men with more powerful ambitions: first Caesar and Pompey, and then Antony and Octavian. As you will learn from Cicero's correspondence in Chapter 66, he felt trapped between fear of Caesar and loyalty to Pompey, who now represented the interests of the Senate. These letters include one to his family in Rome, one to his closest friend Atticus (to whom the *De amicitia*, featured in Chapter 63, was dedicated), and letters to Cicero from Pompey and Caesar.

1 **A.d. xiii Kal. Febr.**: = 18 January because, prior to Caesar's reform of the calendar in 46 B.C., January had 29 days, not 31.
Lānuvium: home town of Milo, about 20 miles southeast of Rome along the Appian Way.
mūnicipium, -ī, n., *town.*
ex quō erat mūnicipiō: = **mūncipium ex quō erat**; the antecedent **mūnicipium** has been drawn into the relative clause.
dictātor: Milo was the chief magistrate of Lanuvium, similar to a mayor.

2 **flāmen, flāminis**, m., *priest.*
prōdō, prōdere, prōdidī, prōditus, *to give forth, nominate, appoint.*
***posterus, -a, -um**, *next, following.*

***circā**, prep. + acc., *around, about.*
nonus, -a, -um, *ninth.*

3 **Bovillās . . . Arīciā**: Bovillae (modern Albano) was a small town south of Rome. Aricia (modern Ariccia), a bit further south, was the first way station on the Appian Way. See the map above.
autem: = **enim**, explaining the previous clause.
alloquor, alloquī, allocūtus sum, *to address, speak to.*
decuriō, decuriōnis, m., *town councilman.*

4 ***vehō, vehere, vexī, vectus**, *to carry, convey*; in passive, *to travel.*
equō vehī, *to ride* (literally, *to be carried by a horse*).
trīgintā ferē: *about 30.*
expedītus, -a, -um, *unhampered* (by baggage), *traveling light.*
iter facientibus: *for travelers*; literally, *for those making a journey*. **Facientibus** is a substantive.

5 **cingō, cingere, cīnxī, cīnctus**, *to surround, encircle; equip with a weapon, gird.*
gladiīs cīnctī: *armed with swords.*

6 ***plēbs, plēbis**, f., *plebeians, common people.*
***nōtus, -a, -um**, *known, well-known.*

LXIV

A Political Murder (Asconius' Account)

A. Clodius and Milo on the Appian Way

This chapter contains selections from Asconius' commentary on Cicero's speech on behalf of Milo. Asconius presents what he believed to be the most accurate account of the murder of Clodius, which you can compare with the account given in Cicero's speech in the next chapter.

A.d. xiii Kal. Febr. Milō Lānuvium, ex quō erat mūnicipiō et ubi tum dictātor, profectus est ad flāminem prōdendum posterā diē. Occurrit eī circā hōram nōnam Clōdius paulō ultrā Bovillās, rediēns ab Arīciā; erat autem allocūtus decuriōnēs Arīcinōrum. Vehēbātur Clōdius equō; servī trīgintā ferē expedītī, ut illō tempore mōs erat iter facientibus, gladiīs cīnctī sequēbantur. Erant cum Clōdiō praetereā trēs comitēs eius, ex quibus eques Rōmānus ūnus, duo dē plēbe nōtī hominēs.

(*continued*)

---

1. Where was Milo going? What was his connection to this town? (1–2)
2. For what purpose was Milo traveling to this place? (1–2)
3. When and where did Clodius meet Milo? (2–3)
4. For what purpose was Clodius on the Appian Way? (3)
5. By what means was Clodius traveling? (4)
6. Who followed Clodius on the journey? How are they described? (4–5)
7. Who else accompanied Clodius? (5–6)

7 **Fausta**: Fausta Cornelia Sulla was the daughter of Sulla's third wife and was the twin of her brother Faustus, who married a daughter of Pompey the Great.

L. Sullae dictātōris: Lucius Cornelius Sulla (138–78 B.C.) had been a military dictator and champion of the Senate.

***familiāris, -is, -e,** *belonging to the household; intimate, friendly*; as substantive, *close friend.*

8 ***agmen, agminis**, n., *line of march, column.*

9 **Eī**: = **gladiātōrēs.**

***ultimus, -a, -um,** *last, least, farthest.*

in ultimō agmine: *at the rear of the column.* The two parties were passing one another, going in opposite directions.

euntēs: present participle of **eō, īre.**

10 **rixam committere**, *to begin a quarrel.*

Reading Note

Adjectives with the Dative

In Chapter 63 you learned the adjective **idōneus, -a, -um**, *suitable (for)*, which can be completed by a noun in the dative, e.g.,

> Forum est locus idōneus **ōrātiōnibus habendīs.**
> *The Forum is a suitable place* ***for delivering speeches.***

There are several other adjectives that can be used with the dative. They include:

amīcus, -a, -um, *friendly (to)*
aptus, -a, -um, *fit (for), suitable (for)*
cārus, -a, -um, *dear (to)*
inimīcus, -a, -um, *unfriendly (to), hostile (to)*
similis, -is, -e, *similar (to)*
ūtilis, -is, -e, *useful (for)*

The Appian Way

Milō raedā vehēbātur cum uxōre Faustā, fīliā L. Sullae dictātōris, et M. Fufiō familiārī suō. Sequēbātur eōs magnum servōrum agmen, inter quōs gladiātōrēs quoque erant, ex quibus duo nōtī, Eudamus et Birria. Eī in ultimō agmine tardius euntēs cum servīs P. Clōdiī rixam commīsērunt.

---

8. By what means was Milo traveling? (7)
9. Who were his traveling companions? (7–8)
10. Who were following Milo on the journey? (8–9)
11. Who began the quarrel? (9–10)

Weapons and armor of a gladiator
Funerary stele of a gladiator, Ephesus, Turkey, 330–27 B.C.

Et latrō et cautus praecingitur ēnse viātor, ille sed īnsidiās, hic sibi portat opem.
Both the highwayman and the cautious traveler are equipped with a sword, but the former carries it for an ambush, the latter carries it as protection for himself. (Ovid, *Tristia* II.1.271)

---

11 **minitābundus, -a, -um,** *menacing.*
umerus, -ī, m., *shoulder.*
rumpia, -ae, f., *pike, spear.*
12 **trāiciō, trāicere, trāiēcī, trāiectus,** *to throw through, pierce.*

***orior, orīrī, ortus sum,** *to arise; to begin.*

13 **Bovillānus, -a, -um,** *belonging to Bovillae.*
in Bovillānō: = *in the vicinity of Bovillae*; a noun such as **agrō** is understood.

Milō . . . exturbārī tabernā iussit (15–16): the complexity of this sentence may reveal the difficulty in Milo's mind of making the decision to do away with Clodius.
vulnerātum: = **vulnerātum esse.**
14 **cum . . . intellegeret**: a **cum** causal clause, as is **(cum) . . . esset habitūrus** (15).
sibi: = Milo.
perīculōsius: what is the degree of this adjective? What does it modify?
illud: = the wounding of Clodius.
vīvō eō . . . occīsō (eō): ablative absolutes.
eō: = Clodius.
futūrum (esse): future infinitive dependent on **intellegeret** in indirect statement with **illud** as the subject.
15 **sōlācium, -ī,** n., *consolation, relief.*
esset habitūrus: *he was going to have.*
etiam sī subeunda esset poena: *even if he had to undergo punishment;* literally, *even if punishment had to be undergone by him.*
exturbō, -āre, -āvī, -ātus, *to force out, drag out.*
exturbārī tabernā iussit: *ordered (him) to be dragged from the tavern.* **Tabernā** is in the ablative because of **ex**, the prepositional prefix of **exturbārī.**

16 ***lateō, latēre, latuī,** *to lie in hiding.*
cōnfectus: = **cōnfectus est.**

cadāver, cadāveris, n., *corpse, body.*
Cadāver: object of **sustulit** (18) and **iussit** (19).
17 **saucius, -a, -um,** *wounded, hurt.*
18 **revertor, revertī, reversus sum,** *to turn back, return.*
19 **ipse:** = Sextus Teidius.
eōdem, adv., *to the same (place).*
unde, adv., *from where.*

B. The Murder of Clodius

Ad quem tumultum cum respexisset Clōdius minitābundus, umerum eius Birria rumpiā trāiēcit. Inde cum orta esset pugna, plūrēs Milōniānī accurrērunt. Clōdius vulnerātus in tabernam proximam in Bovillānō dēlātus est. Milō, ut cognōvit vulnerātum Clōdium, cum sibi perīculōsius illud etiam vīvō eō futūrum intellegeret, occīsō autem magnum sōlācium esset habitūrus, etiam sī subeunda esset poena, exturbārī tabernā iussit. Atque ita Clōdius latēns extractus est multīsque vulneribus cōnfectus. Cadāver eius in viā relictum, quia servī Clōdiī aut occīsī erant aut graviter sauciī latēbant, Sex. Teidius senātor, quī forte ex rūre in urbem revertēbātur, sustulit et lectīcā suā Rōmam ferrī iussit; ipse rūrsus eōdem unde erat ēgressus sē recēpit.

(*continued*)

---

1. What happened to escalate the quarrel into a battle? (11–12)
2. How did Milo's men react to the fighting? (12)
3. Where was Clodius taken? (13)
4. What did Milo think would happen if he allowed Clodius to remain alive? (14)
5. Of what advantage would it be for Milo to kill Clodius? (14–15)
6. What might be the consequence of his action? (15)
7. How did Clodius meet his end? (15–16)
8. What happened to the body at first? (17)
9. Why was this allowed to happen? (17–18)
10. Who eventually found the body and under what circumstances? (18)
11. What became of the corpse? (18–19)
12. What did the senator do then? (19)

This illustration shows the death of Cicero, who was attacked by agents of Antony while traveling in a *lectīca*, similar to the one used by Sextus Teidius (above: 17–19).
Lithograph by Comeleran in Jose Coroleu's, "Las Supersticiones de la Humanidad" 1891

20 **perferō, perferre, pertulī, perlātus**, irreg., *to deliver, bring in.*
ante prīmam noctis hōram: about 5 P.M.
īnfimus, -a, -um, *lowest, most vile.*
21 **lūctus, -ūs**, m., *mourning.*
circumstō, circumstāre, circumstetī, *to stand around, surround.*

augeō, augēre, auxī, auctus, *to increase, magnify.*
22 ***invidia, -ae**, f., *ill will, hatred, outrage.*
factī invidiam: *anger at the deed*, i.e., the killing of Clodius.
Fulvia: Fulvia Flacca Bambula (77–40 B.C.) was a member of the Gracchi, a famous Roman family. A lady of some ambition, she was the first non-mythical woman to be depicted on Roman coins. Fulvia probably financed Clodius' political career.
effūsus, -a, -um, *effusive, unrestrained.*
lāmentātiō, lāmentātiōnis, f., *weeping, wailing, sobbing.*
23 ***ostendō, ostendere, ostendī, ostentus**, *to show, point out.*

eiusdem: genitive singular of **īdem, eadem, idem**, *the same.*
cōnfluō, cōnfluere, cōnflūxī, *to flow together; to gather.*

24 **Eīs . . . hortantibus**: ablative absolute.
imperītus, -a, -um, *ignorant, common.*
25 **calcō, -āre, -āvī, -ātus**, *to trample, crush with the feet.*
26 ***rostra, -ōrum**, n. pl., *rostra*; literally, **rostra** = *beaks of ships* (i.e., battering rams), which decorated the speaker's platform in the Forum and gave it its name.

prō contiōne: *before a public meeting.* A **contiō** was an open public meeting, usually rowdy and boisterous, where the issues involved in an upcoming vote for a law or magistrate were discussed. **Contiō** is a contraction of **conventiō**, *a coming together.*
(T. Munātius) Plancus et (Q.) Pompeius (Rufus): tribunes who supported Milo's political opponents and who contributed to the general civil disorder of this period. Milo was running for the consulship in 53 for the year 52.
competītor, competītōris, m., *political rival, fellow candidate.*
27 ***studeō, studēre, studuī** + dat., *to be eager for, support.*

duce Sex. Clōdiō scrībā: ablative absolute.
scrība, -ae, m., *scribe, clerk.* Sextus Clodius was probably a freedman of Publius Clodius.

28 **subsellium, -ī**, n., *bench.*
tribūnal, tribūnālis, n., *platform.*
cōdicibus librāriōrum: *secretaries' ledgers.*
29 **quō igne**: ablative of cause, equivalent to **propter** + acc.
flagrō, -āre, -āvī, *to burn, blaze up.*
item, adv., *likewise, in the same way.*
Porcia Basilica: this basilica, or public courthouse, the earliest in Rome, was built by Marcus Porcius Cato in 184 B.C. See the plan on page 147.
30 **iungō, iungere, iūnxī, iūnctus**, *to join, connect.*
ambūrō, ambūrere, ambussī, ambustus, *to scorch, burn.*

C. The Burning of the Senate House

Perlātum est corpus Clōdiī ante prīmam noctis hōram, īnfimaeque plēbis et servōrum maxima multitūdō magnō lūctū corpus in ātriō domūs positum circumstetit. Augēbat autem factī invidiam uxor Clōdiī Fulvia, quae cum effūsā lāmentātiōne vulnera eius ostendēbat. Maior posterā diē lūce prīmā multitūdō eiusdem generis cōnflūxit, complūrēsque nōtī hominēs vīsī sunt. Eīsque hortantibus vulgus imperītum corpus nūdum ac calcātum, sīcut in lectō erat positum, ut vulnera vidērī possent in Forum dētulit et in rostrīs posuit. Ibi prō contiōne Plancus et Pompeius, quī competītōribus Milōnis studēbant, invidiam Milōnī fēcērunt. Populus, duce Sex. Clōdiō scrībā, corpus P. Clōdiī in Cūriam intulit cremāvitque subselliīs et tribūnālibus et mēnsīs et cōdicibus librāriōrum, quō igne et ipsa quoque Cūria flagrāvit et item Porcia Basilica, quae erat eī iūncta, ambusta est.

—Asconius, *In Milonianam Ciceronis* (extract)

---

1. Who came to mourn Clodius? (20–21)
2. Cite the Latin that describes the manner in which the news of Clodius' death was received in Rome. (21)
3. How did Fulvia magnify the outrage against her husband's death? (22–23)
4. What happened on the following day? (23–24)
5. How did the mob treat the body of Clodius? (24–26)
6. How did Milo's political rivals attempt to subvert his candidacy? (26–27)
7. What finally happened to the body of Clodius? (27–29)
8. What consequences did this act have for the city of Rome? (29–30)

The *Forum Rōmānum* in Cicero's time

BUILDING THE MEANING

The Passive Periphrastic (Gerundive of Obligation)

In Book II, you met several phrases containing gerundives, e.g., **epistula est cōnficienda**, *the letter must be finished* (47:23). You may deduce from this example that the gerundive **cōnficienda**, when found with a form of the verb **esse**, here **est**, expresses necessity or obligation, i.e., *must.* Here is another example:

> Semper aliquī **anquīrendī sunt** quōs dīligāmus. . . . (63C:1–2)
> *Some (people)* ***must*** *always* ***be sought out*** *whom we may hold dear. . . .*

The gerundive plus a form of **esse,** provided or understood, is translated *must be, should be, has to be.* This use is known as the *passive periphrastic* (a Greek term that means "roundabout") or, more descriptively, the *gerundive of obligation.*

Any tense of the verb **esse** may be used, e.g.,

Amīcī sunt dīligendī.	*Friends have to be cherished.*
Amīcī erant dīligendī.	*Friends had to be cherished.*
Amīcī erunt dīligendī.	*Friends will have to be cherished.*

When an intransitive verb (a verb that does not take a direct object) appears in the passive periphrastic, the gerundive is used *impersonally*, i.e., has *it* as the subject. For better English, transform the passive voice to the active, e.g.,

> Domum **nōbīs redeundum est.** (48:20)
> *We must return home*, literally, *It must be returned home by us.*

Dative of Agent

In the example above, note that **nōbīs** is in the *dative* case. In the passive periphrastic, the person who must perform the obligation expressed in the verb is found in the dative case, a use known as the *dative of agent.* It serves the same function as the *ablative of agent* (**ā/ab** + abl.) with other passive forms of the verb, e.g.,

> Liber **Cicerōnī** scrībendus est. (dative of agent)
> *The book has to be written* ***by Cicero.***
> ***Cicero*** *has to write the book.*

> Liber **ā Cicerōne** scrīptus est. (ablative of agent)
> *The book has been written* ***by Cicero.***

Carthāgō dēlenda est! *Carthage must be destroyed!*
(Spoken by Cato the Elder at Senate meetings prior to the Third Punic War)

EXERCISE 64a

Read aloud, identify all passive periphrastics and datives of agent, and translate:

1. Amīcitia semper cōnservanda est.
2. Vōbīs fidēliōrēs amīcī quaerendī erant.
3. Ennius dīxit amīcōs omnibus habendōs esse.
4. Quot amīcī cuique habendī sunt?
5. Persuāsitne Laelius tibi ut amīcī omnibus dīligendī sint?
6. Inter amīcōs vēra dīcenda erunt.
7. Diēs nātālis amīcī memoriā tibi semper tenenda est.
8. Mentiendō amīcōs repellēs.
9. Nunc ad rostra Cicerōnī redeundum erit.
10. Scrīpsit Catullus, "Nōbīs est dormienda ūna perpetua nox."
11. Gladiātōribus rixa nōn fuit committenda.
12. Clōdius vulnerātus ad tabernam amīcīs dēferendus est.
13. Num Clōdius extrahendus et multīs vulneribus cōnficiendus fuit?
14. In Cūriā populō nōn erat cremandum corpus Clōdiī.

cuique, dative of **quisque**, *each one, each person*
mentior, mentīrī, mentītus sum, *to tell a lie, lie*
rixam committere, *to start a fight*

EXERCISE 64b

Supply the dative case of the pronoun in parentheses, then read aloud and translate:

1. Sī nōbīscum venīre nōn vīs, ___ domī manendum est. (tū)
2. Hic ōrātor ___ laudandus est quod optimē in rēbus difficilibus locūtus est. (ego)
3. Ubi Rōmam pervēneritis, Cūria incēnsa ___ vīsitanda erit. (vōs)
4. Milō erat dictātor Lānuviī; ___ igitur eundum fuit ad flāminem prōdendum. (ille)
5. Haec rēs difficilis ___ agenda erit. (nōs)

The Senate House *(Cūria)* was rebuilt by Caesar after the fire described in Reading C of this chapter. Its present form (as shown in this photograph) dates from the end of the third century A.D.
Rome

1 ***interim**, adv., *meanwhile.*
cum scīret Clōdius: *since Clodius knew*, a **cum** causal clause.
Clōdius: elsewhere in his speech, Cicero recalls for the jury that Clodius, a member of the illustrious Claudian family, had changed his name to the more plebeian Clodius in order to win favor with the lower classes. Cicero suggests that such a man could easily be tempted to murder his political rival.
sollemnis, -is, -e, *customary, traditional; annual.*
lēgitimus, -a, -um, *legal, proper.*
iter sollemne, lēgitimum, necessārium: Cicero states this for the reason that, since Milo's journey was undertaken habitually, legally, and out of necessity, it would be impossible to believe that he had set out with the deliberate intent to murder Clodius.
2 **Milōnī esse**: *Milo had (to make)*, literally, *there was for Milo*, dative of possession.
esse: following **scīret** in indirect statement, the subject of which is **iter** (1).
3 **ad flāminem prōdendum**: note that the very same phrase appears in Asconius, 64A:2.
ipse: = Clodius.
4 **prīdiē**, adv., *on the day before.*
ut . . . collocāret: purpose clause.
fundus, -ī, m., *farm, estate.*
quod rē intellēctum est: *as subsequent events proved*; literally, *which was learned from the event.*
Milōnī: *for Milo*; for dative of reference, see page 92.
īnsidiae, -ārum, f. pl., *ambush.*
collocō, -āre, -āvī, -ātus, *to arrange, set up.*
5 **ita profectus est**: i.e., his departure was timed in such a way. **Ita** anticipates the result clause **ut . . . relinqueret** (5–6).
contiōnem: see 64C:26; this serves as the antecedent of the following relative pronouns **quā, quae**, and **quam.**
turbulentus, -a, -um, *rowdy, boisterous.*
eius: i.e., of Clodius.
furor: Cicero knew that Clodius had the ability to whip crowds into a frenzy through his oratory.
6 **illō ipsō diē:** *on that very day*, i.e., when Milo was traveling.
***obeō, obīre, obīvī** or **obiī, obitūrus**, irreg., *to go to, appear at.*
facinus, facinoris, n., *villainy, crime, foul deed.*

Silent lēgēs inter arma. *Amid arms, laws are silent.*
Spoken by Cicero during his attempted delivery of the speech for Milo.
(*Pro Milone* 11)

LXV

A Political Murder (Cicero's Account)

A. The Setting of the Murder

The court trial of Milo began on 4 April 52 B.C., and for the next three days the testimony of various witnesses was heard in the open Forum. On 8 April, the final day of the trial, the Forum was under armed guard, stationed there by Pompey as sole consul, while the prosecution delivered its summation within the prescribed two hours. Cicero, in his summation, tried to disprove the prosecution's contention that Milo had murdered Clodius with premeditation by attempting to prove, rather, that Clodius had deliberately ambushed Milo and that the latter was acting in self defense. Despite the presence of soldiers, Clodius' supporters were so intimidating that Cicero was prevented from completing his prepared speech.

Interim cum scīret Clōdius (neque enim erat difficile scīre) iter sollemne, lēgitimum, necessārium ante diem trēdecimam Kalendās Februāriās Milōnī esse Lānuvium ad flāminem prōdendum, quod erat dictātor Lānuviī Milō, Rōmā subitō ipse profectus prīdiē est, ut ante suum fundum (quod rē intellēctum est) Milōnī īnsidiās collocāret; atque ita profectus est, ut contiōnem turbulentam, in quā eius furor dēsīderātus est, quae illō ipsō diē habita est, relinqueret, quam, nisi obīre facinoris locum tempusque voluisset, numquam relīquisset.

(continued)

1. Why was it possible for Clodius to learn of Milo's journey to Lanuvium? (1)
2. How does Cicero characterize Milo's journey? (1–2)
3. What was the date of his journey? (2) Does this agree with Asconius? (64A:1)
4. Why was Milo traveling, according to Cicero? (2–3) Does this agree with Asconius' account? (64A:2)
5. When did Clodius leave Rome? (3–4)
6. Why did Clodius leave Rome suddenly? (4)
7. What was happening in Rome when Clodius departed? (5)
8. For what reasons does Cicero feel that the timing of Clodius' departure was suspicious? (5–6, 6–7)
9. What Latin words does Cicero use to suggest Clodius' violent tendencies? Do words such as these appear in Asconius' account?

8 **cum . . . fuisset**: causal clause.
eō diē: i.e., 18 January.
quoad, adv., *until.*
9 **calceus, -ī**, m., *shoe.* Senators wore special red leather half-boots.
calceōs et vestīmenta mūtāvit: when traveling in bad weather, a senator took off his toga and put on a **paenula**, which was a traveling cloak of wool or leather similar to a poncho. See lines 14 and 18.
paulisper, adv., *for a little while*; take with **commorātus est**.
ut fit: *as usual.* Note the use of the indicative with **ut** here and below, line 12.
***comparō, -āre, -āvī, -ātus**, *to prepare.*
commoror, -ārī, -ātus sum, *to wait.*
10 **profectus**: = **profectus est**.
id temporis: *at that point in time.*
cum iam Clōdius . . . redīre potuisset: *when Clodius could have already returned*, a thought completed by the simple condition **sī . . . ventūrus erat**, *if he was going to come (back).*

11 **obviam fit** + dat.: *(he) encounters, (he) meets*; literally, *gets in the way.*
nūllā . . . nūllīs . . . nūllīs: note the asyndeton and anaphora, used to emphasize what was missing from Clodius' party.
12 **Graecīs comitibus**: i.e., dancers, musicians, party-people.
quod numquam ferē: *which he almost never (was)*; **erat** is understood.
cum hic īnsidiātor: *while this (so-called) highwayman*, speaking ironically of Milo.
13 **quī . . . apparāsset**: = **quī . . . apparāvisset**. Note Cicero's sarcasm.
ad caedem faciendam: note that the gerundive of purpose **ad caedem faciendam** is embedded in the clause **quī . . . apparāsset**, which itself is embedded in the clause **cum . . . veherētur**.
cum uxōre: the preposition **cum** extends to **magnō et impedītō . . . comitātū**.
14 **paenulātus, a-, -um**, *wearing the* **paenula**.
impedītus, -a, -um, *loaded down.* This and the following adjectives modify **comitātū**.
muliebris, -is, -e, *womanly.*
dēlicātus, -a, -um, *dainty, effeminate.*
ancillārum puerōrumque: perhaps young people for the choral hymns at the religious ceremony in Lanuvium the following day.
15 **comitātus, -ūs**, m., *company, retinue.*

B. On the Appian Way

Milō autem, cum in senātū fuisset eō diē quoad senātus est dīmissus, domum vēnit, calceōs et vestīmenta mūtāvit, paulisper, dum sē uxor, ut fit, comparat, commorātus est, dein profectus id temporis, cum iam Clōdius, sī quidem eō diē Rōmam ventūrus erat, redīre potuisset. Obviam fit eī Clōdius, expedītus, in equō, nūllā raedā, nūllīs impedīmentīs, nūllīs Graecīs comitibus, ut solēbat, sine uxōre, quod numquam ferē: cum hic īnsidiātor, quī iter illud ad caedem faciendam apparāsset, cum uxōre veherētur in raedā, paenulātus, magnō et impedītō et muliebrī ac dēlicātō ancillārum puerōrumque comitātū.

(*continued*)

1. Where had Milo been on the day of his journey? Until when? (8)
2. What things did Milo do before leaving for Lanuvium? (8–9)
3. What humorous aside does Cicero make in line 9?
4. Why does Cicero make a point of mentioning Milo's late departure? (10–11)
5. In what style does Clodius travel? (11–12) What does Asconius say about Clodius' travel arrangements? (64A:4–6)
6. What comment does Cicero make about Clodius' wife? (12)
7. How does Cicero characterize Milo? (13)
8. How was Milo traveling? (13–15) How does this compare with Asconius' account? (64A:7–9)

Reading Note

Parallel Structure

In the readings of this chapter, you will find examples of one of Cicero's favorite devices: *parallelism*. This is the balance of two or more words, phrases, or clauses in the same sentence to indicate that they have the same level of importance. Note in lines 11–12 and 13–15 above how Cicero balances his description of the traveling parties of Clodius and Milo. Note, too, how the parade of nouns in these lines suggests the arrangement of the travelers in each column. Look for other examples of parallelism in the lines that follow.

Raeda Rōmāna
Tomb relief, Virunum

16 **fit obviam**: see the note on B:11. Note the use of the present tense throughout this passage, even though the actions described are in the past. What is this figure of speech called and what is its purpose? (Review the Reading Note on page 61.)

ante fundum eius: elsewhere in the *Pro Milone*, Cicero claims that the murder had taken place in front of the shrine of the Bona Dea.

ūndecimus, -a, -um, *eleventh.*

nōn multō secus: *not much later*, literally, *not otherwise by much.*

17 **complūrēs**: = **complūrēs hominēs**; substantive.

hunc: = Milo, as **hic** and **hunc**, below. Imagine that Cicero is gesturing toward Milo at these points.

impetum: this word is emphasized by being placed at the end of the clause, separated from the verb that governs it (**faciunt**).

superiōre: *higher*, the literal meaning of this word, describing the position (**locō**) from which Clodius' men attack; you have met this word before used in reference to time, where it meant *previous.*

adversī: *those standing opposite, those in the way* (of the carriage); substantive.

18 ***reiciō, reicere, reiēcī, reiectus**, *to throw back, throw off.*

reiectā paenulā: ablative absolute.

paenula, -ae, f., *traveling cloak.*

dēsiliō, dēsilīre, dēsiluī, *to leap down.*

ācrī animō: *with stout heart.*

19 **dēfenderet**: a continuation of the circumstantial clause **cum . . . dēsiluisset** begun in the previous line.

sēque ācrī animō dēfenderet: in defense of Milo's actions, Cicero is arguing that, when a man's life is immediately threatened, he is allowed to protect himself.

partim, adv., *partly* or *some*, when used as a noun; with **illī** = *some of those.* The next **partim** will then mean *others.*

recurrere . . . caedere (19–20): dependent on **incipiunt** (20).

20 **adorior, adorīrī, adortus sum**, *to rise up against, attack.*

quod . . . putārent: this causal clause gives the reasoning of the slaves. The verb is in the subjunctive to show that Cicero is giving the reasoning as theirs, not his.

interfectum: = **interfectum esse.**

***incipiō, incipere, incēpī, inceptus**, *to begin.*

C. The Attack

Milō fit obviam Clōdiō ante fundum eius hōrā ferē ūndecimā aut nōn multō secus: statim complūrēs cum tēlīs in hunc faciunt dē locō superiōre impetum; adversī raedārium occīdunt; cum autem hic dē raedā, reiectā paenulā, dēsiluisset sēque ācrī animō dēfenderet, illī, quī erant cum Clōdiō, gladiīs ēductīs, partim recurrere ad raedam, ut ā tergō Milōnem adorīrentur, partim, quod hunc iam interfectum putārent, caedere incipiunt eius servōs, quī post erant.

(*continued*)

---

1. How does the time of the attack, as presented here, differ from that given by Asconius? (16; 64A:2)
2. How does Cicero claim the fight began? (17) How does this compare with the version presented by Asconius? (64A:9–10)
3. After the attack had begun, what happened first? (17–18)
4. Describe how Milo reacted to the attack, according to Cicero. (18–19)
5. After drawing their swords, what did some of Clodius' men do? (19–20) Why? (20)
6. What did others of Clodius' men do? (20–21) Why? (20)

Tombstone of a Roman cavalryman

RVFVS·SITA·EQVES·C(o)HO(rtis) VI
TRACVM·ANN(ōrum)·XL·STIP(endiōrum)·XXII
HEREDES·EXS·TEST(āmentō)·F(aciendum)·CVRAVE(runt)
H(īc) S(itus) E(st)

Rufus Sita, cavalryman of the 6th cohort of Thracians, 40 years old, 22 years of service. (His) heirs had this set up according to his will. He is buried here.
Tombstone, Gloucester, England, first century A.D.

22 **Ex quibus servīs**: *of those slaves*, referring to those of Milo under attack in lines 20–21.

*__praesēns, praesentis,__ *present, at hand, immediate; resolute.*

animō fidēlī . . . et praesentī: *of faithful and resolute spirit, with a faithful and resolute spirit*, an ablative of description (see the Reading Note on page 105). Below, **praesente** has its more common meaning of *present*.

partim . . . partim (23): in contrast with the description of Clodius' men in lines 19–21.

23 **cum . . . pugnārī vidērent**: literally, *when they saw that (it) was being fought, when they saw that there was fighting*, an impersonal use of the passive infinitive in indirect statement dependent on **vidērent. Cum** governs **vidērent** and **prohibērentur** (line 23), and **audīrent** and **putārent** (line 24). Note the cumulative effect of these **cum** clauses, which highlight the confusion and uncertainty of Milo's slaves.

*__prohibeō, -ēre, uī, -itus,__ *to prevent, prevent from* (+ infinitive).

24 **occīsum**: = **occīsum esse**; infinitive in indirect statement after **audīrent et . . . putārent.**

rē vērā, *really, actually.*

rē vērā putārent: supply **Milōnem occīsum esse.**

id: the antecedent of **quod** in line 26.

servī Milōnis: superfluous after the second **partim** in line 23, but after such a long parenthesis, Cicero inserts these words to remind the audience what the subject is (remember that this was composed as a speech to be heard, not read). It also helps emphasize Cicero's claim that it was not Milo himself who had killed Clodius, but Milo's slaves.

25 **apertē**, adv., *openly.*

dērīvō, -āre, -āvī, -ātus, *to divert, turn aside, shift.*

crīmen, crīminis, n., *charge, accusation* (i.e., against Milo).

nec . . . nec . . . nec: note the effective anaphora here.

imperō, -āre, -āvī, -ātus, *to order, command.*

imperante . . . dominō: *at the bidding of (their) master*; part of an extended ablative absolute.

26 **quod**: the antecedent is **id**, line 24.

quod . . . quisque . . . voluisset: *what everyone would have wanted.* This clause describes the general type of behavior masters expected from their slaves. In this case, such behavior meant Milo's slaves taking a life to avenge the (reported) death of their master and to save their own lives. Cicero addresses here a point raised by the prosecution. After the events of 18 January, Milo had manumitted his slaves, according to Cicero, as a reward for saving his life, but according to the prosecution, to prevent them from being tortured into testifying against their master, which was within the jurisdiction of the prosecution.

*__tālis, -is, -e,__ *such, of this kind.*

Cēdant arma togae, concēdat laurea linguae.

Let arms yield to the toga, let the (general's) laurels yield to the (orator's) tongue.

(Cicero, *De officiis* I.22.27)

D. Clodius' Death

Ex quibus servīs quī animō fidēlī in dominum et praesentī fuērunt, partim occīsī sunt, partim, cum ad raedam pugnārī vidērent, dominō succurrere prohibērentur, Milōnem occīsum et ex ipsō Clōdiō audīrent et rē vērā putārent, fēcērunt id servī Milōnis—dīcam enim apertē nōn dērīvandī crīminis causā, sed ut factum est—nec imperante nec sciente nec praesente dominō, quod suōs quisque servōs in tālī rē facere voluisset.

—Cicero, *Pro Milone* X

---

1. What Latin phrases describe the behavior of Milo's men during the fight? (22)
2. What happened to some of Milo's slaves? (22–23)
3. What combination of circumstances led Milo's men to attack Clodius? List these circumstances in the sequence of their occurrence. (23–24)
4. What parenthetical comment does Cicero make in line 25?
5. According to Cicero, was Milo himself involved in the decision to kill Clodius? (25–26) How does this differ from Asconius' account? (64B:14–16)
6. What is the dramatic effect of the repeated use of **partim** in this and the previous passage? (19, 20, 22, 23)
7. What does Cicero imply that masters should expect from their slaves in such circumstances? (26)

A sarcophagus (stone coffin) with a relief showing a funeral procession
Relief, Aquileia, Italy, first or second century A.D.

2 **tribūnus aerārius:** *official of the treasury, paymaster*. Originally assistants to the **quaestor**, these officials later served as judges. The **aerārium** was the public treasury of Rome, kept in the lower level of or behind the Temple of Saturn in the Roman Forum.

3 **Vidēbantur**: the subject is **iūdicēs**.
ignōrō, -āre, -āvī, -ātus, *to be unaware.*
iūdex, iūdicis, m., *judge; member of the jury, juror.*
***īnscius, -a, -um**, *not knowing, ignorant.*
īnsciō Milōne: ablative absolute.
vulnerātum esse: infinitive in indirect statement following **ignōrāvisse**, which is dependent upon **vidēbantur**.
initiō: *in the beginning, early on.*
4 **comperiō, comperīre, comperī, compertus**, *to find out for certain.*
iussū, *by order.*
occīsum: = **occīsum esse**. Supply the pronoun **eum** (= **Clōdium**) as subject of the infinitive in indirect statement after **compererant**.

5 **Massilia, -ae**, f., *Massilia* (a city in Gaul, modern Marseilles; see the map on page 23.)

bona: *goods, property, possessions.*
aes aliēnum: *debt*; literally, *another's money*, where **aes, aeris**, n., refers to bronze and copper coins. In 54 B.C., Milo had inaugurated his candidacy for the consulship with games costing one million silver coins.
6 **sēmuncia, -ae**, f., *a coin worth one twenty-fourth of an* ***ās****; an insignificant amount.*
vēneō, vēnīre, vēniī, vēnitūrus, irreg., *to go on sale, be sold.* This is a compound of the prefix **vēn-** and the verb **īre**; it is not the same as the verb **veniō, venīre** *to come* (note the long **ē** in the prefix **vēn-**; this same prefix is found in the verb **vēndere**, *to put on sale, sell*).

Reading Note

Litotes

In line 3 opposite, the phrase **vidēbantur nōn ignōrāvisse**, *seemed not to have been unaware*, is equivalent to *seemed to have been aware*. This is a figure of speech called *litotes*, in which an idea is expressed by negating its opposite.

On this coin from the Roman Republic, a juror is shown dropping his ballot into an urn.

E. The Verdict

During the first day of Milo's five-day trial, some 81 potential jurors had been selected by Pompey. After the summations and before the vote was taken on the final day, both prosecution and defense rejected five jurors from each of the three classes, 30 in all, leaving 51 to decide the verdict. Each juror erased one of the letters on his voting tablet, one side of which was marked **A** (**absolvō**) *and the other* **C** (**condemnō**). *Here is the decision:*

Senātōrēs condemnāvērunt duodecim, absolvērunt sex; equitēs condemnāvērunt trēdecim, absolvērunt quattuor, tribūnī aerāriī condemnāvērunt trēdecim, absolvērunt trēs. Vidēbantur nōn ignōrāvisse iūdicēs īnsciō Milōne initiō vulnerātum esse Clōdium, sed compererant, postquam vulnerātus esset, iussū Milōnis occīsum. Milō in esilium Massiliam intrā paucissimōs diēs profectus est. Bona eius propter aeris aliēnī magnitūdinem sēmunciā vēniērunt.

—Asconius, *In Milonianam Ciceronis* (extract)

---

1. What was the total vote for acquittal? (1–3) Against acquittal? (1–2)
2. What groups made up the members of the jury? (1–2)
3. On what grounds did the jury convict Milo? (3–4)
4. What happened to Milo? (4–5)
5. What happened to his property? (5–6)

Although Cicero was unable to complete the delivery of his speech in defense of Milo, he later sent a written copy to the exiled Milo. The latter replied, "If you had been able to finish delivering this speech, I would not be here in Massilia enjoying such wonderful red mullets." During his absence, Milo was convicted of bribery, unlawful association, and violence (**vīs**). *A certain Marcus Saufeius, who had been Milo's slave overseer, was later indicted but was acquitted! After returning to Italy four years later Milo was executed for insurrection.*

Questions for Thought and Discussion

1. Summarize your comparison of Cicero's narrative of Clodius' murder with that of Asconius. In what respects do they agree? How are they different?
2. Given the sources used by Asconius and the context of Cicero's speech *Pro Milone*, do you agree with the verdict?
3. What have you learned from this speech about how Roman attorneys defended their clients? What have you learned about Cicero's ability as an orator?

Iūstitia est cōnstāns et perpetua voluntās iūs suum cuique tribuendī.
Justice is the firm and lasting intention of granting every man his rights.
(*Corpus iuris civilis, Institutiones* I.1, after Cicero, *De finibus* V.23.65)

Building the Meaning

Indefinite Pronouns and Adjectives

Throughout *Ecce Romani*, you have seen several pronouns and adjectives related to the interrogative pronoun **quis** and the relative pronoun **quī**. These are known as *indefinites*, because they designate some person or thing without specifying which one. Observe the following:

Titus noster **aliquid** malī accēpit. (54:8)
*Our Titus experienced **something** bad.*

Catilīna . . . coniūrāvit cum **quibusdam** clārīs virīs. (55A:2–3)
*Catiline . . . formed a conspiracy with **certain** eminent men.*

In the first example, **aliquid** is an indefinite pronoun; in the second, **quibusdam** is an indefinite adjective. Note how **aliquid** is related to **quis** and **quibusdam** to **quis** or **quī**. Note also that the meaning of **quīdam** is less vague, or "less indefinite," than that of **aliquis**; writers use **quīdam** when they know the identities of the people involved but may not wish to identify or mention them. Observe the following paired examples:

Pronoun	Adjective
Servus **aliquid** portat. *The slave is carrying **something**.*	Servus **aliquās** epistulās portat. *The slave is carrying **some** letters.*
Exīstimō **quōsdam** bonōs nātūrā esse. *I think that **certain** people are naturally good.*	**Quīdam** mīles fortiter pugnāvit. ***A certain** soldier fought bravely.*
Quisque sē optimum esse exīstimat. ***Each one** thinks that he is the best.*	Dominus **cuique** servō laudem dedit. *The master gave **each** slave praise.*
Iūstitia numquam nocet **cuiquam**. *Justice never harms **anyone**.*	(The adjectival form of **quisquam** is rarely found.)
Quisquis dē caede audīverit dolēbit. ***Whoever** hears about the murder will be sad.*	Clōdius, **quōquō** modō poterat, effugere volēbat. *Clodius wanted to escape in **whatever** way he could.*

On the following page you will find a summary of indefinite pronouns and adjectives; for a complete list of these forms refer to the charts at the end of this book. Note that it is only the **quis** or **quī** (in boldface) part of the word that changes.

Cum dēbēre carnufex cuiquam quicquam quemquam, quemque quisque conveniat, neget. *Since the rascal denies that anyone owes anything to anyone, let each one sue the other.* (Ennius, fragment of a comedy)

Pronoun	Adjective
m. **f.** **n.**	**m.** **f.** **n.**
ali**quis**, ali**quis**, ali**quid** (*someone, something, anyone, anything*)	ali**quī**, ali**qua**, ali**quod** (*some, any*)
quīdam, **quae**dam, **quod**dam (*a certain one*)	**quī**dam, **quae**dam, **quod**dam (*a certain*)
quisque, **quis**que, **quid**que (*each one*)	**quis**que, **quae**que, **quod**que (*each*)
quisquam, **quis**quam, **quid**quam (*anyone, anything*)	same as pronoun but rarely found (*any*)
quisquis, quisquis, quidquid (*whoever, whatever*)	same as pronoun (*whatever, any . . . that*)

NOTES

1. Forms of **quīdam** are commonly found with the preposition **ex** and meaning *some of* when a partitive idea is expressed, e.g., **quīdam ex mīlitibus**, *some of the soldiers.*
2. The Romans used forms of **quis**, instead of **aliquis** or **quisquam**, after **sī, nisi, num**, and **nē**. The forms of **quis** are declined like **aliquis** without the prefix **ali-**. For example, **Sī quis in Forum ierit, multōs hominēs vidēbit**, *If anyone goes into the Forum, he/she will see many people.*
3. **Quisquam** is usually found in a negative context; that is, the sentence contains a word such as **nōn, nec, numquam**, or **negāre**. See the fourth example in the chart on page 160 and the **sententia** at the bottom of page 160.
4. **Quicquam** is used as an alternative to **quidquam**, as the assimilation of the sound **d** to the sound **q** makes **quicquam** easier to pronounce.
5. Avoid confusing the conjunction **quamquam**, *although*, and the adverbs **quidem**, *indeed*, and **quoque**, *also*, with forms of the indefinite pronoun/adjective.

EXERCISE 65a

Read aloud, identify examples of indefinites, and translate:

1. Neque quisquam est quī sine custode iter faciat.
2. Quīdam ē senātōribus putābant Milōnem Lānuvium nōn perventūrum esse.
3. Coniūrāvitne Clōdius cum quibusdam senātōribus?
4. "Quicquid velit aliquis facere potest," inquit Clōdius.
5. Milō ipse cuiquam nocēre nōlēbat.
6. Accidetne aliquid malī comitibus quoque Clōdiī?
7. Clōdius vulnerātus in quandam tabernam ā complūribus servīs dēlātus est.
8. Vidēmus quōsdam adesse quī, Clōdiō occīsō, Cūriam incendissent.
9. Poteratne Cicerō dīcere aliquid dē Milōne absolvendō?
10. Sī quis Milōnem nōn condemnandum esse putāverit, ipse condemnētur.

1 **Tullius**: the name by which Marcus Tullius Cicero was affectionately known to his wife Terentia.

Tulliolae: Tullia was Cicero's daughter, 27 at the time; Tulliola is a diminutive.

duābus animīs suīs: in apposition to **Terentiae et . . . Tulliolae.**

***anima, -ae**, f., *soul, darling.*

Cicerō: this is Cicero's son Marcus who was with this father in Campania. Therefore **mātrī** refers to his mother (i.e., Cicero's wife Terentia) and **sorōrī** to his sister Tullia.

suaviss.: = **suāvissimae**; ***suāvis, -is, -e**, *sweet.*

2 **S.P.D.**: **salūtem plūrimam dīcit.**

3 **cōnsilium**: translate as *concern* rather than *plan.*

4 **ille**: = Caesar, as is **homō** in line 5.

***modestē**, adv., *modestly, with restraint, under control.*

rēctē . . . esse: *to be all right.*

in praesentiā: *at present, for the time being.*

5 **sīn**: = **sī** + **-ne**, *but if, if on the other hand.*

āmēns, āmentis, *mad, insane, mindless.*

dīripiendam: *to be plundered* (by his soldiers). At the time, Cicero was unaware that Caesar was bypassing Rome in pursuit of Pompey, who had abandoned the city.

vereor ut . . . possit: *I am afraid that . . . may not be able.*

Dolābella: Publius Cornelius Dolabella, whom Tullia had married the previous year, was a supporter of Julius Caesar.

6 **prōsum, prōdesse, prōfuī**, irreg. + dat., *to help, benefit.*

***metuō, metuere, metuī, metūtus**, *to fear, be afraid of.*

illud metuō nē . . . interclūdāmur: *I fear this, that we may be cut off.* Note how the pronoun **illud** anticipates the following clause.

interclūdō, interclūdere, interclūsī, interclūsus, *to cut off, shut off.*

ut . . . nōn liceat: a result clause; understand **vōbīs** with **liceat.**

Reading Note

Fear Clauses

You have learned that **ut** and **nē** introduce several different types of subjunctive clauses. Another type, the *fear clause*, is found in lines 5–6 and 6 on the opposite page:

Vereor **ut** Dolābella ipse satis nōbīs prōdesse **possit**.
I fear ***that*** *Dolabella himself* ***cannot*** *be of sufficient help to us.*

Metuō **nē** iam **interclūdāmur**.
I am afraid ***that we may be cut off*** *already.*

A fear clause is a noun clause expressing the object of the fear. A word expressing fear or danger introduces the clause, which is completed by a verb in the subjunctive (usually the present or imperfect tense). The word that anticipates the clause is usually a verb, but may be a noun such as **metus** or **timor**. Note that in fear clauses, **ut** is translated *that . . . not* and **nē** is translated *that*—the opposite of their usual meanings.

LXVI

EYEWITNESS TO CIVIL WAR

A. From Cicero to His Family

These four selections from Cicero's correspondence date from the early months of the civil war between Caesar and Pompey. They reveal his personal and political anxieties, as he witnessed what were to become the death throes of the Republic. In Reading A, Cicero is writing en route to Capua on 22 January 49 B.C., in reply to a letter from his wife Terentia. At Pompey's request, he had taken charge of levying troops for Pompey in Campania, leaving his family in Rome. Caesar had crossed the Rubicon on 10 January and was on his way south in pursuit of Pompey.

Tullius Terentiae et pater Tulliolae, duābus animīs suīs, et Cicerō mātrī optimae, suāviss. sorōrī S.P.D.

Sī vōs valētis, nōs valēmus. Vestrum iam cōnsilium est, nōn sōlum meum, quid sit vōbīs faciendum. Sī ille Rōmam modestē ventūrus est, rēctē in praesentiā domī esse potestis; sīn homō āmēns dīripiendam urbem datūrus est, vereor ut Dolābella ipse satis nōbīs prōdesse possit. Etiam illud metuō, nē iam interclūdāmur, ut, cum velītis, exīre nōn liceat.

(*continued*)

---

1. Which members of Cicero's family does he greet? (1–2) How does the son's greeting differ from his father's?
2. How does Cicero greet his family? (3)
3. With what must Cicero's family concern itself? (3–4)
4. Under what conditions does Cicero think his family can safely remain in Rome? (4)
5. What may happen when Caesar enters Rome? (5) What does Cicero fear in this case? (5–6)
6. What additional fear does Cicero express? (6–7)

8 **Reliquum est quod**: *There remains (a matter) which.*
vestrī similēs: *like you*; **vestrī** is genitive of the pronoun **vōs.**
sintne: *whether (or not) there are*; a double indirect question, with the second part omitted.

9 **videndum est**: supply **vōbīs,** *(you) must consider*; literally, *it must be considered by you.*
ut: *how* or *whether* in an indirect question.
honestē . . . esse: i.e., in Rome.

Quōmodo quidem nunc sē rēs habet: *As things stand now*; literally, *How indeed the situation holds itself now.*
10 **modo ut**: *provided that,* followed by a subjunctive verb.
loca: the noun **locus,** masculine in the singular, is often neuter in the plural.
haec . . . loca: i.e., the area of Campania, centering on Capua, where Cicero was in charge and where he owned several estates (see the map on page 18).
bellissimē: *in great comfort.*
11 **praedium, -ī,** n., *property, estate.*

illud verendum est, nē: *there should be concern that*; literally, *this must be feared, that.*

12 **velim . . . cōnsīderētis, . . . sītis** (13): *I would like you to make plans, . . . (and) (I would like you) to be.* Note the use of asyndeton, which suggests urgency.
Pompōniō . . . Camillō: Titus Pomponius Atticus was Cicero's literary adviser and confidant. Camillus was a friend and fellow lawyer.
cum quibus vōbīs vidēbitur: *with whom(ever) it will seem (best) to you.*
13 **ad summam**: *in short.*
animō fortī: *courageous*, literally, *of brave spirit,* an ablative of description (see the Reading Note on page 105).
***cārus, -a, -um**, *dear, beloved.*
14 **quid agātis et quid . . . agātur**: indirect questions after **scrībite.**
istīc, adv., *over there* (i.e., in Rome).

Reading Note

Potential Subjunctive

In line 12 opposite, you see the form **velim**, which is present subjunctive of the irregular verb **volō.** When the independent subjunctive expresses an action that is possible or conceivable, it is translated as *could, may, should,* or *would.* This use of the subjunctive is known as the *potential subjunctive.* Thus, **velim** is translated *I would wish* or *I would like . . . .* In the context of line 12, Cicero uses the subjunctive to express in a polite but firm way some possibilities that he would like his family to consider.

Reliquum est quod ipsae optimē cōnsīderābitis, vestrī similēs fēminae sintne Rōmae. Sī enim nōn sunt, videndum est ut honestē vōs esse possītis. Quōmodo quidem nunc sē rēs habet, modo ut haec nōbīs loca tenēre liceat, bellissimē vel mēcum vel in nostrīs praediīs esse poteritis. Etiam illud verendum est, nē brevī tempore famēs in urbe sit. Hīs dē rēbus velim cum Pompōniō, cum Camillō, cum quibus vōbīs vidēbitur, cōnsīderētis, ad summam, animō fortī sītis. Vōs, meae cārissimae animae, quam saepissimē ad mē scrībite et vōs quid agātis et quid istīc agātur. Valē.

—Cicero, *Epistulae ad familiares* XIV.14

---

7. What fact should his family consider in deciding whether to stay in Rome? (8)
8. What further option must they consider? (9–11)
9. Where does Cicero suggest that his family seek refuge? (10–11) Under what conditions will this be possible? (11)
10. What else does Cicero fear? (11)
11. What two pieces of advice does Cicero give in lines 12–13?
12. What final request does Cicero make of his family? (13–14)

Several days after this letter was written, Cicero's family left for their villa at Formiae (see the map on page 18).

Reading Note

Interpreting ut

When **ut** comes after a main clause that contains a key word such **tantus, tālis, sīc**, etc., it introduces a result clause and means *that*; look for a subjunctive verb to complete the clause:

Senātōrēs quīdam Caesarem **adeō** timēbant **ut** Rōmā **effugerent**.
Certain senators feared Caesar ***so much that they fled*** *from Rome.*

When **ut** follows a verb such as **rogāre, ōrāre, persuādēre** or **imperāre**, it introduces an indirect command with a subjunctive verb, which we express by an infinitive in English:

Cicerō propinquōs **rogat ut** cōnsilia bona **caperent**.
Cicero ***is asking*** *his relatives* ***to make*** *good plans.*

When **ut** follows **timēre, verērī**, or **metuere, ut** will mean *that . . . not*, introducing a fear clause with a subjunctive verb:

Cicerō **verēbātur ut** satis cibī in urbe **esset**.
Cicero ***was afraid that*** *there* ***would not be*** *enough food in the city.*

If none of these things applies, keep reading until you see the verb that completes the **ut** clause. If the verb introduced by **ut** is subjunctive, you are dealing with a purpose clause and **ut** means *(in order) to*:

Cicerō epistulam mīsit **ut** familiam suam **adiuvāret**.
Cicero sent a letter (in order) ***to help*** *his household.*

If the verb introduced by **ut** is indicative, **ut** means *when* or *as*:

Cicerō, **ut** epistulae eius **dēmōnstrant**, līberōs maximē amābat.
Cicero, ***as*** *his letters* ***show****, loved his children very much.*

1 **Sal.**: **Salūtem.**

2 **Pedem**: one **pēs**, or Roman foot, = .97 English feet or .29 meters. Cicero uses the phrase **Pedem in Italiā . . . nūllum** to indicate the fact that all of Italy was now in Caesar's control.
istīus: genitive singular of **iste**. The word refers to Caesar, here and in line 4 below.

3 **nisi in nāvem sē contulerit**: *unless he boards a ship*, literally, *unless he will have boarded a ship.*
exceptum īrī: *will be captured*, an example of the rare future passive infinitive.

Ego quid agam?: *What should I do?*

Quā aut terrā aut marī: *On what land or sea.* Note that **marī** is ablative here, not dative.
4 ***persequor, persequī, persecūtus sum**, *to follow, pursue.*
qui ubi sit, nesciō: literally, *who where he is, I don't know*, i.e., *when I don't know where he is.* The linking **quī** refers to **eum**, Pompey.

5 **Fac posse**: = **Fac (mē) posse (trādere)**, *Suppose that I can surrender (to Caesar).*
tūtō, adv., *safely.*
num . . . honestē?: = **num (mē trādere possum) honestē?**
6 **explicō, -āre, -āvī, -ātus**, *to unfold; to explain, settle* (a difficulty), *resolve.*

Reading Note

Deliberative Questions

In lines 3 and 4 opposite, you met three examples of the subjunctive used in a *deliberative question.* In line 3, **Ego quid agam?** means *What should I do?* or *What am I to do?* and in line 3 **persequar eum?**, *should I follow him?* or *am I to follow him?* How would you translate **Trādam** on line 4, another example of this usage? The deliberative question is a question asked of oneself and can imply doubt, indignation, surprise, or confusion. It does not necessarily expect an answer.

Ubi nihil erit quod scrībās, id ipsum scrībitō.
When there is nothing for you to write, write and say so.
(Cicero, *Epistulae ad Atticum* IV.8.4)

B. What to Do?

This letter was written on 8 or 9 February 49 B.C. from Formiae, where Cicero had retreated after giving up his duties as recruiting officer. He had lost faith in Pompey for abandoning Rome and fleeing from Caesar. The addressee is Titus Pomponius Atticus, Cicero's close friend and confidant.

Cicerō Atticō Sal.

Pedem in Italiā videō nūllum esse, quī nōn in istīus potestāte sit. Dē Pompeiō sciō nihil, eumque, nisi in nāvem sē contulerit, exceptum īrī putō. Ego quid agam? Quā aut terrā aut marī persequar eum, quī ubi sit, nesciō? Trādam igitur istī mē? Fac posse tūtō (multī enim hortantur), num etiam honestē? Nūllō modō. Equidem ā tē petam cōnsilium, ut soleō. Explicārī rēs nōn potest.

—Cicero, *Epistulae ad Atticum* VII.22 (extract)

1. According to Cicero, what progress has Caesar made during the war thus far? (2)
2. In contrast, what does he write about Pompey? (2–3)
3. Discuss the options Cicero presents to Atticus. (3–5)
4. What reservation does Cicero have about delivering himself over to Caesar? (4–5)
5. What is Cicero's final request of Atticus? (5–6) Why does he want advice? (6)

During these trying months, Cicero wrote to Atticus almost daily, in search of a decision. Atticus sympathized with the position of the Senate but refused to engage in politics himself.

Marcus Tullius Cicero
Marble bust, first century B.C.

1 **Cn. Magnus**: Pompey was called Magnus after 81 B.C. because of victories in Italy, Sicily, and Africa.

Prōcōs.: Pompey was officially governor (**prōcōnsul**) of Spain.

M. Cicerōnī Imp.: Cicero is greeted as a victorious general (**imperātor**) by virtue of his conquest of native bandits while governing in Asia Minor the previous year. The abbreviation **M.** is for **Mārcus**, Cicero's **praenōmen** (not part of the salutation **S.D.**).

2 **S.V.B.**: = **Sī valēs, bene (est).**

Tuās litterās: this letter is in reply to one received from Cicero several days earlier, asking whether he should stay in Capua or join Pompey, who intended to take his army to Greece.

prīstinus, -a, -um, *previous, former.*

3 **in salūte commūnī**: *with regard to the common welfare* (of the Republic).

Cōnsulēs: the consuls, nominally commanders in chief, had been elected for the year 49 because they opposed Julius Caesar. They were ineffective in raising an army and eventually fled to Greece with Pompey.

Āpulia: still the name of a region of southeastern Italy.

4 **prō**: *in accordance with, by virtue of.*

singulāris, -is, -e, *outstanding, unique, extraordinary.*

***studium, -ī**, n., *eagerness, enthusiasm, support.*

tē . . . cōnferās: *you should come*; literally, *you should bring yourself.*

5 **afflīgō, afflīgere, afflīxī, afflīctus**, *to strike down.*

afflīctae: *stricken*, i.e., in desperate straits.

6 ***cēnseō, cēnsēre, cēnsuī, cēnsus**, *to be of the opinion, think, advise, suggest.*

Cēnseō: followed by the indirect commands **ut . . . faciās** and **(ut) . . . veniās.**

In Rome, letters were most often written on waxed wooden tablets, less often on plain wooden tablets, parchment (cured animal skin), or papyrus. A set of waxed tablets is shown in this Pompeian wall painting, leaning against the *capsa* (case) that holds papyrus scrolls. The tablets would be folded (the dark strip in the center is the location of the hinge), tied with string, and sealed with wax stamped by the author's signet ring. Upper-class Roman citizens usually sent their mail either by a trusted slave or by hired messenger. Sometimes letters would be carried by a friend traveling to or near the same destination.

Fresco, Naples, first century A.D.

C. An Invitation from Pompey

Pompey wrote this letter on 20 February 49 B.C. *from Canusium, near Brundisium. He invites Cicero to join him as he marshals his forces shortly before abandoning Italy for Greece. Despite his famous* **celeritās**, *Caesar was unable to catch him. Pompey, who had helped in Cicero's recall from exile in 58, corresponded often with Cicero. Cicero was in the habit of forwarding to Atticus copies of his letters both to and from Pompey and Caesar. What is the tone of Pompey's letter?*

Cn. Magnus Prōcōs. S.D. M. Cicerōnī Imp.

S.V.B. Tuās litterās libenter lēgī. Recognōvī enim tuam prīstinam virtūtem etiam in salūte commūnī. Cōnsulēs ad eum exercitum, quem in Āpuliā habuī, vēnērunt. Magnopere tē hortor prō tuō singulārī perpetuōque studiō in rem pūblicam, ut tē ad nōs cōnferās, ut commūnī cōnsiliō reī pūblicae afflīctae opem atque auxilium ferāmus. Cēnseō ut viā Appiā iter faciās et celeriter Brundisium veniās.

—Cicero, *Epistulae ad Atticum* VIII.11C

---

1. What comment does Pompey make about Cicero's letter? (2–3)
2. What news does Pompey provide about his military status? (3)
3. What is Pompey urging Cicero to do? (4–5)
4. What is his justification for making this request? (4)
5. In what way does Pompey feel that Cicero can help? (5)
6. What final request does Pompey make? (6)

A portrait of Pompey. Note his facial expression, which suggests the war weariness of a man who was in his late 50s during the civil war against Caesar.
Marble bust, first half of first century B.C.

1 **Caesar Imp. . . . Cicerōnī Imp.**: note how both Caesar and Pompey address Cicero as an equal in military status, even though his title of **imperātor** came from one insignificant victory.

2 **cum**: *although*. What word in the main clause suggests this meaning of **cum**? (See the Reading Note on page 61.)

***properō, -āre, -āvī, -ātus**, *to hurry.*

in itinere: Caesar is on the march in pursuit of Pompey.

praemittō, praemittere, praemīsī, praemissus, *to send ahead.*

praeterīre . . . nōn potuī: *I could not neglect (the opportunity).*

3 **quīn et scrīberem ad tē et grātiās tibi agerem**: *to write to you and thank you* (literally, *that I should write . . .*). **Quīn**, following a negative verb or phrase, introduces a clause with the subjunctive.

etsī, conj., *even if, although.*

etsī hoc et fēcī saepe: Cicero tried several times, unsuccessfully, to mediate Caesar's conflict with Pompey, and it is perhaps for this reason that Caesar is thanking him.

et saepius mihi factūrus (esse) videor: *and it seems to me that I will do this more often* (literally, *I seem to myself to be about to do this*).

4 ***mereor, merērī, meritus sum**, *to deserve, earn.*

Ita dē mē merēris: *You deserve this from me.*

In prīmīs: *First of all.*

petō: governs the indirect command **ut . . . videam** (5).

cōnfīdō, cōnfīdere, cōnfīsus sum, semi-deponent + dat., *to trust, believe.*

5 **ventūrum**: = **ventūrum esse**.

grātiā: *favor, influence*; a different meaning of the word **grātia** than is found in the expression **grātiās agere** (3) or in the use of the genitive + **grātiā** = *for the sake of, for the purpose of.*

dignitās, dignitātis, f., *prestige, good name, reputation.*

ope omnium rērum: *the help of all (your) resources,* i.e., his skills as an orator.

6 **ūtī**: present infinitive of **ūtor**, whose object is in the ablative case. (Review the Reading Note on page 100.)

festīnātiō, festīnātiōnis, f., *haste.*

brevitās, brevitātis, f., *brevity, shortness.*

ignōscō, ignōscere, ignōvī, ignōtus + dat., *to pardon.*

D. A Request from Caesar

Caesar wrote this letter to Cicero in March 49 B.C. while approaching Brundisium by forced marches in an attempt to cut off Pompey from Greece.

Caesar Imp. S.D. Cicerōnī Imp.

Cum properārem atque essem in itinere, praemissīs iam legiōnibus, praeterīre tamen nōn potuī quīn et scrīberem ad tē et grātiās tibi agerem, etsī hoc et fēcī saepe et saepius mihi factūrus videor. Ita dē mē merēris. In prīmīs ā tē petō, quoniam cōnfīdō mē celeriter ad urbem ventūrum, ut tē ibi videam, ut tuō cōnsiliō, grātiā, dignitāte, ope omnium rērum ūtī possim. Festīnātiōnī meae brevitātīque litterārum ignōscēs.

—Cicero, *Epistulae ad Atticum* IX.6A (extract)

---

1. Under what circumstances is Caesar writing this letter? (2)
2. What news does Caesar provide about his military status? (2)
3. Why is Caesar writing to Cicero? (3)
4. What does he state about his previous relationship with Cicero? About his future relationship? (3–4)
5. What compliment does Caesar pay Cicero in line 4?
6. What request does Caesar make of Cicero? (4–5)
7. How does Caesar feel that Cicero will help his cause? (5–6)
8. For what does he ask Cicero's pardon? (6)

After vacillating for several months in despair over what his position should be, Cicero finally wrote that he would "rather be conquered with Pompey than conquer with Caesar." His decision was greatly influenced by his debt of gratitude toward Pompey for bringing him back from exile ten years previously.

Accompanied by his brother Quintus and son Marcus, Cicero sailed from Formiae on 7 June 49 B.C. and, after spending several months at Atticus' estate in Epirus, joined the Republican forces in Greece. In the meantime, Caesar made himself master of Italy and restored order in Rome, defeated Pompey's forces in Spain, and crossed the Adriatic in January 48 B.C. You learned in Chapter 55C how Caesar eventually defeated the Republican army at the battle of Pharsalus, thereby making himself undisputed master of the Roman world.

Nec quemquam iam ferre potest Caesarve priōrem, Pompeiusve parem.

Caesar cannot tolerate a superior, nor Pompey an equal.

(Lucan, *De bello civili* I.125-26)

EXERCISE 66a

In a subsequent letter, after Cicero had joined Pompey in Greece, Caesar replied as follows. Read aloud and translate:

Quod nē faciās, prō iūre nostrae amīcitiae ā tē petō. Postrēmō quid virō bonō et quiētō et bonō cīvī magis convenit quam abesse ā cīvīlibus contrōversiīs?

—quoted by Cicero in *Epistulae ad Atticum* X.8b

Quod: = to join Pompey
nē faciās: indirect command dependent on **petō**
prō iūre: *by right (of), by virtue (of)*
quid . . . magis convenit?: *what is more appropriate?*

EXERCISE 66b

1. Compare the letter Pompey wrote to Cicero with the one Caesar wrote (Readings C and D). How are the content, language, and tone similar? How are they different?
2. What does each general hope to gain from Cicero? On what does each base his appeal?
3. What do these two letters reveal about the personalities of the opponents? How does each seem to feel about his cause?
4. What do all four letters tell us about Cicero as a private citizen? As a man of public affairs?

EXERCISE 66c

Read aloud, identify the type of clause introduced by **ut** or **nē**, and translate the entire sentence. Note that some are fear clauses (see the Reading Note on page 162).

1. Quīdam amīcī Cicerōnis hortābantur nē sē Caesarī trāderet.
2. Cicerō proficīscitur Capuam ut Pompeiī iuvandī causā mīlitēs cōnscrībat.
3. Timēbatne Pompeius nē Cicerō auxilium Caesarī lātūrus esset?
4. Tanta famēs Rōmae erat ut nēmō satis cibī habēret.
5. Pompeius, ut omnēs scītis, plūrēs mīlitēs quam Caesar habuit.
6. Pompeius Cicerōnī scrīpsit ut auxilium obtinēret.
7. Cicerō metuēbat ut familia sua tūta in urbe esset.
8. Cicerō familiam suam monuit ut Rōmā proficīscerentur.
9. Caesar adeō volēbat Cicerōnem sibi conciliāre ut epistulam adulantem eī mīserit.
10. Pompeius Cicerōnem ad Campaniam mittet ut mīlitēs cōnscrībat.
11. Erat Pompeiō metus ut satis mīlitum habēret ad Caesarem vincendum.

conciliō, -āre, -āvī, -ātus, *to win over*
adulāns, adulantis, *flattering*

AN EXCEPTIONAL WIFE

As you learned in Chapter 54, it was customary in Rome for a family member to deliver a speech, referred to as a **laudātiō fūnebris**, in praise of a person who had died. The readings in this chapter come from such a speech delivered by a husband in praise of his deceased wife. We do not know the identity of the couple, but two important things become clear from reading this inscription.

The first is the genuine love that existed between the husband and wife. You know from Book II that it was usual for a girl's parents to arrange a marriage for her, and presumably this was the case for the wife described here. Although the practice of arranged marriages may seem strange today, there is abundant evidence that in many cases a strong bond developed between the partners. The author of this speech leaves no doubt about his affection and admiration for his wife and cites many examples of their mutual love.

Second, this inscription gives us some insight into how women functioned in the legal and social environment of the late Republic. Under Roman law, a woman usually had to be under the guardianship of a male relative and could not manage her own property or take legal actions on her own behalf. In practice, however, things were more complicated. Some women did take active measures to look out for their own interests or those of their husbands. The woman described in this oration inherited property from her father who died shortly after she was married. Some of her relatives tried to invalidate the will so that they could obtain the property. Her husband praises her energetic and successful efforts to prevent this from happening in his absence. After Antony, Octavian, and Lepidus formed the Second Triumvirate in 43 B.C. (see Chapter 56B), they outlawed a number of their enemies, including the husband who delivered this speech. You will read below how his wife took great risks to save him.

This woman was not the only one who took decisive action to save her husband during the proscriptions. The historian Appian of Alexandria describes in Book IV of his *Roman Histories* a number of such women. Here are some:

> The wife of Apuleius threatened that if he should flee without her, she would give information against him. So he took her with him unwillingly, and he succeeded in avoiding suspicion in his flight by traveling with his wife and his male and female slaves in a public manner. The wife of Antius wrapped him up in a clothes-bag and gave the bundle to some porters to carry from the house to the seashore, whence he made his escape to Sicily. The wife of Rheginus concealed him by night in a sewer, into which the soldiers were not willing to enter in the daytime, on account of the foul odor. The next night she disguised him as a charcoal dealer, and furnished him an ass to drive, carrying coals. Lucretius, who had been wandering about with two faithful slaves and had become destitute of food, set out to find his wife . . . by whom he was concealed between the planks of a double roof until his friends got his name erased from the proscription.

1 **diūturnus, -a, -um,** *long-lasting.*
dīvertium, -ī, n., *divorce.*

contingō, contingere, contigī, contactus, *to touch; to happen, fall to, be granted to* (+ dat.).
2 **perdūcō, perdūcere, perdūxī, perductus,** *to lead along, to continue.*
perdūcerētur: the subject is *it*, the marriage.

utinam, adv., *if only* (with subjunctive).
vetustus, -a, -um, *old, long-lasting.*
coniūnctiō, coniūnctiōnis, f., *joining together, union.*
3 **mūtātiō, mūtātiōnis,** f., *change*; here a euphemistic way of saying *end.*
vice meā: *through my turn, on my part.*
quā: *through which*, ablative of means.
iūstius: what form does the **-ius** ending indicate?
***cēdō, cēdere, cessī, cessūrus,** *to go, move; to submit, yield.*
cēdere fātō: *to yield to fate*; another euphemism = *to die.*
maiōrem: supply **mē**, *me (as) the elder*; subject accusative with the infinitive **cēdere**.

Domestica bona: a neuter plural substantive, object of **memorem** (5) and modified by several nouns in the genitive (note the asyndeton in this list).
4 **pudicitia, -ae,** f., *chastity, fidelity* (in marriage).
obsequium, -ī, n., *obedience.*
comitās, comitātis, f., *friendliness, kindliness.*
facilitās, facilitātis, f., *good nature.*
lānificium, -ī, n., *working wool, wool-spinning.*
5 **ōrnātus, -ūs,** m., *equipment, clothing; adornment, wearing of jewelry.*
nōn cōnspiciendī: *not to be noticed, inconspicuous, moderate, restrained.*
cultus, -ūs, m., *care (of one's person); clothing, style of dress.*
modicus, -a, -um, *modest.*
memorō, -āre, -āvī, -ātus, *to recall.*
cūr memorem: *why should I recall*, a deliberative question, as is **dīcam**; see page 166.

cāritās, cāritātis, f., *love.*
6 ***pietās, pietātis,** f., *sense of duty, devotion.*
cāritāte familiae pietāte: = **cāritāte et pietāte familiae**; the genitive **familiae** modifies both nouns, as its placement between them and the lack of a conjunction shows.
cum: completed by three verbs: **colueris, cūrāveris** (7), and **habueris** (7), with asyndeton.
aequē . . . ac: *in the same way as.*
nōn aliā mente: *with no other mind, with no different attitude.*
illī: dative, *to her* (the husband's mother).
7 **tuīs**: *your own people, your own relatives*, a substantive.
mātrōna, -ae, f., *married woman.*
8 **dignus, -a, -um,** *worthy, suitable, appropriate.*

proprius, -a, -um, *particular, unique.*
propria . . . tua: *your unique (traits)*, a neuter plural substantive.
vindicō, -āre, -āvī, -ātus, *to support, uphold, champion.* The husband means that he will devote much of what follows to the characteristics that were special in his wife.
9 **incidērunt**: deduce from **in** + **cadere**.
paterentur: from **patior**, not **pateō** (how can you tell them apart in the imperf. subj.?)
praestō, -āre, praestitī, *to surpass, excel; to be responsible for, take upon onself, perform.*

A. A Happily Married Couple

Rāra sunt tam diūturna mātrimōnia, fīnīta morte nōn dīvertiō interrupta. Contigit nōbīs ut ad annum XXXXI sine offēnsā perdūcerētur. Utinam vetusta coniūnctiō habuisset mūtātiōnem vice meā, quā iūstius erat cēdere fātō maiōrem. Domestica bona pudicitiae, obsequiī, comitātis, facilitātis, lānificiī, studiī religiōnis sine superstitiōne, ōrnātūs nōn cōnspiciendī, cultūs modicī, cūr memorem? Cūr dīcam dē cāritāte familiae pietāte, cum aequē mātrem meam ac tuōs parentēs colueris, nōn aliā mente illī quam tuīs cūrāveris, cētera innumerābilia habueris commūnia cum omnibus mātrōnīs dignam fāmam colentibus? Propria sunt tua quae vindicō ac paucae uxōrēs in similia incidērunt ut tālia paterentur et praestārent.

—*Corpus Inscriptionum Latinarum* VI.1527 (extract)

1. How does the husband compare his marriage with that of many couples? (1)
2. What kind of married life did they have and for how long? (1–2)
3. What wish does the husband express? Why would this have been appropriate? (2–3)
4. What things does the husband not think it necessary to discuss? (3–5)
5. What other qualities will he not deal with at length? What evidence is there that his wife possessed these qualities? (5–7)
6. What other general statement does the husband make about his wife? (7–8)
7. What will be the focus of the husband's speech? In what way was his wife different from most other women? (8–9)

Reading Note

Preterition

An author or speaker may say that he is not going to talk about something. At the same time, by mentioning the topic that will not be discussed, he has brought it to the attention of the reader or the audience. This is a rhetorical device called *preterition*, from the verb **praeterīre**, *to go by, bypass*. The two examples of preterition in Reading A above are introduced by the subjunctive phrases **cūr memorem** and **cūr dīcam** (5).

Questions for Thought and Discussion

1. Why is the preterition in this section appropriate and effective?
2. Based on the information in Reading A, how does it seem that Roman men usually defined a "good" wife?

This relief shows the *iūnctiō dextrārum*, the joining of hands that was part of a Roman wedding.

Relief, Rome, Imperial Roman, first to second century A.D.

1 **subsidium, -ī,** n., *assistance, support.*

subsidia: the plural suggests that the wife did this many times (an idea reinforced by **subinde** in line 2), but the singular sounds better in English.

fugae: *exile* (an additional meaning of the word **fuga** = *flight, escape*).

praestitistī: *you supplied*; from **praestō**, the same verb as on line A:9, but with a different meaning.

ōrnāmentum, -ī, n., *equipment; ornament, embellishment; luxury.* **Ōrnāmenta**, like **frūctūs** in line 3, refers to things that were not necessary for survival but contributed to the husband's ability to live as a senator was expected to, thereby maintaining his **dignitās**.

īnstruō, īnstruere, īnstrūxī, īnstrūctus, *to prepare, arrange; to equip, provide with* (+ abl.).

cum: what verbs complete the clause introduced by **cum**? Are these verbs indicative or subjunctive? How does this affect the meaning? (See the Reading Note on page 76.)

2 ***aurum, -ī,** n., *gold.*

margarītum, -ī, n., *pearl.*

dētracta: deduce from **dē** + **trahō**.

corporī tuō: *from your own body*, a dative of separation; these objects were the wife's personal jewelry that she chose to sell in order to assist her husband.

subinde, adv., *over and over, repeatedly.*

familiā: remember that **familia** means *household* (i.e., slaves), not *family* in the English sense.

3 **nummus, -ī,** m., *coin; money.*

frūctus, -ūs, *fruit; income, profit.* Note the asyndeton; what is its effect?

callidē, adv., *cleverly.*

dēcipiō, dēcipere, dēcēpī, dēceptus, *to deceive.*

callidē dēceptīs . . . custōdibus: ablative absolute.

4 **locuplētō, -āre, -āvī, -ātus,** *to supply with wealth, enrich.*

locuplētāstī: short for **locuplētāvistī**.

5 **agmen**: this neuter noun could be subject or direct object. You must read through the entire sentence before you can tell for certain; what words at the end of the sentence clarify the function of **agmen**?

ex repertīs hominibus: *from men who had been found*; Milo had returned to Italy on his own and gathered whatever followers he could find.

domūs: genitive object of **potītus eram**.

ēmptiō, ēmptiōnis, f., *purchase.*

ēmptiōne: ablative of means.

6 **occāsiō, occāsiōnis,** f., *opportunity.*

occāsiōnibus: *because of the opportunities*, an ablative of cause. The situation in Italy was so chaotic that Milo felt free to make such an attack.

irruptūrum, dīreptūrum: what noun earlier in the sentence do these future participles modify? Hint: the participles are neuter, not masculine.

7 **reiēcistī**: deduce from **re-** + **iaciō, iacere**.

dēfendistī: with the help of the household slaves and perhaps guards whom the wife had hired.

B. In Time of Civil War

The husband opposed Caesar's attempts to become sole ruler of Rome, probably joining the senatorial forces at the battle of Pharsalus (48 B.C.); see Reading 55C. After Pharsalus those who fought against Caesar were not allowed to return to Italy without special permission. During this time the wife contrived to support her husband in his exile.

Amplissima subsidia fugae meae praestitistī. Ōrnāmentīs vītam meam īnstrūxistī cum omne aurum margarītaque corporī tuō dētracta trādidistī mihi et subinde familiā, nummīs, frūctibus, callidē dēceptīs nostrōrum adversāriōrum custōdibus, absentiam meam locuplētāstī.

---

1. What did the wife supply for her husband? (1)
2. How else did she assist her husband? (1)
3. Where did she get the funds to do this? (1–2)
4. What did the wife do repeatedly? (2–4)
5. What measures did the wife have to take while doing this? (3)

After taking control of Italy, Caesar allowed many political exiles to return home. Titus Annius Milo was not included in this group, however, probably because Caesar wanted to respect the memory of his supporter Clodius who had been killed by Milo (see Chapters 64 and 65). After Caesar left Italy to fight his opponents in Spain and then in Greece, Milo returned (48 B.C.) and joined in a short-lived rebellion against Caesar, in which he was killed. The following incident took place sometime between Milo's return to Italy and his death.

Intereā agmen collectum ex repertīs hominibus ā Milōne, cuius domūs ēmptiōne potītus eram cum ille fuisset exul, bellī cīvīlis occāsiōnibus irruptūrum et dīreptūrum prosperē reiēcistī et dēfendistī domum nostram.

—*Corpus Inscriptionum Latinarum* VI.1527 (extracts)

---

6. Whom was the wife able to drive off? (5)
7. How had the husband obtained the house? Under what circumstances? (5–6)
8. What did the group of men intend to do? Why were they able to engage in such behavior? (6)
9. How does the husband summarize what his wife did? (6–7)

A Roman couple
Sardonyx, two layers, circa A.D. 230

1 **Quid**: = **Cūr.**
interior, interior, interius, gen., **interiōris**, *interior, inner; private.*
reconditus, -a, -um, *hidden.*
***sermō, sermōnis**, m., *speech, conversation.*
arcānus, -a, -um, *secret.*
ēruō, ēruere, ēruī, ērutus, *to dig up; to draw out, reveal.*
ēruam: deliberative subjunctive (see the Reading Note on page 166).
ut: *how*, introducing a series of indirect questions with verbs in the perfect subjunctive.
2 **repentīnus, -a, -um**, *sudden.*
immineō, imminēre, *to hang over, threaten.*
ēvocātus: as soon as a man's name was posted on the proscription lists, he could be hunted down and killed. Once the husband learned, probably from friends, that his name was to be added, he had to make an immediate decision whether to flee or go into hiding; so the husband describes himself as *called out to*, i.e., confronted by, the dangers.
3 **experīrī**: supply **mē** with **experīrī** as the object of **passa sīs.**
cāsus, -ūs, m., *accident; misfortune; disaster.*
experīrī cāsūs audācius: *too recklessly to attempt disasters*, i.e., to attempt a course of action that would have turned out disastrously. Because he had received a pardon from Caesar, the husband was surprised and angered to find himself proscribed. So his first thought was to join the forces fighting against the triumvirs, as many proscribed senators did.
temere, adv., *rashly, thoughtlessly*, modifying **passa sīs.**
modestiōra: neuter plural substantive, object of **cōgitantī** (not agreeing with **fida receptācula**).
cōgitantī: supply **mihi.**
modestiōra cōgitantī: *thinking more modest things*, i.e., *making more modest plans*. The husband abandoned his plans to join the opposition and agreed with his wife's idea of going into hiding.
fīdus, -a, -um, *faithful, reliable.*
4 **receptāculum, -ī**, n., *receptacle, container; shelter, hiding place.*
parāris: short for **parāveris.**
sociōs: *(as) allies*, in apposition with **sorōrem . . . et virum** (4–5).
5 **virum**: *husband.*
coniūnctō omnium perīculō: the proscription edicts specified that anyone who aided or hid a proscribed man would also be proscribed, so the family members were taking a very real risk by hiding the husband.

sint: present subjunctive in a future hypothetical condition (see pages 96–97). The unexpressed subject *they* refers to the plans (**cōnsilia**, 1), which explains the neuter adjective **īnfīnīta.**
attingō, attingere, attigī, attactus, *to touch; to touch upon, mention.*
attingere: supply **omnia (cōnsilia)** as object.
6 **sat**: short for **satis.**
sit: *let it be*, jussive subjunctive.
salūtāriter, adv., *safely.*

C. Caught Up in the Proscriptions

In a section of the funeral oration not included here, the husband describes how his wife was able to secure a pardon from Caesar by pleading his case to Caesar's representatives in Italy; so the husband returned home. After Caesar's murder and the formation of the Second Triumvirate by Antony, Lepidus, and Octavian, the triumvirs outlawed a number of their political enemies. Despite Caesar's pardon, the husband found himself among the proscribed. He reacted by planning to join either Sextus Pompeius (son of Pompey the Great), who was fighting the triumvirs in Sicily, or Brutus and Cassius in Greece. His wife talked him out of this plan.

Quid ego nunc interiōra nostra et recondita cōnsilia sermōnēsque arcānōs ēruam, ut repentīnīs nūntiīs ad praesentia et imminentia perīcula ēvocātus tuīs cōnsiliīs cōnservātus sim, ut neque audācius experīrī cāsūs temere passa sīs et modestiōra cōgitantī fīda receptācula parāris sociōsque cōnsiliōrum tuōrum ad mē servandum dēlēgeris sorōrem tuam et virum eius C. Cluvium, coniūnctō omnium perīculō? Īnfīnīta sint sī attingere cōner; sat sit mihi tibique salūtāriter mē latuisse.

—*Corpus Inscriptionum Latinarum* VI.1527 (extract)

---

1. What is the husband not going to discuss in detail? (1) What figure of speech is used here? (See the Reading Note on page 175).
2. Under what circumstances did these conversations take place? (1–2)
3. What happened as a result? (2–3)
4. What did the wife not allow? (3)
5. What did the wife do for the husband when he changed his plans? (3–4)
6. Whom did the wife enlist as allies? For what purpose? (4–5)
7. As a result, in what situation did they all find themselves? (5)
8. What would be the result if the husband tried to list all his wife's plans on his behalf? (5–6)
9. How does the husband summarize what happened at this point in their lives? (6)

Reading Note

Syncopated Verbs

In line B:4 you saw the verb **locuplētāstī**, short for **locuplētāvistī**, and in 4 above **parāris**, a contracted form of **parāveris**. Verbs that use the letter **-v-** as the marker of the perfect stem sometimes drop the syllable that begins with **-v-**; such forms are called *syncopated*. Other examples that you have seen include **petīstī**, 59C:8; **nōsse**, 62F:1; and **apparāsset**, 65B:13. What would be the uncontracted form of each of these?

1 **acerbus, -a, -um,** *bitter.*
tuā vice: *on your account.*
***fateor, fatērī, fassus sum,** *to admit, confess.*

reddō, reddere, reddidī, redditus, *to give back, restore.*
redditō . . . cīve: ablative absolute.
cīve: *as a citizen*, in apposition to **mē**.
2 ***beneficium, -ī,** n., *kindness.*
beneficiō et iūdiciō: ablatives of means.
restitūtiō, restitūtiōnis, f., *restoration.*
3 **interpellō, -āre, -āvī, -ātus,** *to interrupt; to confront.* The wife had approached Lepidus in public and begun to plead her husband's case, either because Lepidus would not see her privately or because she thought it better to do so in public.
prōstrātus, -a, -um, *lying on the ground, prostrate.*
***humus, -ī,** f., *ground, earth*; note the gender; **humī** is locative case.
4 **allevō, -āre, -āvī, -ātus,** *to raise, lift up.*
allevāta: supply **es** here and with **tracta** and **rapsāta** in the next line.
rapsō, -āre, -āvī, -ātus, *to drag along.*
livor, livōris, m., *bruise.*
repleō, replēre, replēvī, replētus, *to fill.*
cum: not the preposition, but the conjunction, completed by the verb **admonērēs**.
5 ***admoneō, admonēre, admonuī, admonitus,** *to remind X* (acc.) *of Y* (gen.).
grātulātiō, grātulātiōnis, f., *congratulation(s), expression of happiness.*
6 **contumēliōsus, -a, -um,** *insulting.*
palam, adv., *in public, openly.*
conqueror, conquerī, conquestus sum, *to complain.*
7 ***auctor, auctōris,** m., *creator, author, person responsible.*
nōtēscō, nōtēscere, *to become known*; the unexpressed subject of **nōtēsceret** is *he*, Lepidus.

Cui nocuit mox ea rēs: Lepidus was soon forced to give up control of Italy and Gaul and govern only the province of Africa. The husband may have enjoyed thinking that Lepidus' mistreatment of his wife caused this, but Antony and Octavian had earlier decided that Lepidus was to be pushed aside.

hāc virtūte: *than this courage (of yours)*, ablative of comparison with **efficācius** (8).
8 **efficāx, efficācis,** *effective.*
Quid . . . efficācius: supply **erat**.
praebeō, praebēre, praebuī, praebitus, *to offer, provide.*
praebēre: this infinitive completes the meaning of **efficācius**; we would say *at providing.*
Caesarī: dative of reference, almost equivalent to a possessive.
***clēmentia, -ae,** f., *mercy, clemency.*
locum: *opportunity*, i.e., an opportunity to display.
***spīritus, -ūs,** m., *breath; spirit, life.*
custōdiā spīritūs meī: *concern for my life.*
notō, -āre, -āvī, -ātus, *to mark off; to indicate, call attention to.*
notāre: parallel to **praebēre** (8) and so may be translated *at calling attention to.*
9 **importūnus, -a, -um,** *oppressive.*
patientia, -ae, f., *suffering; endurance.*

D. Lepidus' Abusive Behavior

The wife managed to gain Octavian's support for her husband, which should have resulted in his name being removed from the proscription lists. Octavian, however, had left Italy to fight the senatorial opposition in Greece. Lepidus remained in charge of Italy, so the wife had to make sure that he would respect Octavian's wishes before her husband could safely return.

Acerbissimum tamen in vītā mihi accidisse tuā vice fatēbor. Redditō mē iam cīve patriae, beneficiō et iūdiciō absentis Caesaris Augustī, cum per tē dē restitūtiōne meā M. Lepidus collēga praesēns interpellārētur, et ad eius pedēs prōstrāta humī nōn modo nōn allevāta sed trācta et servīlem in modum rapsāta, livōribus corporis replēta, cum firmissimō animō eum admonērēs ēdictī Caesaris cum grātulātiōne restitūtiōnis meae atque, vōcibus etiam contumēliōsīs et crūdēlibus exceptīs vulneribus, palam conquerēris ut auctor meōrum perīculōrum nōtēsceret. Cui nocuit mox ea rēs. Quid hāc virtūte efficācius praebēre Caesarī clēmentiae locum et cum custōdiā spīritūs meī notāre importūnam crūdēlitātem Lepidī firmā tuā patientiā.

—*Corpus Inscriptionum Latinarum* VI.1527 (extract)

---

1. What will the husband admit? (1)
2. What had happened to the husband? How? (1–2)
3. What was the wife doing? (2–3)
4. How was the wife treated when she was prostrate before Lepidus? (3–4)
5. What was the result of this treatment? (4)
6. What was the wife doing? (5)
7. How does the husband summarize the treatment his wife received? (6)
8. What else did she do? Why? (6–7)
9. What effect did Lepidus' treatment of the wife ultimately have on him? (7)
10. What was one effect of the wife's actions? (7–8)
11. What was a second effect? By what means did the wife achieve this? (8–9)

After the civil wars were over, the husband describes how he and his wife lived happily together. They were disappointed, however, because they could not have children. The wife suggested that they divorce so that he could marry someone else, an idea he summarily rejected. The husband concludes the speech by saying that, despite his wife's good example and good advice, he cannot put aside the sorrow he feels at her passing.

Meter : Alcaic strophe

1 **Nunc**: note the emphasis indicated by the anaphora.
est bibendum: impersonal; literally, *it must be drunk*; *we must drink*. These opening words imitate a poem of the early Greek poet Alcaeus in which he celebrated a tyrant's death.
pede līberō: *with free foot*, i.e., *with uninhibited dancing*.

2 **pulsō, -āre, -āvī, -ātus**, *to pound, stamp, beat*. Understand **est** with **pulsanda**.
***tellūs, tellūris**, f., *ground*.
Saliāris, -is, -e, *Salian, relating to the Salii*. The Salii were a college of twelve priests of Mars who dressed in military outfits and held processions through Rome on the Kalends of March. The name *Salii* derives from **salīre**, *to leap*; leaping was part of their ritual.

3 **pulvīnar, pulvīnāris**, n., *couch, cushioned seat*, on which were placed images of the gods during the **lectisternium** (*couch spreading*), when a ceremonial meal was set out in front of the couch as a thanksgiving feast (**supplicātiō**).

4 **dapibus**: *feasts*; the Salii were noted for their lavish banquets.

5 **antehāc**, adv., *beforehand, earlier, previously;* pronounced as two syllables, **ant'hāc**.
***nefās**: = **nefās erat**; **nefās**, n., indeclinable: *without religious or divine sanction; sinful, improper*. It was deemed sacrilegious to revel while Rome was at war.
dēprōmō, dēprōmere, dēprompsī, dēpromptus, *to take out, produce; pour out, serve*.
Caecubus, -a, -um, *Caecuban*, famous wine of Latium; substantive for **Caecubum vīnum**.

6 **cella, -ae**, f., *room; wine cellar*.
avītus, -a, -um, *of forefathers, ancestral*. The adjective **avītīs** modifies **cellīs** grammatically, but its meaning is more appropriate for describing the wine, **Caecubum** (**vīnum**).
Capitōlium, -ī, n., *the Capitol, temple of Jupiter Optimus Maximus*; metonymy for Rome.

7 **rēgīna**: any suggestion of royalty was loathsome to the Romans; Cleopatra's name does not appear in Augustan poetry. Note the juxtaposition of **rēgīna** with **Capitōliō**.
***dēmēns, dēmentis**, *mad, insane, mindless*.

8 **fūnus et**: = **et fūnus**; here **fūnus** = *catastrophe, destruction*; emphatic position and metonymy.

9 **contāminō, -āre, -āvī, -ātus**, *to contaminate, infect, pollute*.
contāminātō . . . grege: note that **contāminātō** modifies **grege** and not **morbō**.
contāminātō . . . grege turpium . . . virōrum: this probably refers to the palace retinue of Queen Cleopatra, which consisted of eunuchs (**virōrum** is ironic). Romans would have typically considered such individuals contemptible and immoral.
grex, gregis, m., *pack, herd, flock, brood*.

10 **morbō**: take with **turpium** as *foul because of disease* (or *perversion*). Horace does not clarify his use of **morbus**, which might be either physical or psychological.
quidlibet: *anything at all*; direct object of **spērāre**. Cleopatra's hopes were limitless.
impotēns spērāre: *mad (enough) to hope*.

11 **fortūnā dulcī**: perhaps referring to Cleopatra's ability to get what she wanted first from Julius Caesar and then from Antony, or perhaps to her general position as queen.

LXVIII

A Roman Looks at Cleopatra

The following poem, written after the suicide of Cleopatra at the age of 39, one year after the battle of Actium, serves as a song of victory and thanksgiving for Augustus' delivery of the Roman people from the ambitions of a foreign woman. (Notice the omission of any reference to Antony in the poem.) Horace labels Cleopatra as a **fātāle mōnstrum** *but ends the poem in an unexpected way.*

Nunc est bibendum, nunc pede līberō
pulsanda tellūs, nunc Saliāribus
  ōrnāre pulvīnar deōrum
    tempus erat dapibus, sodālēs.

Antehāc nefās dēprōmere Caecubum
cellīs avītīs, dum Capitōliō
  rēgīna dēmentēs ruīnās,
    fūnus et imperiō parābat

contāminātō cum grege turpium
morbō virōrum, quidlibet impotēns
  spērāre fortūnāque dulcī
    ēbria.

(*continued*)

1. In what two ways does Horace invite celebration in lines 1–2?
2. How else is everyone invited to celebrate? (2–4)
3. What was it previously forbidden to do? (5–6)
4. What plans did Cleopatra have for Rome? (6–8)
5. To whom does Horace refer in lines 9–10? Who was helping/accompanying the queen?
6. How does the poet describe the queen in lines 10–12?

Reading Note

Transferred Epithet

In line 7 above, the adjective **dēmentēs** grammatically modifies **ruīnās** (both are acc. pl.), but more logically describes **rēgīna**—*insane queen* rather than *insane ruin*. This is called a *transferred epithet*. (Note that "epithet" originally meant any kind of descriptive phrase, not necessarily a negative or insulting one.) Another such transferred epithet is found in line 6, **cellīs avītīs**.

12 **furōrem**: what previous characterization of Cleopatra does this continue?

13 ***vix**, adv., *scarcely*, *hardly*. Take with **ūna.**

sospēs, sospitis, *safe*, *unharmed.*

vix ūna sospes nāvis ab ignibus: we learn from other sources that 60 ships accompanied Cleopatra back to Alexandria. Horace now moves from the celebration at Cleopatra's death to her flight from Actium some eleven months before.

14 **mentem**: i.e., Cleopatra's.

lymphātus, -a, -um, *driven crazy*, *deranged.*

mentem lymphātam: **lympha**, *spring water*, is a parallel form of **nympha**, *a spirit of nature*, the sight of which could produce hallucinations, irrational fears, or loss of wits.

Mareōticum, -ī, n., *Mareotic wine*, from the area around Lake Mareotis, near Alexandria.

15 **redigō, redigere, redēgī, redāctus**, *to drive back*, *reduce to a specific state.*

in vērōs timōrēs: as opposed to fantasies produced by wine.

16 **Caesar**: note the emphatic position of this word. **Caesar** serves as the subject of **redēgit** (line 15), **adurgēns** (17), and **daret** (20).

ab Ītaliā: more accurately, Horace should say *from Actium*, as Cleopatra's fleet set sail for Alexandria even before the battle was over. The poet is perhaps suggesting that Cleopatra was compelled to flee from her ultimate objective, which was Italy.

volō, -āre, -āvī, -ātus, *to fly*. (Do not confuse with **volō**, **velle**, *to want.*)

volantem: understand **rēgīnam.** This metaphor, used to emphasize Cleopatra's haste in escaping, is carried down into the next few lines to suggest Octavian's hot pursuit.

17 **rēmus, -ī**, m., *oar.*

adurgeō, adurgēre, *to press hard upon*, *pursue closely.*

rēmīs adurgēns: **rēmīs**, *oars*, stands for *ships*. Actually, Octavian returned to Italy for six months after the battle of Actium in order to deal with public unrest.

accipiter, accipitris, m., *hawk.*

accipiter velut: = **velut accipiter**. Note how **accipiter** is placed outside of and before its clause for emphasis.

18 ***mollis, -is, -e**, *soft.*

columba, -ae, f., *dove.*

accipiter . . . mollēs columbās: supply **adurgēns**, as in the following simile. Cleopatra now seems to be portrayed as a victim.

***citus, -a, -um**, *swift.*

citus / vēnātor: hunters usually ran behind their hounds when on a hunt.

19 **vēnātor, vēnātōris**, m., *hunter.*

nivālis, -is, -e, *snowy*, *snow-covered.*

20 **Haemonia, -ae**, f., *Haemonia*, a poetic equivalent of Thessaly.

daret ut: = **ut daret**, a purpose clause and another instance of a word placed outside its clause.

catēna, -ae, f., *chain.*

daret ut catēnīs: literally, *to give fatal chains*, i. e., *to put in chains.*

21 ***fātālis, -is, -e**, *given by fate*, *destined; fatal*, *destructive.*

Sed minuit furōrem
vix ūna sospes nāvis ab ignibus,
mentemque lymphātam Mareōticō
redēgit in vērōs timōrēs
Caesar, ab Ītaliā volantem

rēmīs adurgēns, accipiter velut
mollēs columbās aut leporem citus
vēnātor in campīs nivālis
Haemoniae, daret ut catēnīs
fātāle mōnstrum.

(*continued*)

---

7. To what historical event does line 13 refer? How is the outcome of this event described?
8. What effect did this event have on Cleopatra? (12)
9. What did Caesar (i.e., Octavian) do, as described in lines 14–16?
10. How is Cleopatra characterized in line 14? Where previously in the poem has she been described in these terms?
11. What is Cleopatra doing in line 16? What is Caesar doing? (17)
12. What comparisons are made in lines 17–20?
13. For what purpose was Caesar "hunting" Cleopatra? (20)
14. How does Horace characterize her in line 21?

Reading Note

Metonymy

Metonymy is a figure of speech in which an object is referred to by mentioning something else that is closely related. In line 6 on the previous page, **Capitōlium**, the temple of Jupiter, stands for Rome as a whole and **fūnus** (line 8), literally *funeral*, stands for *destruction*.

Portion of the outer wall of the temple of the goddess Hathor at Dendera, Egypt, showing Cleopatra and Caesarion (her son by Julius Caesar)
Outer wall of the Hathor Temple, Egypt, late Ptolemaic period, 47–30 B.C.

21 **Quae**: the antecedent of the linking **quī** is **rēgīna**, rather than the neuter **mōnstrum** as would be expected. The poet makes a striking change to the feminine **Quae**: *But she . . .*
generōsius: *more nobly, with greater dignity*. Horace's tone now becomes more sympathetic.
generōsius / perīre quaerēns: i.e., than Octavian had planned, which included display in the triumphal procession through the Forum (see lines 31–32) and then execution.

22 **muliebriter**, adv., *in womanly fashion, like a woman*. In saying that Cleopatra did not act "like a woman," Horace is indirectly praising the queen whom he had previously described as a madwoman and fugitive.

23 **expavēscō, expavēscere, expāvī**, *to fear especially, dread.*
***ēnsis, ēnsis**, m., *sword.*
expāvit ēnsem: perhaps an allusion to Cleopatra's attempt to stab herself, which was prevented by Proculeius, a friend of Octavian sent to Egypt after the battle of Actium.
latēns, latentis, *hidden, secret.*

24 **reparō, -āre, -āvī, -ātus**, *to get again, reach; get in exchange* (i.e., for her kingdom in Egypt).
***ōra, -ae**, f., *shore, coast.*
latentēs / . . . reparāvit ōrās: Horace is saying that Cleopatra did not flee into exile. She did, however, attempt to haul her ships over the isthmus of Suez to the Red Sea, but was prevented by Arabs from Petra, who burned them.

25 **ausa**: = **ausa est**, from **audeō** (not **audiō**).
et, adv., *even.*
iacentem . . . rēgiam: **iacēre** (note that this is not **iacientem**, from **iacere**) can mean *to lie in ruins* or *to lie prostrate, lie vanquished*. The palace (**rēgia**) stands by metonymy for Cleopatra's kingdom. (There is no evidence that Octavian destroyed Cleopatra's palace.)
vīsō, vīsere, vīsī, vīsus, *to look upon.*
rēgia, -ae, f., *palace.*

26 **vultū serēnō**: the Romans admired Stoic forebearance in facing life's difficulties.
***asper, aspera, asperum**, *harsh, rough; scaly.*
asperās / . . . serpentēs: these asps were both deadly poisonous and scaly to the touch.

27 **tractō, -āre, -āvī, -ātus**, *to manage; handle.*
fortis . . . tractāre: literally, *brave to handle, brave (enough) to handle.* In one account Cleopatra thrust her arm into a basket of figs that contained the asps; in another she held them to her breast. Cleopatra may have chosen the asp because it was a symbol of Egyptian royalty.
***āter, ātra, ātrum**, *black, dark; deadly.*

28 **combibō, combibere, combibī, combibitus**, *to drink in or deeply*. With **corpore**, *to drink by means of her body, to drink into her body*; an unusual ablative.
venēnum, -ī, n., *venom, poison.*

29 ***dēlīberō, -āre, -āvī, -ātus**, *to consider, weigh, choose; premeditate.*
dēlīberātā morte: ablative absolute.
ferōx, ferōcis, *fierce, wild; defiant.*

30 **Liburna, -ae**, f., *Liburnian galley*, a fast, light craft used in Octavian's fleet at Actium.
saevīs Liburnīs: ablative of means with **dēdūcī**.
invidēns: *hating, refusing to permit.*

(*vocabulary and notes continued on opposite page*)

Quae generōsius
perīre quaerēns nec muliebriter
expāvit ēnsem nec latentēs
classe citā reparāvit ōrās;

ausa et iacentem vīsere rēgiam
vultū serēnō, fortis et asperās
tractāre serpentēs, ut ātrum
corpore combiberet venēnum,

dēlīberātā morte ferōcior;
saevīs Liburnīs scīlicet invidēns
prīvāta dēdūcī superbō
nōn humilis mulier triumphō.

—Horace, *Odes* I.37

---

15. What two things did Cleopatra not do? (22–24) What reason does the poet give for these decisions? (21–22)
16. What two things did the queen dare to do? (25–27)
17. What was her purpose in doing the second? (27–28)
18. How is Cleopatra described after she made her choice? (29)
19. What was the queen reluctant to do? (30–32)
20. Cite from this poem five descriptive words or phrases in Latin that characterize Cleopatra.

31 **prīvātus, -a, -um,** *a private person* (vs. **rēgīna**, line 7), substantive.
***dēdūcō, dēdūcere, dēdūxī, dēductus,** *to lead, lead down.*
dēdūcī: this infinitive serves as the direct object of **invidēns**.
superbus, -a, -um, *proud, exalted; magnificent, splendid.*

32 **humilis, -is, -e,** *humble.*
nōn humilis: *not humble*, litotes for **superbus**, *proud.*
superbō . . . triumphō: the most obvious way to construe these words is as a dative of purpose with **dēdūcī**, *for the proud triumph*; i.e., Cleopatra would have been taken to Rome to be exhibited in Octavian's triumphal procession. (See the note on 56B:7.) However, these words might also be ablative with **nōn humilis mulier**. Could Horace be suggesting that Cleopatra had triumphed over the Romans by depriving them of the opportunity to humiliate and then execute her?

This is a marble bust of Cleopatra VII. She was of Macedonian, rather than Egyptian descent. She was the last member of the dynasty of Ptolemy, which ruled Egypt until it was incorporated into the Roman empire. Compare this depiction of Cleopatra with that shown on the coin on page 41.
Marble bust, before 31 B.C.

EMPEROR AND EMPIRE: THE RISE OF THE ROMAN PRINCIPATE

Overview of Part IV

In Chapter 57, you received an overview of events that took place between 27 B.C. and A.D. 14, with special attention to the career of Augustus, the first emperor of Rome. In Part IV you will read the emperor's actual words and, in addition, you will gain several perspectives on his imperial rule by reading about individuals both inside and outside of the imperial family. Part IV has the following specific objectives:

- to present the character and accomplishments of Augustus, the first Roman emperor
- to increase your ability to read Latin prose and poetry by working with selections from the *Res gestae divi Augusti*, Suetonius' *Vita Augusti*, and Ovid's *Tristia*
- to provide insight into the workings of imperial government, the activities of the imperial family, and the attitudes of those affected by imperial rule

In Chapters 56B and 68, you learned that it was near Actium, in Greece, that Octavian defeated the combined naval forces of Antony and Cleopatra to become master of the Mediterranean world. After his victory, Octavian gradually assumed autocratic powers under the guise of restoring the Republic and ushered in a period of **Pāx Rōmāna**. Command of the entire Roman Empire thus came into the hands of this one man, Gaius Julius Caesar Octavianus, called **Augustus** (*worthy of respect, venerable*), a title conferred on him by the Senate. His rule, which ended the Republic (509–27 B.C.), has come to be known as the Principate, from the unofficial title **prīnceps**, *first citizen*, which Augustus used to describe himself. The next 500 years of Roman history were dominated by over ninety-five rulers, or emperors, who reigned over the more than fifty million people of the Empire. The emperor, whose official title was **Imperātor**, was formally granted his powers through senatorial decree and through ratification by the people, but the real basis of his power was the allegiance of the military. The role of the Senate gradually became ceremonial, and its functions were assumed by a vast bureaucracy, mainly dependent upon the **auctōritās**, or personal prestige, of the emperor himself.

(*opposite page*) A marble statue, slightly over life size, of the Emperor Augustus found in the villa of his wife Livia at Prima Porta, just outside Rome. Note the cupid riding a dolphin at the emperor's feet, suggesting Augustus' descent from the goddess Venus. What other messages are sent by the gesture and pose, facial expression, and dress?
Marble sculpture, Augustus of Prima Porta, first century A.D.

Beginning with Augustus, both the military and civilian populations of the Empire swore an oath of allegiance to the new emperor and renewed it on each anniversary of his accession. The following oath was sworn to the Emperor Gaius (better known as Caligula) by a community in Spain in A.D. 37:

> I solemnly swear that I will be an enemy to those who I learn are enemies to Gaius Caesar Germanicus. If anyone brings or shall bring danger to him and his welfare, I will not cease to pursue him with arms and deadly war on land and on sea until he has paid the penalty to him; I will hold neither myself nor my children dearer than his welfare; and I will regard as enemies of mine those who have hostile intentions against him. If I knowingly swear or shall swear falsely, then may Jupiter Optimus Maximus and the deified Augustus and all the other immortal gods cause me and my children to be deprived of fatherland, safety, and all good fortune.
>
> —*Corpus inscriptionum Latinarum* II.172

In addition to oaths of allegiance, the relationship between ruler and ruled was fostered by emperor worship, through the imperial cult established by Augustus, and by emperor deification. Julius Caesar was the first Roman ruler to be declared a god posthumously by the Senate, and emperors as early as Caligula began to seek divinity during their reigns.

Imperial Propaganda

The symbolic linking of military victory, internal order, and happiness through divine providence is seen everywhere in the art and literature of the Augustan era. A good example of Augustan propaganda is the Ara Pacis, about which you will read in Chapter 69. The detail

The Ara Pacis was discovered during the 19th century, buried under a palace built during the Renaissance. It was recovered in the 1930s, despite great difficulties, and is now housed in a museum near Augustus' tomb. The actual altar, not visible in this photograph, is surrounded by an enclosure decorated with some of the finest Roman sculptural reliefs that have survived.
Marble, Rome, 13 B.C.

The goddess Pax from the Ara Pacis
Marble, Rome, circa 13 and 9 B.C.

in the picture below shows Pax; from another part of the altar comes a relief showing the family of Augustus in a sacrificial procession (reproduced on the cover of this book).

The breastplate of the Prima Porta statue (shown in detail below) offers symbolic messages that suggest the same imperial plan seen elsewhere in the art and architecture, coinage, and literature of the Augustan Age. The scene depicts an achievement of which Augustus was justly proud, a Parthian returning to the Romans the legionary standards lost in the East at Carrhae in 53 B.C. (See also the coin on page 49.) In a more general way, this scene represents the new imperial ideology of prosperity through peace. Below the central figures, Mother Earth (or possibly the goddess Pax) reclines holding an overflowing cornucopia. Barely visible to each side are figures of the deities Apollo and Diana. At the top left of the breastplate's pectoral zone hover Sol, riding in his chariot, and at right, the goddess Luna carrying a torch and the winged figure of Dawn. Above all, Caelus supports the vault of heaven. These earth and sky deities represent the eternal in nature. Their presence symbolically suggests that the gods approve of and protect Augustus; that the new **saeculum aureum** or Golden Age of Augustus is an event of cosmic significance.

These same virtues of the Augustan regime, which reach their highest form of expression in Vergil's epic poem the *Aeneid*, are celebrated in a hymn written to Apollo and Diana by the imperial poet Horace in honor of the Secular Games of 17 B.C.:

> And whatever the illustrious descendant of Anchises and Venus reverently entreats of you with sacrifice of milk-white oxen may he, triumphant over the war-maker but merciful to the vanquished foe, be granted his wish.
>
> Now the Parthian fears our forces, mighty by land and sea, and (dreads) the Alban axes; and now the Indians and Scythians, recently so arrogant, await our commands.
>
> Now Faith and Peace and Honor and Modesty of old and neglected Virtue venture to return, and blessed Plenty appears with a full horn.

—Horace, *Carmen saeculare* 49–60

1 **Annōs ūndēvīgintī nātus**: literally, *born for 19 years; at the age of 19.*
exercitum: Octavian raised an army because of his rivalry with Antony and his desire to exact vengeance from Caesar's murderers.
cōnsilium: *responsibility, initiative.*
impēnsa, -ae, f., *expense.*
comparāvī: note that Augustus is writing in the first person; these are his actual words.
prīvātō cōnsiliō . . . prīvātā impēnsā: why are these forms in the ablative case?
2 **per quem**: what is the antecedent of this relative pronoun?
ā dominātiōne factiōnis: Augustus is referring here to the political faction led by Marc Antony, who had challenged his rights as Caesar's heir in 44 B.C.
vindicō, -āre, -āvī, -ātus, *to claim as free, liberate; deliver.*
in libertātem vindicāvī: this refers to Octavian's freeing of Rome from the dominance of Antony's faction by defeating him in 43 B.C. in a battle at Mutina, Italy (see the map on page 18).

Eō nōmine: *For that reason.*
3 **senātus**: the subject of both main verbs in this sentence, **allēgit** (3) and **dedit** (4).
dēcrētum, -ī, n., *edict, decree.*
dēcrētīs honōrificīs: the decree granting Augustus the special powers mentioned here was moved by Cicero on 1 January 43 B.C.
allegō, allegere, allēgī, allēctus, *to elect, enroll.*
C. Pānsā et A. Hirtiō cōnsulibus: Pansa and Hirtius were consuls in 43 B.C.
4 **cōnsulārem locum**: *consular prerogative* or *privilege.*
sententiae dīcendae: *of giving an opinion.* The consuls had the privilege of being the first to speak in any debate in the Senate; this privilege was also extended to Augustus.
et: joins the two main clauses, **Eō nōmine . . . allēgit** (2–3) and **imperium . . . dedit** (4).
imperium, -ī, n., the *imperium* or *right to command* was the discretionary authority to do whatever the interests of the State required, especially the right to command armies.

5 **Rēs pūblica**: this phrase appears before the word **nē** that begins the clause.
nē quid dētrīmentī: literally, *not anything of harm, no harm*; **dētrīmentī** is partitive genitive. This clause contains official wording of the **senātūs cōnsultum ultimum**, *the final decree of the Senate*, which was passed during times of emergency. The decree, granting Octavian powers equivalent to those of a dictator, authorized Octavian and the consuls to lead troops against Antony in Cisalpine Gaul, which ultimately led to the battle of Mutina (for which, see line 2).
prō praetōre: *in place of a praetor, as a propraetor.* A propraetor was a magistrate with the powers of a praetor, who was a judicial official elected annually. Praetors also held the **imperium**, but this was subordinate to that of the consuls.
prōvideō, prōvidēre, prōvīdī, prōvīsus, *to look out, take precautions.*
6 **iussit**: governs **prōvidēre** on which depends the indirect command **nē . . . caperet**, line 5. The subject of **iussit** is **senātus**, carried over from the previous sentence (line 3).

LXIX

AUGUSTUS

A. Augustus Before the Principate (43–42 B.C.)

The Res gestae divi Augusti *survives as an inscription carved in Greek and in Latin on the wall of the temple of Rome and Augustus in Ankara, Turkey. (See the photographs below and on page 195.) The text was composed by Augustus himself shortly before his death. This inscription, called "the queen of Latin inscriptions," is a copy of the one that was ordered cut in bronze and erected in front of Augustus' mausoleum in Rome as a testament to the achievements of his principate. As you read, consider the purposes that such a text would have served and whether or not Augustus is giving an accurate account of his own principate.*

Annōs ūndēvīgintī nātus exercitum prīvātō cōnsiliō et prīvātā impēnsā comparāvī, per quem rem pūblicam ā dominātiōne factiōnis oppressam in lībertātem vindicāvī. Eō nōmine senātus dēcrētīs honōrificīs in ōrdinem suum mē allēgit, C. Pānsā et A. Hirtiō cōnsulibus, cōnsularem locum sententiae dīcendae tribuēns, et imperium mihi dedit. Rēs pūblica nē quid dētrīmentī caperet, mē prō praetōre simul cum cōnsulibus prōvidēre iussit.

(*continued*)

1. What did Augustus do at the age of nineteen? (1)
2. By what means did he achieve this? (1)
3. What had happened to the Roman state at this time? (2)
4. What was Augustus able to do as a consequence of his action? (2)
5. As a result, what did the Senate do? (3)
6. In what two ways did the Senate honor Augustus? (3–4)
7. For what purpose was Augustus declared propraetor? (5)

A portion of the *Res gestae*

7 **mē cōnsulem**: Augustus fails to mention that he compelled the Senate to validate his exceptional consulship by marching on Rome after defeating Antony at Mutina. In reality, the **populus** had little to do with it.

cōs.: inscriptional abbreviation for **cōnsul.**

in bellō: this refers to the battle at Mutina, mentioned above.

cecidisset: a form of the verb **cadō.**

8 **triumvirum reī pūblicae cōnstituendae**: *triumvir for the organization of the state.* After the battle of Mutina, Antony and Octavian were reconciled (see Chapter 56A, page 37) and together with Lepidus formed the Second Triumvirate and were given this legal title. See the coin on page 40, where the title appears to the right of Antony's head in the abbreviated form **III V R P C.**

creāvit: what is the direct object of this verb? How do the words **cōnsulem** and **triumvirum** relate to this direct object?

Quī . . . trucidāvērunt: refers to **eōs**. Relative clauses sometimes precede their antecedents.

parentem meum: who was this?

trucidō, -āre, -āvī, -ātus, *to murder.*

eōs: Brutus, Cassius, and the other senatorial assassins.

9 **iūdiciīs lēgitimīs**: *through legitimate tribunals*, set up in 43 B.C. by decree of the Senate.

ulcīscor, ulcīscī, ultus sum, *to punish, avenge.*

ultus: remember that the past participle of a deponent verb has an active meaning.

facinus, facinoris, n., *wicked deed, crime.*

bellum īnferre, idiom + dat., *to bring war to, wage war (on).*

reī pūblicae: dative with the compound verb **īnferō.**

10 **bis,** adv., *twice.*

aciēs, aciēī, f., *line of troops in attack formation, battle line*; here the word **aciēs** stands for the battle itself. (What figure of speech is this? Review the Reading Note on page 185.)

vīcī bis aciē: this refers to the two battles at Philippi, in Greece, where Brutus and Cassius were defeated in 42 B.C. See Chapter 56A.

Tēnē magis salvum populus velit an populum tū?
Servet in ambiguō, quī cōnsulit et tibi et urbī, Iuppiter.

Would the people wish you to be more secure, or would (you wish) the people (to be more secure)?
May Jupiter, who looks after the interests of both you and of Rome, keep the answer in doubt.

(L. Varius Rufus, *Panegyricus Augusti*)

Populus autem eōdem annō mē cōnsulem, cum cōs. uterque in bellō cecidisset, et triumvirum reī pūblicae cōnstituendae creāvit. Quī parentem meum trucidāvērunt, eōs in exsilium expulī iūdiciīs lēgitimīs ultus eōrum facinus, et posteā bellum īnferentēs reī pūblicae vīcī bis aciē.

—Augustus, *Res gestae* 1–2

---

8. What circumstances led to Augustus becoming consul? (7)
9. From whom did he receive this honor? (7–8)
10. Why was Augustus made a triumvir? (8)
11. Whom did he drive into exile? (8–9)
12. To what is Augustus referring in his use of the word **facinus**? (9)
13. For what other reason did he make war upon these men? (9) How did this conflict end? (10)

The Temple of Rome and Augustus in Ankara, Turkey (Roman *Āncȳra*), on whose walls the *Res gestae divi Augusti* was carved both in Latin and in a Greek translation.

1 **In cōnsulātū sextō et septimō**: 28 and 27 B.C.
exstīnxeram: from the verb **exstinguō**. Note the metaphor for putting out a fire.
cōnsēnsus, -ūs, m., *agreement, consent.*

2 **senātūs populīque Rōmānī**: embedded within the prepositional phrase **in . . . arbitrium** (3). The phrase **senātus populusque Rōmānus**, abbreviated **SPQR**, was the official, legal way of referring to the Roman government. The initials SPQR are still found in Rome today in many places as a marker of the city government—including stamped on manhole covers.
rem pūblicam . . . trānstulī (3): By laying aside all the extraordinary powers that the Senate had granted him during the civil wars, Augustus claims to have restored the Republic; however, he retained the powers of a tribune, which included the right to veto legislation and the power to command soldiers.

3 **arbitrium, -ī,** n., *mastery, control.*

Quō: *this*, a linking **quī,** modifying **meritō**.
meritum, -ī, n., *service.*
***cōnsultum, -ī,** n., *decree, decision, edict.* Do not confuse **cōnsultum** with **cōnsulem**.
Augustus appellātus sum: Augustus is also said to have considered the name Romulus. Some ancient writers date the beginning of the imperial monarchy to 16 January 27 B.C., when Octavian received the title Augustus.

4 **laurea, -ae,** f., *(leaves of) the bay tree; laurels, symbols of victory.*
***aedēs, aedis,** gen. pl., **aedium,** f., *building, temple*; pl., *house.*
vestiō, vestīre, vestīvī, vestītus, *to clothe, dress; to decorate, adorn.*
vestītī: = **vestītī sunt**. Can you locate another example of ellipsis in line 5?
***corōna, -ae,** f., *garland, wreath, crown.* The **corōna cīvica** was a crown of oak leaves awarded to a citizen soldier for saving the life of a comrade in battle. Augustus had saved lives by bringing the civil wars to an end.
***super**, prep. + acc., *over, above.*

5 **fīgō, fīgere, fīxī, fīxus,** *to fasten, attach.*
clipeus, -ī, m., *a large round shield,* also awarded to a soldier who had saved a life in battle.
***aureus, -a, -um,** *golden, of gold.*
Cūria Iūlia: the Curia was rebuilt by Julius Caesar after the Clodian fire (see page 147).
Senātum . . . dare (6): indirect statement governed by **testātum est** (6–7).

6 **clēmentia, -ae,** f., *mercy, forgiveness.*
pietās, pietātis, f., *duty, respect, devotion.*
virtūtis . . . pietātis: Augustan virtues were also represented on coins and inscriptions.
testor, testārī, testātus sum, *to bear witness, give evidence of, prove.*
testātum est per . . . īnscrīptiōnem (7): *the inscription proved,* literally, *it was proven through the inscription.*

7 ***auctōritās, autōritātis,** f., *influence, prestige; authority.* For this term, see page 4.
auctōritāte: *with respect to (my) influence*; ablative of respect.
auctōritate omnibus praestitī: Augustus claims to have ruled through the influence or prestige (**auctōritās**) he had obtained as a result of his preeminent service to Rome, rather than through his use of political power or official authority (**potestās**).

8 **autem**: Augustus uses this word to concede the fact that his authority had limits.
nihilō amplius . . . quam: *nothing more . . . than.* Take **nihilō amplius** with **potestātis** as partitive genitive.
mihi: *with reference* or *respect to me*, i.e., *my.*
magistrātus, -ūs, -m., *magistracy, office.*
collēga, -ae, m., *fellow official, colleague.*

B. Augustus at the Time of Transition to the Principate (28–27 B.C.)

In cōnsulātū sextō et septimō, postquam bella cīvīlia exstīnxeram, per cōnsēnsum ūniversōrum potītus rērum omnium, rem pūblicam ex meā potestāte in senātūs populīque Rōmānī arbitrium trānstulī. Quō prō meritō meō senātūs cōnsultō Augustus appellātus sum et laureīs postēs aedium meārum vestītī pūblicē corōnaque cīvica super iānuam meam fixa est et clipeus aureus in Cūriā Iūliā positus, quem mihi Senātum populumque Rōmānum dare virtūtis clēmentiaeque et iūstitiae et pietātis causā testātum est per eius clipeī īnscrīptiōnem. Post id tempus auctōritāte omnibus praestitī, potestātis autem nihilō amplius habuī quam cēterī quī mihi quōque in magistrātū collēgae fuērunt.

—Augustus, *Res gestae* 34

---

1. When does Augustus claim that the civil wars came to an end? (1)
2. According to Augustus, what was the source of his authority? (1–2)
3. What does the emperor claim to have done? (2–3)
4. For what reason was Octavian granted the title Augustus? From whom did he receive this title? (3–4)
5. What public honors were bestowed upon his house? (4–5)
6. What special item was placed in the Senate House? (5)
7. For what personal qualities was he recognized? By whom? (5–6)
8. In what way were these qualities publicly acknowledged? (6–7)
9. What does Augustus say about his **auctōritās**? (7) His **potestās**? (7–9)

The obverse of this coin of Augustus shows the *corōna cīvica* (above: 4–5) with the legend *OB CĪVĪS SERVĀTŌS* (*cīvīs* is an alternate spelling for *cīvēs*). The reverse shows the laurel branches that were also granted to Augustus (above: 4).

1 **bellum gerere**: idiom, *to wage war.* Cf. **bellum īnferre**, A:9.
Bella . . . cīvilia externaque: the direct objects of **gessī.**
orbis terrārum: *the world;* literally, *the circle of lands.*
2 **venia, -ae**, f., *pardon, forgiveness.*
pepercī: from the verb **parcō**, which takes the dative (**omnibus . . . petentibus cīvibus**).
omnibus . . . pepercī: as had Julius Caesar, who was famous for his clemency.

tūtō, adv., *safely.*
quibus tūtō ignōscī potuit: *who could be safely pardoned*, literally, *to whom it could be safely pardoned.* **Ignōscī** is the passive infinitive and is used impersonally.
3 **excīdō, excīdere, excīdī, excīsus**, *to exterminate.*

Omnium prōvinciārum: this genitive modifies **fīnēs**, the direct object of **auxī** (4).
populī Rōmānī: nominative plural or genitive singular?
quibus . . . fuērunt (4): literally, *to which there were; which had, that had.* **Quibus** is dative of possession. What is its antecedent?
4 **fīnitimus, -a, -um**, *neighboring, bordering.*
quae nōn pārērent imperiō nostrō: what type of clause? (See page 59.) This clause refers to those people who were not subject to Roman authority.
fīnēs, fīnium, m. pl., *territory*; plural of **fīnis.**
augeō, augēre, auxī, auctus, *to increase, extend, enlarge.*
fīnēs auxī: for the enlargement of the empire under Augustus, see the map on page 23.

5 **Cum ex Hispāniā Galliāque**: **cum** introduces the clause that ends with **rediī**. What is the meaning of **cum** when it is completed by a verb in the indicative? (Review page 76.)
eīs prōvinciīs: = **in eīs prōvinciīs.**
gerō, gerere, gessī, gestus, *to manage, supervise, oversee;* cf. the phrase **rēs gestae.**
rēbus . . . gestīs: what is this grammatical construction?
Ti. Nerōne P. Quīntiliō cōnsulibus: Nero and Quintilius were consuls in 13 B.C.
6 **āra, -ae**, f., *altar.*
Augustus, -a, -um, *Augustan, relating to Augustus.*
prō reditū meō: Augustus often left Rome to visit the provinces; he had left three years earlier, in 16 B.C. The altar was commissioned by the Senate in 13 B.C. and dedicated in 9 B.C.
cōnsecrandam: = **cōnsecrandam esse**, *ought to be/should be dedicated*; a passive periphrastic (see page 148). The infinitive in indirect statement is introduced by the main clause **senātus . . . cēnsuit** (6–7).
7 **ad campum Mārtium**: the Altar of Augustan Peace was located in the Field of Mars.
sacerdōs, sacerdōtis, m., *priest.*
virginēs Vestālēs: the Vestal virgins were the six chief priestesses of the state cult of Vesta and were chosen from the most aristocratic families. Vesta was the goddess of the hearth and home; a fire burned continuously in her temple, symbolizing the State as one "family." The most important job of the Vestals was to keep the fire burning.
8 **anniversārius, -a, -um**, *annual.*
sacrificium facere: the sculptured frieze around the altar depicts the first occasion of this annual procession. See the front cover of this book and page 190 for illustrations.
iussit: the subject is still **senātus.**

C. *Pāx Rōmāna*: The Augustan Peace (27 B.C.–9 B.C.)

Bella terrā et marī cīvilia externaque tōtō in orbe terrārum saepe gessī victorque omnibus veniam petentibus cīvibus pepercī. Externās gentēs, quibus tūtō ignōscī potuit, cōnservāre quam excīdere māluī. Omnium prōvinciārum populī Rōmānī quibus fīnitimae fuērunt gentēs quae nōn pārērent imperiō nostrō fīnēs auxī.

Cum ex Hispāniā Galliāque, rēbus eīs prōvinciīs prosperē gestīs, Rōmam rediī, Ti. Nerōne P. Quīntiliō cōnsulibus, āram Pācis Augustae senātus prō reditū meō cōnsecrandam cēnsuit ad campum Mārtium in quā magistrātūs et sacerdōtēs virginēsque Vestālēs anniversārium sacrificium facere iussit.

(*continued*)

---

1. In what types of wars did Augustus engage? Where? (1)
2. What does he say about his clemency? (2)
3. How did Augustus deal with defeated foreign peoples who no longer posed a threat to Rome (2–3)?
4. What claim does the emperor make in the sentence **Omnium . . . auxī**? (3–4)
5. How was Augustus honored on his return from Spain and Gaul? (6–7)
6. What special provisions did the Senate make regarding this structure? (7–8)

9 **Iānum**: Janus was a deity associated with entrances and exits and in the capacity designated here seems to have been protector (**nūmen**) of the gates of Rome.

Quirīnum: Quirinus was a local spirit associated with the Quirinal Hill and later was a god of war. At some point he became associated with Janus.

Iānum Quirīnum: Janus Quirinus refers to what was apparently an arched gate or temple in the Roman Forum, near the Palatine Hill. There are no remains of this structure, and its exact purpose and location are uncertain (see a later version depicted on the coin opposite). Some think that it was the gate through which the Roman armies marched en route to war.

Iānum . . . cēnsuit (12): this is a complex sentence. Read through the entire sentence to locate the boundaries of the various phrases and clauses. **Iānum Quirīnum** serves as the subject of the infinitive **claudendum esse** in indirect statement after **senātus . . . cēnsuit** (12) at the end of the sentence.

clausum esse: what is the tense and voice of this infinitive?

maiōrēs nostrī: *our ancestors.*

10 **imperium**: in this context, **imperium** means *empire.*

pariō, parere, peperī, partus, *to give birth to, produce, bring about.* Do not confuse this verb with **parcō** in line 2 or with **parō, parāre,** *to prepare,* or with **pāreō, pārēre,** *to obey.*

victōriīs: literally, *by means of victories; through conquest.*

pāx: note the emphatic position.

cum: *although.*

priusquam nāscerer: *before I was born.* Note that the clause **priusquam nāscerer** is nested within another clause, **cum . . . prōdātur memoriae.**

11 **ā conditā urbe**: remember that Rome was founded in 753 B.C., according to Roman tradition.

clausum fuisse: = **clausum esse.** This infinitive follows the verbal phrase **prodātur memoriae** in indirect statement.

prōdō, prōdere, prōdidī, prōditus, *to record, bring forth.*

prōdātur memoriae: literally, *it is handed down to memory that; tradition records that.*

ter, adv., *three times, thrice.* The three closings of Janus Quirinus took place in 29 B.C., 25 B.C., and at another unknown date. The gates had been closed only twice (**bis**) in the nearly seven hundred years between the founding of Rome and Augustus' birth.

mē prīncipe: what is this grammatical construction?

12 **claudendum esse**: *ought to be closed*; passive periphrastic in an indirect statement following **senātus . . . cēnsuit.**

Iānum Quirīnum quem clausum esse maiōrēs nostrī voluērunt cum per tōtum imperium populī Rōmānī terrā marīque esset parta victōriīs pāx, cum priusquam nāscerer ā conditā urbe bis omnīnō clausum fuisse prōdātur memoriae, ter mē prīncipe senātus claudendum esse cēnsuit.

—Augustus, *Res gestae* 3, 12, 13, 26 (extracts)

---

7. When had ancestral Romans closed the gates of Janus Quirinus? (9–10)
8. Since Rome's beginning, how many times had the gateway of Janus been closed? (11)
9. How many times was the gateway shut during Augustus' principate? (11–12)
10. Who decided that the emperor should be recognized in this way? (12)

Reading Note

Summary of Cum Clauses

When you encounter a **cum** clause, note first whether it is completed by a verb in the indicative; if so, the meaning must be *when* (temporal clause) as in line 5 on page 199. If the verb in the **cum** clause is subjunctive, observe whether **tamen** appears in the main clause; if so, **cum** must mean *although* (see the Reading Note on page 61). If **tamen** is not present in the main clause, try one meaning of **cum**, then another, to see which meaning makes the best sense in the context of the sentence. Be aware that *although* is the least common meaning of **cum**; *when* or *after* and *since* or *because* are much more frequent.

The shrine of Janus. The legend on this coin of Nero reads Pāce p(opulī) R(ōmānī) terrā marīq(ue) partā Iānum clūsit; compare this with Augustus' language in lines 9–10 above. The letters SC stand for senātūs cōnsultō, ***by order of the Senate.***

1 **Capitōlium, -ī**, n., *the Capitolium* or *Capitol* (the temple of Jupiter, Juno, and Minerva on the Capitoline Hill).

Pompeium theātrum: built by Pompey the Great, this was the first and most important stone theater in Rome. Julius Caesar was assassinated here.

Capitōlium et Pompeium theātrum: note that the pattern of the direct object at the beginning of the sentence and **refēcī** at the end is repeated in an almost formulaic way in this passage.

opus, operis, n., *(public) work.*

impēnsā grandī: *at great cost;* the ablative is used to indicate the cost of something.

reficiō, reficere, refēcī, refectus, *to rebuild, restore.*

sine . . . meī (2): it was customary for the emperor or other individual who was responsible for the construction or restoration of a public work to claim recognition by having his name and titles inscribed in the stone. Note the irony of the emperor's words here, given the fact that he is recording them in an inscription!

2 **rīvus, -ī**, m., *stream; water channel of an aqueduct* (**aqua**).

vetustās, vetustātis, f., *old age.*

lābentēs: present participle of the deponent verb **lābor.** (This verb does not mean *work.*)

3 **Marcia appellātur**: the Aqua Marcia, built in 144 B.C., was the first to contain arches.

duplicō, -āre, -āvī, -ātus, *to double*; i.e., he doubled the amount of water delivered by the Aqua Marcia.

***fōns, fontis**, m., *spring, source.*

fonte novō: remember that springs from the Appennine Mountains provided the source of the water brought by aqueducts into Rome.

Forum Iūlium: the Julian Forum (also called the Forum of Caesar), named after Julius Caesar, was dedicated in 47 B.C. along with the Basilica Julia (**basilicam**) in the Forum Romanum.

4 **aedem Castoris et aedem Saturnī**: the temple of Castor (Castor and Pollux were the Gemini) and the temple of Saturn (mythical god-king of early Rome) were also located in the Roman Forum. See the plan on page 147.

coeptus, -a, -um, *begun, undertaken.*

prōflīgātus, -a, -um, *nearly completed.*

5 **ā patre meō**: who was this?

eandem basilicam cōnsūmptam: the Basilica Julia burned in A.D. 12.

ampliō, ampliāre, ampliāvī, ampliātus, *to enlarge, increase.*

solum, -ī, n., *floor, foundation.*

sub titulō nōminis fīliōrum meōrum: Augustus means that he gave his adopted sons, Gaius and Lucius, all the credit (**sub titulō**, *under the title*) in the inscription.

6 **incohō, incohāre, incohāvī, incohātus**, *to undertake, begin.*

sī . . . nōn perfēcissem: *if I had not completed*; for conditional clauses, see pages 96–97.

perficī: do not confuse this with **perfēcī**. What is the subject of this infinitive?

7 **hērēs, hērēdis**, m., *heir.*

octōgintā, *eighty.*

deum: = **deōrum.**

sextum: *for the sixth time.*

D. Augustus During the Principate: The Building Program

Capitōlium et Pompeium theātrum, utrumque opus impēnsā grandī, refēcī sine ūllā īnscrīptiōne nōminis meī. Rīvōs aquārum complūribus locīs vetustāte lābentēs refēcī, et aquam quae Marcia appellātur duplicāvī fonte novō in rīvum eius immissō. Forum Iūlium et basilicam quae fuit inter aedem Castoris et aedem Saturnī, coepta prōflīgātaque opera ā patre meō, perfēcī et eandem basilicam cōnsūmptam incendiō, ampliātō eius solō, sub titulō nōminis fīliōrum meōrum incohāvī, et, sī vīvus nōn perfēcissem, perficī ab hērēdibus meīs iussī. Duo et octōgintā templa deum in urbe cōnsul sextum et auctōritāte Senātūs refēcī.

—Augustus, *Res gestae* 20

---

1. Of what two public works was Augustus especially proud, and for what reasons? (1–2)
2. In what specific ways did the emperor improve Rome's water supply? (2–3)
3. Which works begun by Julius Caesar did Augustus complete? (4–5) What was the location of the basilica? (4)
4. What special provisions did he make for the Basilica Julia? What had happened to this building? (5–6)
5. How many temples did Augustus restore? When and under whose auspices? (7–8)

The obverse of this coin shows Augustus, wearing a laurel wreath. On the reverse are Gaius and Lucius, his grandsons and adopted sons, who are mentioned above in line 6. The reverse reads C(āius) L(ūcius) CAESARES AVGVSTI F(īliī) CO(n)S(ulēs) DESIG(nātī) PRINC(ipēs) IVVENT(ūtis), *Gaius and Lucius Caesar, sons of Augustus, consul designates, leaders of the youth.* Prīnceps iuventūtis was a title that Augustus invented as part of his plan to prepare his grandsons to succeed him as rulers of Rome. See Chapter 70A and B for more about Gaius and Lucius.

Urbem excoluit adeō ut iūre sit glōriātus marmoream sē relinquere quam latericiam accēpisset. *He improved Rome to such an extent that he could rightly boast of having found it brick and left it marble.* (Said of Augustus, Suetonius, *Vita Augusti* XXVIII.3)

Exercise 69a

Read the following additional selections from Augustus' *Res gestae* and think about why he took the actions that he did and why he describes them as he does.

During the consulship of Marcus Vinius and Quintus Lucretius [19 B.C.], and afterward during that of Publius Lentulus and Cnaeus Lentulus [18 B.C.], and for a third time during that of Paullus Fabius Maximus and Quintus Tubero [11 B.C.], when the Senate and people of Rome agreed that I alone should be made overseer of laws and morals with supreme power, I accepted no office that was offered contrary to the customs of our ancestors. The things that the Senate wanted to be done by me at that time, I accomplished through the tribunician power, of which power I myself voluntarily five times asked for and received a colleague from the Senate. (*Res gestae* 6)

Note: Augustus did not actually hold the office of tribune, but was granted the same powers that tribunes had—including the right to propose and veto legislation. This tribunician power was one of the legal bases on which his rule rested; his colleagues in this power were his general and son-in-law Agrippa, and later his stepson Tiberius.

I refused to become high priest in place of my colleague who was still alive, when the people offered me this priesthood which my father had held. I received this priesthood some years later, after he who had seized it through the opportunity of civil unrest had died; a huge crowd gathered from all Italy for my election [as high priest], such as is said never to have been in Rome before that time, during the consulship of Publius Sulpicius and Gaius Valgius [12 B.C.]. (*Res gestae* 10)

Note: Marcus Lepidus, who formed the second triumvirate with Octavian and Antony (see Chapter 56A), took the office of **pontifex maximus** after the assassination of Julius Caesar. In 36 B.C. Octavian stripped him of all his powers except that of **pontifex maximus.**

Questions for Thought and Discussion

1. Was the *Res gestae* simply an autobiographical account of Emperor Augustus' life, or was there some other purpose for its publication? Cite an instance in which Augustus distorts the facts or omits important truths about what we know to have taken place historically.
2. Summarize the powers and honors received by Augustus during the years of his ascendancy. Are these consistent with his claim to have "transferred the Republic from my authority to that of the Senate and people of Rome"? What source of his power does he avoid mentioning?
3. Is there any inconsistency between the emperor's claim to have expanded the Empire and that of having brought peace to the world?
4. How might a building program contribute to the idea of imperial propaganda?
5. Elsewhere in the *Res gestae*, Augustus mentions that he received the title **Pater Patriae.** Based upon what you've learned about the emperor in these readings, do you think that he deserved this title? Why or why not?

LXX

An Emperor's Daughter

Several generations after Augustus died, a man from North Africa rose to prominence in Rome as a historian and biographer. That man was Gaius Suetonius Tranquillus (A.D. 69–after 130). During the reign of Emperor Hadrian, Suetonius, who was the emperor's personal secretary, produced his best known work, *De vita Caesarum*, commonly known as *The Twelve Caesars*. This collection of biographies of the twelve Roman rulers from Julius Caesar through Domitian covers the critical period of the end of the Republic and the transition to the Principate. It is from his *Vita Augusti* (*Life of Augustus*) that you will read in this chapter about Emperor Augustus' daughter (Julia the Elder, 39 B.C.–A.D. 14) and granddaughter (Julia the Younger, 19 B.C.–A.D. 28).

Because Suetonius is chatty and anecdotal in his writing style, he has much to say about the private life of the Emperor Augustus, the "kitchen details" of the imperial family, and, by association, the roles of men and women in Roman society. Julia the Elder had a difficult life. Augustus divorced her mother Scribonia on the eve of her birth. Julia subsequently became the only blood heir of the Emperor in a political world dominated by men and in a culture that gave pre-eminence to the birth of sons to carry on the family name. Taken from her mother, Julia was raised as an aristocratic Roman girl by her stepmother Livia, whom Augustus had married just a few days after Julia's birth. Although Augustus doted on his daughter, it was his desire that she should be exemplary, so her upbringing appears to have been strict and somewhat old-fashioned. This was, in part, motivated by political considerations, as Augustus was promoting a return to the moral virtues of earlier days, even while he was usurping the power of Republican governance. When Julia grew up, she became a pawn in the game of her father's political ambitions and was married successively to her cousin Marcellus (at age 14), her father's best friend Agrippa (at age 18), and her stepbrother Tiberius (at age 27). Augustus adopted her only sons, by Agrippa, as his own in 12 B.C. In 2 B.C., however, Julia was arrested for adultery and treason.

As you read about the women in Augustus' life, compare the public man, about whom you learned in the previous chapter, with the private man. Also think about what the story of the emperor's daughter might reveal about the role of women in Roman society.

Julia, daughter of Augustus
39 B.C. to 14 A.D.

1 **Agrippa**: Marcus Vipsanius Agrippa (64–12 B.C.), lifelong friend and right-hand man of Augustus. He married Julia (she was 18 to Agrippa's 43), who bore him five children. The relief shown on the cover of this book depicts Agrippa (the tall man with his toga drawn over his head) accompanied by his son Gaius and his wife Julia (in the background with her hand on Gaius' head).

habuit: the unexpressed subject is Augustus, who was still Octavian at this time.

Agrippam: also known as Postumus Agrippa or Agrippa Postumus. Postumus Agrippa was named after his father Agrippa, who had died before he was born.

neptis, neptis, gen. pl. **neptium**, f., *granddaughter*.

2 **Gāium et Lūcium**: see the coin shown on page 203.

per assem et lībram: a legal phrase often appearing as **per aēs et lībram**, literally, *by way of coin and the scales*, i.e., in the manner of a sale. The legal process of adoption, like that of freeing a slave, involved a fictitious "sale."

ēmptōs: modifies **Gāium et Lūcium**, the objects of **adoptāvit**.

3 ***tener, tenera, tenerum**, *young*.

adhūc, adv., *still*; take with **tenerōs**, modifying **Gāium et Lūcium**, understood.

***admoveō, admovēre, admōvī, admōtus**, *to move to, apply to, advance to*.

ad cūram reī pūblicae admōvit: i.e., he began to train them to become rulers of the state.

dēsignātus, -a, -um, *elect, designate*.

cōnsulēs dēsignātōs: in apposition to **Gāium et Lūcium** (2). During the Republic, the right to determine consuls had been in the hands of a popular assembly, albeit one in which the richest citizens held the majority. This right had been usurped by Augustus.

5 ***īnstituō, īnstituere, īnstituī, īnstitūtus**, *to establish, set up*; *to educate, instruct*.

lānificium, -ī, n., *working in wool; spinning, weaving*; from **lāna** + **faciō**.

assuēfaciō, assuēfacere, assuēfēcī, assuēfactus, *to accustom someone* (acc.) *to something* (dat.).

assuēfaceret: understand **eās** = **fīliam et neptēs**.

6 **prōpalam**, adv., *publicly, openly*, i.e., with the family. Understand **referrētur** with both **prōpalam** and the clause introduced by **quod**.

quod . . . referrētur: i.e., something of the type that might be reported; relative clause of characteristic.

diūrnus, -a, -um, *daily*; related to **diēs**.

diūrnōs commentāriōs: *daily journal, household notebook* or *diary*.

extrāneus, -ī, m., *foreigner, stranger*.

7 **coetus, -ūs**, m., *meeting*; from **cum** + **eō**.

coetū: *from meeting*; ablative of separation after **prohibuit**; understand **eās** (his daughter and granddaughters) as direct object of **prohibuit**.

ut . . . scrīpserit: what previous word anticipates this clause?

decōrus, -a, -um, *decent, well brought up*.

***iuvenis, iuvenis**, m., *young man*.

8 **parum**, adv. from **parvus, -a, -um**, *little, a little, too little*.

parum modestē: *with too little modesty, with a lack of modesty*.

fēcisse: *acted, behaved*.

eum: Vinicius.

salūtātum: *to greet*. See the Reading Note on the supine, opposite.

A. A Strict Upbringing

Nepōtēs ex Agrippā et Iūliā trēs habuit Gāium et Lūcium et Agrippam, neptēs duās Iūliam et Agrippīnam. Gāium et Lūcium adoptāvit domī, per assem et lībram ēmptōs ā patre Agrippā, tenerōsque adhūc ad cūram reī pūblicae admōvit, et cōnsulēs dēsignātōs circum prōvinciās exercitūsque dīmīsit.

Fīliam et neptēs ita īnstituit ut etiam lānificiō assuēfaceret vetāretque loquī aut agere quicquam nisi prōpalam et quod in diūrnōs commentāriōs referrētur. Extrāneōrum quidem coetū adeō prohibuit ut L. Viniciō, clārō decōrōque iuvenī, scrīpserit quondam parum modestē fēcisse eum, quod fīliam suam Baiās salūtātum vēnisset.

—Suetonius, *Vita Augusti* LXIV

---

1. How many grandchildren did Augustus have? (1–2)
2. What arrangements did the Emperor make for two of his grandsons? (2–3)
3. In what ways did he groom them for imperial rule? (3–4)
4. What was a main activity in the upbringing of the granddaughters? (5)
5. What specific things were they forbidden to do? (5–6)
6. How did Augustus try to make sure that Julia's behavior would always be socially acceptable? (5–6)
7. Why did the emperor scold Vinicius? (7–8)

Reading Notes

The Supine

In line 8 above, you met **salūtātum**, a form that looks like a perfect passive participle. This form, when used in the accusative case with a verb of motion (**vēnisset**) indicates purpose and is called a *supine*. The clue that you are dealing with a supine and not a perfect participle is the presence of the verb of motion in a context that indicates purpose; also, in this sentence, **salūtātum** clearly cannot agree with **Iūliam**. The only other use of the supine is in the ablative, with the 4th declension ending **-ū**, in adjectival phrases such as **mīrābile vīsū**, *amazing to see*, and **facile dictū**, *easy to say*.

• • •

Subordinate Clauses Inside Indirect Statement

In line 8 above, you noticed that **quod** is completed by the subjunctive verb **vēnisset**. A subordinate clause with the indicative becomes subjunctive when it is governed by an indirect statement. So this sentence:

Vinicius parum modestē fēcit quod Iūliam salūtātum **vēnerat**.

becomes an indirect statement such as:

Augustus scrīpsit Vinicium parum modestē fēcisse quod Iūliam salūtātum **vēnisset**.

This rule also explains why **nāscerer** (69C:11) is subjunctive.

1 **eum**: Augustus; object of **dēstituit**.
fīdēns, fīdentis, *confident in* + abl.
subolēs, subolis, f., *sprout, shoot; offspring*.
disciplīna, -ae, f., *instruction, training; management, orderliness*.
dēstituō, dēstituere, dēstituī, dēstitūtus, *to forsake, desert*.

Iūliās: both Augustus' daughter and granddaughter were named Julia.
2 **probrum, -ī**, n., *reproachful conduct, vice, depravity*. Their most objectionable behavior was promiscuity and infidelity. Their general disrespect of the conservative traditions of Roman womanhood defied Augustus' program to restore the family values of earlier times.
contāminō, -āre, -āvī, -ātus, *to render unclean, infect, pollute*.
relēgō, -āre, -āvī, -ātus, *to send away, banish*.
(Iūliās) . . . relēgāvit: Julia the Elder was confined to a remote island named Pandateria (modern Ventotene), where she spent six years, 2 B.C.. to A.D. 4. Julia the Younger was banished to the island of Trimerus, off the Apulian coast, where she died in A.D. 28 after twenty years of exile.
3 **Lycia, -ae**, f., *Lycia*, a region on the southern coast of Asia Minor (Turkey). See the map on page 270.
Massilia, -ae, f., *Massilia*, a seaport in Gaul (modern Marseilles).
dēfungor, dēfungī, dēfūnctus sum, *to perform, discharge; to die*.
dēfūnctīs: Note that the participle is in the plural because it modifies both **Gāiō** and **Lūciō** in this ablative absolute. Note also the asyndeton.

4 **aliquantō**, adv., *considerably, somewhat*.
patientius: comparative adverb of **patiēns**, from **patior**.
mortem: understand **suōrum** with both **mortem** and **dēdecora**.
dēdecus, dēdecoris, n., *shame, dishonor, disgrace*. Cf. **decōrus**, A:7.

5 ***frangō, frangere, frēgī, fractus**, *to break*.
fractus: take as a past participle modifying Augustus, understood.
nōn adeō fractus: *not broken*, i.e., affected, *so very much*; Suetonius implies that Augustus' heart was not so broken by the deaths of his two grandsons as it was by the disgraceful behavior of his daughter and granddaughter (2–3).
dē fīliā: take with **nōtum senātuī fēcit** (5–6).
absēns: *(Augustus) being absent, without being present*; serves as the present participle of **absum**.
libellus, -ī, m., *little book; letter*, referring to **nōtum . . . fēcit** (5–6). **Libellō** is a diminutive (note the double **l**; see the Reading Note on page 121).
per quaestōrem, *by the quaestor*; the quaestor read the letter aloud on behalf of Augustus.
nōtum facere, idiom, *to notify, inform*.
6 **abstineō, abstinēre, abstinuī, abstentus**, *to stay away, refrain from*. From **ab** + **teneō**.
congressus, -ūs, m., *gathering, social interchange, company*.
prae, prep. + abl., *on account of, because of*.
***pudor, pudōris**, m., *sense of honor, sense of shame*.
dē necandā: = **dē necandā eā** (= **Iūliā**).

7 **sub idem tempus**: *at the very same time*.

(vocabulary and notes continued on opposite page)

B. An Angry Father

Sed laetum eum atque fīdentem et subole et disciplīnā domūs fortūna dēstituit. Iūliās, fīliam et neptem, omnibus probrīs contāminātās relēgāvit; Gāium et Lūcium in duodēvīgintī mēnsium spatiō āmīsit ambōs, Gāiō in Lyciā, Lūciō Massiliae dēfūnctīs. Aliquantō autem patientius mortem quam dēdecora suōrum tulit. Nam Gāī Lūcīque cāsū nōn adeō fractus, dē fīliā absēns ac libellō per quaestōrem recitātō nōtum senātuī fēcit abstinuitque congressū hominum diū prae pudōre; etiam dē necandā dēlīberāvit. Certē cum sub idem tempus ūna ex cōnsciīs līberta Phoebē suspendiō vītam fīnīsset, māluisse sē ait Phoebēs patrem fuisse.

(*continued*)

---

1. How did Augustus feel toward his family? Why? (1)
2. What then happened? (1)
3. What did Augustus do regarding his daughter and his granddaughter? (2)
4. Why did he take this action? (2)
5. What happened to two of his grandsons? In what span of time? (2–3)
6. How did he feel about his daughter's behavior, compared to the loss of his grandsons? (4)
7. Describe Augustus' subsequent behavior. (4–6)
8. To what extent did his thoughts take him? (6)
9. What happened to one of Julia's confidantes? (7)
10. What did Augustus say about this? (8)

cōnscia, -ae, f., *a trusted person, confidante*. From **cum** + **sciō**.
Phoebē, Phoebēs, f., *Phoebe* (Greek name of a freedwoman).
suspendium, -ī, n., *hanging* (i.e., herself).
8 **māluisse**: a form of what irregular verb? This infinitive is in indirect statement after **ait**, the subject of which is Augustus (**sē**).
fuisse: complements **māluisse**.

Reading Note

Greek Noun Forms

Roman authors frequently used Greek names and Greek loan words, and they often kept the Greek case endings on such words instead of putting Latin endings on them. In Chapter 45, you met **Thisbēn**, the accusative of **Thisbē**, and in line 8 above you saw a Greek genitive, **Phoebēs**. This is similar to the practice of preserving the Latin plural form of words such as *alumni* when they are used in English.

9 **Relēgātae**: past participle of **relēgō** (see B:2); a substantive, referring to Julia, in the dative case with the compound verb **adimō**.
dēlicātiōrem: comparative of **dēlicātus, -a, -um**, *extravagant, luxurious.*
cultus, -ūs, m., *culture, refinement.*
adimō, adimere, adēmī, ademptus, *to take away something* (acc.) *from someone* (dat.)
adīrī: *to be approached*; present passive infinitive of **adeō, adīre** and dependent upon **permīsit** (10), with **eam** (= **Iūliam**) understood.
quōquam: from the indefinite pronoun **quisquam**, for which, see pages 160–161.
10 **-ve**: an alternate spelling of **vel**, both of which mean *or*. This enclitic, like **-que**, is attached to the end of the second of the two words that it binds together.
nisi sē cōnsultō: *unless he had been consulted*, an ablative absolute.
certior fierī, idiom, *to be informed.*
quā is aetāte: understand **esset** in this and the following clauses. Why subjunctive?
11 **statūra, -ae**, f., *stature, height.*
corporis notīs: *marks on the body; birthmarks.*
cicātrīx, cicātrīcis, m., *scar.*

12 **quīnquennium, -ī**, n., *a period of five years* (**quīnque** + **annus**).
dēmum, adv., *finally, at last.*
continēns, continentis, f., *the mainland*; actually, Regium (modern Reggio di Calabria). See the map on page 18.
lēniōribus: comparative of **lēnis, lēnis, lēne**, *more gentle*, i.e., *less severe.*

13 **ut omnīnō revocāret**: i.e., to Rome. This clause is governed by **exōrārī**, following.
exōro, -āre, -āvī, -ātus, *to entreat successfully, prevail upon.*
dēprecor, dēprecārī, dēprecātus sum, *to entreat, intercede, plead.*
14 **īnstō, īnstāre, īnstitī**, *to persist, insist.*
dēprecantī . . . populō Rōmānō et . . . īnstantī: dative object of **imprecātus** (15).
pertinācius: comparative adverb from **pertināx, pertinācis**, *tenacious, insistent.*
***coniūnx, coniugis**, m./f., *husband, wife, spouse.*
15 **prō contiōne**: *in public assembly*. For this term, see 64C:26
imprecor, -ārī, -ātus sum, *to invoke against, call down on.*
tālēs fīliās tālēsque coniugēs . . . imprecātus: i.e., he expressed a wish that the crowd asking for Julia's return might have wives and daughters who behaved as Julia did.

16 **damnātiō, damnātiōnis**, f., *condemnation, guilty verdict.*
ēdō, ēdere, ēdidī, ēditus, *to produce, bring forth; bear a child.*
agnōscī: present passive infinitive of **agnōscō**, *to recognize, acknowledge*. The legitimacy of a Roman child was acknowledged by the father, who picked up the child that had been laid at his feet; otherwise, the child would be left outside, where it could be found and raised by anyone, or could die of neglect. The cruel custom of exposure was rarely practiced.
alō, alere, aluī, altus, *to feed; to rear.*

Agrippam: Postumus Agrippa, the third son of Marcus Vipsanius Agrippa and Julia the Elder (see note on A:1).
17 **nihilō**, adv., *not at all, in no way.*
tractābilis, -is, -e, *compliant, manageable.*
in diēs, idiom, *day by day, every day.*
āmēns, āmentis, *foolish, senseless; insane, mad.*

(*vocabulary and notes continued on opposite page*)

C. The Fate of the Two Julias and Postumus Agrippa

Relēgātae ūsum vīnī omnemque dēlicātiōrem cultum adēmit neque adīrī ā quōquam līberō servōve, nisi sē cōnsultō, permīsit, et ita ut certior fieret, quā is aetāte, quā statūrā, quō colōre esset, etiam quibus corporis notīs vel cicātrīcibus.

Post quīnquennium dēmum ex īnsulā in continentem lēniōribusque paulō condiciōnibus trānstulit eam. Nam ut omnīnō revocāret, exōrārī nūllō modō potuit, dēprecantī saepe populō Rōmānō et pertinācius īnstantī, tālēs fīliās tālēsque coniugēs prō contiōne imprecātus.

Ex nepte Iūliā post damnātiōnem ēditum īnfantem agnōscī alīque vetuit. Agrippam nihilō tractābiliōrem, immō in diēs āmentiōrem, in īnsulam trānsportāvit saepsitque īnsuper custōdiā mīlitum. Cāvit etiam senātūs cōnsultō ut eōdem locī in perpetuum continērētur. Atque ad omnem et eius et Iūliārum mentiōnem ingemēscēns prōclāmāre etiam solēbat: αἴθ' ὄφελον ἄγαμός τ' ἔμεναι ἄγονός τ' ἀπολέσθαι, nec aliter eōs appellāre quam trēs vomicās ac tria carcinōmata sua.

—Suetonius, *Vita Augusti* LXV

---

11. After Julia was banished, what things was she denied? (9)
12. Under what conditions was a man allowed to come near her? (9–11)
13. What happened five years later? (12–13)
14. Who pressed for her return to Rome? In what manner? (13–14)
15. How did Augustus respond? (14–15)
16. What happened after Julia the Younger was banished? How did the Emperor react? (16)
17. What happened to Augustus' grandson? Why? (16–18)
18. What was the content of the senatorial decree? (18–19)
19. What would Augustus cry out at the mention of these family members? (19–20)
20. In what terms did he allude to his daughter, granddaughter, and grandson? (20–21)

saepiō, saepīre, saepsī, saeptus, *to enclose, confine.*
18 **īnsuper**, adv., *besides, moreover, furthermore.*

caveō, cavēre, cāvī, cautus, *to guard against, take precautions; to provide, order.*
eōdem locī: = **in eōdem locō**.
in perpetuum: *forever.*

19 **ingemēscō**: can you deduce from **gemō**?
20 **αἴθ' ὄφελον . . . τ' ἀπολέσθαι**: the Greek, which is transliterated *aith' ophelon agamos t'emenai agonos t'apolesthai*, means "I wish I had remained unmarried and had died without offspring." This is an adapted quotation from the *Iliad*, III.40, where Hector is venting his rage on Paris for ever having been born or married. Note that Augustus delivered this in Greek, a language learned by all educated Romans.
nec aliter . . . quam: *nor (and not) other . . . than, nothing else than.*
appellāre: dependent upon **solēbat**.
21 **vomica, -ae**, f., *sore, boil.*
carcinōma, carcinōmatis, n., *cancerous ulcer*

Meter: Elegiac couplet

1 **Triptolemus, -ī**, m., *Triptolemus*, the first human to whom the goddess Demeter taught the art of farming. He in turn spread this knowledge to all of Greece, riding in a winged chariot.
cuperem: *I would desire.*
***cōnsistō, cōnsistere, cōnstitī, cōnstitūrus**, *to come to a stop, stand still, stand.*
currus, -ūs, m., *chariot.*

2 **mīsit in ignōtam**: these words come outside the clause **quī . . . humum** to which they belong.
***ignōtus, -a, -um**, *unknown.*
rudis, -is, -e, *rough, wild.* The seed is **rude** because humans are just starting to learn agriculture, and **ignōtam** refers both to the newness of farming and the unfamiliar places to which Triptolemus brought this knowledge.
sēmen, sēminis, n., *seed.*

3 **frēnō, -āre, -āvī, -ātus**, *to put a bridle* (**frēnum**) *on, control, harness.*
dracō, dracōnis, m., *serpent, snake.* Winged serpents carried Medea away from Corinth in a chariot after she killed Jason's new wife and her own children by Jason.

4 **arx, arcis**, f., *citadel.*
arce: the ablative expresses the idea of *from . . .*; what is the clue to this?
Corinthus, -ī, f., *Corinth* (city in Greece where Jason and Medea took refuge).
Corinthe: vocative case; the speaker addresses the city as though it were a person.

5 **iactō, -āre, -āvī, -ātus**, *to beat repeatedly, flap.*
iactandās: *to be beaten, to be flapped*; a future passive participle.
optō, -āre, -āvī, -ātus, *to wish.*
***penna, -ae**, f., *feather*; here referring to the *wings* that were made from the feathers.

6 ***sīve . . . sīve**, *whether . . . or.*
Perseu: vocative case (Greek form). Perseus used winged sandals lent by Mercury.
Daedale: Daedalus made wings for himself and his son Icarus to escape from imprisonment in Crete. Note the chiasmus and asyndeton in this line, which links Perseus and Daedalus as the two examples of humans who used wings. The story of Daedalus appears in Chapter 73.

7 **ut**: introduces a purpose clause whose verb is **aspicerem** (8).
volātus, -ūs, m., *flight* (poetic plural here).
***aura, -ae**, f., *breeze.*
tenerā . . . cēdente . . . aurā: *while the soft breeze yielded to, gave passage to*, an ablative absolute.

8 ***aspiciō, aspicere, aspexī, aspectus**, *to look at, see.*
solum, -ī, n., *ground, land, soil.*

9 **dēsertaeque domūs vultūs**: *the faces of my deserted house*, i.e., the faces of those who lived in the house in Rome that Ovid was forced to abandon.
***memor, memoris**, *remembering, mindful.*

10 **coniugis**: Ovid's first marriage ended in divorce, the second with his wife's death. His third marriage lasted to the end of his life and he was apparently much in love with this woman (whose name we do not know). Several of the *Tristia* are addressed to her, and Ovid praises her devotion in his time of misfortune.

LXXI

POET AND PRINCEPS

In this poem, written after he was sent into exile, Ovid expresses his desire to escape from Tomis where he is so unhappy; even if he cannot go home, he might be sent to some less brutal place. The only way to accomplish this is to petition the all-powerful Augustus. (For more about Ovid's life, see the introduction to Chapter 74, page 261.) As you read, note particularly the lines that express Ovid's attitude toward the emperor.

A. Ovid's Desire to Return Home

Nunc ego Triptolemī cuperem cōnsistere currū,
    mīsit in ignōtam quī rude sēmen humum;
nunc ego Mēdēae vellem frēnāre dracōnēs,
    quōs habuit fugiēns arce, Corinthe, tuā;
nunc ego iactandās optārem sūmere pennās,
    sīve tuās, Perseu, Daedale, sīve tuās:
ut tenerā nostrīs cēdente volātibus aurā
    aspicerem patriae dulce repente solum,
dēsertaeque domūs vultūs, memorēsque sodālēs,
    cāraque praecipuē coniugis ōra meae.

Persephone and Demeter bid farewell to Triptolemus as he sets out to spread the knowledge of agriculture. They hold torches, which were symbols of the cult of Demeter at Eleusis, and sheaves of wheat. The wings on the chariot are clearly visible, and Triptolemus' chariot, like that of Medea, is drawn by snakes.
Greek vase painting, 490–480 B.C.

---

1. What four characters from mythology would Ovid like to emulate? What could these characters all do? By what means? (1–6)
2. What places and people would Ovid like to see? (8–10) How does he hope to do this? (7)

Reading Note

Synecdoche

Synecdoche is the use of a part of something to stand for the entire object. In line 5 above, the feathers (**pennās**) are used to indicate the wings as a whole. Other common examples are the use of **carīna**, *keel*, to stand for **nāvis**, *ship*, or **tēctum**, *roof*, for **domus**, *house*. Synecdoche is not the same as metonymy (page 185), where an idea is represented by a related (but separate) concept.

11 **Stulte**: *You fool;* the poet addresses himself.
quid: = **cūr** (as often in poetry).
vōtum, -ī, n., *vow, prayer, wish.*
puerīlis, -is, -e, *boyish, childish.*
12 **nōn ūlla**: equivalent to **nūlla**.

13 **semel**, adv., *once; at some time.*
optandum est: supply **tibi.** When a passive periphrastic is used impersonally, as here, it is better to translate it in the active (review page 148).
14 **quem**: the antecedent of **deum**; the relative clause appears before the main clause.
quem sēnsistī: *whom you have perceived*, i.e., whose power you have felt.
rīte, adv., *properly.*
precor, -ārī, -ātus sum, *to pray to.*
precāre: imperative singular of a deponent verb.

15 **volucer, volucris, volucre**, *winged, flying.*
16 **det**: present subjunctive of **dō, dare**. How is the subjunctive translated when it is the main verb? (Review pages 117–118.)
prōtinus, adv., *immediately.*
āles, ālitis, *winged.*

18 **modesta parum**, *too little modest*, i.e., *immodest, overreaching, asking too much.*

19 **forsitan**, adv., *perhaps.*
hoc: this word was originally spelled **hocce**; for this reason it scans as a long syllable. **Hoc** is the object of **rogandus erit** and refers to permission for Ovid to return to Rome.
satiō, -āre, -āvī, -ātus, *to satisfy, satiate.*

21 **Quod minus**: *A lesser thing.*
īnstar, indeclinable, n., plus genitive, *image, likeness.* This word is often translated with the adjective *like*, so **īnstar mūneris amplī** = *like a great gift.*
22 **quōlibet**, *anywhere* (literally, *to where it is pleasing*, **quō** + **libet**).

23 **faciunt**: supply something like **mē fēlīcem**.
24 **ei mihi**, *oh, poor me.*
corpora: plural, but translate in the singular.
languor, languōris, m., *weakness.*

25 **seu**: alternate form of **sīve**.
vitiō, -āre, -āvī, -ātus, *to weaken.*
***artus, -ūs**, m., *limb, part of body.*
contāgium, -ī, n., *disease, contagion.*
26 **malī**: *bad thing, trouble, difficulty, distress*; a substantive.
27 ***tangō, tangere, tetigī, tactus**, *to touch; to reach, arrive at.*
Pontus, -ī, m., *the Black Sea*, called in antiquity the Pontus Euxīnus. For this and the location of Tomis, see the map on page 23.
28 **ōs, ossis**, n., *bone.*
maciēs, maciēī, f., *thinness.*

Stulte, quid haec frūstrā vōtīs puerīlibus optās,
quae nōn ūlla tibī fertque feretque diēs?
Sī semel optandum est, Augustī nūmen adōrā,
et, quem sēnsistī, rīte precāre deum.
Ille tibī pennāsque potest currūsque volucrēs
trādere. Det reditum, prōtinus āles eris.
Sī precer hoc (neque enim possum maiōra rogāre)
nē mea sint, timeō, vōta modesta parum.
Forsitan hoc ōlim, cum iam satiāverit īram,
tum quoque sollicitā mente rogandus erit.
Quod minus intereā est, īnstar mihi mūneris amplī;
ex hīs mē iubeat quōlibet īre locīs.

---

3. What rhetorical question does Ovid ask? (11–12)
4. What does the poet urge himself to do? (13–14)
5. What can Augustus do for the poet? (15–16)
6. What might happen if Ovid asked to return home? (17–18)
7. When will it be proper to make such a request? (19) In what frame of mind would such a request be made? (20)
8. What might Augustus do even if he did not allow Ovid to return home? (22) How would Augustus regard this? How would the poet regard it? (21)

B. Ovid's Unhappiness in Exile

Nec caelum nec aquae faciunt nec terra nec aurae;
ei mihi, perpetuus corpora languor habet!
Seu vitiant artūs aegrae contāgia mentis,
sīve meī causa est in regiōne malī,
ut tetigī Pontum, vexant īnsomnia, vixque
ossa tegit maciēs nec iuvat ōra cibus;

(*continued*)

---

1. How does Ovid feel physically? (23–24)
2. What two possible explanations does he give for his condition? (25–26)
3. What symptoms has Ovid experienced since arriving in Pontus? (27–28)

29 **quī**: the relative clause comes before its antecedent **color** (30); *and the color which . . .*
percutiō, percutere, percussī, percussus, *to strike.*
frīgus, frīgoris, n., *cold.*
30 **folium, -ī,** n., *leaf.*
***hiems, hiemis,** f., *winter.*
laesit: the onset of winter (**nova hiems**) "harms" or "attacks" the leaves by freezing them, turning them shriveled and brown. Ovid states that his physical appearance is like shriveled leaves, but this is also a reflection of his mental condition.
31 **is**: i.e., **is color.**
***vīribus**: ablative plural of **vīs**; remember that this word means *strength* in the plural.
allevō, -āre, -āvī, -ātus, *to lift up.*
32 **querulus, -a, -um,** *complaining, full of complaints.*

33 **melius valeō**: *I am in better health, I am healthier.*
corpore, mente: *in body, in mind,* ablatives of specification; **mente** completes the idea of **melius valeō**, which is then followed by the comparative **quam.**
34 **bīnī, -ae, -a,** *two at a time, double.*
damnum, -ī, n., *loss, damage; hurt.*

35 **velutī**: alternate form of **velut,** *just as.*
spectābilis, -is, -e, *visible.*
36 **astō, astāre, astitī [ad + stō],** *to stand before.*
fortūnae forma . . . meae: *the shape of my fortune,* i.e., the dramatic changes in Ovid's circumstances when he was sent into exile. Notice how Ovid progresses from describing his physical condition (23–32) to his mental condition (33–36); his unhappiness is almost like a physical presence, a constant reminder of what he has lost.
legenda: *to be read.*
37 **locum**: the place of his exile, Tomis.
cultus, -ūs, m., *cultivation; culture, civilization.*
sonus, -ī, m., *sound* (of the language spoken in Tomis).
38 **cernō, cernere, crēvī, crētus,** *to discern, distinguish, perceive.*
cernimus: Roman poets often use the first person plural where the singular is meant.
quī sim quī fuerimque: this relative clause is the subject of **subit.** Again Ovid stresses the contrast between his earlier life in Rome and his current life in exile.
subeō, subīre, subiī or **subīvī, subitūrus,** irreg., *to come up under, come before, approach, come to.*
subit: supply **mē.**
39 **nex, necis,** f., *killing, death.*
queror, querī, questus sum, *to complain, find fault (with).*
querar: this verb belongs with the result clause introduced by the following **ut.**
cum: how can you tell that this is the preposition *with* and not the conjunction?
40 **offēnsās . . . suās**: *his offenses = offenses against him.*
vindicō, -āre, -āvī, -ātus, *to avenge.*

41 **est . . . ūsus**: = **ūsus est**; in this context **ūtor** = *act upon, express.* Remember that **ūtor** is one of the deponent verbs that take their object in the ablative (see the Reading Note on page 100).
odium, -ī, n., *hatred.*
cīvīliter, adv., *politely, in a civil way, gently*; i.e., he exiled Ovid rather than executed him.
42 **mūtātō . . . locō**: ablative absolute.
sit: *may be,* potential subjunctive.

quīque per autumnum percussīs frīgore prīmō
    est color in foliīs, quae nova laesit hiems,
is mea membra tenet, nec vīribus allevor ūllīs,
    et numquam querulī causa dolōris abest.
Nec melius valeō, quam corpore, mente, sed aegra est
    utraque pars aequē bīnaque damna ferō.
Haeret et ante oculōs velutī spectābile corpus
    astat fortūnae forma legenda meae:
cumque locum mōrēsque hominum cultūsque sonumque
    cernimus, et, quī sim quī fuerimque, subit,
tantus amor necis est, querar ut cum Caesaris īrā,
    quod nōn offēnsās vindicet ēnse suās.
At, quoniam semel est odiō cīvīliter ūsus,
    mūtātō levior sit fuga nostra locō.

—Ovid, *Tristia* III.8

---

4. What does his body look like? (29–31)
5. What is never lacking? (32)
6 How does Ovid's mental condition compare with his physical condition? (33–34)
7. To what are the changes in Ovid's fortune similar? (35–36)
8. What things does Ovid perceive? (37)
9. What awareness presses upon him? (38)
10. What desire does Ovid have when he considers his situation? (39)
11. Why does the poet complain about the emperor's anger? (39–40)
12. Why does Ovid hope that his exile may become more bearable? Under what circumstances? (41–42)

Reading Note

Future Passive Participles

In Chapters 63 and 64, you learned some uses of the gerundive or future passive participle. One common use is the passive periphrastic, such as **Liber mihi legendus est**, *I must read the book.* A more literal translation is *The book is to be read by me*, which clearly shows the identity of the gerundive as a future passive participle.

Sometimes such future passive participles are found by themselves (i.e., not in a passive periphrastic), as in line 36 above;

The shape of my fate stands to be read (**legenda**); also **iactandās** in line 5.

Here is another example:

Ovidius magistrō nāvis carmina Rōmam afferenda dedit.
Ovid gave the captain of the ship poems to be taken to Rome.

This Roman mosaic from Tunisia shows Vergil seated between two Muses. He holds a scroll that is open to Book I, line 8 of the *Aeneid*: Mūsa, mihī causās memorā, quō nūmine laesō.

Mosaic, Vergil and Two muses, Tunis, early third century A.D.

POETS IN THE AGE OF AUGUSTUS

Overview of Part V

The reign of Augustus (27 B.C.–A.D. 14) was a time when poetry flourished. Three of Rome's greatest poets—Vergil, Horace, and Ovid—lived and worked during this time. Part V has the following objectives:

- to review what you learned in Book II of *Ecce Romani* about the *Aeneid* and to present selections from *Aeneid* IV that deal with the love of Dido and Aeneas
- to provide additional background about the poet Horace, whose work you first met in Chapter 68, and some additional poems by him
- to present two episodes from Ovid's *Metamorphoses*, about which you learned in Chapter 45, along with more information about Ovid's life and work
- to help you become more adept at reading Latin poetry by working through the selections in these three chapters
- to develop greater appreciation for the stylistic features that make reading poetry in the original language interesting and rewarding

Chapter 72: Vergil's *Aeneid*

In Chapters 38–39, you met Vergil's great epic, the *Aeneid*. The poem was not quite finished when Vergil died in 19 B.C. His executors disobeyed his instructions to burn the poem; instead, they published it. It was immediately recognized as a great masterpiece and was soon read by students in school, as you saw in Chapter 38. Books I–VI deal with the destruction of Troy and Aeneas' adventures before arriving in Italy, while Books VII–XII describe how he fought against great odds to settle there. Many of Aeneas' difficulties were caused by the goddess Juno, who knew that her favorite city, Carthage, would ultimately perish if the Trojans established a new city in Italy.

In Book I, we encounter Aeneas in the midst of a great storm caused by Juno, which drives his fleet from Sicily down toward the African coast near Carthage. Juno and Venus make Dido, the queen of Carthage, fall madly in love with Aeneas, because they believe that this will ensure his safety and that of his men; Juno also hopes that he will stay in Carthage permanently. Aeneas relates the fall of Troy to the audience at Dido's banquet (Book II) and then describes his seven years of wandering (Book III).

In Book IV, Dido and Aeneas become lovers. Dido convinces herself that she and Aeneas are, in effect, married, and they live together for several months. Observing Aeneas' long stay in Carthage, Jupiter finally sends Mercury to order Aeneas to resume his trip to Italy without delay and accomplish what fate had in store for him.

305 **dissimulō, -āre, -āvī, -ātus**, *to conceal, cover up.*
dissimulāre: a complementary infinitive with **posse** (306).
spērāstī: = **spērāvistī**. See the Reading Note on syncopated verbs, page 179. Observe that **dissimulāre etiam spērāstī** is the first of five rhetorical questions (see page 69).
perfidus, -a, -um, *treacherous*; as substantive, *traitor.*
306 **nefās**, indeclinable, *unspeakable*; as neuter substantive, *crime, wickedness.*
meā . . . terrā: *from my land.*

307 **tē**: direct object of **tenet** (308). Note how the anaphora emphasizes *you.*
dextera: *right hand* given as a pledge. Earlier in Book IV, Dido convinced herself that she and Aeneas were for all practical purposes married, even though no actual marriage had taken place nor had Aeneas made any commitment to stay with her permanently.
308 **moritūra**: Dido may have already decided to commit suicide, although this is not completely clear. Aeneas probably thought **moritūra** would refer to being captured and killed by her brother or by the African tribes (see lines 325–326).
Dīdō: the separation of the name from the participle **moritūra** and its placement at the end of the sentence add great emphasis. Lines 307–308 also form a tricolon crescens; see the Reading Note opposite.

309 **Quīn etiam**: *In fact, are you even . . .*
hibernus, -a, -um, *winter* (adjective not noun). Greeks and Romans avoided sailing in the winter if they could, due to the storms, so Dido is skeptical about the reasons for Aeneas' sudden departure during the winter.
mōlior, -īrī, -ītus sum, *to struggle, work hard at; to build, equip.*
sīdus, sīderis, n., *star, constellation.* Since the stars that are visible change with the seasons, **hibernō . . . sīdere** = *during the winter season*; **sīdere** stands for **tempore**.
310 **Aquilō, Aquilōnis**, m., *north wind* (more prominent during the winter). **Aquilō** is used to mean **tempestās**, *storm.*
mediīs . . . Aquilōnibus: ablative of time when.
***altum**: *the deep, the sea*; a neuter substantive.

311 ***arvum, -ī**, n., *region, land, field.*
aliēnus, -a, -um, *belonging to another, foreign.*
313 **undōsus, -a, -um**, *full of waves, billowy.*
***aequor, aequoris**, n., *flat surface, sea.*

Reading Note

Preposition Omitted with Compound Verbs

In line 306 opposite, you noticed that **meā . . . terrā** is in the ablative case without a preposition and means *from my land.* The prefix **dē-** on **dēcēdere** means *from*, so Vergil did not feel it necessary to include a separate preposition. Such omission of prepositions happens frequently with compound verbs.

DIDO AND AENEAS

A. Dido Confronts Aeneas

After being told by Mercury that he must leave Carthage to pursue his destiny in Italy, Aeneas ordered his men to prepare for departure while he searched for the best way to tell Dido. She, however, heard about the preparations and angrily confronted Aeneas.

"Dissimulāre etiam spērāstī, perfide, tantum
posse nefās tacitusque meā dēcēdere terrā?
Nec tē noster amor nec tē data dextera quondam
nec moritūra tenet crūdēlī fūnere Dīdō?
Quīn etiam hībernō molīrīs sīdere classem
et mediīs properās Aquilōnibus īre per altum,
crūdēlis? Quid, sī nōn arva aliēna domōsque
ignōtās peterēs, et Troia antīqua manēret,
Troia per undōsum peterētur classibus aequor?

(*continued*)

---

1. What two things does Dido accuse Aeneas of hoping to be able to do? (305–306)
2. Dido asks whether three things might influence Aeneas to stay. What are they? (307–308)
3. What is Aeneas doing that seems unusual to Dido? (309–310)
4. What hypothetical question does Dido ask in lines 311–313?

Reading Note

Tricolon

In lines 307–308 above, you met a sentence with three clauses:

nec tē noster amor (tenet)
nec tē data dextera quondam (tenet)
nec (tē) moritūra tenet crūdēlī fūnere Dīdō?

A series of three phrases or clauses, parallel in structure, is called a *tricolon*. (Observe that the verb **tenet** is gapped in the first two clauses and the pronoun **tē** in the third.) Note also the anaphora with **nec**; such repetition is common in tricola. It is also common for the last member of the tricolon to be the longest and/or most important, as here. The name *tricolon crescens* is used to describe such an arrangement. A tricolon reinforces the writer's point through the sequential buildup of ideas or examples.

314 **Mēne fugis?**: the emphatic placement of **Mē** and the short sentence, contrasted with the complex sentences that precede and follow, make Dido's point very effectively.

Per: in oaths, *by*.

ego: subject of the verbs **meruī** (317) and **ōrō** (319). Note how this word interrupts the prepositional phrases introduced by **Per**. The placement of this word and its separation from **tē** and from the verbs that complete it make it particularly emphatic.

tē: object of **ōrō** (319).

***lacrima, -ae**, f., *tear*.

315 **quandō**: *since*, a less common meaning of this word.

aliud . . . nihil: *nothing else*, i.e. than my tears and the pledge of your right hand.

316 **cōnūbium, -ī**, n., *marriage*. See the note for line 307.

hymenaeus, -ī, m., a Greek refrain used at weddings; in the plural, *wedding*.

317 **sī . . . quid**: what is the meaning of this indefinite expression (review page 161, note 2, if necessary). Another example occurs below in line 319, **sī quis**.

(sī) fuit aut tibi quicquam / dulce meum: *or (if) anything of mine has been sweet for you.*

318 ***misereor, miserērī, miseritus sum** + gen., *to take pity on, feel sorry for*.

miserēre: how do you know this is an imperative and not an infinitive?

domūs lābentis: *(my) falling house*; *house* can mean *family* or *dynasty*. Dido's position is precarious (see 320–321 and 325–326), and she has no children to carry on her line.

istam: modifies **mentem** (319).

319 **prex, precis**, f., *prayer, entreaty*.

locus: supply **est**.

exuō, exuere, exuī, exūtus, *to take off; to put aside*.

mentem: here, *intention, plan* (of leaving).

320 **Tē propter**: the **Tē** is strongly emphasized by being placed in front of the preposition.

Libycus, -a, -um, *Libyan*.

Nomas, Nomadis, m., *Numidian*, member of a tribe in North Africa whose territory was west and south of Carthage.

tyrannus, -ī, m., *ruler, king*.

321 **ōdī, ōdisse**, *to hate*.

ōdēre: an alternate form of **ōdērunt**, *they hate*.

īnfēnsus, -a, -um, *hostile*.

Tyrius, -a, -um, *Tyrian, from Tyre* (city in Phoenicia from which Dido and her followers had fled; see the map on page 23). Vergil often refers to Carthaginians as Tyrians.

īnfēnsī Tyriī: supply **sunt**.

tē propter eundem: *because of the same you = likewise because of you*. The word **īdem** is often used this way. Note the emphatic anaphora of **tē propter**. This sentence continues on page 225.

Reading Note

The Ending -ēre

In line 321 opposite, you met **ōdēre**. Recall that **-ēre** is an alternative ending for **-ērunt** in the third person plural of the perfect tense (review the Reading Note on page 116).

Mēne fugis? Per ego hās lacrimās dextramque tuam tē
(quandō aliud mihi iam miserae nihil ipsa relīquī),
per cōnūbia nostra, per inceptōs hymenaeōs,
sī bene quid dē tē meruī, fuit aut tibi quicquam
dulce meum, miserēre domūs lābentis et istam,
ōrō, sī quis adhūc precibus locus, exue mentem.
Tē propter Libycae gentēs Nomadumque tyrannī
ōdēre, īnfēnsī Tyriī; tē propter eundem

(*continued*)

5. What is the central question in Dido's mind? (314)
6. Why does Dido call upon her tears and Aeneas' right hand to witness her request? (315)
7. What two other things does she call upon as witnesses? (316)
8. For what reasons might Aeneas be moved? (317–318)
9. What two things does Dido ask of Aeneas? (318–319)
10. Under what condition might Aeneas listen? (319)
11. What two difficulties does Dido claim she faces because of Aeneas? (320–321)

Reading Notes

Intransitive Verbs with Genitive

In line 318 above, you met the phrase **miserēre domūs lābentis**. The words **domūs lābentis** are the object of **miserēre**, which is one of a small group of verbs that take their object in the genitive. Here is a list of these verbs:

meminī, meminisse, *to remember*
misereor, miserērī, miseritus sum, *to take pity on, feel sorry for*
oblīvīscor, oblīvīscī, oblītus sum, *to forget*
potior, potīrī, potītus sum, *to get control, get possession of* (**potior** can also take the ablative)

This group is the last of the special verbs that take a case other than the accusative as their object. You already know about intransitive verbs that take the dative (see page 31) and about the five deponent verbs that take the ablative (see page 100).

• • •

Verbs with Forms in the Perfect System Only

In line 321 above, you met **ōdēre**, *(they) hate*; you also saw **ōdī**, *I hate*, in 62G:1. This verb is found only in the perfect, pluperfect, and future perfect tenses; the perfect is translated as a present, the pluperfect as a perfect, and the future perfect as a simple future. The verb **meminī**, *to remember*, given in the Reading Note above, works the same way: so **meminit** = *he remembers*, **meminerat** = *he remembered*, and **meminerit** = *he will remember*.

322 **exstīnctus**: supply **est**; this verb is the predicate to both **pudor** and **fāma** (323).
pudor, pudōris, m., *sense of honor, sense of shame*. Dido had vowed to remain true to her husband Sychaeus, killed by her brother Pygmalion (see line 325), and not remarry.
quā: the relative clause comes before its antecedent **fāma** (323); **quā** is ablative of means.
sīdera adībam: *I was approaching the stars = I was becoming famous, had hopes of immortality.*
323 **prior, prior, prius**, gen. **priōris**, *first, previous, former.*

moribundus, -a, -um, *dying.*
***dēserō, dēserere, dēseruī, dēsertus**, *to desert, abandon.*
hospes: *my guest*, said sarcastically.
324 **restō, restāre, restitī**, *to stay behind, be left, remain.*

325 **Quid**: = **Cūr.**
moror: not the same as **morior.**
An: here this word introduces a direct question, but it need not be translated by a separate word in English.
Pygmaliōn: Dido's brother, king of Tyre in Phoenicia, who had murdered her husband Sychaeus in order to get his hands on Sychaeus' wealth.
dum: when completed by a verb in the subjunctive (**dēstruat** and **dūcat** in the next line), **dum** = *until* (not *while*).
***moenia, moenium**, n. pl., *walls, fortifications.*
326 **captam**: supply **mē.**
Gaetūlus, -a, -um, *Gaetulian*; the Gaetulians were a North African tribe.
Iarbās: king of the Gaetuli, who permitted the Tyrian colonists to settle in Africa and who was angry because Dido took Aeneas as a lover rather than accept his marriage proposal. Note that the i in **Iarbās** is a vowel, not a semiconsonant (y-sound), so the name has three syllables.

327 **saltem**, adv., *at least.*
sī qua: remember the special meaning of **quis** after **sī** (see lines 317 and 319 and page 161, note 2).
suscipiō, suscipere, suscēpī, susceptus, *to pick up, support; to bear* (children).
328 **subolēs, subolis**, f., *offspring, child.*
subolēs: the wide separation of **subolēs** from **qua** and its placement at the end of the clause serve to emphasize it; likewise with **quis** and **Aenēās** in the next clause.
parvulus, -a, -um, *small, little.*
aula, -ae, f., *hall, palace.*
aulā: = **in aulā.**
329 **quī . . . referret**: *who would bring you back*, i.e., who would remind me of you; a relative clause of characteristic.
tamen: *nevertheless, still* (i.e., although you have deserted me).
330 **equidem**, adv., *certainly, surely.*
capta: *deceived* in this context.

exstīnctus pudor et, quā sōlā sīdera adībam,
fāma prior. Cui mē moribundam dēseris, hospes
(hoc sōlum nōmen quoniam dē coniuge restat)?
Quid moror? An mea Pygmaliōn dum moenia frāter
dēstruat aut captam dūcat Gaetūlus Iarbās?
Saltem sī qua mihi dē tē suscepta fuisset
ante fugam subolēs, sī quis mihi parvulus aulā
lūderet Aenēās, quī tē tamen ōre referret,
nōn equidem omnīnō capta ac dēserta vidērer."

—Vergil, *Aeneid* IV.305–330

---

12. What two things have been destroyed because of Aeneas? (322–323)
13. How does Dido refer to Aeneas at this point? Why? (323–324)
14. Dido asks rhetorically whether she should wait for two things; what are they? (325–326)
15. Under what circumstances would Dido not feel deceived and deserted? (327–330)

Questions for Thought and Discussion

1. Dido's speech may be analyzed in three sections: lines 305–314, 314–319, and 320–330. What is the point of each section? How is the tone of each section different? How does the arrangement of material play on the emotions of the listener for maximum impact?
2. Dido is clearly very upset, yet she delivers an elaborate and carefully organized speech. Identify the rhetorical devices that are present in her speech (some, but not all, are pointed out in the notes).
3. How do you react to this speech? Does it seem like a speech that a woman in Dido's position would be likely to make? Do the careful structure and rhetorical devices make the speech more or less effective? Why or why not?

This painting shows Tityrus playing the pipes. It comes from the Vergilius Romanus, an illuminated (illustrated) manuscript of the fifth century A.D. that contains almost all of Vergil's works. It is one of the few manuscripts from the Roman empire that have survived. Note the writing, in all capital letters, with dots (not spaces) between the words.
The Roman Vergil manuscript, from the Aeneid, *fifth century A.D.*

331 **monitum, -ī**, n., *warning, advice, command.*
Iovis monitīs: Jupiter had sent Mercury to Carthage with orders for Aeneas to seek his destiny in Italy.
332 ***lūmen, lūminis**, n., *light*; in plural, *eyes.*
obnītor, obnītī, obnīxus sum, *to strain, struggle.*
obnīxus: *with a struggle.*

333 **refert**: *brings back = replies.*
Ego tē: note how Aeneas places the two pronouns next to each other to show that he still feels a connection with Dido.
tē: accusative, completed by the infinitive **prōmeritam (esse)** in line 335, dependent on the head verb **negābō** (334).
plūrima: this word belongs to the main clause, not the relative clause **quae . . . valēs**; it is a neuter plural substantive and serves as the object of **prōmeritam (esse)**.
***for, fārī, fātus sum**, *to say, speak.*
fandō: *by speaking, in your speech.*
334 **valēs**: = **potes.**
335 **prōmereor, prōmererī, prōmeritus sum**, *to deserve.*
piget, pigēre, piguit, *it annoys, it makes one regret.*
Elissae: Dido's original Phoenician name was Elissa; Vergil uses both names.
336 **dum memor**: the verb **sum** is understood.
meī: genitive of the pronoun **ego**, not the possessive **meus, -a, -um**.

337 **rē**: *(my) case*, a common meaning of **rēs** in legal contexts.

abscondō, abscondere, abscondidī, absconditus, *to hide, conceal.*
fūrtum, -ī, n., *theft; trick, deception.*
338 ***fingō, fingere, finxī, fictus**, *to imagine, think.*
nē finge: **nē** with the imperative is sometimes found in poetry as a negative command, instead of **nōlī** with an infinitive.
339 **praetendō, praetendere, praetendī, praetentum**, *to hold out in front; to offer.*
taeda, -ae, f., *torch*. Torches were carried in wedding processions; therefore *torches* are often used by metonymy to stand for *marriage*.

340 ***fāta, -ōrum**, n. pl., *the fates.*
341 **auspicium, -ī**, n., *auspices* (signs in nature believed to show the will of gods).
meīs (340) **. . . / auspiciīs**: *under my own auspices*, i.e., as I myself would prefer.
342 **meōrum**: *of my own (people)*, a substantive.
343 **rēliquiae, -ārum**, f. pl., *remains, relics.*
Priamus, -ī, m., *Priam*, king of Troy.
344 **recidīvus, -a, -um**, *revived, restored.*
manū: = **manū meā.**
posuissem: from **posuī**, perfect of **pōnō**, not from **potuī**, perfect of **possum**.
Pergama, -ōrum, n. pl., *Pergama*, the citadel of Troy; by metonymy, *Troy.*
victīs: *for the vanquished*, a substantive.

B. Aeneas Replies

Dīxerat. Ille Iovis monitīs immōta tenēbat
lūmina et obnīxus cūram sub corde premēbat.
Tandem pauca refert: "Ego tē, quae plūrima fandō
ēnumerāre valēs, numquam, rēgīna, negābō
prōmeritam, nec mē meminisse pigēbit Elissae
dum memor ipse meī, dum spīritus hōs regit artūs.
Prō rē pauca loquar. Neque ego hanc abscondere fūrtō
spērāvī (nē finge) fugam, nec coniugis umquam
praetendī taedās aut haec in foedera vēnī.
Mē sī fāta meīs paterentur dūcere vītam
auspiciīs et sponte meā compōnere cūrās,
urbem Troiānam prīmum dulcēsque meōrum
rēliquiās colerem, Priamī tēcta alta manērent,
et recidīva manū posuissem Pergama victīs.

(*continued*)

1. Does Aeneas show that he is affected by Dido's words? How does he deal with his feelings? (331–332)
2. What does Aeneas acknowledge to Dido? (333–335)
3. How will Aeneas feel about his relationship with Dido? (335) For how long? (336)
4. What does Aeneas claim he did not intend to do? (337–338)
5. What does Aeneas say about his relationship with Dido? How is this different from her view as expressed in line 316? (338–339)
6. What hypothetical situation does Aeneas describe in lines 340–341?
7. Under these circumstances, what would Aeneas be doing now? What would be the status of Troy? (342–343)
8. What would Aeneas have done to bring this about? (344)

Reading Note

Impersonal Verbs of Feeling

Several impersonal verbs express feelings. **Pigēbit** (line 335) is one such example. The person who feels goes in the accusative and the cause of the feeling in the genitive, if a noun, or in the infinitive, if a verb. So **nec mē meminisse pigēbit Elissae** = *it will not annoy me to remember Elissa, I will not be annoyed to remember Elissa*. **Mē piget morae** would mean *It makes me annoyed at the delay, I am annoyed at the delay*. It is usually best to translate such verbs with a person as the English subject. In addition to **piget**, you will meet the following:

miseret, miserēre, miseruit, *it makes one pity, feel sorry for something*
paenitet, paenitēre, paenituit, *it makes one regret something, repent of something*
pudet, pudēre, puduit, *it makes one ashamed of something*
taedet, taedēre, taeduit or **taesum est**, *it bores, makes one tired of something*

345 **Grȳnēus, -a, -um,** *of Grynium* (Asia Minor), where there was a wood sacred to Apollo.
Ītaliam magnam Grȳnēus Apollō: How do you know that the verb **iussit** is gapped here?
346 **Lycius, -a, -um,** *Lycian, of Lycia* (territory in southwest Asia Minor see the map on page 270). There was an oracle of Apollo at Patara in Lycia.
iussēre: how do you know this is not an infinitive? (See the Reading Note on page 116.)
capessō, capessere, capessīvī, capessītus, *to make for, try to reach.*
***sors, sortis,** f., *lot; prophecy; oracle.*
347 **hic**: the **i** is short, but the syllable scans as long (the word was originally spelled **hicce**).

arx, arcis, f., *citadel.*
348 **Phoenissus, -a, -um,** *Phoenician.*
aspectus, -ūs, m., *sight.*
dētinet: deduce from **dē + teneō**. The verb is singular because it is next to the singular subject **aspectus**, but it is gapped also with the plural subject **arcēs** (347).
349 **quae**: modifies **invidia** (350).
Ausonia, -ae, f., *Ausonia*, another name for Italy.
Ausoniā . . . terrā: = **in Ausoniā terrā.**
Teucrī, -ōrum, m. pl., *Teucrians*, another name for the Trojans.
cōnsīdō, cōnsīdere, cōnsēdī, *to sit down; to settle.*

350 **Et nōs**: referring to Aeneas and the Trojans; Dido and her people, refugees from Tyre after the murder of Dido's husband Sychaeus, have already found shelter in a new land.
***fās,** indeclinable, n., *right, proper*. Supply **est** with **fās.**
exterus, -a, -um, *external; foreign.*

351 **Mē**: accusative, object of **admonet** and **terret** (353), whose subject is **turbida . . . imāgō** (353).
Anchīsēs, Anchīsae, m., *Anchises* (deceased father of Aeneas).
patris Anchīsae: genitive, modifying **imāgō** (353).
quotiēns, adv., *as often as.*
ūmēns, ūmentis, *moist, damp.*
352 ***operiō, operīre, operuī, opertus,** *to cover, hide.*
astrum, -ī, n., *star*
igneus, -a, -um, *fiery.*
353 **turbidus, -a, -um,** *wild, troubled, agitated.*
***imāgō, imāginis,** f., *likeness, image; phantom, ghost.*
354 **puer Ascanius**: son of Aeneas and his first wife Creusa. There is no verb in this clause; the idea of **admonet** and **terret** is continued from the previous line. How do you know this?
capitis iniūria cārī: *the wrong done to that dear person*; **caput** can mean *life* or *person* as well as *head.*
355 **Hesperia, -ae,** f., *Hesperia, the land in the west* (a Greek term for Italy).
fraudō, -āre, *to cheat, deprive someone* (acc.) *of something* (abl.).
fātālis, -is, -e, *given by fate, fated, destined.*

356 **interpres, interpretis,** m., *messenger*. Cf. note for line 331.
dīvum: contracted form of **dīvōrum.**
357 **testor, testārī, testātus sum,** *to bear witness; to swear (by).*
utrumque caput: *both our lives*, i.e., his own and Dido's; as on line 354, **caput** = *life.*
358 **manifestus, -a, -um,** *plain, distinct, clear.*

(*vocabulary and notes continued on opposite page*)

Sed nunc Ītaliam magnam Grȳnēus Apollō,
Ītaliam Lyciae iussēre capessere sortēs;
hic amor, haec patria est. Sī tē Karthāginis arcēs
Phoenissam Libycaeque aspectus dētinet urbis,
quae tandem Ausoniā Teucrōs cōnsīdere terrā
invidia est? Et nōs fās extera quaerere rēgna.
Mē patris Anchīsae, quotiēns ūmentibus umbrīs
nox operit terrās, quotiēns astra ignea surgunt,
admonet in somnīs et turbida terret imāgō;
mē puer Ascanius capitisque iniūria cārī,
quem rēgnō Hesperiae fraudō et fātālibus arvīs.
Nunc etiam interpres dīvum Iove missus ab ipsō
(testor utrumque caput) celerēs mandāta per aurās
dētulit: ipse deum manifestō in lūmine vīdī
intrantem mūrōs vōcemque hīs auribus hausī.
Dēsine mēque tuīs incendere tēque querēlīs;
Ītaliam nōn sponte sequor."

—Vergil, *Aeneid* IV.331–361

---

9. What two factors are influencing Aeneas' decision to go to Italy? (345–346)
10. How does Aeneas use Dido's own situation as queen of Carthage to argue that he should go on to Italy? (347–350)
11. What is the ghost of Aeneas' father Anchises doing? (351–353)
12. How often does this happen? (352)
13. What other consideration is urging Aeneas to go to Italy? (354–355)
14. What has Mercury done? Why? (356–358)
15. How does Aeneas attempt to show Dido that his meeting with Mercury was real? (358–359)
16. What request does Aeneas make of Dido? (360)
17. What does Aeneas say he is not doing? (361)

359 **mūrōs**: of Carthage.
*__auris, auris__, gen. pl., **aurium**, f., *ear*. How do you distinguish this from **aurās** (line 357)?

360 **dēsinō, dēsinere, dēsiī, dēsitus**, *to give up, abandon, stop.*
querēla, -ae, f., *complaint.*

361 **sequor**: this line is incomplete, like a number of others in the *Aeneid*, because Vergil died before he put the finishing touches on the poem.

365 **dīva, -ae**, f., *goddess*. Supply **erat** in both clauses in this line.
generis: modifies **auctor** and belongs inside the second clause introduced by **nec**.
Dardanus, -ī, m., *Dardanus*, legendary ancestor of the Trojans.
auctor, auctōris, m., *person responsible, creator, founder*.

366 **perfidus, -a, -um**, *treacherous*; as substantive, *traitor*.
dūrus, -a, -um, *hard, harsh*.
gignō, gignere, genuī, genitus, *to bear, give birth to*.
cautēs, cautis, f., *crag, rock*.
dūrīs . . . cautibus: = **ē dūrīs cautibus**. Dido's point is that Aeneas cannot be human if he remains unmoved by her pleas.
horrēns, horrentis, *dreadful, terrible; rugged, jagged*.

367 **Caucasus, -ī**, m., *the Caucasus Mountains*, at the western end of the Black Sea.
Hyrcānus, -a, -um, *Hyrcanian*; Hyrcania was an area near the Caucasus Mountains and the Caspian Sea.
admōrunt: = **admōvērunt**, a syncopated verb.
admōrunt ūbera: *suckled*. This is another way of saying that Aeneas is less than human; **tigrēs** is emphasized by being separated from the adjective that modifies it and by being placed at the end of the sentence.

368 **dissimulō, -āre, -āvī, -ātus**, *to cover up, conceal*.
quae . . . ad maiōra: *for what greater things*. Dido is saying that she has no reason to hold back any of her anger against Aeneas; she will give free rein to her rage. Note the series of rhetorical questions.

369 **flētus, -ūs**, m., *crying, weeping*.
***flectō, flectere, flexī, flectus**, *to bend, turn*.
Num lūmina flexit: cf. lines 331–332 where Aeneas' eyes gave no indication of his true feelings. Note the use of the third person, which emphasizes the emotional distance that Dido now feels between herself and Aeneas, as does the formal rhetoric with the anaphora of **num** and the tricolon (369–370).

370 **dedit**: *gave forth, shed*.
victus: *overcome* by Dido's appeal.
miseror, miserārī, miserātus sum, *to pity*.
amantem: *his lover*, a present participle used as a substantive.

371 **Quae quibus anteferam**: *What shall I put in front of what*, i.e., *What shall I say first?*
Iam iam: emphatic; *for some time now*, connected with **aspicit** in the next line.

372 **Saturnius . . . pater**: Jupiter, who was the son of Saturn.
aspicit: *has been regarding*, present tense to show an action begun in the past and still continuing in the present.
aequus, -a, -um, *equal; fair, just*.

373 ***nusquam**, adv., *nowhere*.
fidēs: supply **est. Fidēs** is a word often used with reference to fidelity of lovers; cf. Catullus, 62D:3.
***lītus, lītoris**, n., *shore, coast*.
lītore: = **in lītore**.
Ēiectum, egentem: these participles refer to Aeneas (note the asyndeton); Dido expresses her disdain by using neither the pronoun **tē** nor his name; *I welcomed (a man) cast out . . .*

374 **egeō, egēre**, *to lack, want, be in need, be destitute*.
rēgnī: genitive, modifying **parte**.
dēmēns: nominative, agreeing with the subject of **locāvī**.
locō, -āre, -āvī, -ātus, *to locate, establish*; supply **eum** as direct object.

C. Dido's Response

"Nec tibi dīva parēns generis nec Dardanus auctor,
perfide, sed dūrīs genuit tē cautibus horrēns
Caucasus Hyrcānaeque admōrunt ūbera tigrēs.
Nam quid dissimulō aut quae mē ad maiōra reservō?
Num flētū ingemuit nostrō? Num lūmina flexit?
Num lacrimās victus dedit aut miserātus amantem est?
Quae quibus anteferam? Iam iam nec maxima Iūnō
nec Sāturnius haec oculīs pater aspicit aequīs.
Nusquam tūta fidēs. Ēiectum lītore, egentem
excēpī et rēgnī dēmēns in parte locāvī.

(*continued*)

---

1. What statement does Dido make about Aeneas' birth? (365–367)
2. What rhetorical questions does Dido ask to show her anger that Aeneas was not moved by her pleas? (369–370)
3. How have the gods been treating Dido recently? (371–372)
4. What does Dido say about trust? (373)
5. In what situation was Aeneas when Dido welcomed him? (373–374)
6. How did Dido treat Aeneas after she took him in? In what state of mind was she when she did this, as she now sees it? (374)

This painting shows the final conversation between Aeneas and Dido, with Anna, Dido's sister, at the right. Is this the way you would imagine them during this conversation, based on the passages from Vergil in this chapter?
Aeneas Takes Leave of Dido, *oil on canvas, circa 1630, Guido Reni*

375 **Āmissam classem**: Aeneas' ships had been split into two groups during the storm that drove them from Sicily to Carthage. The larger group had arrived in Carthage before Aeneas did, and Dido had welcomed them and provided food and help in repairing their ships.

376 **furiae, -ārum**, f. pl., *madness, frenzy* (for revenge).

feror: *I am carried (along), I am swept (along)*.

augur, auguris, m. or f., *augur* (priest who foretold the future from signs in nature), *prophet*. Here the noun is equivalent to an adjective, *prophetic*.

augur Apollo / Lyciae sortēs: see notes for lines 345–346.

378 **interpres dīvum**: see note for line 356.

iussa, -ōrum, n. pl., *commands, orders*.

379 **superī, -ōrum**, m. pl., *the gods above*.

ea cūra: i.e., paying special attention to Aeneas, seeing that he carries out his destiny.

quiētōs: masculine plural referring to the gods.

380 **sollicitō, -āre, -āvī, -ātus**, *to worry, trouble*.

dictum, -ī, n., *word*.

refellō, refellere, *to refute, contradict*.

381 **sequere**: how do you know that this is an imperative, not an infinitive?

***unda, -ae**, f., *wave*.

382 **quid**: remember the special meaning of **quid** after **sī** (see page 161, note 2).

***pius, -a, -um**, *dutiful*. In the *Aeneid*, Aeneas is often referred to as **pius**; here Dido ironically applies the word to the gods she hopes will punish him.

possunt: an infinitive such as *to accomplish* is understood here.

383 **hausūrum**: an infinitive in indirect statement, introduced by **Spērō** (382); **tē** and **esse** are understood here, as well as with **vocātūrum** in the next line. For the metaphorical use of this verb, see the note on line 359.

scopulus, -ī, n., *rock, cliff*.

mediīs . . . scopulīs: Dido imagines Aeneas dying in a shipwreck somewhere.

384 **āter, ātra, ātrum**, *black*.

ātrīs ignibus: this refers to the smoky torches carried by the Furies (goddesses who took vengeance on those who committed terrible crimes such as killing family members); Dido imagines herself as a Fury. There may also be an anticipation of Dido's funeral pyre (**ignem**, line 661).

absēns: concessive, *although absent*, since she will not be there in person to get revenge.

385 **animā**: what case? How does the verb **sēdūxerit** help you interpret this? (See the Reading Note on page 220.)

sēdūcō, sēdūcere, sēdūxī, sēductus, *to lead apart, separate*.

386 **umbra**: *as a ghost*. Dido will be in the underworld (387) but her memory will haunt Aeneas wherever he goes (**omnibus . . . locīs**), especially if he feels guilty about causing her death.

poenās dare, *to pay the price, be punished*.

improbus, -a, -um, *evil, wicked, shameless*. What case is **improbe**?

387 **mānēs, mānium**, m. pl., *spirits of the dead, ghosts*; modified by **īmōs**.

haec . . . fāma: i.e., the reports of Aeneas' shipwreck and death. **Fāma** can mean *rumor* or *report* as well as *fame, reputation* (cf. Dido's concern for her **fāma** in line 323).

īmus, -a, -um, *lowest, deepest*; here referring to the ghosts in the underworld.

Āmissam classem, sociōs ā morte redūxī
(heu furiīs incēnsa feror!): nunc augur Apollō,
nunc Lyciae sortēs, nunc et Iove missus ab ipsō
interpres dīvum fert horrida iussa per aurās.
Scīlicet is superīs labor est, ea cūra quietōs
sollicitat. Neque tē teneō neque dicta refellō:
ī, sequere Ītaliam ventīs, pete rēgna per undās.
Spērō equidem mediīs, sī quid pia nūmina possunt,
supplicia hausūrum scopulīs et nōmine 'Dīdō'
saepe vocātūrum. Sequar ātrīs ignibus absēns
et, cum frīgida mors animā sēdūxerit artūs,
omnibus umbra locīs aderō. Dabis, improbe, poenās.
Audiam et haec mānēs veniet mihi fāma sub īmōs."

—Vergil, *Aeneid* IV.365–387

---

7. What did she do regarding Aeneas' ships and men? (375)
8. How does Dido describe her own state of mind at the moment? (376)
9. How does Dido throw Aeneas' own words back at him? (376–378; compare lines 345–347 and 356–358). What word does Dido add?
10. What sarcastic comment does Dido make about Aeneas' claim that the gods have told him to go to Italy? (379–380)
11. What is Dido not doing? (380)
12. What does Dido tell Aeneas to do? (381)
13. What does Dido hope will happen to Aeneas? (382–384)
14. What does Dido say that she will do? When will she do this? (384–386)
15. What will happen to Aeneas? (386)
16. How will Dido know about this? (387)

One of the Furies throws a vase around which a snake is coiled. Note the snaky hair on the Fury. This comes from a relief on the altar of Zeus at Pergamum, Asia Minor, that shows the battle between the gods and the giants.
Relief, circa 180 B.C.

651 **exuviae, -ārum**, f. pl., *reminder, memento.* Dido is addressing Aeneas' possessions that have been heaped up on the pyre, including his sword.

fāta deusque sinēbat: the verb is singular because it is closer to **deus**, but both **fāta** and **deus** are its subjects. See line 348 for a similar situation.

652 **exsolvō, exsolvere, exsolvī, exsolūtus**, *to release from, free from.*

653 ***cursus, -ūs**, m., *course.*

cursum: the antecedent of the relative clause **quem dederat . . . fortūna**, placed inside the clause, as often in Vergil.

peragō, peragere, perēgī, perāctus, *to carry through to the end, complete.*

656 **ulcīscor, ulcīscī, ultus sum**, *to avenge, get revenge for.*

ulta: *avenging.* The perfect participle of a deponent verb is sometimes best translated as in the present.

virum: *husband.*

poenās . . . recēpī: *I exacted punishment.* Dido took her brother's ships and money with her into exile as revenge for his murder of her husband.

657 **nimium**, adv., *too, too much, excessively.*

fēlīx: supply **fuissem** as part of a hypothetical condition with **sī . . . tetigissent** (658). See pages 96–97 for conditional sentences.

sī . . . tantum: *if only.*

658 **Dardanius, -a, -um**, *Dardanian, Trojan.*

tetigissent: from **tangō**.

carīna, -ae, f., *keel*; by synecdoche, *ship.*

659 **imprimō, imprimere, impressī, impressus**, *to press down, press into.*

torus, -ī, m., *mattress, bed.* The bed that Dido and Aeneas had shared is among the things to be burned on the pyre.

ōs impressa torō: *having pressed her face into the bed.* The perfect participle **impressa** is completed by the accusative **ōs**, a Greek construction often copied by Latin poets. **Torō** is dative object of the compound verb **impressa**.

moriēmur, moriāmur (660): poetic plural, as is **nostrae** (662); note the change of tense and mood.

inultus, -a, -um, *unavenged* (cf. **ulcīsor**, 656).

660 **iuvat**: *it is pleasing*, an impersonal use of the verb **iuvāre**.

661 **Hauriat . . . oculīs**: *let (him) drink in with (his) eyes*, an unusual phrase. Dido wants Aeneas to keep in his mind forever the image of her death. For this verb used metaphorically, see the note on line 359 and cf. line 383.

crūdēlis: modifies **Dardanus** (662).

ab altō: Dido imagines Aeneas seeing the smoke of her funeral pyre from far out at sea. In fact the Trojans do see the smoke and fear that it indicates something terrible, although they do not know the exact cause (*Aeneid* V.1–7).

662 **Dardanus**: Dido is so angry that she does not even want to say Aeneas' name.

nostrae: = **meae**.

ōmen, ōminis, n., *omen, sign (from the gods).*

ōmina: the Romans were particularly sensitive to bad omens that occurred at the beginning of a new venture. So for Aeneas to arrive in Italy under a cloud because of Dido's death would not be propitious for his success there. **Mortis** is emphasized by being separated from its modifier **nostrae** and by being placed at the end of the sentence.

D. The Death of Dido

Aeneas longs to comfort Dido but instead returns to his ships. Dido sends her sister Anna to make one last appeal to Aeneas, but he is not persuaded to stay. Haunted by dreadful signs from the gods and by terrible nightmares, Dido finally decides to commit suicide. She tells Anna to build a pyre on which she will burn the possessions that Aeneas left behind and thereby free herself from love for him. Mercury appears to Aeneas and orders him to depart immediately. From her palace Dido watches the Trojan fleet sail away and calls down curses on Aeneas and all his descendants; then she climbs onto the pyre.

"Dulcēs exuviae, dum fāta deusque sinēbat,
accipite hanc animam mēque hīs exsolvite cūrīs.
Vīxī et quem dederat cursum fortūna perēgī,
et nunc magna meī sub terrās ībit imāgō.
Urbem praeclāram statuī, mea moenia vīdī,
ulta virum poenās inimīcō ā frātre recēpī,
fēlīx, heu nimium fēlīx, sī lītora tantum
numquam Dardaniae tetigissent nostra carīnae."
Dīxit, et ōs impressa torō "moriēmur inultae,
sed moriāmur" ait. "Sīc, sīc iuvat īre sub umbrās.
Hauriat hunc oculīs ignem crūdēlis ab altō
Dardanus et nostrae sēcum ferat ōmina mortis."

(*continued*)

---

1. What objects does Dido address? (651)
2. What does she ask them to do? (652)
3. What has Dido achieved? (653)
4. What will happen now? (654)
5. List three things that Dido accomplished during her life. (655–656)
6. Under what conditions would Dido have been happy? (657–658)
7. What gesture does Dido make? (659)
8. How does she describe her impending death? (659–660)
9. What wishes does Dido express? (661–662)

Dido's simple and dignified summary of her life in lines 655–656 recalls the style of Roman epitaphs such as the following, which dates perhaps to about 150 B.C. As often in such inscriptions, the deceased is imagined as speaking to the person who looks at the tomb.

> Traveler, what I have to say is short: stop and read it through. This is the tomb, not beautiful, of a beautiful woman: her parents named her Claudia. She loved her husband with all her heart. She had two sons; of these she leaves one on the earth, the other she buried under the earth. Her speech was charming and her gait pleasant. She kept house. She worked wool. I have spoken; go along.

663 **ferrum, -ī**, n., *iron; an iron object, a sword* (metonymy).
ferrō: with **collāpsam** (664), *on the sword* or *over the sword.*
664 **ēnsis, ēnsis**, m., *sword.*
cruor, cruōris, m., *gore, blood.*
665 **spumō, -āre**, *to foam.*

666 **concutiō, concutere, concussī, concussus**, *to strike, shake.*
bacchor, -ārī, -ātus sum, *to act like a worshipper of Bacchus; to run wild.*
fāma: *rumor, report.*
667 **gemitus, -ūs**, m., *groaning.*
ululātus, -ūs, m., *howling, wailing.*
668 **fremō, fremere, fremuī, fremitus**, *to roar, resound.*
resonō, -āre, -āvī, -ātus, *to resound.*
plangor, plangōris, m., *striking, beating; wailing.*
aethēr, aetheris, m., *upper air, sky.*
669 **nōn aliter quam**, *not otherwise than*; this phrase is equivalent to "just as" and introduces a simile, based upon Homer's *Iliad* XXII.410, which describes the lamentations for the slain Hector.
immissīs . . . hostibus: ablative absolute.
ruō, ruere, ruī, rutus, *to collapse, fall in ruins.*
670 **Tyros, Tyrī**, f., *Tyre* (see note on line 321). Note the gender.
671 **culmen, culminis**, n., *peak, top; roof.*
culmina: object of the first **per** and to be supplied with the second **per. Culmina hominum** is a poetic way of saying *houses* and **(culmina) deōrum** *temples.*
volvō, volvere, volvī, volūtus, *to roll.*

Reading Notes

Onomatopoeia

In line 667 opposite, you met the word **ululātū**, which is an example of *onomatopoeia.* This is a figure of speech in which the sound of the word imitates or suggests the sound one hears, as in the English words "buzz" and "hiss."

• • •

Similes in Epic Poetry

Lines 669–671 opposite contain a simile, introduced by the phrase **nōn aliter**. The use of similes at key moments in the story is a characteristic feature of Greek and Roman epic poetry. Such similes act as signposts to alert the reader that a turning point in the story has come or to demonstrate the importance of a particular event. Similes in Latin are introduced by words such as **ut, velut, sīcut, tamquam**, and **quālis**, as well as **nōn aliter quam**. You will meet more such similes in Chapter 74.

Dīxerat, atque illam media inter tālia ferrō
collāpsam aspiciunt comitēs ēnsemque cruōre
spūmantem sparsāsque manūs. It clāmor ad alta
ātria: concussam bacchātur fāma per urbem.
Lāmentīs gemitūque et fēmineō ululātū
tēcta fremunt, resonat magnīs plangōribus aethēr,
nōn aliter quam sī immissīs ruat hostibus omnis
Karthāgō aut antīqua Tyros, flammaeque furentēs
culmina perque hominum volvantur perque deōrum.

—Vergil, *Aeneid* IV.651–671

---

10. What do Dido's companions see? (663–665)
11. What is the reaction when they see this? (665–666)
12. What sounds reflect the people's grief at Dido's actions? (667–668)
13. What event might provoke a similar reaction? (669–670)
14. What would be happening in such a situation? (670–671)

This painting of a scene from the *Aeneid* was done in 1740. It shows an early episode in Book IV, in which Vergil describes how Dido and Aeneas went hunting; note the hunters and dogs at the left. Juno sent a storm that drove Dido and Aeneas into a cave.
Aeneas and Dido in the storm, by Corrado Giaquinto (1703–1765)

693 **omnipotēns, omnipotentis**, *all-powerful.*
miseror, miserārī, miserātus sum, *to pity.*
694 **obitus, -ūs**, m., *death.*
Īris, Īris, f., *Iris*, the goddess of the rainbow and messenger of Juno.
Olympō: to understand the meaning of this ablative, note the prefix **dē-** on the verb **dēmīsit** (see the Reading Note on page 220).
695 **quae . . . resolveret**: *to release.* The subjunctive is used when a relative clause expresses the purpose of an action.
luctor, -ārī, -ātus, *to wrestle; to struggle.*
nectō, nectere, nexuī, nexus, *to tie, connect, bind.*
nexōs . . . artūs: Dido's body is bound to her soul, since her proper time for death had not yet come, as explained in the following lines.
696 **quia**, conj., *because.*
nec fātō meritā nec morte: Dido chose death, since it was neither her fate to die at this time nor had she done anything to deserve death. Note that **meritā** modifies **morte.**
pereō, perīre, periī or **perīvī, perītus**, irreg., *to perish.*
697 **ante diem**: *before the (appointed) day, before her time.*
subitus, -a, -um, *sudden.*
accendō, accendere, accendī, accēnsus, *to set on fire, inflame.*
furor, furōris, m., *rage, madness, frenzy.*
698 **illī**: referring to Dido; dative of reference.
flāvus, -a, -um, *yellow, blonde.*
Prōserpina, -ae, f., *Proserpina* (= Greek Persephone, queen of the underworld). Vergil alludes to the belief that she cuts a lock of a dying person's hair, thereby consigning the person to the underworld.
vertex, verticis, m., *peak, top; head.*
vertice: how do you know that this means *from (her) head*? (Review the Reading Note on page 220 if necessary.)
crīnem: this word is usually found in the plural; here the singular means *a lock of hair.*
699 **Stygius, -a, -um**, *Stygian, of the river Styx* (in the underworld).
caput: *life* in this context.
Orcus, -ī, m., *the underworld.*

700 **croceus, -a, -um**, *saffron-colored, yellow.*
roscidus, -a, -um, *dewy.*
701 **adversō sōle**: *with the sun turned toward*, i.e., in the sunlight, since a rainbow can only be seen if the sun is shining.
702 **dēvolō, -āre, -āvī, -ātus**, *to fly down.*
assistō, assistere, astitī, *to stand by, stand near.*
Hunc: agrees with **sācrum** (703); both are masculine because **crīnem** is understood.
Dīs, Dītis, m., *Dis*, another name for Pluto or Hades.
703 ***sācer, sācra, sācrum**, *sacred, consecrated.*
iussa: Iris normally would not have the power of life and death over a person, but in this case she has been specifically ordered by Juno.
ferō: = **auferō**, *I take away.*
istō corpore: *from that body*, ablative of separation with **solvō.**
***solvō, solvere, solvī, solūtus**, *to release, untie.*

(vocabulary and notes continued on opposite page)

Anna rushes to the pyre and attempts to stop the bleeding from Dido's wound, but she is too late; Dido cannot be saved, but she does not die immediately.

Tum Iūnō omnipotēns longum miserāta dolōrem
difficilēsque obitūs Īrim dēmīsit Olympō
quae luctantem animam nexōsque resolveret artūs.
Nam quia nec fātō meritā nec morte perībat,
sed misera ante diem subitōque accēnsa furōre,
nōndum illī flāvum Prōserpina vertice crīnem
abstulerat Stygiōque caput damnāverat Orcō.
Ergō Īris croceīs per caelum roscida pennīs
mīlle trahēns variōs adversō sōle colōrēs
dēvolat et suprā caput astitit. "Hunc ego Dītī
sācrum iussa ferō tēque istō corpore solvō:"
sīc ait et dextrā crīnem secat, omnis et ūnā
dīlāpsus calor atque in ventōs vīta recessit.

—Vergil, *Aeneid* IV.693–705

---

15. What did Juno feel? (693–694)
16. For what purpose did she send Iris? (695)
17. Under what circumstances was Dido dying? (696–697)
18. What had not happened because of these circumstances? (698–699)
19. Describe how Iris looked as she flew down from Olympus. (700–702)
20 What did Iris say? (702–703)
21. What did she do as she said this? (704)
22. What resulted from Iris' actions? (704–705)

704 **ait**: this word is pronounced as two syllables, *a-yit*.
secō, secāre, secuī, sectus, *to cut*.
***ūnā**, adv., *together; at the same time*.

705 **dīlābor, dīlābī, dīlāpsus sum**, *to slip away*; supply **est** with **dīlāpsus**.
calor, calōris, m., *heat, warmth*; modified by **omnis** in the previous line.

BUILDING THE MEANING

Expressing Purpose (Consolidation)

You have now met all the ways in which Latin normally expresses purpose. In Book II, you learned that purpose is often expressed by a clause with the subjunctive:

Iūnō Īrim dēmīsit **ut** animam Dīdōnis **resolveret**, **nē** diūtius **paterētur**.
Juno sent Iris down ***to release*** *Dido's soul,* ***so that she would not suffer*** *any longer.*

Unlike result clauses, fear clauses, and indirect commands, purpose clauses do not have any special markers that make them easy to identify; however, they always answer the question *why*. The most common English equivalents are *(in order) to* . . . (affirmative) or *so that . . . not, lest, to prevent,* or *to avoid* (negative).

In Chapter 63 (pages 134–135), you met gerunds and gerundives expressing purpose, with either **ad** + accusative or **causā/grātiā** + preceding genitive:

Īris **ad animam** Dīdōnis **resolvendam** vēnit.
Īris **animae** Dīdōnis **resolvendae causā** vēnit.
Iris came ***to release*** *Dido's* ***soul****.*

In Chapter 70, purpose was expressed by a supine in the accusative with a verb of motion (review the Reading Note on page 207):

Iūnō Īrim dēmīsit animam Dīdōnis **resolūtum**.
Juno sent Iris down ***to release*** *Dido's soul.*

The supine looks like a perfect participle but always has the neuter accusative ending -**um** when expressing purpose, and the verb that governs it must involve motion.

In lines 694–695 of the current chapter there is a *relative clause of purpose*:

Iūnō . . . Īrim dēmīsit Olympō / **qua**e luctantem animam nexōsque **resolvere**t artūs.
Juno sent Iris down from Olympus ***to release*** *the struggling soul and the bound limbs.*

Such clauses are introduced by a relative pronoun, have their verbs in the subjunctive, and are governed by a verb of motion. The presence of a verb of motion, as well as the context, can help you distinguish a relative clause of purpose from a relative clause of characteristic, which also has its verb in the subjunctive.

HORACE ON LIFE AND LOVE

You met the poet Quintus Horatius Flaccus in Chapter 68, where he celebrated Octavian's victory over Queen Cleopatra. Born in 65 B.C., Horace lived during the most volatile period of the civil wars of the late Republic. He spent much of his early life in Venusia, a poor country town where he no doubt developed his love of nature. Horace describes himself as a man "of slight build, prematurely gray, devoted to sunshine, and quick-tempered but easily placated." He was the son of a freedman who was apparently affluent enough to afford for his son an education in Athens. Most likely it was here that Horace was introduced to Epicurean philosophy and began his literary preoccupation with the inevitability and universality of death. In many of his poems, Horace encourages the reader to adopt the Epicurean view of enjoying life while one can and living for the moment (see Readings 73B and C). It was also probably in Athens that he met the tyrannicide Brutus, whose army he subsequently joined as a junior officer and with whom he suffered defeat at Philippi in 42 B.C. Horace was able to return to Italy under the general amnesty of Octavian, but found his father dead and the family farm confiscated. Good fortune and connections led him to a job as a civil servant, during which time he met Vergil and the wealthy patron Gaius Cilnius Maecenas. Horace devoted the next years, after he had received his Sabine farm near Tibur (modern Tivoli), to the production of three book-rolls of poems known as *Carmina* (*Odes*), which became his best-known writings and from which come the four poems presented in this chapter. In the *Odes*, he adapted and transformed Greek lyric verse into poems on love (see Readings A and D), politics, and other areas of life that were particularly appealing to Roman taste. Published in 23 B.C. when Horace was 42, these poems exhibit a wide variety of lyric meters, ranging from those used by Alcaeus (6th century B.C.) to Callimachus (3rd century B.C.), who strongly influenced Catullus.

Horace is best known for what has been called **callida iūnctūra**, *skillful or artful joining*, which refers to his ability to get the most out of the words he uses. Friedrich Nietzsche describes the dense and compact effect of Horace's verse as "a mosaic of words, in which every unit spreads its power to the left and to the right over the whole, by its sound, by its place in the sentence, and by its meaning" (*Twilight of the Idols*). Embedded within his poems are many pithy aphorisms, of which **Carpe diem** (*Odes* I.11.8, Reading C in this chapter) is perhaps the most familiar.

Meter: Fourth Asclepiadean

1 **Quis?** = **Quī?**, interrogative adjective, describing **gracilis puer**. The youth is unnamed.
multā . . . in rosā: the exact setting is unclear. The grotto mentioned in line 3 might be decorated with flowers or the lovers might be reclining on a bed of rose petals.
gracilis, -is, -e, *graceful; slight, slim, slender.*
tē: = **Pyrrha**, (3), direct object of **urget** (2). How does the word order of line 1 suggest the erotic setting?

2 **perfundō, perfundere, perfūdī, perfūsus,** *to pour over, soak, drench.*
liquidīs . . . odōribus: fashionable Romans anointed themselves, especially their hair, with scented oils.
urgeō, urgēre, ursī, ursūrus, *to press (on); embrace.*

3 **Pyrrha, -ae**, f., *Pyrrha*, a name deriving from the Greek word for fire and suggesting that Pyrrha had either reddish-gold hair or a fiery personality, or both.
antrum, -ī, n., literally, *a natural cave*; here, *a grotto*, probably one that takes the form of a rustic arbor or bower. The image is used here as literary decoration.

4 **flāvus, -a, -um,** *yellow, golden, the color of honey; blonde*, a rarity among Romans.
religō, -āre, -āvī, -ātus, *to fasten up, tie back.*
coma, -ae, f., *hair.*
religās cōmam: i.e., wearing the hair off the face in a knot, in a simple style.

5 **simplex, simplicis,** *without artifice, straightforward, uncomplicated; natural, simple.*
munditia, -ae, f., *that which is clean and neat, good grooming; taste, refinement, elegance.*
simplex munditiīs: *simple in (your) elegance.*
Heu: = **Ēheu.**
quotiēns, adv., *how often, how many times.*
fidem: supply **mūtātam** from **mūtātōs** in the next line.

6 **(fidem) / mūtātōsque deōs**: Pyrrha is fickle and has transferred her devotion (**fidem mūtātam**) to another. The gods are "changed" now, i.e., they no longer favor the young man and his interest in Pyrrha.
***fleō, flēre, flēvī, flētus,** *to weep, lament.*
flēbit: the subject of this and of **ēmīrābitur** below is **puer**, from line 1.
asper, aspera, asperum, *harsh, cruel.*
aspera / nigrīs aequora ventīs: note the interlocking of adjectives and nouns. The comparison between women and the sea is ages old. Ancient poets felt that women, like the sea, can be both alluring and treacherous. Pyrrha is the sea on which the youth has set sail and her nature is tempestuous.

7 **nigrīs**: this adjective agrees with **ventīs** but transfers its meaning to **aequora**. Review the Reading Note on page 183.
aequora: plural for singular. The phrase **aspera . . . aequora** starts a metaphor in which the young man's experience with Pyrrha is compared to a storm at sea.

8 **ēmīror, -ārī, -ātus sum,** *to wonder at, marvel at, be astonished* or *utterly astounded at.*
īnsolēns, īnsolentis, *unaccustomed, inexperienced; naively, in surprise*, i.e., at Pyrrha's stormy temper. **Īnsolēns** derives from **soleō, solēre,** *to be accustomed, be in the habit of.*

A. Pyrrha

This ode is one of Horace's most famous. There is a book devoted entirely to translations of this poem, which describes an inexperienced youth caught in the web of a fickle older woman.

Quis multā gracilis tē puer in rosā
perfūsus liquidīs urget odōribus
    grātō, Pyrrha, sub antrō?
        Cui flāvam religās comam,
simplex munditiīs? Heu quotiēns fidem
mūtātōsque deōs flēbit et aspera
    nigrīs aequora ventīs
        ēmīrābitur īnsolēns,

(*continued*)

---

1. How is the young lover described in lines 1–2?
2. What are we told about the setting of the lovers' rendezvous? (1, 3)
3. What does the poet ask Pyrrha in line 4?
4. What is the meaning of the phrase **simplex munditiīs**? (5)
5. How will the youth respond to Pyrrha's behavior? (5–8)
6. What imagery is used to describe Pyrrha in lines 6–7?

9 **quī**: = **puer** (1), which continues to be the subject of this sentence.

tē . . . aureā: the ablative object of the special deponent verb **fruor**, for which, see page 100. **Aureā** likely refers both to Pyrrha's golden hair and, metaphorically, to the quality of her beauty. Note how the boy (**quī . . . crēdulus**) and Pyrrha (**tē . . . aureā**) verbally "embrace" in the line through the interlocking of the words.

crēdulus, -a, -um, *trusting, too trusting, gullible.*

10 **vacuam:** *empty; free (of passion for another), available.*

vacuam: = **tē vacuam esse**, in indirect statement after **spērat**, as is **(tē) amābilem (futūram esse).**

amābilis, -is, -e, *lovable, able to be loved.* The youth imagines Pyrrha to be **aurea, vacua**, and **amābilis.**

11 **nescius, -a, -um** + gen., *unaware (of), unsuspecting (of)*; cf. **īnsolēns** (8) and **crēdulus** (9).

aurae: note how **aurae** plays on **aureā.**

12 **fallāx, fallācis,** *false, shifting, treacherous.*

aurae / fallācis: extends the stormy sea metaphor introduced in line 7. The wind is *treacherous* because it shifts without warning, which can cause problems for sailors.

Miserī: = **Miserī sunt. Miser** commonly describes one suffering because of love.

13 **intemptātus, -a, -um**, *untried, untested*; **intemptāta** modifies Pyrrha, to whom the subject of **nitēs** refers.

niteō, nitēre, *to sparkle, gleam, shine.*

Mē: emphatic and in contrast to **puer** (1), and **miserī** (12). Horace has been both a victim and a survivor of Pyrrha, whom the sea represents. The pronoun **mē** serves as the subject of **suspendisse** (15) in indirect statement introduced by **indicat** (14).

tābulā . . . / vōtīvā: sailors who escaped from some danger at sea commonly dedicated a tablet of thanks (called a votive tablet) to Neptune. The tablet with a suitable inscription was mounted on the wall of a shrine (**sacer / . . . pariēs**) of the tutelary deity. Note the mosaic-like placement of the word pairs in lines 13–16. Might this poem itself be Horace's **tābula vōtīva**?

14 **indicō, -āre, -āvī, -ātus**, *to indicate, show.*

ūvidus, -a, -um, *soaked, dripping wet, drenched.*

15 **suspendō, suspendere, suspendī, suspēnsus**, *to hang up.*

suspendisse: a votive offering of the clothes in which a sailor had been rescued (**ūvida . . . vestīmenta**, 16) would accompany the votive tablet mentioned above. What does the relative placement of **suspendisse** and **vestīmenta** suggest, visually?

potentī . . . deō: *to the powerful god*; dative indirect object.

16 **maris deō**: i.e., Neptune.

qui nunc tē fruitur crēdulus aureā,
quī semper vacuam, semper amābilem
    spērat, nescius aurae
        fallācis. Miserī, quibus
intemptāta nitēs. Mē tabulā sacer
vōtīvā pariēs indicat ūvida
    suspendisse potentī
        vestīmenta maris deō.

—Horace, *Odes* I.5

7. What is the young man's attitude toward Pyrrha? (9) What does he hope? (10–11)
8. Of what is he unaware? (11–12)
9. Who are **miserī**? (12–13)
10. How does the sacred wall show what happened to the poet? (13–14)
11. What did the poet hang up? (14-16) To whom did he dedicate these items? (15–16)
12. What is the poet implying in lines 13–16 about his own relationship with Pyrrha?

Questions for Thought and Discussion

Explore the ways in which the poet uses imagery to express his experiences with and feelings about Pyrrha. What do we learn about her youthful lover? What do we learn about Pyrrha? What do we learn about Horace himself? What do we learn about the fate of any man who loves Pyrrha?

This votive tablet comes from a sanctuary on the island of Melos in the Aegean. A woman named Tyche had a problem with her leg; after being healed, she set this up as a thank-offering to Asclepius, god of healing, and to Hygeia, the goddess Health.
Votive relief, circa A.D. 100–200

Meter: Alcaic strophe

1 **Vidēs**: a statement, but more likely to be taken as a question, = **Vidēsne?**, or perhaps **Nōnne vidēs?** The opening stanzas of this poem derive from a poem of Alcaeus, who was a Greek lyric poet of the 7th century B.C.; see the quotation on the opposite page.

ut . . . stet . . . / . . . sustineant (2)**/ . . . / cōnstiterint** (4): render **ut** as *how*, introducing three indirect questions.

altā: *deep*; take with **nīve**, ablative of respect depending on **candidum.**

nix, nivis, f., *snow*.

2 **Sōracte, Sōractis**, n., *Mt. Soracte* (modern Soratte), located about 28 miles north of Rome.

nec iam: *and no longer*.

sustineō, sustinēre, sustinuī, sustentus, *to sustain, hold up, support*.

sustineant: the subject is **silvae labōrantēs** (3) and the direct object **onus.**

onus: i.e., of snow.

3 **labōrantēs**: *struggling, straining, bending*.

gelū, gelūs, n., *icy* or *biting cold; ice*; one of the rare 4th declension neuter nouns.

4 **cōnsistō, cōnsistere, cōnstitī, cōnstitus**, *to stand fast, stand still; be frozen, freeze over*.

acūtus, -a, -um, *pointed, sharp; hard-* or *sharp-edged*.

5 **dissolvō, dissolvere, dissolvī, dissolūtus**, *to set free from, dissolve; thaw, melt*.

frīgus, frīgōris, n., *cold*.

lignum, -ī, n., *wood; firewood, log*.

focus, -ī, m., *fireplace, hearth*.

6 **largē**, adv., *plentifully, copiously, generously*.

repōnēns: perhaps replacing logs that have burned. This participle modifies **Thaliarche** (5), who is the addressee of the imperative verbs **Dissolve** (5) and **Permitte** (9).

benignius: *more generously, more liberally* (than usual).

7 **dēprōmō, dēprōmere, dēprōmpsī, dēprōmptus**, *to bring out*, i.e., from the store room.

quadrīmus, -a, -um, literally, *four winters old*; *four year old*.

Sabīnus, -a, -um, *Sabine*; Horace's farm was in Sabine country, to the northeast of Rome. See the picture on page 249.

8 **Thaliarchus, -ī**, m., *Thaliarchus*, a Greek name probably made up by Horace and indicating a young man.

***merus, -a, -um**, *pure, undiluted*; substantive for **merum vīnum.**

diōta, -ae, f., *two-handled wine jar*, literally, "two eared."

diōtā: what about the verb **dēprōme** (7) helps you understand the meaning of the ablative? (See the Reading Note on page 220.) Note the interlocked word order in lines 7–8.

B. Soracte

In the Soracte ode, one of the best-loved of Horace's poems, the poet develops the theme of carpe diem, *which is further elaborated in the next poem,* Odes *I.11. The poem in this reading is a dramatic monologue in which Horace gives advice to a young man named Thaliarchus. Observe how Horace employs images from nature to express his theme in both poems.*

Vidēs ut altā stet nive candidum
Sōracte nec iam sustineant onus
    silvae labōrantēs gelūque
        flūmina cōnstiterint acūtō?

Dissolve frīgus ligna super focō
largē repōnēns atque benignius
    dēprōme quadrīmum Sabīnā,
        ō Thaliarche, merum diōtā.

(*continued*)

---

1. How is Mt. Soracte described? (1)
2. Why are the trees struggling to stay standing? (2–3)
3. What has happened to the rivers? Why? (3–4)
4. What does the poet bid Thaliarchus (line 8) to do? (5)
5. How does he suggest that Thaliarchus is to do this? (5–6)
6. By what other means can Thaliarchus combat the weather? (6–8)

Zeus sends rain, a great winter storm comes from the sky, the streams of waters are frozen. . . . Defeat the storm, build up the fire, mix sweet wine unstintingly, around your temples place a soft pillow.

—Alcaeus, fragment 338

Mt. Soracte
Lazio, Italy

9 **permittō, permittere, permīsī, permissus,** *to give up, leave to.*
cētera: i.e., everything but the pleasures just described; neuter plural substantive.
Permitte dīvīs cētera: Horace is moralizing in these lines: it is not for us to worry about things, such as the seasons or weather, that are not in our control. A higher power, perhaps the gods or nature, will see to it that winter will not last forever.
simul: = **simulac** or **simul ac**, *as soon as.*
10 **sternō, sternere, strāvī, strātus,** *to lay low or flat, spread out; make smooth, calm.*
strāvēre: = **strāvērunt** (review the Reading Note on page 116).
aequore fervidō: = **(in) aequore fervidō**; prepositions are often omitted in poetry.
fervidus, -a, -um, *boiling, seething;* of water, *turbulent, churning, foaming.*
11 **dēproeliāns, dēproeliantis,** *struggling, wrestling, battling.*
ventōs aequore fervidō / dēproeliantēs: how does the word order contribute to the meaning?
cupressus, -ī, f., *cypress tree*; a tall, thin, evergreen, shaped like an artist's paint brush. See the photograph on the opposite page.
12 ***vetus, veteris,** *old, aged, ancient.*
agitō, -āre, -āvī, -ātus, *to drive about, put in constant motion; toss, shake.*
ornus, -ī, f., *ash tree.*

13 **Quid sit futūrum**: indirect question introduced by **quaerere**, which follows.
fuge quaerere: = poetic equivalent of **nōlī quaerere.**
14 **quīcumque, quaecumque, quodcumque**, indefinite pronoun, *whoever, whatever.*
quem . . . cumque: tmesis for **quemcumque**. *Tmesis* is the separation of parts of a compound word by one or more intervening words.
fors, forte (nom. sing. and abl. sing. only), f., *chance, luck, fortune*; related to **fortūna**; both are often personified.
diērum: take with **quemcumque**, *whatever (of) days, whatever sort of day*; the entire clause **quem . . . dabit** serves as the direct object of **appōne** (15).
lucrum, -ī, n., *profit, return, gain.*
lucrō / appōne: *set down as profit, credit to your account*; a bookkeeping metaphor.
15 **appōnō, appōnere, apposuī, appositus,** *to set down (as), credit (to).*
nec: = **neve (neu)**, *and don't. . . .*
16 **spernō, spernere, sprēvī, sprētus,** *to reject, scorn, spurn.*
puer: adverbial, *while young, as a boy.*
chorea, -ae, f., *dance*; formally, *a group dance in a ring.*
17 ***dōnec,** *while, as long as.*
virēns, virentis, *green*; figuratively, *in bloom, youthful.*
virentī . . . abest: understand **tibi** with **virentī**, *is absent (from you) in your youth*; the dative **tibi** indicates separation.
cānitiēs, cānitiēī, f., *the color white/gray; gray hair; old age.*
18 **morōsus, -a, -um,** *gloomy, moody; cranky, irritable.*
dōnec virentī cānitiēs abest / morōsa: the juxtaposition of **virentī** and **cānitiēs** creates an effective contrast and also demonstrates how Horace uses nature to describe the human condition.

Permitte dīvīs cētera, quī simul
strāvēre ventōs aequore fervidō
dēproeliantēs, nec cupressī
nec veterēs agitantur ornī.

Quid sit futūrum crās, fuge quaerere, et
quem fors diērum cumque dabit, lucrō
appōne nec dulcēs amōrēs
sperne puer neque tū choreās,
dōnec virentī cānitiēs abest
mōrōsa.

(*continued*)

---

7. In line 9, what does the poet advise Thaliarchus to do?
8. What have the gods done in lines 10–11? With what effect? (11–12)
9. What further advice does the poet give in line 13?
10. What does he advise Thaliarchus to consider as profit? (14–15)
11. What two activities should Thaliarchus not ignore? (15–16)
12. At what stage in life will all this advice be taken? (16)
13. How long will Thaliarchus be able to follow this advice? (17)
14. How is old age (**cānitiēs**) described?

The remains of Horace's Sabine farm northeast of Rome. Note the tall, thin cypress trees (above: 11) in the background.

18 **Nunc**: i.e., while young; repeated for emphasis in line 21.
campus, -ī, m., *field; any open space*; here, the Campus Martius. The colonnades and porticoes probably served as meeting places for young lovers.
āreae: the open areas or squares around public buildings.
19 **lēnis, -is, -e**, *gentle; faint, subdued.*
sub noctem: *at nightfall.*
susurrus, -ī, m., *sigh, whisper.*
20 **compositus, -a, -um**, *appointed, predetermined, arranged*; with **hōrā**, a "date."
repetō, repetere, repetīvī, repetītus, *to seek* or *search out again.*
repetantur: *let . . . be sought*; jussive subjunctive, for which, see pages 117–118. The subjects of this verb are **campus, āreae, susurrī** (18–19) and **rīsus** and **pignus** (22–23).
21 **prōditor, prōditōris**, m., *traitor, betrayer, tell-tale.*
prōditor: this word is in apposition to **grātus . . . rīsus** in the next line and it modifies **latentis** (22) **. . . puellae.**
intimus, -a, -um, *innermost, remotest.*
22 **rīsus, -ūs**, m., *laughter, giggle.*
angulus, -ī, m., *corner.*
23 **pignus, pignoris**, n., *pledge, keepsake; love token* (such as a bracelet or ring).
dēripiō, dēripere, dēripuī, dēreptus, *to snatch away, tear away.*
lacertus, -ī, m., *(upper) arm.*
lacertīs: *from the upper arm*, ablative of separation with **dēreptum**, as is **digitō** (24).
24 **pertināx, pertinācis**, *gripping firmly, holding tightly.*
male pertinācī: *faintly* or *half-heartedly resisting.*

Nunc et campus et āreae
lēnēsque sub noctem susurrī
compositā repetantur hōrā,
nunc et latentis prōditor intimō
grātus puellae rīsus ab angulō
pignusque dēreptum lacertīs
aut digitō male pertinācī.

—Horace, *Odes* I.9

---

15. Where are the recommended activities to take place? (18)
16. What should be sought out at nightfall? How does sound suggest the meaning here? (19)
17. At what time should these activities take place? (20)
18. What betrays the presence of the girl? Where is she and what is she doing there? (21–22)
19. How does the tone change between lines 21–22 and 23–24? What seems to have happened?

Questions for Thought and Discussion

1. What contrasts does the poet draw between stanzas 1 and 2? How do these introduce or contribute to the theme of the poem?
2. What words in the second stanza contribute to a sense of urgency?
3. How do trees help convey symbolically the message of the first three stanzas?
4. What aspects of youth does the poet recommend in the final three stanzas?
5. With reference to lines 18–24, describe what you see and hear as an imaginary bystander.
6. What seems to be the difference in age and life experience between Horace and Thaliarchus? Support your position by citing evidence from the poem.

Meter: Fifth or Greater Asclepiadean

1 **nē quaesieris**: an alternative to the prohibition **nōlī quaerere.**
quaesieris: = **quaesīveris**, perfect subjunctive with **nē.**
scīre nefās: = **scīre nefās est.**
quem mihi, quem tibi: = **quem . . . / fīnem (vītae) mihi, quem (fīnem vītae) tibi.** See the Reading Note on gapping, page 42. What kind of clause is this?
2 **Leuconoē**: a woman's name that means "having a clear mind" in Greek. Think about why Horace chose this name for the woman in the poem.
nec . . . / temptāris: = **et nē temptāveris**, parallel to **nē quaesieris** (1).
Babylōniōs / . . . numerōs: *Babylonian tables*, a reference to the casting of horoscopes. Belief in astrology was widespread among the Romans, who often ascribed its invention to the Babylonians or Chaldeans.

3 **Ut melius**: *How (much) better*, exclamatory.
4 **plūrēs hiemēs**: *more winters*, i.e., more years than one has already lived.
tribuō, tribuere, tribuī, tribūtus, *to allocate, grant, allot.*
ultimam: = **ultimam hiemem.** How do you know that **hiemem** is to be understood here?

5 **oppositīs . . . pūmicibus**: *by means of* or *on opposing cliffs.*
dēbilitō, -āre, -āvī, -ātus, *to weaken, break down, break the force of.*
pūmex, pūmicis, m., *pumice*, a porous volcanic rock commonly found in Italy.
quae . . . / Tyrrhēnum (6): the image is unexpected, since we normally think of the sea as wearing down the rocks.
6 **Tyrrhēnus, -a, -um**, *Tyrrhenian, Etruscan.* The Tyrrhenian Sea was to the west of Italy.
sapiō, sapere, sapīvī, *to be sensible, be wise.* Cf. **homō sapiēns.**
sapiās . . . liquēs . . . / resecēs: these independent subjunctives in the 2nd person express a kind of mild command. See pages 117–118.
liquō, -āre, -āvī, -ātus, *to remove the sediment* or *dregs, strain; purify.*
vīna liquēs: wine was strained through cloth or a sieve before drinking in order to remove sediment. The speaker is bidding Leuconoe to prepare to enjoy life.
spatiō brevī: *since the space (of our life) is short*, ablative absolute.
7 ***spēs, speī**, f., *hope.*
resecō, -āre, -āvī, -ātus, *to cut back, prune* (vegetation).
spem longam resecēs: hope for a long life is to be "pruned back" in the manner of a grapevine.
invidus, -a, -um, *grudging, envious.*
8 **aetās**: not *age*, but *time.*
***carpō, carpere, carpsī, carptus**, *to pluck, pick* (a flower or fruit).
carpe diem: the image of picking the day (like a grape) carries along the vine metaphor of **resecēs** in the previous line.
quam minimum: *as little as possible.*
crēdulus, -a, -um + dat., *believing (in), trusting (in).*
posterō: supply **diēī** (from **diem** earlier in the line), *the next day, tomorrow.*

C. Carpe Diem

This poem is the source of the well-known saying carpe diem. *Pay close attention to the poetic context in which this saying is found and be alert to the similarities between this poem and the previous one.*

Tū nē quaesieris (scīre nefās) quem mihi, quem tibi
fīnem dī dederint, Leuconoē, nec Babylōniōs
temptāris numerōs. Ut melius, quicquid erit, patī,
seu plūrēs hiemēs seu tribuit Iuppiter ultimam,
quae nunc oppositīs dēbilitat pūmicibus mare
Tyrrhēnum: sapiās, vīna liquēs et spatiō brevī
spem longam resecēs. Dum loquimur, fūgerit invida
aetās: carpe diem, quam minimum crēdula posterō.

—Horace, *Odes* I.11

---

1. What does the poet bid Leuconoe not to do in lines 1–2?
2. What parenthetical reason is given for her to take this advice? (1)
3. What does the poet mean by what he says in lines 2–3?
4. What does he suggest that it is better to do? (3)
5. In what way does the poet measure a human lifetime? (4) Who is responsible for the length of human life? (4)
6. What poetic imagery does Horace use to describe the passage of time in lines 5–6?
7. What three pieces of advice does the poet give Leuconoe? (6–7)
8. How does the imagery in lines 6–7 help the writer convey this?
9. What is happening as he is giving this advice? (7–8)
10. What final suggestion does the poet make? (8)

Quid cinerī ingrātō servās bene olentia serta?
  Anne corōnātō vīs lapide ossa tegī?
Pōne merum et tālōs; pereat quī crāstina cūrat:
  Mors aurem vellēns "Vīvite" ait, "veniō."

Why do you save sweet-smelling garlands for your ungrateful ashes?
  Do you want your bones to be covered by a garlanded gravestone?
Bring out the undiluted wine and the dice; let him perish who thinks about tomorrow:
  Death, tugging at my ear, says, "Live now, I'm coming for you."

—*Appendix Vergiliana: Copa*, 35–38

Meter: Second Asclepiadean

1 **nec quisquam**: = **et nūllus.**

potior: *preferable, more favored*; comparative of **potis.**

nec quisquam potior . . . / . . . iuvenis (3): take these words together.

***bracchium, -i**, n., *arm.*

2 **cervīx, cervīcis**, f., *neck.*

dabat: = **circumdabat**; the datives **candidae cervīcī** are governed by this compound verb. The poet is describing the embracing of the girl (**bracchia . . . / [circum]dabat**) around the neck (**candidae / cervīcī**). Note the interlocking of these words.

3 **Persae, -ārum**, m. pl., *the Persians, people of the Persian Empire.*

Persārum . . . rēge: to the Romans, a Persian king was symbolic of power and wealth.

vigeō, vigēre, viguī: *to be vigorous; thrive, flourish, prosper.*

4 **nōn aliā**: = **nūllā (puellā)**; ablative of cause with **ārsistī** (6).

5 **ārsistī**: how does Lydia's description of the young man's love for her differ from that given by the **iuvenis** in line 1?

Lȳdia: Lydia speaks of herself in the third person, to bring a contrast with Chloe. Horace addresses several poems to Lydia, a Greek name that was common among female slaves and freedwomen. Lydia was a territory in western Asia Minor famous as the kingdom of Croesus (see the map on page 270).

post: *less important than.*

Chloē, Chloēs, f., *Chloe*, a Greek name meaning young or green shoot or sprout.

Chloēn: Greek accusative (see the Reading Note on page 209). The mention of Chloe by name suggests that it was the boyfriend who had been unfaithful.

6 **multī . . . nōminis**: = **fēmina multī nōminis,** *a woman of fine reputation* or *great renown.*

7 **Īliā**: another name for Rhea Silvia, mother of Romulus and Remus. Note the sound play of **aliā** (5), **Lȳdia** (6 and 7), and **Īliā.**

D. Lovers' Dialogue

The woman Lydia and her youthful lover, who is unnamed, are caught up in a squabble brought on by recent infidelities. Note how the poet uses parallel vocabulary and phrasing, as well as balanced structure, to illustrate the back-and-forth nature of the quarrel. Is the unnamed lover Horace himself?

Iuvenis

Dōnec grātus eram tibi
nec quisquam potior bracchia candidae
cervīcī iuvenis dabat,
Persārum viguī rēge beātior.

Puella

Dōnec nōn aliā magis
ārsistī neque erat Lȳdia post Chloēn,
multī Lȳdia nōminis,
Rōmānā viguī clārior Īliā.

(*continued*)

1. What led the young man (**iuvenis**, line 3) to compare himself to a Persian king? (1–3)
2. To whom does Lydia compare herself? (8) What has led her to feel this way? (5–6)
3. How does Lydia characterize herself? (7)
4. In what way or ways does Lydia's expression of love top that of her lover?

Mars and Rhea Silvia, with two cupids

Mars and Rhea Silvia, *originally oil on wood, transferred onto canvas, circa 1616–1617, Peter Paul Rubens*

9 **Mē**: emphatic position.
Thressus, -a, -um, *Thracian, of Thrace* (a wild area of northern Greece).
regit: thus far, the youth associates love with power and possession (**potior**, 2, **rēge**, 4).

10 **docta**: past participle of **doceō**.
***modus, -ī**, m., *measure, rhythm; measure of verse, poem, song* (additional meanings of the noun you have previously met meaning *way, method*).
cithara, -ae, f., *cithara, lyre* (a stringed instrument; see the photograph on the opposite page).
citharae sciēns: the adjective **sciēns**, *knowledgable (about), skilled (in)*, takes the genitive.

12 ***parcō, parcere, pepercī, parsūrus** + dat., *to spare, be sparing to; treat mercifully, set free.*
superstēs, superstitis, *remaining alive, surviving.*
superstitī: *and allow her to live*; modifies **animae**. This is an example of *prolepsis* or speaking of something future (**sī parcent animae fāta**) as already completed or existing, i.e., her soul survives before it is spared.

13 **Mē**: Lydia is equally emphatic; cf. line 9.
torreō, torrēre, torruī, tostus, *to sear, singe, scorch, burn.*
***fax, facis**, f., *a torch*, often used as a symbol of marriage or death. Lydia associates love with passion.

14 **Thūrīnus, -a, -um**, *of Thurii, belonging to Thurii*, a Greek colony in Magna Graecia (southern Italy). This area was known for its luxury.
Calaïs: the name of Lydia's new lover. The **-ai-** is pronounced in two syllables, as is shown by the long mark on the **i**.
Ornytus, -ī, m., the name of Calais' father, apparently a man of note in Thurii, since Lydia bothers to mention his name.

15 **bis**: cf. line 11; Lydia again trumps her lover.
patiar morī: poetic variation for something like **volam morī**; perhaps a more forceful statement than the boyfriend's **nōn metuam morī** (11).

The threads which the Fates spin are so unchangeable, that, even if they decreed to someone a kingdom which at the moment belonged to another, and even if that other slew the man of destiny, to save himself from ever being deprived by him of his throne, nevertheless the dead man would come to life again in order to fulfil the decree of the Fates . . . He who is destined to become a carpenter, will become one even if his hands have been cut off: and he who has been destined to carry off the prize for running in the Olympic games, will not fail to win even if he broke his leg: and a man to whom the Fates have decreed that he shall be an eminent archer, will not miss the mark, even though he lost his eyesight.

—Flavius Philostratus, *Life of Apollonius of Tyana* 8.7, trans. F. C. Conybeare

Iuvenis

Mē nunc Thressa Chloē regit,
dulcēs docta modōs et citharae sciēns,
prō quā nōn metuam morī,
sī parcent animae fāta superstitī.

Puella

Mē torret face mūtuā
Thūrīnī Calaīs fīlius Ornytī,
prō quō bis patiar morī,
sī parcent puerō fāta superstitī.

(*continued*)

---

5. What does the youth confess in line 9?
6. What skills does Chloe possess? (10)
7. Under what circumstance would he not be afraid to give his life for her? (12)
8. With what metaphor does Lydia counter the youth's claim regarding Chloe? (13) In what context earlier in the poem does a similar image appear? Cite the Latin.
9. How does Lydia gain the advantage in the faceoff? (15)
10. Under what circumstance would she not be afraid to give her life for Calais? (16)

Muse playing the lyre on a Greek vase
Painting of a lekythos by Peter Connolly, watercolor. The lekythos dates back to 440–430 B.C.

17 **prīscus, -a, -um,** *ancient; previous, former.*
prīsca . . . Venus: i.e., previous or former feelings of love. What figure of speech is **Venus**?
redit: the present tense is used here (also **cōgit, excutitur,** and **patet** in the next lines), rather than the expected future, to bring the reader into the moment.

18 **dīdūcō, dīdūcere, dīdūxī, dīductus,** *to draw apart, separate.*
dīductōs: i.e., the lovers; the masculine is preferred when the gender is mixed or uncertain.
***iugum, -ī,** n., literally, a *yoke* or *collar* on the necks of oxen or horses; also refers to a crossbar under which an enemy defeated by the Romans was required to pass as a sign of submission (cf. English *subjugate*). Note also **cōgit**, from **cōgere**, *to compel, force.*
aēneus, -a, -um, *made of bronze.*
iugō . . . aēneō: a bronze yoke is used figuratively to represent the bond of love. Also, if the two get married, they will go side by side through life; the idea of submission to love is not out of place here.

19 **excutiō, excutere, excussī, excussus,** *to shake; push or drive away* (with blows).

20 **reiectae . . . Lȳdiae**: best translated as a clause, e.g., *Lydia, who has been . . . .*
patet iānua: an open or closed door is an image often used in love poetry to indicate access to or denial of affection.

21 **sīdus, sīderis,** n., *star.*
sīdere pulchrior: in answer to **flāva** (19).

22 **ille**: Calais. Note the asyndeton of **ille est** and **tū** and the chiasmus in 22–23.
tū: = **tū es**, paralleling **ille est**; ellipsis.
cortex, corticis, m. or f., *the bark of a tree; the bark of a Spanish oak, cork.*
improbus, -a, -um, *shameless*; often used to describe the sea, *tempestuous, restless, wild.*

23 **īrācundus, -a, -um,** *irritable, inclined to anger, temperamental, unstable.*
Hadria, -ae, m., *the Adriatic Sea*, lying between the peninsula of Italy and the western coast of the Balkans. This nearly landlocked sea had a reputation for being stormy and unpredictable because of its winds and currents. See the map on page 18 or 23.

24 **tēcum . . . tēcum**: note the parallel structure and balance here, including the assonance of -e-. What does this suggest about the resolution of the quarrel?
amem: *I would love*, a potential subjunctive, as is **obeam** (see the Reading Note on page 164).
libēns, libentis, *willing, glad.*

Iuvenis

Quid sī prīsca redit Venus
dīductōsque iugō cōgit aēneō,
sī flāva excutitur Chloē
rēiectaeque patet iānua Lȳdiae?

Puella

Quamquam sīdere pulchrior
ille est, tū levior cortice et improbō
īrācundior Hadriā,
tēcum vīvere amem, tēcum obeam libēns.

—Horace, *Odes* III.9

---

11. What offer does the young man make in line 17?
12. In what alternative way does he put this proposal? (18)
13. What does the youth say about Chloe? (19) About Lydia? (20)
14. With what comparison does Lydia describe Calais? (21–22)
15. What images does she use to describe the **iuvenis**? (22–23) Does this picture seem consistent with her previous characterization of the young man?
16. What does Lydia finally admit that she would gladly do? (24)

Questions for Thought and Discussion

1. How does Lydia one-up or get the advantage on the youth in each of the three sets of stanzas?
2. Is the ending of this poem surprising? Why or why not?
3. What other images do the **iuvenis** and Lydia use to describe themselves? Each other?
4. What role does fate play in this poem? What about the idea of death?
5. How does the poem's final line reflect the first two stanzas, and then the next two?
6. In what ways does line 24 reflect the initial line of Catullus 5 (Chapter 61A, reprinted below)?
7. What imagery found in this poem has appeared previously in the poems of Horace?
8. How does the poet use words and phrases, images, and word placement to create a sense of balance in the dialogue?
9. What evidence, if any, is there in the poem that the **iuvenis** is Horace himself?

Vīvāmus, mea Lesbia, atque amēmus.
Let us live, my Lesbia, and let us love. (Catullus 5.1)

BUILDING THE MEANING

Latin Word Order (Consolidation)

1. You already know that the most common word order in Latin places the subject first, then objects and other modifiers, with the verb last. The verb (or participle, in a participial phrase or an ablative absolute) very often acts as a signpost for the end of a clause or phrase:

illam media inter tālia ferrō / **collāpsam** (72D:663)

But sometimes a word appears outside its own clause, to the left of the clause marker:

Mē sī fāta meīs paterentur dūcere vītam/auspiciīs (72B:340)

Adjectival modifiers (adjectives, nouns in the genitive, and relative clauses) usually come after the nouns they modify; numbers, adjectives of quantity, and demonstratives usually come first:

senātōrēs Rōmānī	Āra Pācis	vir quī Rōmae habitat
septem senātōrēs	magnum aedificium	hae mulierēs

2. When writers depart from the general principles of word order, it is usually to create emphasis or a special effect; the more unusual the position, the more emphatic. The first and last words in a sentence are very strong/emphatic positions. E.g., in the phrase is **Tē propter** (72A:320), **Tē** is strongly emphasized through the breaking of the normal pattern of preposition followed by object, with the result that **Tē** comes first in the sentence. You know that figures of speech such as chiasmus (page 99) and hyperbaton (page 133) involve unusual word order. These figures illustrate the general principle that departures from normal word order serve to create emphasis.

3. A relative clause occasionally appears before its antecedent, and other modifiers appear before their head words—the latter is particularly common in poetry:

Quī parentem meum trucidāvērunt, eōs in exsilium expulī . . . (69A:8–9)
Vidēs ut altā stet nive candidum / Sōracte (73B:1–2)

4. Word order may be used to "paint a picture" for the reader; e.g., see 73A:1 where the order of words shows visually how Pyrrha and the young man are surrounded by roses:

Quis multā gracilis tē puer in rosā

5. In poetry the line is the basic unit. One word of a phrase may be carried onto the next line, a technique called *enjambment*; this often creates emphasis on the enjambed word:

Hauriat hunc oculīs ignem et crūdēlis ab altō / Dardanus (72D:661–662)

Here **Dardanus** is emphasized both by the enjambment and by being separated from its modifier **crūdēlis**, which comes before it.

OVID'S *METAMORPHOSES*

In Book II, you read the story of Pyramus and Thisbe and were introduced to Ovid's great poem, the *Metamorphoses*. Publius Ovidius Naso was born in the town of Sulmo (modern Sulmona) on March 23, 43 B.C. From an early age he showed a talent for writing verse, and consequently rejected the legal career that his father intended for him. As a young man he published several collections of love poetry: the *Amores (Loves)*, that describe an affair between the narrator and a woman he calls Corinna; the *Heroides (Heroines)*, letters from women in mythology to their lovers; and the *Ars amatoria (Art of Love)*, which gives advice both to men and to women about how to find and keep a lover. All these poems are in elegiac couplets and derive from the genre of love elegy that had been practiced by earlier poets such as Propertius and Tibullus.

Sometime before the end of the first century B.C., Ovid turned from love poetry to the writing of his epic masterpiece, the *Metamorphoses (Changes of Form)*. This poem consists of fifteen books in dactylic hexameter. It is organized around the theme of transformation; almost every story includes characters who change from one form to another, usually under the power of a god or goddess. Most of the stories come from Greek mythology, but the last two books include myths and legends that are specifically Roman. It was completed before A.D. 8. As he completed the *Metamorphoses*, Ovid began work on another long poem, the *Fasti (Calendar)*. This poem describes the festivals of the Roman year, beginning in January and advancing through the year.

The *Fasti* was half completed when Ovid received an order from Augustus to leave Rome for exile in the isolated village of Tomis on the Black Sea in Dacia (modern Romania; see the map on page 23). The reasons for his exile are not precisely known. Ovid himself says in a poem written during his exile that it was due to **carmen et error**, *a poem and a mistake*. Many scholars believe that the poem was the *Ars amatoria*. Augustus was trying to promote a return to traditional standards of morality and behavior and might very well have been offended by a poem that gave advice on extramarital affairs. The mistake has been the subject of much speculation. It might have involved Augustus' granddaughter Julia, whose extramarital affairs embarrassed the emperor (cf. Chapter 70B and C). But we do not know for sure.

Ovid lived in exile for nine years, dying in A.D. 17. During his exile he wrote two groups of poems, the *Tristia (Sad Poems)*, one of which appears in Chapter 71, and the *Epistulae ex Ponto (Letters from the Black Sea)*. Despite Ovid's pleas for a pardon—a recurrent theme of these poems—Augustus never relented. In this chapter, you will read two selections from the *Metamorphoses*: the story of Midas and the golden touch, followed by the ill-fated flight of Daedalus and Icarus.

Meter: Dactylic hexameter

100 **Huic**: = Midas. The first two lines, written in a simpler word order, would be: **Deus, gaudēns altōre receptō, fēcit huic arbitrium, grātum sed inūtile, optandī mūneris.**
inūtilis, -is, -e, *useless.*
grātum sed inūtile: Midas may enjoy having the choice, but it is useless because he is incapable of choosing an appropriate reward.
fēcit: i.e., gave, granted.
101 **arbitrium, -ī**, n., *choice.*
altor, altōris, m., *foster father, guardian* (referring to Silenus).

102 **male ūsūrus**: *destined to misuse.*
efficiō, efficere, effēcī, effectus, *to bring it about that*, with the subjunctive clause **(ut) vertātur in aurum** (103).
103 **contingō, contingere, contigī, contactus**, *to touch.*
fulvus, -a, -um, *tawny, yellow.*

104 **annuō, annuere** + dat., *to nod to* (in assent).
optātum, -ī, n., *wish.*
solvit: this verb often means *to pay* (a debt); here it means *grant* (the gift Bacchus promised).
105 **Līber**: another name for Bacchus or Dionysus.
indolēscō, indolēscere, indoluī, *to feel sorry, feel bad.*

106 **malō**: *the bad thing, the evil*, a substantive.
Berecynthius, -a, -um, *of Mt. Berecynthus* (a mountain in Phrygia sacred to the goddess Cybele, who was the mother of Midas).
Berecynthius hērōs: a roundabout way of referring to Midas.
107 **pollicitum, -ī**, n., *promise.*
108 **frōns, frondis**, f., *foliage, leaves.*
fronde: modifies **virentem**, *green with foliage.*
virēns, virentis, *green.*
109 **īlex, īlicis**, f., *holm-oak.*
nōn altā . . . īlice: note the litotes and the meaning *from* (note the prefix on **dētrāxit**).
virga, -ae, f., *twig, small branch.*
110 **humō**: *from the ground*; the preposition is usually omitted with this word, as it is with the words **domus** and **rūs.**
saxum, -ī, n., *rock, stone.*
pallēscō, pallēscere, palluī, *to become pale, grow yellow, be yellow.*
111 **glaeba, -ae**, f., *lump of earth, clod.*
112 **massa, -ae**, f., *nugget* (of metal).
āreō, ārēre, *to be dry.*
Cerēs, Cereris, f., *Ceres*, equivalent to the Greek Demeter, goddess of agriculture.
Cereris: Ceres is used by metonymy (page 185) to stand for an important crop, *wheat.*
dēcerpō, dēcerpere, dēcerpsī, dēcerptus, *to pick, pluck.*
arista, -ae, f., *ear* (of grain).

A. Midas Chooses a Gift

Silenus, the old tutor and friend of the god Bacchus, had wandered off after drinking too much. He was found by some farmers and brought to King Midas of Phrygia. Midas recognized Silenus, entertained him hospitably for ten days, and finally took Silenus back to Bacchus.

Huic deus optandī grātum, sed inūtile, fēcit
mūneris arbitrium gaudēns altōre receptō.
Ille male ūsūrus dōnīs ait 'effice, quicquid
corpore contigerō, fulvum vertātur in aurum.'
Annuit optātīs nocitūraque mūnera solvit
Līber et indoluit, quod nōn meliōra petīsset.
Laetus abit gaudetque malō Berecynthius hērōs
pollicitīque fidem tangendō singula temptat
vixque sibi crēdēns, nōn altā fronde virentem
īlice dētrāxit virgam: virga aurea facta est;
tollit humō saxum: saxum quoque palluit aurō;
contigit et glaebam: contactū glaeba potentī
massa fit; ārentēs Cereris dēcerpsit aristās:

(*continued*)

1. What did the god do for Midas? (100–101) Why? (101)
2. What did Midas ask for? (102–103)
3. How did the god react to Midas' request? (104–105) How did he feel about this? (105)
4. How did Midas feel at this point? (106)
5. Why does Midas touch various things? (107)
6. Name three things that Midas touches; what is the result in each case? (108–112)

Silenus is traditionally shown riding on a donkey. In this mosaic, the donkey is not being very cooperative! Note that Silenus is holding the *thyrsus*, a pole tipped with leaves, a symbol of Bacchus.
Detail from a mosaic, Pompeii, first century B.C.

113 **messis, messis**, gen. pl., **messium**, f., *harvest*.
dēmō, dēmere, dēmpsī, dēmptus, *to take (from)*.
pōmum, -ī, n., *fruit*.
114 **Hesperidae, -ārum**, f. pl., *the Hesperides* (nymphs who tended a garden in which grew a tree with golden apples).
putēs: *you would think*, a potential subjunctive (see the Reading Note on page 164).
115 **radiō, -āre, -āvī, -ātus**, *to gleam, glisten, shine*.
116 **palmīs**: *from his hands* (ablative).
117 **fluō, fluere, flūxī, flūctus**, *to flow*.
ēlūdō, ēlūdere, ēlūsī, ēlūsus, *to make fun of, mock; to deceive*.
Danaēn: Greek accusative (see the Reading Note on page 209). Danae's father locked her up after receiving an oracle that her son would kill him. Jupiter visited Danae in the form of a shower of gold and she gave birth to the hero Perseus.
118 **spēs . . . capit**: i.e., he accepts that what he hoped for has really come true.
fingō, fingere, finxī, *to imagine*.
119 **Gaudentī**: *for the one rejoicing, for him as he rejoiced*, a substantive.
posuēre: = **posuērunt**, from **pōnō**, not **possum**.
minister, ministrī, m., *servant*.
120 **exstruō, exstruere, exstrūxī, exstrūctus**, *to heap up, pile up*.
daps, dapis, f., *banquet, feast*.
torreō, torrēre, torruī, tostus, *to scorch, parch, toast*.
frūx, frūgis, f., *grain*.
tostae frūgis: *toasted grain* = *bread*.
egeō, egēre, eguī + gen., *to want, need, lack, be without*.

---

121 **Cereālis, -is, -e**, *of Ceres*.
122 **rigeō, -ēre**, *to be stiff, stiffen*.
123 **avidus, -a, -um**, *greedy, eager*.
convellō, convellere, *to pluck, seize, tear at*.
dēns, dentis, m., *tooth*.
124 **lammina, -ae**, f., *thin sheet of metal, skin, film*.
fulvus, -a, -um, *tawny, yellow*.
premēbat: *pressed upon*, i.e., *covered*.
125 **auctōrem mūneris**: *the author of the gift*. Bacchus was responsible for Midas' golden touch, so this phrase refers to Bacchus, which then stands by metonymy for the wine; see the Reading Note on page 185.
miscuerat: remember that in the ancient world it was customary to mix water into wine before drinking it (recall the **arbiter bibendī** from Chapter 34).
126 **fūsilis, -is, -e**, *molten, liquid*.
rictus, -ūs, m., *open mouth, smile*; by metonymy, *teeth*.
fluitō, -āre, *to flow*.
vidērēs: *you would see*.
127 **novitās, novitātis**, f., *novelty, strangeness*.
128 **modo**: *recently*.
vōverat: *had wished for*, in this context.

aurea messis erat; dēmptum tenet arbore pōmum:
Hesperidās dōnāsse putēs; sī postibus altīs
admōvit digitōs, postēs radiāre videntur;
ille etiam liquidīs palmīs ubi lāverat undīs,
unda fluēns palmīs Danaēn ēlūdere posset;
vix spēs ipse suās animō capit, aurea fingēns
omnia. Gaudentī mēnsās posuēre ministrī
exstrūctās dapibus nec tostae frūgis egentēs.

—Ovid, *Metamorphoses* XI.100–120

---

7. What two items of food does Midas pick up? What happens to each? (112–114)
8. What happens if Midas touches doorposts? (114–115)
9. What could the water that Midas uses to wash his hands have done? (116–117)
10. What hopes does Midas have in his mind? (118–119)
11. What do the servants do for Midas? (119–120)
12. How does Midas feel at this point? (119)

B. Consequences of the Choice

Tum vērō, sīve ille suā Cereālia dextrā
mūnera contigerat, Cereālia dōna rigēbant,
sīve dapēs avidō convellere dente parābat,
lammina fulva dapēs admōtō dente premēbat;
miscuerat pūrīs auctōrem mūneris undīs:
fūsile per rictūs aurum fluitāre vidērēs.
Attonitus novitāte malī dīvesque miserque
effugere optat opēs et quae modo vōverat ōdit.

(*continued*)

---

1. What happened if Midas touched the bread? (121–122)
2. When did a gold film cover the food? (123–124)
3. What had Midas done with the wine? (125)
4. What happened when Midas drank the wine? (126)
5. What is Midas' emotional state at this point? (127)
6. How does he feel about the gold? (128)

129 **relevō, -āre, -āvī, -ātus**, *to reduce, lighten, relieve.*
sitis, sitis, gen. pl., **sitium**, f., *thirst.*
āridus, -a, -um, *dry.*
ārida: a transferred epithet (see the Reading Note on page 183).
guttur, gutturis, n., *throat.*
130 **ūrō, ūrere, ussī, ustus**, *to burn.*
torqueō, torquēre, torsī, tortus, *to twist; to torture, torment.*
132 **venia, -ae**, f., *pardon, forgiveness.*
Lēnaeus: a title of Bacchus meaning "lord of the wine press."
peccō, -āre, -āvī, -ātus, *to sin, do wrong.*
peccāvimus: poetic plural.
133 **speciōsus, -a, -um**, *showy, (outwardly) beautiful*, i.e., attractive but harmful.
ēripe: supply **mē**.
damnum, -ī, n., *damage, injury, loss.*
speciōsō damnō: what case are these words? See the Reading Note on page 220.
134 **mītis, -is, -e**, *mild, gentle.*
deum: contracted form of **deōrum**.
nūmen: supply **est**.
peccāsse fatentem: = **(Midam sē) peccāsse fatentem.**
135 **pactī fidē**: *in good faith of his agreement*, i.e., as a sign that he did in fact grant Midas' wish.
restituō, restituere, restituī, restitūtus, *to restore.*
solvit: in this context = *released*, i.e., *took away, annulled*. Note that this is, ironically, the same verb used when Bacchus granted the gift (line 104).
136 **-ve**: here equivalent to **et**.
nē . . . maneās: a negative purpose clause.
male: modifies **optātō**, i.e., hoped for in error, unwisely hoped for.
circumlinō, circumlinere, —, circumlitus, *to smear, cover (with).*
137 **vādō, vādere**, *to go, make one's way.*
Sardēs, Sardium, f. pl., *Sardis*, capital of the ancient kingdom of Lydia in Asia Minor. See the map on page 270.
magnīs . . . Sardibus: dative with **vīcīnum**, *near great Sardis.*
ad magnīs vīcīnum Sardibus amnem: note the interlocked word order (synchysis); see page 103.
amnis, amnis, gen. pl., **amnium**, m., *river*. This refers to the River Pactolus in Lydia.
138 ***iugum, -ī**, *yoke; mountain ridge.*
nītor, nītī, nīxus sum, *to strain, struggle; to advance, climb.*
obvius, -a, -um, *in the way, exposed*; with dative (**lābentibus . . . undīs**) and verbs of motion, *to meet*; that is, Midas is to go upstream, against the current.
139 ***dōnec**: this conjunction can mean *until* as well as *while*.
ortus, ortūs, m., *rising; source.*
140 **spūmiger, spūmigera, spūmigerum**, *foam-bearing, full of foam, foamy.*
spūmigerō . . . fontī: dative object of the compound verb **subde** (141).
tuum: modifies **caput corpusque** (141).
fōns, fontis, m., *spring.*
quā plūrimus exit: *where it (the spring) comes up out of the ground in greatest amount.*
141 **subdō, subdere, subdidī, subditus**, *to place under, put under, submerge.*
ēluō, ēluere, ēluī, ēlūtus, *to wash off, wash away.*

(vocabulary and notes continued on opposite page)

Cōpia nūlla famem relevat; sitis ārida guttur
ūrit, et invīsō meritus torquētur ab aurō
ad caelumque manūs et splendida bracchia tollēns
'dā veniam, Lēnaee pater! peccāvimus' inquit,
'sed miserēre, precor, speciōsōque ēripe damnō!'
Mīte deum nūmen: Bacchus peccāsse fatentem
restituit pactīque fidē data mūnera solvit
'nē' ve 'male optātō maneās circumlitus aurō,
vāde' ait 'ad magnīs vīcīnum Sardibus amnem
perque iugum nītēns lābentibus obvius undīs
carpe viam, dōnec veniās ad flūminis ortūs,
spūmigerōque tuum fontī, quā plūrimus exit,
subde caput corpusque simul, simul ēlue crīmen.'
Rēx iussae succēdit aquae: vīs aurea tīnxit
flūmen et hūmānō dē corpore cessit in amnem;
nunc quoque iam veteris perceptō sēmine vēnae
arva rigent aurō madidīs pallentia glaebīs.

—Ovid, *Metamorphoses* XI.121–145

---

7. What practical problem confronts Midas? (129–130)
8. To whom does Midas pray? What does the king acknowledge? (132)
9. What is Midas' request? (133)
10. Why is the god willing to grant the request? (134–135)
11. Where must Midas go first? (137)
12. What route should he then follow? How far? (138–139)
13. How will Midas be able to rid himself of the golden touch? (140–141)
14. What happened when the king followed the god's instructions? (142–143)
15. What effect did Midas' actions have on the river and the surrounding land? (144–145)

142 **succēdō, succēdere, successī, successūrus**, + dat., *to come up under, approach.*
tingō, tingere, tīnxī, tinctus, *to color.*

144 **percipiō, percipere, percēpī, perceptus**, *to get hold of, seize; to gather in, absorb.*
sēmen, sēminis, n., *seed.*
vēna, -ae, f., *vein, artery; vein of metal* (in the ground). The River Pactolus was famous as a source of gold; Ovid imagines that the golden touch was like a seed that took root and grew in the ground, producing the nuggets of gold that could be found in the riverbed.

145 **rigeō, rigēre, riguī**, *to be stiff.*
madidus, -a, -um, *soaking wet, dripping wet.*

172 **-que**: connects the two nouns **iūdicium** and **sententia**.
sānctī . . . montis: the mountain god Tmolus, on whose slopes the contest was held.
sententia, -ae, f., *opinion*.
173 **arguō, arguere, arguī, argūtus**, *to prove; to find fault with, disapprove of.*
174 **Dēlius**: *the Delian*, i.e., Apollo, who was born on the island of Delos. See the map on page 270.
aurēs: object of **patitur** (175), **trahit** and **implet** (176), and **facit** (177). Remember to distinguish **auris**, *ear*, **aura**, *breeze*, and **aurum**, *gold*.
175 **stolidus, -a, -um**, *dull, stupid*.
figūra, -ae, f., *appearance, shape*.
176 **trahit in spatium**: *he drags (out) into space*, i.e., *he lengthens*.
villus, -ī, m., *hair*.
albeō, albēre, *to be white*.
impleō, implēre, implēvī, implētus, *to fill*.
177 **īmus, -a, -um**, *lowest, bottom, at the bottom*.
posse: the infinitive is the equivalent of a noun here, *the power*. It is the direct object of **dat**; supply **eīs** (= **auribus**) as the indirect object.
178 **damnō, -āre, -āvī, -ātus**, *to find guilty, sentence, condemn*.
179 **induō, induere, induī, indūtus**, *to put on*. The passive form **induitur** is completed by the accusative word **aurēs** and can be translated actively; see 72D:659 for another example of this Greek construction sometimes copied by Roman poets.
gradior, gradī, gressus sum, *to go, walk*.
asellus, -ī, m., *donkey*.

180 **pudor, pudōris**, m., *shame*.
181 **tempora**: this word can mean *temple* (of the forehead) as well as *time*.
relevō, -āre, -āvī, -ātus, *to lift up, lighten; to relieve* (the shame).
tiāra, -ae, f., *headdress, cap*. This may refer to the typical Phrygian cap, peaked at the top and with pieces that fell down the sides and were tied under the chin.
182 **solitus**: perfect participle of the verb **soleō, -ēre**.
ferrum: by metonymy, *an object made of iron, knife, scissors*.
resecō, -āre, resecuī, resectus, *to cut back, trim*.
capillus, -ī, m., *hair*.
183 **famulus, -ī**, m., *servant*.

Quī: this connecting relative is the subject of the **cum** clauses (**audēret** in 184 and **posset** in 185; note that the **cum** clause is interrupted by the participial phrase **cupiēns . . . aurās**) as well as the main verbs in lines 185–187.
184 **dēdecus, dēdecoris**, n., *disgrace, shame*.
cupiēns: the participle here has a concessive force, *although desiring*.
sub aurās: *into the open air, into the open*.
185 **reticeō, reticēre, reticuī**, *to keep quiet, remain silent*.
sēcēdō, sēcēdere, sēcessī, sēcessūrus, *to go away, go apart*.
186 **effodiō, effodīre, effōdī, effossus**, *to dig up*.
quālēs . . . aurēs: an indirect question that serves as the direct object of **refert** and **immurmurat** (187).
187 **haustae: hauriō** = *to dig up*, in this context.

C. Midas Makes Another Poor Choice

Midas now hated wealth and lived in the woods as a follower of the rustic god Pan. He was present at a musical contest between Pan and Apollo, where the mountain god Tmolus declared the smooth, sophisticated music of Apollo much superior to the crude music of Pan.

Iūdicium sānctīque placet sententia montis
omnibus, arguitur tamen atque iniūsta vocātur
ūnīus sermōne Midae; nec Dēlius aurēs
hūmānam stolidās patitur retinēre figūram,
sed trahit in spatium villīsque albentibus implet
īnstabilēsque īmās facit et dat posse movērī:
cētera sunt hominis, partem damnātur in ūnam
induiturque aurēs lentē gradientis asellī.
Ille quidem cēlāre cupit turpīque pudōre
tempora purpureīs temptat relevāre tiārīs;
sed solitus longōs ferrō resecāre capillōs
vīderat hoc famulus. Quī, cum nec prōdere vīsum
dēdecus audēret, cupiēns efferre sub aurās,
nec posset reticēre tamen, sēcēdit humumque
effodit et, dominī quālēs aspexerit aurēs,
vōce refert parvā terraeque immurmurat haustae

(*continued*)

1. What pleased all the spectators except Midas? (172)
2. How did Midas react? (173–174)
3. How did Apollo punish Midas? (174–175)
4. Describe the changes Apollo made to Midas' body. (175–177)
5. What was the result of these changes? (178–179)
6. How did Midas react? (180–181)
7. Who knew the truth? (182–183)
8. What conflicting emotions did this person experience? (183–185)
9. What did he do after digging in the ground? (185–187)

A musician playing panpipes, an instrument invented by Pan and used in his contest with Apollo.
Mosaic, second century A.D.

188 **indicium, -ī**, n., *information, evidence.*
tellūs, tellūris, f., *earth.*
regerō, regerere, regessī, regestus, *to carry back, throw back.*
189 **obruō, obruere, obruī, obrutus**, *to hide, bury.*
scrobis, scrobis, gen. pl., **scrobium**, m., *ditch, trench.*
operiō, operīre, operuī, opertus, *to cover, fill in.*

190 **crēber, crēbra, crēbrum**, *thick.* With what word does **Crēber** agree?
harundō, harundinis, f., *reed.*
lūcus, lūcūs, m., *grove, stand* (of vegetation).
191 **ut prīmum**, *as soon as.*
192 **prōdō, prōdere, prōdidī, prōditus**, *to betray.*
agricola, -ae, m., *farmer*; here referring to the servant who dug the hole.
lēnis, -is, -e, *soft, gentle.*
auster, austrī, m., *the south wind* (sometimes used to stand for any wind).
193 **coarguō, coarguere, coarguī**, *to prove conclusively, demonstrate; to reveal, expose.* The subject of **refert** and **coarguit** is *it* (the stand of reeds). The fully grown reeds whisper the secret as they are moved in the breeze.

indiciumque suae vōcis tellūre regestā
obruit et scrobibus tacitus discēdit opertīs.
Crēber harundinibus tremulīs ibi surgere lūcus
coepit et, ut prīmum plēnō mātūruit annō,
prōdidit agricolam: lēnī nam mōtus ab austrō
obruta verba refert dominīque coarguit aurēs.

—Ovid, *Metamorphoses* XI.172–193

---

10. How did he try to conceal what he had done? (188–189)
11. What grew up on the spot? (190)
12. In what way was the digger "betrayed"? (192–193)

Questions for Thought and Discussion

1. What kind of person is Midas in the story of the golden touch? Is he depicted similarly or differently in the story of the music contest? Support your answer with evidence from the text. Could he have behaved any differently than he did?
2. Ovid describes Midas' reaction to receiving the golden touch at some length (lines 107–119). What does Midas' reaction tell us about him? How does it prepare for what comes next?
3. How would you describe Midas' treatment by Bacchus? Fair? Appropriate? Wise? What about his treatment by Apollo?
4. Many of the stories in the *Metamorphoses* are aetiological, that is, they explain the origin of something. What is the aetiological element in the story of the golden touch? In the story of the musical contest?

King Midas (with crown and scepter) is listening to Apollo perform. Note that Apollo is playing an instrument from the Renaissance, not a Roman lyre. The figure at the right is Tmolus, the mountain god, with a crown of leaves. At the left is Pan, holding his pipes in his right hand.
Judgment of King Midas, *oil on canvas, Jacopo da Empoli (1554–1640)*

Meter: Dactylic hexameter

183 **Crētēn**: Greek accusative case; see the Reading Note on page 209.

perōdī, perōdisse, perōsus, *to hate thoroughly* (**per-**). For verbs that exist only in the perfect, pluperfect, and future perfect tenses, see page 223. The perfect participle **perōsus** has the sense of a present participle, *hating*.

184 **nātālis, -is, -e**, *natal, connected with one's birth.*

185 **pelagus, -ī**, n., *sea.*

186 **obstruō, obstruere, obstruxī, obstructus**, *to obstruct, block.*

obstruat: the subjunctive is used here to complete **licet** (185), *he (Minos) may block.*

illāc, adv., *that way.*

187 **possideat**: present subjunctive, *may possess*, continuing the idea of **licet** (185).

possideat, possidet: two main verbs; the asyndeton and use of the same verb twice in different forms stress the contrast between the two ideas.

āēr, āeris, m., *air*. The two vowels are pronounced separately (note the macrons).

āera: Greek accusative form; see the Reading Note on page 209.

188 **ignōtus**: *unknown*, because no human had ever made wings and flown before.

dīmittō, dīmittere, dīmīsī, dīmissus, *to send away, send forth.*

189 **novō, -āre, -āvī, -ātus**, *to make new, refresh, change, alter.*

190 **longam breviōre sequentī**: = **longam (pennam) breviōre (pennā) sequentī**, an ablative absolute.

191 **clīvus, -ī**, m., *slope.*

clīvō: = **in clīvō.**

crēvisse: perfect infinitive of **crēscō** in indirect statement, with **eās** (= **pennās**) understood.

ut . . . putēs: *that you would think*, a result clause.

quondam: *on occasion, sometimes.*

192 **fistula, -ae**, f., *pipe* (musical instrument). The phrase **rūstica fistula** refers to the shepherd's pipes or panpipes; see the note and picture on page 269.

dispār, disparis, *unequal, of different lengths.*

avēna, -ae, f., *oats; stalk, reed.*

Reading Note

Hyperbaton II

On page 133, you learned that hyperbaton is the wide separation of words that belong together, most often an adjective from the noun it modifies. An example is found on line 188 opposite, where **ignōtās** modifies **artēs**. This is a particularly artful example, since **ignōtās** comes at the end of the first half of the line, marked by the caesura, and **artēs** at the end of the line. (See page 311 for the explanation of caesura.) Hyperbaton emphasizes the words that are separated. What is the effect of such separation?

D. Daedalus Fashions Wings

The famous craftsman and inventor Daedalus was exiled from Athens after killing his nephew Perdix in a fit of jealousy. He then went to Crete, which was ruled by King Minos, whose powerful fleet controlled the Aegean Sea. At the royal palace in Gnossos Daedalus built the labyrinth to contain the Minotaur, a monster half man and half bull. King Minos then refused to allow Daedalus to leave the island.

Daedalus intereā Crētēn longumque perōsus
exsilium tactusque locī nātālis amōre
clausus erat pelagō. "Terrās licet," inquit, "et undās
obstruat: at caelum certē patet; ībimus illāc:
omnia possideat, nōn possidet āera Mīnōs."
Dīxit et ignōtās animum dīmittit in artēs
nātūramque novat. Nam pōnit in ōrdine pennās
ā minimā coeptās, longam breviōre sequentī,
ut clīvō crēvisse putēs: sīc rūstica quondam
fistula disparibus paulātim surgit avēnīs.

(*continued*)

---

1. How did Daedalus feel about being on Crete? (183–184)
2. What ways of leaving were closed to Daedalus? How did he solve this problem? (185–187)
3. How is his solution described? (188–189)
4. How did Daedalus arrange the feathers? (189–190)
5. To what two things is the shape of the wings compared? (191–192)

Remains of the palace at Gnossos, capital of Crete during the Bronze Age. The complex layout of this building may have given rise to the legend of the labyrinth.
Minoan palace ruins, north entrance, Gnossos, Crete

193 **līnum, -ī**, n., *flax; string* (made from the fibers of the flax plant).
mediās: **pennās** is understood here and also with **īmās** and **compositās** (194). How do you know that **pennās** is to be supplied?
cēra, -ae, f., *wax*.
alligō, -āre, -āvī, -ātus, *to bind together*.
īmus, -a, -um, *lowest, bottom, at the bottom*.
194 **curvāmen, curvāminis**, n., *curve*.
flectō, flectere, flexī, flexus, *to bend*.
195 ***avis, avis**, gen. pl., **avium**, f., *bird*.
Puer: note the stress on Icarus as a young child; cf. the description of his play in lines 197–200.
196 **ignārus, -a, -um**, *unaware*, introducing an indirect statement.
sua perīcla: *his own dangers*, i.e., *things dangerous to himself*.
perīcla: a syncopated form of **perīcula**.
tractō, -āre, -āvī, -ātus, *to handle*.
197 **renīdēns, renīdentis**, *glistening, shining*.
ōre renīdentī: ablative of manner modifying the verbs **captābat** (198), **mollībat** (199), and **impediēbat** (200).
modo . . . modo (198): *now . . . now*, correlatives.
quās . . . aura: this relative clause comes before its antecedent, which is **plūmās** (198).
vagus, -a, -um, *wandering*.
198 ***captō, -āre, -āvī, -ātus**, *to catch at eagerly, try to catch, keep catching*.
plūma, -ae, f., *feather*.
flāvus, -a, -um, *yellow*.
pollex, pollicis, m., *thumb*.
199 **molliō, mollīre, molliī** or **mollīvī, mollītus**, *to soften*.
mollībat: = **molliēbat**. Note that Ovid continues to use the imperfect to indicate that Icarus keeps on playing and getting in his father's way.
lūsus, -ūs, m., *play*.
mīrābilis, -is, -e, *wonderful*.
mīrābile: agrees with **opus** (200), another example of hyperbaton (see the Reading Note on page 133).
200 **manus ultima**: in English we would say *final touch*.
coeptum, -ī, n., *beginning, thing begun, undertaking, work*.
201 **imposita est**: deduce from **in** + **pōnere**.
geminus, -a, -um, *twin, double*.
opifex, opificis, m., *craftsman*.
lībrō, -āre, -āvī, -ātus, *to balance*.
āla, -ae, f., *wing*.
lībrāvit in ālās: this phrase describes Daedalus' first experiment with flight. He lifts off the ground and finds that the wings work, but he does not fly any distance. The accusative phrase **in ālās** suggests how Daedalus finally entrusts all his weight to the wings. Note how the order of the words shows Daedalus suspended between the two wings.
202 **ipse**: modifying **opifex** (201). Daedalus experiments with flight on his own before allowing Icarus to do so.
mōtā . . . in aurā: i.e., in the air moved by the flapping of the wings.
pendeō, pendēre, pependī, *to hang, be suspended, hover*.

Tum līnō mediās et cērīs alligat īmās
atque ita compositās parvō curvāmine flectit,
ut vērās imitētur avēs. Puer Īcarus ūnā
stābat et, ignārus sua sē tractāre perīcla,
ōre renīdentī modo, quās vaga mōverat aura,
captābat plūmās, flāvam modo pollice cēram
mollībat lūsūque suō mīrābile patris
impediēbat opus. Postquam manus ultima coeptō
imposita est, geminās opifex lībrāvit in ālās
ipse suum corpus mōtāque pependit in aurā.

—Ovid, *Metamorphoses* VIII.183–202

---

6. By what two means did Daedalus bind the feathers together? (193)
7. How did he shape the finished wings? What was the result? (194–195)
8. What did Icarus not know? (196)
9. What two things did Icarus keep doing? (197–199)
10. What effect did Icarus' playing have on his father? (199–200)
11. How did Daedalus test the wings after he finished them? (201–202)

Daedalus making wings
From Thesaurus Graecarum Antiquitatum, *Jacob Gronovius, 1699*

203 ***nātus, -ī**, m., *son.*

mediō: note that the **-que** is attached to the first word of the quotation rather than to the verb **ait** (204); in English the **ait** would come first since it introduces the words of Daedalus.

līmes, līmitis, m., *path.*

mediō . . . līmite: = **in mediō līmite**. Note the emphatic position of **mediō**, the first word of the quotation, coming directly after the caesura; this word contains the essence of Daedalus' advice.

ut . . . currās: indirect command introduced by **moneō** in the next line.

204 **ait**: this word contains two syllables, pronounced *a-yit.*

nē . . . pennās (205): notice how the **sī** clause is nested inside the negative purpose clause.

dēmissus, -a, -um, *low.*

dēmissior: remember that comparative adjectives can be translated *too. . . .*

205 **gravō, -āre, -āvī, -ātus**, *to make heavy, weigh down.*

celsus, -a, -um, *high.*

sī celsior: = **nē, sī celsior ībis**, where **nē** introduces another negative purpose clause with an if-clause nested inside. How do you know that the words **nē** and **ībis** are gapped?

ignis: i.e., the heat of the sun.

adūrō, adūrere, adussī, adustus, *to burn, scorch.*

206 **inter utrumque**: = **inter utrumque līmitem.**

volō, -āre, -āvī, -ātus, *to fly* (do not confuse with **volō, velle**, *to want*).

Nec: negates **spectāre**. The phrase **Nec tē spectāre** is governed by **iubeō** (207).

Boōtēs, -ae, m., *Boötes*, a constellation with the bright star Arcturus that points toward the Great Bear. Boötes is seen as a human figure watching or chasing the Bear.

207 **Helicē, Helicēs**, f., *the Great Bear* (constellation also known as Ursa Major).

Boōtēn, Helicēn: Greek accusative singular forms.

stringō, stringere, strīnxī, strictus, *to draw* (pull out a sword)

Ōrīōn, Ōrīonis, m., *Orion* (constellation in the form of a hunter with a sword on his belt). Boötes and Helice are in the northern sky, while Orion is in the south, so they serve to define direction for Daedalus' flight. At the same time Daedalus is warning his son to stay close to him and not be carried away by the novelty of flight.

208 **mē duce**: ablative absolute.

pariter, adv., *equally, together, at the same time.*

praeceptum, -ī, n., *rule; instruction.*

209 **ignōtās**: cf. **ignōtās** (188) and **ignārus** (196), all emphasizing the strangeness of what is happening.

umerus, -ī, m., *shoulder.*

umerīs: understand **Īcarī.**

accommodō, -āre, -āvī, -ātus, *to apply to, fit.*

āla, -ae, f., *wing.*

E. Preparations for Flight

Īnstruit et nātum "mediō"que "ut līmite currās,
Īcare," ait "moneō, nē, sī dēmissior ībis,
unda gravet pennās, sī celsior, ignis adūrat:
inter utrumque volā. Nec tē spectāre Boōtēn
aut Helicēn iubeō strictumque Ōrīonis ēnsem:
mē duce, carpe viam!" Pariter praecepta volandī
trādit et ignōtās umerīs accommodat ālās.

(*continued*)

---

1. What instructions did Daedalus give his son? (203–204)
2. What will happen if Icarus flies too low? (204–205) If too high? (205) Where should Icarus fly? (206)
3. What does Daedalus order his son not to do? (206–207)
4. What should he do? (208)
5. What does Daedalus do while he gives Icarus instructions about flying? (208–209)

210 **monitus, -ūs**, m., *warning, advice.*
gena, -ae, f., *cheek.*
madēscō, madēscere, maduī, madidus, *to become wet* (with tears).
maduēre: = **maduērunt**.
senīlis, -is, -e, *old man's.*
211 **patrius, -a, -um**, *of a father, father's.*
tremō, tremere, tremuī, *to tremble, shake.*
tremuēre: = **tremuērunt**.
ōsculum, -ī, n., *kiss.*
nātō: modified by **suō** in the next line, another example of hyperbaton (see the Reading Note on page 272).
212 **nōn . . . repetenda**: a future passive participle; see the Reading Note on page 217.
levō, -āre, -āvī, -ātus, *to lift, raise up.*
213 ***velut**, *just as*; this word introduces a simile. Remember that it is a hallmark of epic poetry to have similes at key points in the story (see the Reading Note on page 236).
āles, ālitis, *winged*; as noun, *winged creature, bird.*
altō: modifies **nidō** (214), a striking example of hyperbaton. Notice how Ovid has placed the young bird in the center of the nest through his arrangement of words.
214 **tener, tenera, tenerum**, *tender*, i.e., immature, young.
prōles, prōlis, f., *offspring.*
nīdus, -ī, m., *nest.*
215 **hortātur**: the subject is *he* (Daedalus); Ovid resumes the narrative after the simile.
damnōsus, -a, -um, *causing loss, destructive* (referring to what will happen to Icarus).
ērudiō, ērudīre, ērudīvī, ērudītus, *to teach.*
216 **et . . . et**: remember that **et** used this way = *both . . . and*, emphasizing the two things that Daedalus is doing simultaneously.
suās: how do you know that **ālās** is to be supplied?
217 **Hōs**: = Daedalus and Icarus, the objects of **vīdit et obstipuit** (219).
aliquis tremulā: these words belong inside the clause introduced by **dum**, although they are placed before the clause marker. Notice that there are three parts to this clause; **aliquis . . . piscēs** is the first; the second and third are introduced by **aut . . . -ve** (= **aut . . . aut**).
harundō, harundinis, f., *reed* (used for fishing pole).
piscis, piscis, gen. pl., **piscium**, m., *fish.*
218 **pāstor, pāstōris**, m., *shepherd.*
stīva, -ae, f., *handle* (of a plow in this case).
innīxus, -a, -um + abl., *leaning on.* How do you know that this word is used both with **pāstor** and **arātor**?
arātor, arātōris, m., *plowman.*
219 **obstipēscō, obstipēscere, obstipuī**, *to be amazed, be dumbstruck.*
quīque: relative pronoun **quī** plus **-que**; **-que** links **crēdidit** (220) to **vīdit et obstipuit**. The word **eōs** is understood before **quī** and is the subject of the indirect statement **esse deōs** (220); review the Reading Note on page 79.
aethēr, aetheris, n., *air.*
aethera: Greek accusative form.
aethera carpere: compare the expression **carpe viam** in line 208.

Inter opus monitūsque genae maduēre senīlēs,
et patriae tremuēre manūs; dedit ōscula nātō
nōn iterum repetenda suō pennīsque levātus
ante volat comitīque timet, velut āles, ab altō
quae teneram prōlem prōdūxit in āera nīdō,
hortāturque sequī damnōsāsque ērudit artēs
et movet ipse suās et nātī respicit ālās.
Hōs aliquis tremulā dum captat harundine piscēs,
aut pāstor baculō stīvāve innīxus arātor
vīdit et obstipuit, quīque aethera carpere possent,
crēdidit esse deōs.

—Ovid, *Metamorphoses* VIII.203–220

---

6. How do we know that Daedalus is feeling anxious about the flight? (210–211)
7. What does Daedalus do before setting out? (211–212)
8. To what are Daedalus and Icarus compared? (213–214)
9. Identify four things that Daedalus does as he and Icarus begin the flight. (215–216)
10. What three people observe Daedalus and Icarus flying? How is each one described? (217–218)
11. What do these people think when they see Daedalus and Icarus? Why? (219–220)

Caelum ipsum petimus stultitiā.
Heaven itself we seek in our folly. (Horace, *Odes* I.3.38)

Iuvenīle vitium est regere nōn posse impetūs.
It is a fault of the young to be unable to control (their) impulses. (Seneca, *Troades* 250)

Saepe mōrēs patris imitātur fīlius īnfans.
A young son often imitates the ways of his father. (Medieval)

---

220 **Iūnōnius, -a, -um**, *belonging to Juno, Juno's, sacred to Juno.*
laevus, -a, -um, *left.*
laevā / parte (221): = **in laevā parte**, where **parte** = *side.*
221 **Samos, -ī**, f., *Samos* (island in the Aegean sea). There was a famous temple of Juno on Samos in ancient times. Note that Samos and the other islands are feminine. See the map on page 270 for all the places mentioned here.
fuerant . . . relictae: = **relictae erant.**
Dēlos, -ī, f., *Delos*, an island in the Aegean at the center of the Cyclades group, birthplace of Apollo and Artemis.
Paros, -ī, f., *Paros*, another island in the Cyclades. Daedalus and Icarus are flying northeast away from Crete.
222 **Lebinthos, -ī**, f., *Lebinthos*, another island.
fēcundus, -a, -um, *fertile, rich (in).*
mel, mellis, n., *honey.*
Calymnē, Calymnēs, f., *Calymne*, another island.
223 **volātus, -ūs**, m., *flight.*
224 **cupīdō, cupīdinis**, f., *desire, eagerness.*
225 **rapidus, -a, -um**, *fast-moving, seizing, carrying away;* (of fire, etc.) *consuming, scorching.*
vīcīnia, -ae, f., *nearness.*
226 **mollit**: an ironic echo of **mollībat** (199).
odōrātus, -a, -um, *pleasant-smelling.*
vinculum, -ī, n., *bond.*
cērās: plural, but translate as singular.
227 **tābēscō, tābēscere, tabuī**, *to waste away, distintegrate, fall apart, melt.*
quatiō, quatere, *to shake, wave, flap.*
lacertus, -ī, m., *upper arm, arm.*
228 **rēmigium, -ī**, n., *rowing, oars.* This metaphor compares the repetitive beating of wings to the motion of oars (an appropriate image, given what happens in the next two lines).
careō, carēre + abl., *to lack.*
nōn ūllās: = **nūllās.**
percipiō, percipere, percēpī, perceptus, *to get hold of, catch.*
aura, -ae, f., *breeze.*
229 **ōra**: plural of **ōs, ōris.**
caeruleus, -a, -um, *sky-blue, blue.*
caeruleā: what noun does this adjective modify? What figure of speech is this?
patrius, -a, -um, *belonging to a father, of a father.*
patrium . . . nōmen: *the name 'father';* Icarus calls out **pater** (not **Daedale**) as he falls.
230 **excipiuntur**: notice the wordplay here; Icarus cannot catch the breeze (**percipit**, 228) but is himself caught up in the water.
trāxit: *took* in this context.
quae nōmen traxit: the Icarian Sea, an eastern section of the Aegean.

Reading Note

Poetic Plurals

In Roman poetry, one often finds words in the plural which might seem more logical in the singular. In the passage opposite, we have **cērās** (226) and **ōra** (229). Such words may be translated in the singular.

F. The Fate of Icarus

Et iam Iūnōnia laevā
parte Samos (fuerant Dēlosque Parosque relictae)
dextra Lebinthos erat fēcundaque melle Calymnē,
cum puer audācī coepit gaudēre volātū
dēseruitque ducem caelīque cupīdine tractus
altius ēgit iter. Rapidī vīcīnia sōlis
mollit odōrātās, pennārum vincula, cērās;
tābuerant cērae: nūdōs quatit ille lacertōs,
rēmigiōque carēns nōn ūllās percipit aurās,
ōraque caeruleā patrium clāmantia nōmen
excipiuntur aquā, quae nōmen trāxit ab illō.

(*continued*)

1. Between what islands were they flying? What islands had they passed by? (220–222)
2. What two Latin phrases express the idea that Icarus is caught up in the experience of flying? What does he do as a result? (223–225)
3. What happens to Icarus' wings? (225–226)
4. How does the melting of the wax affect Icarus' flight? (227–228)
5. What happens to Icarus? What is he doing as this happens? (229–230)

It is clear that the painter Brueghel was familiar with Ovid's version of the story of Daedalus and Icarus. What elements in the painting can you find that prove this statement?
Landscape with the Fall of Icarus, *oil on canvas, mounted on wood, circa 1558, Pieter Brueghel the Elder*

231 **īnfēlīx, īnfēlīcis,** *unhappy, unfortunate, unlucky.*

232 **Quā . . . regiōne:** = **In quā regiōne.**

requīrō [re- + **quaerō**], **requīrere, requīsīvī, requīsītus,** *to seek, search for.*

233 **Īcare**: the repetition of Icarus' name three times (231, 232, and 233) suggests the Roman custom of **conclāmātiō**, according to which the name of person who had just died was called three times, as if to call the deceased back to life.

234 **dēvoveō, dēvovēre, dēvōvī, dēvōtus,** *to sacrifice; to curse.*

***sepulcrum, -ī,** n., *tomb.*

235 **condidit**: the verb **condere** can mean *to bury* as well as *to found.*

tellūs, tellūris, f., *land.* This refers to the island of Icaria, near Samos (see the map on page 270). Many of the myths in the *Metamorphoses* explain the origin of something.

dicta: = **dicta est.**

sepultī: *the one buried*, perfect participle of the verb **sepelīre** used as a substantive.

Before reading the following poem by William Carlos Williams, written in 1962, look carefully at the painting by Pieter Brueghel shown on the previous page.

Landscape with the Fall of Icarus

According to Brueghel
when Icarus fell
it was spring

a farmer was ploughing
his field
the whole pageantry

of the year was
awake tingling
with itself

sweating in the sun
that melted
the wings' wax

unsignificantly
off the coast
there was

a splash quite unnoticed
this was
Icarus drowning

At pater īnfēlīx, nec iam pater, "Īcare," dīxit,
"Īcare," dīxit, "ubi es? Quā tē regiōne requīram?"
"Īcare" dīcēbat: pennās aspexit in undīs
dēvōvitque suās artēs corpusque sepulcrō
condidit, et tellūs ā nōmine dicta sepultī.

—Ovid, *Metamorphoses* VIII.220–235

---

6. How is Daedalus described at this point? (231)
7. What does Daedalus do when he cannot see Icarus? (231–233)
8. How does Daedalus realize that his son has fallen into the sea? (233)
9. What is Daedalus' reaction after he realizes that Icarus is dead? (234)
10. How is the memory of Icarus preserved? (234–235)

Questions for Thought and Discussion

1. A frequent theme in the *Metamorphoses* is that of a human who in some way goes beyond what is permissible for mankind. Reread the story of Daedalus and Icarus and note any language that suggests that Daedalus is crossing this boundary.
2. How are the people who observe the flight different from Daedalus? Why did Ovid choose people such as these to be observers? What does the fact that they believe Daedalus and Icarus to be gods contribute to the narrative?
3. Why does Ovid say that Icarus disobeyed his father? Is this consistent with the way Icarus was portrayed earlier in the story? Is there any evidence that Icarus is "pushing the envelope" of acceptable human behavior?
4. How does Ovid draw readers emotionally into the story and make them feel sorry for Daedalus? Cite the Latin text to justify your answer.
5. Roman authors often praise the choice of a middle path between extremes; for example, in one of his poems Horace refers to **aurea mediocritās**, *the golden mean*. Daedalus' instructions to Icarus fit into this tradition, yet they are highly ironic given the circumstances under which Daedalus delivers them. Explain the irony.
6. In what ways is the bird simile (213–215) appropriate to the flight of Daedalus and Icarus? In what ways is it not appropriate? What does it contribute to our understanding of the story?
7. Carefully study the painting on page 281. What evidence is there that Brueghel was familiar with Ovid's account of Icarus? Locate Icarus in the painting and notice how the other people relate to his death. What is the message of Brueghel's painting?
8. Compare the painting with the poem by William Carlos Williams on page 282. Do you think that Williams has understood the painting well? Why or why not?

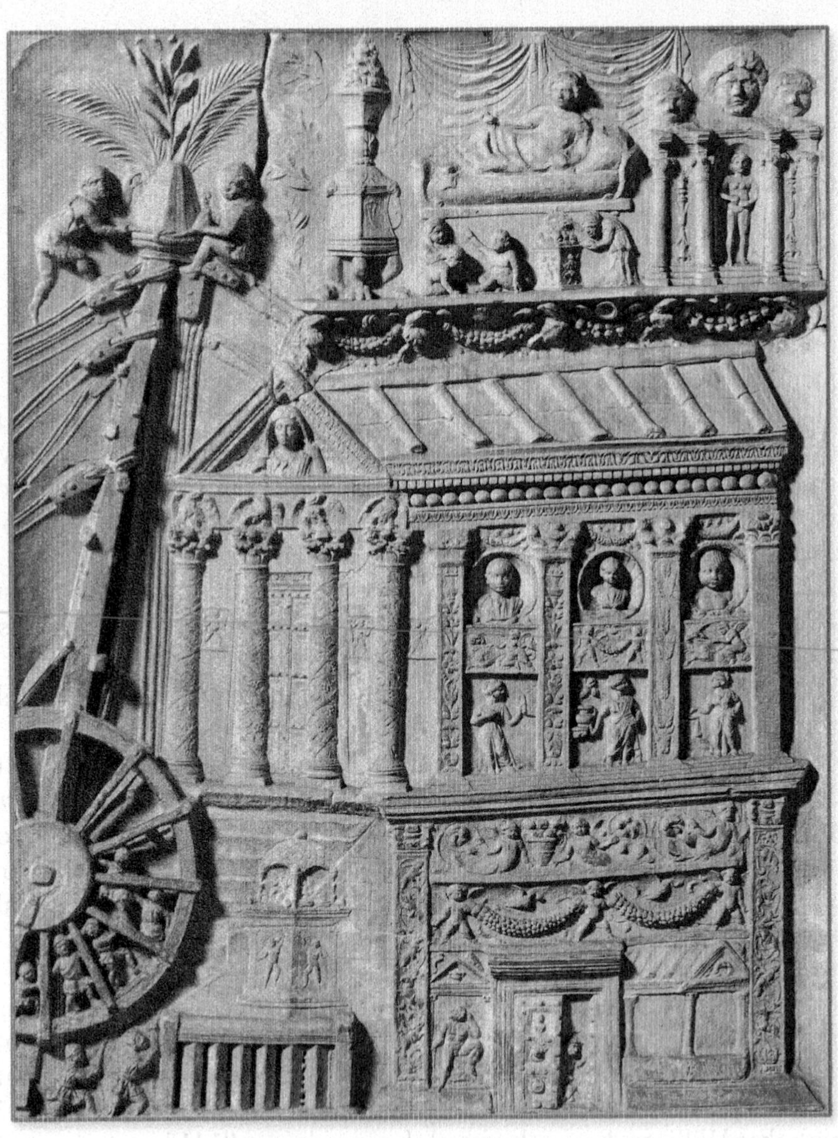

Relief from the tomb of Quintus Haterius Tychicus, a rich building contractor of the late first century A.D. A tomb-temple is shown, every inch of its surface crammed with sculpture. A crane (operated by slaves on a treadwheel) symbolizes the owner's trade. The upper right-hand corner gives an interior view of the temple. Haterius himself reclines on a couch while his three children play on the floor and his old nurse lays a sacrifice on an altar. To their right is a shrine of Venus with ancestor-masks above.
Marble sculpture, Italy

Two Authors of the Early Empire

The readings in Parts I–V were drawn mostly from authors of the late Republic and the Augustan era. So much high quality literature was written during this time that it is often referred to as the "golden age" of Latin. But literary production continued throughout the Empire. You have already read selections from three imperial writers who described events of earlier times: Eutropius (Chapters 55–57), Asconius (Chapter 64), and Suetonius (Chapter 70). This final Part introduces two of the many writers whose works reflect their own lives during the Empire. Chapter 75 presents extracts from the *Satyricon*, a satiric novel of the first century A.D. Chapter 76 contains a letter of Pliny the Younger; see page 287 for information about his life and works.

Objectives for Part VI:

- to read several selections of Latin prose from two authors of the early Empire, Petronius and Pliny, both of whom were personally acquainted with the emperors whom they served
- to become acquainted with the genre of satire and to gain further appreciation of Roman letter writing as a literary genre
- to learn about some of the social changes that took place during the early Empire, such as the growing influence of freedmen
- to read an eyewitness account of one of the most famous events in Roman history

Petronius and the *Satyricon*

The author of the *Satyricon* is usually identified with the Gaius Petronius described by the historian Tacitus as a man who held a privileged but dangerous position as unofficial "Arbiter of Elegance" at the court of Nero. Yet, as governor of Bithynia and later consul, he showed himself a capable and energetic administrator. Eventually, he aroused Nero's suspicions and died by suicide (a form of imperial execution), surrounded by friends who comforted him "not with philosophical doctrines but with frivolous songs and light verse."

The longest and most famous of the surviving fragments of the *Satyricon* is the *Cena Trimalchionis* (*Banquet of Trimalchio*). It describes an elaborate dinner party given by the ex-slave and self-made millionaire Trimalchio. An army of slaves serves a vast array of dishes, most of them disguised as something other than what they are: for example, glowing "coals" made of sliced damsons and pomegranates, a roast boar with sausages for entrails, and a sow with pastry "piglets." From time to time the guests are entertained by musicians, actors, or singing waiters of various degrees of awfulness.

Some of the most interesting and amusing passages of the *Cena* are those in which Petronius lets us eavesdrop on the conversations of Trimalchio and his guests. These conversations are unique in Latin literature for the vividness with which they portray the habits of speech and thought of ordinary people in the ancient Roman world. But the real heart of the *Cena* is the brilliant comic portrait of Trimalchio himself. Every aspect of the banquet reveals some facet of Trimalchio's life and personality: the culinary extravaganzas, the service and entertainment, and the guests' comments on their host and his fabulous wealth.

A Roman banquet scene, as shown in a Pompeiian wall painting
Fresco, Pompeii

Of all the ways Petronius brings to life this great comic figure, Trimalchio's own speeches are the most revealing. The passage contained in readings A and B of Chapter 75, in which Trimalchio describes the preparations he has made for his own death, is an example of this kind of self-characterization. As you read the passage, try to share Petronius' double vision: on the one hand, the way Trimalchio sees himself (i.e., the image he thinks he is presenting to others) and on the other hand the way we, the readers, see him. In this double vision lies much of the humor and humanity of the *Cena*.

Ascyltos, one of the main characters in the *Satyricon*, has come to Trimalchio's house for dinner. He is met by an outlandishly dressed doorkeeper and a magpie in a golden cage:

> While I was staring at all these things, I almost fell and broke my leg. For at the left as you entered, not far from the doorkeeper's room, there was a huge dog, tied up with a chain, painted on the wall and in square letters was written BEWARE OF THE DOG. For sure my friends laughed, but I, after catching my breath, continued to peruse the whole wall. There was a slave market painted with captions, and Trimalchio himself, with the long hair of a young slave, was holding a caduceus and entering Rome while Minerva led the way. Next it showed how he had learned to keep accounts and then had become steward; the careful painter had rendered everything diligently with labels. Indeed, in the painting at the end of the portico Mercury had picked up Trimalchio by his chin and was raising him onto the high magistrates' platform. The goddess Fortune was on hand with her horn of plenty and the three Fates spinning golden threads.
>
> —Petronius, *Satyricon* XXIX.1–6

What facts about Trimalchio's life can you determine or infer from this passage? What kind of person do you think Trimalchio is? Watch to see whether your impressions are confirmed by the Latin readings in this chapter.

A Roman Senator of the Empire

Gaius Plinius Secundus, or Pliny the Younger, was born to a prosperous landowning family at Comum, in the Cisalpine province of northern Italy. Although a lawyer by vocation, Pliny published hundreds of letters, including his official correspondence with the Emperor Trajan, who ruled A.D. 98–117. These letters—perhaps the most famous of which is Pliny's eyewitness account of the eruption of Mt. Vesuvius in A.D. 79—provide an intimate look at the personal and professional life of a member of the Roman ruling class during the reigns of the emperors Domitian and Nerva, as well as Trajan. Pliny was privileged to witness the reconciliation between Senate and emperor after the tyrannical rule of Domitian and the transformation of the empire into what the English historian Gibbon called "the period in the history of the world during which the condition of the human race was most happy and prosperous." As an advocate for the Senate, Pliny prosecuted or defended a number of Roman officials accused of maladministration and embezzlement in their provinces. This, coupled with the fact that he was knowledgeable about financial affairs, having served as head of the state treasury, led to his commission in A.D. 110 as special envoy of the Emperor Trajan, with the title **lēgātus Augustī cōnsulārī potestāte**, to deal with problems of inefficiency and corruption in the province of Bithynia-Pontus. The last of Pliny's ten books of epistles contains over 100 letters to and from Trajan, in which Pliny asks for advice on such matters as procedure, law, finance, building projects, and security. It is believed that Pliny died in office in Bithynia just before A.D. 114.

Here is a translation of part of an inscription that was placed in the baths at Comum, Pliny's hometown, in recognition of his civic generosity:

> Gaius Plinius Caecilius Secundus, son of Lucius of the tribe Oufentina, consul, augur, praetorian commissioner with full consular power for the province of Pontus and Bithynia, sent to that province in accordance with the Senate's decree by the Emperor Nerva Trajan Augustus, curator of the bed and banks of the Tiber and the sewers of Rome, official of the Treasury of Saturn, official of the military Treasury, praetor, tribune of the people, quaestor of the emperor, commissioner for the Roman knights, military tribune of the Third Gallic Legion, magistrate of the Board of Ten, left by his will public baths at a cost of . . . and an additional 300,000 sesterces for furnishing them, with 1,866,666 sesterces to support a hundred of his freedmen, and subsequently to provide an annual dinner for the people of the city. . . . Likewise in his lifetime he gave 500,000 sesterces for the maintenance of boys and girls of the city and also 100,000 for the upkeep of the library.
>
> —*Corpus Inscriptionum Latinarum* V.5262

1 **aequē**: *equally*, i.e., with us free men.
lāc, lactis, n., *milk*, here referring to mother's milk.
lactem: = **lāc**; Trimalchio confuses the gender of nouns; he treats both **lāc** and **fātum** in the following clause as if they were masculine, not neuter.

2 **mē salvō**: *as long as I'm alive, while I'm around.*
cito, adv., *quickly, soon.*

3 **gustō, -āre, -āvī, -ātus**, *to taste.*
aquam līberam gustābunt: *they will taste the water of freedom*, a cliché. Trimalchio in his confusion has jumbled together two incompatible ideas, since the slaves will not be free until Trimalchio is dead.

manū: one meaning of the word **manus** is the *power* that a Roman father exercised over all members of his household; hence **manū mittere** (sometimes written as one word), *to send from one's power*, meant *to free from slavery*.

ideō, adv., *for this reason.*

4 **pūblicō, -āre, -āvī, -ātus**, *to make public.*
***tamquam**, conj., *just as if, as.*

5 **nūgae, nūgārum**, f. pl., *jokes, trifles.*
oblītus nūgārum: *getting down to business* (literally, *forgetting trifles*).
exemplar, exemplāris, n., *copy.*

6 **ingemēscō, ingemēscere, ingemuī**, *to groan.*

7 **Habinnam**: Habinnas, one of Trimalchio's friends, a stonemason.

8 **quemadmodum**, conj., *in what way, as.*

secundum, prep. + acc., *by, beside.*

9 **catella, -ae**, f., *puppy.*
pingō, pingere, pīnxī, pictus, *to paint, portray.*
Petraitis: genitive of **Petraitēs**, a real gladiator of the 1st century A.D.

10 **beneficium, -ī**, n., *kindness.*
ut sint: continuing the indirect command construction from **rogō** (8).
in fronte: *wide.*

11 **in agrum**: *deep.*
dūcentī, -ae, -a, *two hundred.*

Omne genus . . . pōma: *Every kind (of) fruit tree.*
sint: supply **ut**.
circā, prep. + acc., *around.*
***cinis, cineris**, m., *ash.*

12 **vīneārum largiter**: *plenty of grapevines.*
vīvō . . . esse: *for a living man to have*; **vīvō** is dative of possession, and the infinitives (**esse** and **cūrārī**) are the subjects of **falsum est**, *it is wrong.*
cultus, -a, -um, *cultivated, elegant.*

13 **Hoc . . . sequātur**: *Let this monument not pass to* (literally, *follow*). This formula was intended to prevent sale or unauthorized use of the tomb by the heirs of the deceased; it did not "pass to" them (**sequātur**) with the rest of his possessions.

LXXV

THE MILLIONAIRE

A. Trimalchio's Tomb

At this point in the dinner, Trimalchio has just invited his slaves to share the dining couches with his guests; as they scramble to accept this offer, the dining room is thrown into confusion. Trimalchio then addresses his friends and defends his liberal gesture with bits of ill-digested "philosophy."

Trimalchiō, "Amīcī," inquit, "et servī hominēs sunt et aequē ūnum lactem bibērunt, etiam sī illōs malus fātus oppresserit. Tamen mē salvō, cito aquam līberam gustābunt. Ad summam, omnēs illōs in testāmentō meō manū mittō. Et haec ideō omnia pūblicō, ut familia mea iam nunc sīc mē amet tamquam mortuum."

Grātiās agere omnēs indulgentiae coeperant dominī, cum ille oblītus nūgārum exemplar testāmentī iussit afferrī et tōtum ā prīmō ad ultimum ingemēscente familiā recitāvit. Respiciēns deinde Habinnam, "Quid dīcis," inquit, "amīce cārissime? Aedificās monumentum meum, quemadmodum tē iussī? Valdē tē rogō, ut secundum pedēs statuae meae catellam pingās et corōnās et unguenta et Petraitis omnēs pugnās, ut mihi contingat tuō beneficiō post mortem vīvere; praetereā ut sint in fronte pedēs centum, in agrum pedēs dūcentī. Omne genus enim pōma volō sint circā cinerēs meōs, et vīneārum largiter. Valdē enim falsum est vīvō quidem domōs cultās esse, nōn cūrārī eās, ubi diūtius nōbīs habitandum est. Et ideō ante omnia adicī volō: 'Hoc monumentum hērēdem nōn sequātur.'

(*continued*)

1. What is Trimalchio's attitude toward slaves? (1–2)
2. What has Trimalchio decided to do about his slaves? (2–3)
3. Why has he decided to make this known now? (3–4)
4. What does Trimalchio do with the copy of his will? (5–7)
5. What request does he make of Habinnas? (7–8)
6. Describe the tomb Trimalchio wants built. (8–12)
7. Why does he think it is important to plan a tomb? (12–13)
8. What is the last item he wants on his tomb? (13–14)

15 **nāvēs**: Trimalchio's fortune was derived from merchant shipping.
vēlum, -ī, n., *sail.*
16 **tribūnal, tribūnālis**, n., *magistrates' raised platform, tribunal.* Trimalchio was a **sēvir Augustālis**, one of the priests in charge of the worship of the emperor in the towns. A bordered toga, gold ring, and throne were symbols of the office. Cf. line 24.
nummus, -ī, m., *coin.*
17 **sacculus, -ī**, m., *little sack*, a diminutive.
effundō, effundere, effūdī, effūsus, *to pour out.*
quod: *that*, introducing indirect statement, a colloquial usage.
epulum, -ī, n., *feast, dinner.*
bīnī, -ae, -a, *two at a time, two each, two per person.* This was the cost of the dinner that Trimalchio gave.

Faciātur: for **Fīat**, *Let there be made*; the verb is singular either because Trimalchio mistakes **trīclīnia** for a 1st declension noun, or because he is thinking in Greek, in which a neuter plural subject takes a singular verb; either way, his Latin is shaky.

18 **sibi suāviter facientem**: *enjoying themselves.*

19 **Fortūnātae**: *Fortunata*, Trimalchio's wife.
columba, -ae, f., *dove.*
cingulum, -ī, n., *belt; leash.*
20 **alligō, -āre, -āvī, -ātus**, *to tie.*
cicarōnem meum: *my little pet*, probably his favorite slave.
amphorās cōpiōsās gypsātās: *large wine jars sealed with gypsum.*
effluō, effluere, efflūxī, *to flow out; to spill.*

21 **sculpō, sculpere, sculpsī, sculptus**, *to carve.*
licet . . . sculpās: *you may carve.*
plōrō, -āre, -āvī, -ātus, *to weep.*

hōrologium, -ī, n., *clock, sundial.*
in mediō: supply **sit**, *let there be.*
22 **velit nōlit**: *(whether) he wishes to (or) not.*

23 **vidē dīligenter sī haec**: *consider carefully whether this (inscription). . . .*
24 **requiēscō, requiēscere, requiēvī, requiētūrus**, *to rest.*

sēvirātus: *the office of* ***sēvir***; see note on line 16.
absentī: with **huic**, *in his absence*; an additional honor, implying that he neither campaigned nor paid for the office.
dēcernō, dēcernere, dēcrēvī, dēcrētus, *to decide, decree, assign.*

Cum: how does **tamen** (25) affect the meaning (see the Reading Notes on pages 61 and 201)?
25 **decuriīs**: the *boards* that formed the lower ranks of the Roman civil service.
26 **sēstertium . . . trecentiēs**: the usual way of expressing millions of sesterces was simply to use a numerical adverb (ending in **-iēs**) with the words **centēna mīlia** understood: 300 x 100,000 = 30,000,000.

(vocabulary and notes continued on opposite page)

B. More about the Tomb

"Tē rogō ut nāvēs etiam in monumentō meō faciās plēnīs vēlīs euntēs, et mē in tribūnālī sedentem praetextātum cum ānulīs aureīs quīnque et nummōs in pūblicō dē sacculō effundentem; scīs enim, quod epulum dedī bīnōs dēnāriōs. Faciātur, sī tibi vidētur, et trīclīnia. Faciās et tōtum populum sibi suāviter facientem. Ad dexteram meam pōnās statuam Fortūnātae meae columbam tenentem, et catellam cingulō alligātam dūcat, et cicarōnem meum, et amphorās cōpiōsās gypsātās, nē effluant vīnum. Et urnam licet frāctam sculpās, et super eam puerum plōrantem. Hōrologium in mediō, ut quisquis hōrās īnspiciet, velit nōlit, nōmen meum legat.

"Īnscrīptiō quoque vidē dīligenter sī haec satis idōnea tibi vidētur: C. Pompeius Trimalchiō Maecēnātiānus hīc requiēscit. Huic sēvirātus absentī dēcrētus est. Cum posset in omnibus decuriīs Rōmae esse, tamen nōluit. Pius, fortis, fidēlis, ex parvō crēvit, sēstertium relīquit trecentiēs, nec umquam philosophum audīvit. Valē. 'Et tū.' " Haec ut dīxit Trimalchiō, flēre coepit ūbertim. Flēbat et Fortunāta, flēbat et Habinnas, tōta dēnique familia, tamquam in fūnus rogāta, lāmentātiōne trīclīnium implēvit.

—Petronius, *Satyricon* 71–72 (extracts)

---

9. What will appear on Trimalchio's tomb that symbolizes the source of his riches? (15)
10. What will be depicted to show that Trimalchio benefited his fellow citizens? (15–18)
11. How will family members be depicted? (18–20)
12. What symbols of mourning will appear? (21)
13. How will Trimalchio ensure that people stop and look at his tomb? (21–22)
14. What honors given to Trimalchio will be mentioned in the inscription? (23–25)
15. How does Trimalchio describe himself in the rest of the inscription? (25–26)
16. How do the guests and family members react to all this? (27–28)

26 **"Valē. 'Et tū.' "**: *"Farewell (to you, passerby). 'And (to) you, (Trimalchio).' "* Inscriptions on Roman tombs often take the form of an imaginary dialogue between the dead man and the passerby.

27 **ūbertim**, adv., *copiously, abundantly.*
28 **impleō, implēre, implēvī, implētus**, *to fill.*

Tomb relief of the Publius Gessius family
Marble sculpture, Italy, 30–20 B.C. Photograph © 2008 Museum of Fine Arts, Boston

2 **candēlābrum, -ī**, n., *lampstand.* Notice that Trimalchio treats this as a masculine noun.

3 **mētior, mētīrī, mēnsus sum**, *to measure.*
rostrum, -ī, n., *beak (of a bird); chin.*
barbātus, -a, -um, *bearded, with a beard.*
labrum, -ī, n., *lip.*
lucerna, -ae, f., *lamp.*
dē lucernā unguēbam: lamps burned olive oil.

4 **cēterum**, adv., *for the rest, moreover.*
ipsimus, -ī, m., *the man himself;* a form derived from **ipse,** used by slaves to refer to the master.
5 **cerebellum, -ī**, n., *brain.*

Quid multa?: *To put it briefly* (literally, *Why [should I say] much?*).
cohērēs, cohērēdis, m./f., *joint heir (with)* + dat. Rich men often left something to the emperor to avoid his confiscating the whole estate.
patrimōnium, -ī, n., *inheritance.*
lāticlāvius, -a, -um, *with a broad stripe, fit for a senator.* The property qualification for the Senate during the first century A.D. was at least a million sesterces.

6 **concupīscō, concupīscere, concupīvī, concupītus**, *to long for, long to.*
negōtior, -ārī, -ātus sum, *to go into business.*

Nē . . . morer: *To cut a long story short* (literally, *So that I don't delay you with many [words]*).
7 **onerō, -āre, -āvī, -ātus**, *to load.*
tunc: alternate form of **tum**.
contrā: in this context, *equal to, worth its weight in.*

8 **Putārēs**: *You would think*, a potential subjunctive.
naufragō, -āre, -āvī, *to be wrecked.* **naufragārunt** = **naufragāvērunt**.

9 **trecentiēs sēstertium**: see note on B:26.
dēficiō, dēficere, dēfēcī, dēfectus, *to fail, falter.*

10 **iactūra, -ae**, f., *loss.*
gustus, -ūs, m., *appetizer, small portion.*
gustī: *worth a tiny bit,* a genitive (as if 2nd declension) expressing value.

11 **fortitūdō, fortitūdinis**, f., *courage, strength.*

12 **lardum, -ī**, n., *lard.*
faba, -ae, f., *bean.*
sēplasium, -ī, n., *perfume.*
manicipium, -ī, n., *slave.*

Hōc locō: *At this point,* ablative of time when.

14 **pecūlium, -ī**, n., *small savings, nest egg.*
fermentum, -ī, n., *yeast, leavening.*

(*vocabulary and notes continued on opposite page*)

C. The Millionaire's Autobiography

Having regaled his guests with a detailed account of his preparations for death, Trimalchio next treats them to the story of his life, a classic of the rags-to-riches genre.

"Sed, ut coeperam dīcere, ad hanc mē fortūnam frūgālitās mea perdūxit. Tam magnus ex Asiā vēnī, quam hic candēlābrus est. Ad summam, cotīdiē mē solēbam ad illum mētīrī, et ut celerius rostrum barbātum habērem, labra dē lucernā unguēbam. Cēterum, quemadmodum dī volunt, dominus in domō factus sum, et ecce, cēpī ipsimī cerebellum. Quid multa? Cohērēdem mē Caesarī fēcit, et accēpī patrimōnium lāticlāvium. Nēminī tamen nihil satis est. Concupīvī negōtiārī. Nē multīs vōs morer, quīnque nāvēs aedificāvī, onerāvī vīnum—et tunc erat contrā aurum—et mīsī Rōmam. Putārēs mē hoc iussisse; omnēs nāvēs naufragārunt, factum, nōn fābula. Ūnō diē Neptūnus trecentiēs sēstertium dēvorāvit. Putātis mē dēfēcisse? Nōn mehercule̅s; mī haec iactūra gustī fuit, tamquam nihil factī. Alterās fēcī maiōrēs et meliōrēs et fēlīciōrēs, ut nēmō nōn mē virum fortem dīceret. Scītis, magna nāvis magnam fortitūdinem habet. Onerāvī rūrsus vīnum, lardum, fabam, sēplasium, manicipia. Hōc locō Fortunāta rem piam fēcit; omne enim aurum suum, omnia vestīmenta vēndidit et mī centum aureōs in manū posuit. Hoc fuit pecūliī meī fermentum. Cito fit, quod dī volunt. Ūnō cursū centiēs sēstertium corrotundāvī. Statim redēmī fundōs omnēs quī patrōnī meī fuerant. Aedificō domum, vēnālīcia coemō iūmenta; quicquid tangēbam, crēscēbat tamquam favus.

—Petronius, *Satyricon* 75–76 (extracts)

1. In what two ways does the lampstand remind Trimalchio of his childhood? (1–3)
2. What happened to Trimalchio when his master died? (4–6)
3. Describe Trimalchio's first business venture. (6–7)
4. What was the outcome of this first venture? (8–9)
5. How did Trimalchio react to this? (9–10)
6. What did Trimalchio build next, and why? (10–12)
7. What did Trimalchio invest in the second time? (12)
8. Where did he get the money for this investment? (12–14)
9. How did the project turn out? (14–15)
10. What did Trimalchio do with the profits? (15–17)

15 **centiēs sēstertium**: see note on B:26.

corrotundō, -āre, -āvī, -ātus, *to round off, "clear," make (money).*

redimō, redimere, redēmī, redēmptus, *to buy back.* Trimalchio had perhaps sold some of this property to finance his business ventures, or perhaps his former master had sold the properties before he died.

fundus, -ī, m., *farm.*

***patrōnus, -ī**, m., *patron.* Freed slaves became **clientēs** of their former masters.

16 **vēnālīcia, -ōrum**, n. pl., *slaves.*

iūmentum, -ī, n., *draft animal, horse, mule.*

17 **favus, -ī**, m., *honeycomb.*

18 **patria**: Trimalchio's original home in Asia Minor.
manum dē tābulā, *hand(s) off the tablet.* This was an expression used by teachers to tell students to stop working.
19 **negōtiātiō, negōtiātiōnis**, f., *business.*
faenerō, -āre, -āvī, -ātus, *to lend money, finance, underwrite.*

negōtium agere, *to do business.*
20 **exhortor, -ārī, -ātus sum**, *to encourage.* Trimalchio treats this deponent as a regular active verb, yet another example of his shaky Latin.
mathēmaticus, -ī, m., *mathematician, astrologer.*
colōnia, -ae, f., *colony, settlement, town.*
21 **Graeculiō, Graeculiōnis**, m., *a little Greek.*
cōnsiliātor, cōnsiliātōris, m., *adviser.*

22 **ab aciā et acū**, *from thread and needle* (i.e., in great detail).
expōnō, expōnere, exposuī, expositus, *to explain, reveal.*
intestīna, -ōrum, n. pl., *intestines.*
intestīnās meās nōverat: i.e., he knew me inside out. Note again Trimalchio's confusion of genders.
nōverat: *he knew*, from **nōscō**.
tantum: *the only thing.*

23 **Putāssēs**: = **Putāvissēs**, *You would have thought*, another potential subjunctive.

24 **Mercurius**: the god Mercury was the patron of merchants, and Trimalchio believed that Mercury took a special interest in him.
***vigilat**: *watched over (me).*

casula, -ae, f., *a little house, hut.* What type of word are **casula** and **Graeculiō** (21)?

25 **cēnātiō, cēnātiōnis**, f., *dining room.*
porticus, -ūs, f., *portico, colonnade* (a walkway with a roof held up by columns). Trimalchio treats the noun as masculine.
marmorātus, -a, -um, *made of marble.*
26 **sūsum** (= **sūrsum**), adv., *up, above, upstairs.*
vipera, -ae, f., *viper* (a poisonous snake). This is a reference to Fortunata.
sessōrium, -ī, n., *sitting room.*
27 **ōstiārius, -ī**, m., *doorkeeper.*
cella, -ae, f., *small room.*
perbonus, -a, -um, *very good.*
hospitium, -ī, n., *hospitality; lodgings, guest room.*

28 **hospitor, -ārī, -ātus sum**, *to stay as a guest, lodge.*

29 **assem . . . valeās**: *(if) you have a penny, a penny is what you're worth.* An **ās**, gen., **assis**, was a Roman coin, about half an ounce of bronze (cf. 62A:3).
habēs, habēberis: *you have, you will be considered*, i.e., *you are judged by what you have.*

30 **amīcus vester**: i.e., Trimalchio.
rāna, -ae, f., *frog*; metaphorically, *a nobody.*

D. The Millionaire's Autobiography, continued

"Postquam coepī plūs habēre, quam tōta patria mea habet, manum dē tābulā; sustulī mē dē negōtiātiōne et coepī lībertōs faenerāre. Et sānē nōlentem mē negōtium meum agere exhortāvit mathēmaticus, quī vēnerat forte in colōniam nostram, Graeculiō Serāpa nōmine, cōnsiliātor deōrum. Hic mihi dīxit etiam ea, quae oblītus eram; ab aciā et acū mī omnia exposuit; intestīnās meās nōverat; tantum quod mihi nōn dīxerat, quid prīdiē cēnāveram. Putāssēs illum semper mēcum habitāsse.

"Interim, dum Mercurius vigilat, aedificāvī hanc domum. Ut scītis, casula erat; nunc templum est. Habet quattuor cēnātiōnēs, cubicula vīgintī, porticūs marmorātōs duōs, sūsum cēnātiōnem, cubiculum in quō ipse dormiō, viperae huius sessōrium, ōstiāriī cellam perbonam; hospitium hospitēs capit. Ad summam, Scaurus, cum hūc vēnit, nusquam māluit hospitārī, et habet ad mare paternum hospitium. Et multa alia sunt, quae statim vōbīs ostendam. Crēdite mihi; assem habeās, assem valeās; habēs, habēberis. Sīc amīcus vester, quī fuit rāna, nunc est rēx."

—Petronius, *Satyricon* 76–77 (extracts)

---

11. What did Trimalchio do with his money after he retired from business himself? (18–19)
12. Who had encouraged Trimalchio when he wanted to quit? (19–21)
13. Why did Trimalchio believe in this man and his advice? (21–23)
14. Describe the house Trimalchio built. (25–27)
15. How does Scaurus feel about the house? Why might this be surprising? (27–28)
16. How does Trimalchio sum up his feelings about life? (29–30)

Questions for Thought and Discussion

1. What does Trimalchio intend his guests to think about his will? His tomb? His life story?
2. Would you describe Trimalchio as hypocritical? Generous? Altruistic? Humanitarian? Self-centered? How would he describe himself?
3. Is Trimalchio afraid of death?
4. Is it true that Trimalchio "never listened to a philosopher"? What words suggest that he has somehow picked up a smattering of philosophy? Why does he make this claim? As part of an epitaph, what is the effect of the remark?
5. Why does Trimalchio make grammatical mistakes? How does this affect our view of him?
6. Does Trimalchio's story of his own life make you see him any differently than you did after reading about his tomb? If so, how? Are there ways that Trimalchio's life story reinforces the earlier impressions you had of him?
7. What qualities would be needed for a man to rise from slavery to great wealth? Does Trimalchio seem to exhibit these qualities? To what do you attribute Trimalchio's success? To what does he himself attribute it?

1 **Erat**: the subject is *he* (Pliny the Elder).
Mīsēnum, -ī, n., *Misenum* (an important Roman naval base, at the very northern end of the Bay of Naples; see map on page 298).
imperiō: *with* **imperium**, *with authority, in command.*
praesēns: *in person, personally.*

2 **appāreō, appārēre, appāruī**, *to appear.*
nūbēs, nūbis, gen. pl., **nūbium**, f., *cloud.*
speciēs, speciēī, f., *appearance.*
inūsitātā et magnitūdine et speciē: *of unusual size and appearance*, ablatives of description.

3 **Ille**: = Pliny the Elder.
mīrāculum, -ī, n., *strange sight.*

incertus, -a, -um, *uncertain*; supply **erat** with **incertum**.
4 **procul**, adv., *far off, from a distance.*
intuentibus: *to those watching*, a substantive.
5 **similitūdō, similitūdinis**, f., *likeness.*
pīnus, -ūs, f., *pine tree.* Pliny is referring to the umbrella pine of the Mediterranean, which has a tall trunk with no branches until close to the top, where they spread out like an umbrella. See the photograph on the opposite page.
exprimō, exprimere, expressī, expressus, *to press out, express, represent, convey.*

6 **ērudītus, -a, -um**, *learned, scholarly.*
vīsum: supply **est**.
Magnum . . . vīsum: *To him, as a very learned man, it seemed a great thing and one that had to be observed at closer range.* Pliny describes his uncle as **virō ērudītissimō** because he was very interested in the natural world (a curiosity which many Romans did not share) and had written a huge encyclopedia of scientific lore called *Naturalis historia*.

Liburnica, -ae, f., *a light, fast warship*; cf. 68:30.
aptō, -āre, -āvī, -ātus, *to fit, fit out, prepare.*
7 **mihi** (6) **. . . facit cōpiam**: *he gives me the chance.*
quod scrīberem: *what I was to write* (i.e., something to write), a relative clause of purpose, with **id** understood as the antecedent of **quod**.

8 **cōdicillī, -ōrum**, m. pl., *short letter, note.*
Rēctīnae Tascī: *from Rectina, (the wife) of Tascius.*
immineō, imminēre, imminuī, *to project out, hang over, threaten.*
9 **exterritus, -a, -um**, *frightened, terrified.*
subiaceō, subiacēre, subiacuī, *to lie under, lie at the foot of* (Mt. Vesuvius).
10 **discrīmen, discrīminis**, n., *crisis, danger.*

LXXVI

THE DEATH OF PLINY THE ELDER

A. A Rescue Attempt

In this letter, written to the historian Cornelius Tacitus, Pliny the Younger describes how his uncle and adoptive father, Pliny the Elder, was killed in the eruption of the volcano Mt. Vesuvius in A.D. 79—the same eruption that destroyed the towns of Pompeii and Herculaneum. In the first paragraph of the letter (omitted here), Pliny expresses his gratitude to Tacitus for requesting information about his uncle's death and his appreciation that his uncle will be immortalized in the pages of Tacitus' work. He then continues as follows:

Erat Mīsēnī classemque imperiō praesēns regēbat. Nōnum Kal. Septembrēs hōrā ferē septimā māter mea indicat eī appārēre nūbem inūsitātā et magnitūdine et speciē. Ille ascendit locum ex quō maximē mīrāculum illud cōnspicī poterat. Nūbēs—incertum procul intuentibus ex quō monte (Vesuvium fuisse posteā cognitum est)—oriēbātur, cuius similitūdinem et fōrmam nōn alia magis arbor quam pīnus expresserit. Magnum propiusque nōscendum ut ērudītissimō virō vīsum. Iubet Liburnicam aptārī; mihi, sī venīre ūnā vellem, facit cōpiam; respondī studēre mē mālle, et forte ipse quod scrīberem dederat. Ēgrediēbātur domō; accipit cōdicillōs Rēctīnae Tascī imminentī perīculō exterritae (nam vīlla eius subiacēbat, nec ūlla nisi nāvibus fuga): ut sē tantō discrīminī ēriperet ōrābat.

---

1. Why was Pliny the Elder at Misenum? (1)
2. On what day did the events described take place, and at what time? (1–2)
3. What did Pliny's family see? (2)
4. What did Pliny's uncle do in response? (3)
5. Describe the cloud. From where was it coming? (3–5)
6. Why did Pliny the Elder decide to take a closer look? (5–6)
7. Did his nephew go along? Why or why not? (6–8)
8. Why was Rectina frightened? (8–9)
9. What was the content of her message? (9–10)

An Italian umbrella pine

11 **quod . . . maximō**: a free translation of this clause might be *what he had begun as a scholar he completed as a hero.*

incohō, -āre, -āvī, -ātus, *to start, begin.*

obit: *he accepts, he takes on.*

dēdūcō, dēdūcere, dēdūxī, dēductus, *to lead down, launch* (a ship).

12 **quadrirēmis, quadrirēmis**, f., *quadrireme* (a ship with four banks of oars, heavier and larger than the **Liburnica** he had originally ordered).

frequēns, frequentis, *crowded, thickly populated.*

amoenitās ōrae: *the pleasantness of the shore*, i.e., *the pleasant shore.* The Bay of Naples was a resort area for wealthy Romans.

13 **rēctus, -a, -um**, *right, straight.*

14 **gubernāculum, -ī**, n., *a large oar used to steer a ship, steering-oar, helm.*

rēctum cursum (et) rēcta gubernacula: asyndeton (note that the **-que** on **rēctumque** introduces a new clause and does not connect the two nouns **cursum** and **gubernācula**).

solūtus, -a, -um, *free from.*

mōtus, -ūs, m., *motion, movement.*

15 **figūra, -ae**, f., *shape, form.*

omnēs (14) **. . . mōtūs omnēs figūrās**: another example of asyndeton.

ut dēprenderat (= **dēprehenderat**) **oculīs**: *as he had caught them with his eyes*, i.e., as he had observed them.

ēnotō, -āre, -āvī, -ātus, *to note down.*

dictāret ēnotāretque: Pliny presumably had a slave with him who took notes as he dictated.

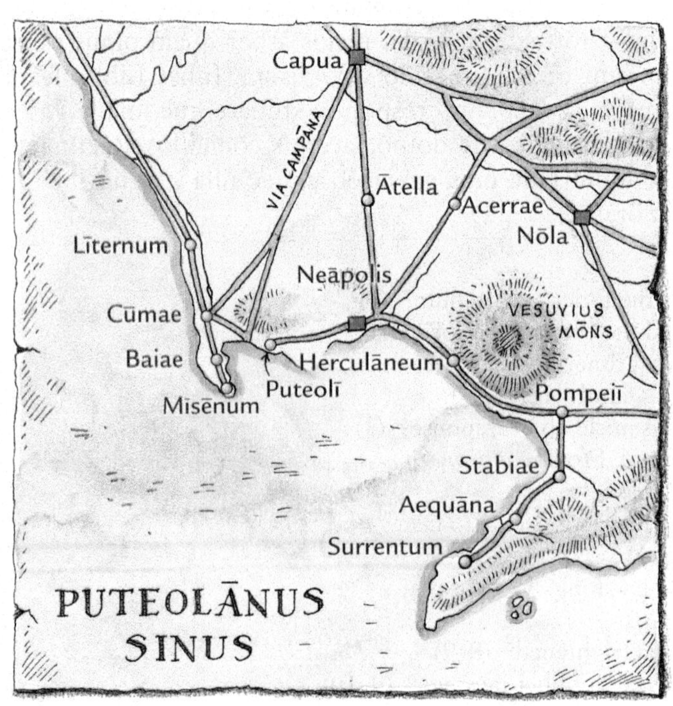

Vertit ille cōnsilium et quod studiōsō animō incohāverat obit maximō. Dēdūcit quadrirēmēs, ascendit ipse nōn Rēctīnae modo sed multīs (erat enim frequēns amoenitās ōrae) lātūrus auxilium. Properat illūc unde aliī fugiunt, rēctumque cursum rēcta gubernācula in perīculum tenet adeō solūtus metū, ut omnēs illīus malī mōtūs omnēs figūrās ut dēprenderat oculīs dictāret ēnotāretque.

(continued)

---

10. What did Pliny the Elder do in response to the message? What was his intention? (11–13)
11. What course did the ship take? (13–14)
12. What did Pliny the Elder do as he sailed into danger? What was his state of mind? (14–15)

After being inactive for about 200 years, Mt. Vesuvius erupted 23 times between 1631 and 1944. This painting shows one of the eruptions in the late 18th century.
The Eruption of Vesuvius, *oil on wood, Jean Baptiste Genillion*

16 **incidēbat**: deduce from **in + cadō**.

quō propius . . . calidior et dēnsior: *the nearer . . . hotter and thicker.*

accēdō, accēdere, accessī, accessūrus, *to come near, approach.*

17 **pūmex, pūmicis**, m., *pumice* (a light, porous volcanic rock).

ambustus, -a, -um, *burned up.*

vadum, -ī, n., *shallow water.*

subitus, -a, -um, *sudden, unexpected.*

18 **obstō, obstāre, obstitī**, *to stand in the way, block the way.*

(erat) vadum subitum ruīnāque montis lītora obstantia: the shape of the sea bottom was changed by the eruption and the accompanying earthquake.

cūnctor, -ārī, -ātus sum, *to delay, hesitate.*

retrō, adv., *backward, back.*

gubernātor, gubernātōris, m., *helmsman* (cf. **gubernāculum**, A:14).

19 **Stabiīs**: Stabiae was a town on the Bay of Naples, south of Pompeii. What case is **Stabiīs**?

dirimō, dirimere, dirēmī, dirēmptus, *to separate, divide, cut off, isolate.*

erat dirēmptus: the subject is Pomponianus.

20 **sinū mediō**: *by the bay (which lay) in between.* The wind was blowing strongly from the northwest, so that the Elder Pliny was able to sail easily from Misenum down to Stabiae. By saying that Pomponianus was cut off *by the bay in between*, Pliny refers to the fact that Pomponianus could not get his ship into the open sea without first sailing north into the Bay of Naples, against the wind, which ancient ships could not do.

quamquam . . . proximō (21): a long ablative absolute; **cōnspicuō** and **proximō** modify **perīculō**. Note how the clause **cum crēsceret** is nested inside the ablative absolute.

cōnspicuus, -a, -um, *clear, obvious, evident.*

21 **sarcina, -ae**, f., *pack, baggage.*

22 **resīdō, resīdere, resēdī**, *to sit down again, calm down.*

avunculus, -ī, m., *mother's brother, uncle.*

secundissimō: = **secundissimō ventō**.

invehō, invehere, invexī, invectus, *to carry toward, bring in.*

complector, complectī, complexus sum, *to embrace.*

trepidāns, trepidantis, *in a panic, panic stricken.* This refers to Pomponianus.

23 **sēcūritās, sēcūritātis**, f., *freedom from anxiety, lack of concern.*

lēniō, -īre, -īvī, -ītus, *to soften, soothe, calm down.*

dēferrī: supply **sē** as the subject of this infinitive.

24 **balineum, -ī**, n., *bath.*

lōtus: perfect passive participle of **lavāre**.

accubō, accubāre, *to recline, lie down.*

hilaris, -is, -e, *cheerful.*

quod (est): *(a thing) which is.*

aequē: Pliny means that it was just as admirable for his uncle to pretend not to be afraid as actually to be unconcerned.

similis hilarī: *similar to a cheerful (person)*, i.e., *apparently cheerful.*

B. At Pomponianus' Villa

Iam nāvibus cinis incidēbat, quō propius accēderent, calidior et dēnsior; iam pūmicēs etiam nigrīque et ambustī et fractī igne lapidēs; iam vadum subitum ruīnāque montis lītora obstantia. Cūnctātus paulum an retrō flecteret, mox gubernātōrī ut ita faceret monentī, "Fortēs," inquit, "fortūna iuvat: Pompōniānum pete." Stabiīs erat dirēmptus sinū mediō; ibi quamquam nōndum perīculō appropinquante, cōnspicuō tamen et cum crēsceret proximō, sarcinās contulerat in nāvēs, certus fugae sī contrārius ventus resēdisset. Quō tunc avunculus meus secundissimō invectus, complectitur trepidantem cōnsōlātur hortātur, utque timōrem eius suā sēcūritāte lēnīret, dēferrī in balineum iubet; lōtus accubat cēnat, aut hilaris aut (quod aequē magnum) similis hilarī.

(continued)

13. Describe what was falling from the sky. (16–17)
14. What problem did the ship encounter? (17–18)
15. What decision did Pliny the Elder have to make? (18)
16. What did he finally tell the helmsman to do? (18–19)
17. Describe the situation in which Pomponianus found himself. (19–21)
18. What did Pomponianus intend to do if the wind changed? What action of his shows this? (21–22)
19. What did Pliny the Elder do immediately after he landed? (22–23)
20. What actions did Pliny the Elder take to reassure Pomponianus? (23–24)
21. What was Pliny the Elder's mood? (24)

Liburnica

A Liburnica, one of the fast, light warships used by Octavian at the battle of Actium (68:30) as well as by Pliny the Elder (A:6).

25 **plūribus locīs**: = **in plūribus locīs.**
lātus, -a, -um, *broad, wide, widespread.*
relūceō, relūcēre, relūxī, *to gleam, shine.*
26 **fulgor, fulgōris**, m., *brilliance.*
clāritās, clāritātis, f., *brightness.*
tenebrae, -ārum, f. pl., *shadows, darkness.*
excitābātur: *was accentuated, was heightened* (literally, *was awakened*).

Ille: Pliny the Elder. **Ille** is the subject of **dictitābat** (28).
agrestis, -is, gen. pl., **agrestium**, *farmer, peasant.*
trepidātiō, trepidātiōnis, f., *fear, panic.*
agrestium trepidātiōne . . . relictōs (27): Pliny means that the terrified peasants fled without putting out their fires, which then spread as the earthquake knocked down the houses.
27 **sōlitūdō, sōlitūdinis**, f., *wilderness, countryside.*
in remedium formīdinis: *as a cure for their fear.*
28 **dictitō, -āre, -āvī, -ātus**, *to keep saying, say over and over, repeat.*

meātus, -ūs, m., *motion, movement.*
meātus animae: *the movement of his breathing*, i.e., snoring.
29 **illī**: *in his case*, dative of reference.
amplitūdō, amplitūdinis, f., *size, large size.*
sonāns, sonantis, *making noise, loud.*
līmen, līminis, n., *threshold, entrance.*
līminī: *at his door, outside his door.*
30 **obversor, -ārī, -ātus sum** + dat., *to move about in front of.*

31 **ārea . . . surrēxerat**: by saying that *the courtyard had risen* Pliny means that the level of the floor rose as the ash fell.
diaeta, -ae, f., *living room.*
adībātur: *was approached, had its entrance.*
oppleō, opplēre, opplēvī, opplētus, *to fill up.*

32 **mora, -ae**, f., *delay.*
prōcēdit: the subject is Pliny the Elder.
sē . . . reddit (33): *he rejoined*; literally, *he gave himself back to.*
33 **pervigilō, -āre, -āvī, -ātus**, *to stay awake, stay up.*

In commūne: *Together.*
34 **subsistant an**: *(whether) they should stay . . . or.*
in apertō: *in the open.*
vagor, -ārī, -ātus sum, *to wander.*

crēber, crēbra, crēbrum, *numerous, crowded, repeated.*
nūtō, -āre, -āvī, -ātus, *to nod, shake.*
35 **ēmōta**: deduce from **ē** + **moveō.**
sēdibus suīs: *from its foundations* (review the Reading Note on page 220).

36 **Sub diō**: *Under the open sky.*
exēsus, -a, -um, *eaten away, corroded, hollowed out, porous.*
cāsus: *fall, falling.*

(*vocabulary and notes continued on opposite page*)

C. Disaster Comes Closer

Interim ē Vesuviō monte plūribus locīs lātissimae flammae altaque incendia relūcēbant, quōrum fulgor et clāritās tenebrīs noctis excitābātur. Ille agrestium trepidātiōne ignēs relictōs dēsertāsque vīllās per sōlitūdinem ardēre in remedium formīdinis dictitābat. Tum sē quiētī dedit et quiēvit vērissimō quidem somnō; nam meātus animae, quī illī propter amplitūdinem corporis gravior et sonantior erat, ab eīs quī līminī obversābantur audiēbātur.

Sed ārea ex quā diaeta adībātur ita iam cinere mixtīsque pūmicibus opplēta surrēxerat, ut sī longior in cubiculō mora, exitus negārētur. Excitātus prōcēdit, sēque Pompōniānō cēterīsque quī pervigilāverant reddit. In commūne cōnsultant, intrā tēcta subsistant an in apertō vagentur. Nam crēbrīs vāstīsque tremōribus tēcta nūtābant, et quasi ēmōta sēdibus suīs nunc hūc nunc illūc abīre aut referrī vidēbantur. Sub diō rūrsus quamquam levium exēsōrumque pūmicum cāsus metuēbātur, quod tamen perīculōrum collātiō ēlēgit; et apud illum quidem ratiō ratiōnem, apud aliōs timōrem timor vīcit. Cervīcālia capitibus imposita linteīs cōnstringunt; id mūnīmentum adversus incidentia fuit.

(continued)

---

22. What was happening on Vesuvius? (25–26)
23. What explanation did Pliny give for this? (26–28)
24. How did the others know that Pliny was really asleep? (28–30)
25. Why could Pliny no longer remain in the bedroom? (31–32)
26. What was the subject of debate at the villa? (33–34)
27. What were the arguments on either side? (34–36)
28. What course of action was finally decided upon? (35–37)
29. According to Pliny, why did his uncle choose this course? Why did the others choose it? (37–38)
30. What precaution did the group take? Why? (38–39)

quod . . . ēlēgit (37): *a thing which a comparison of the dangers chose*, i.e., after comparing the dangers they chose the second option.

37 **apud illum . . . ratiō ratiōnem (vīcit)**: *in his case* (Pliny the Elder's) *one reason overcame the other*, i.e., he made his choice on a logical basis.

38 **cervīcal, cervīcālis**, gen. pl., **cervīcālium**, n., *pillow.*
imposita: deduce from **in** + **pōnō**.
linteum -ī, n., *linen; object made of linen, (piece of) cloth.*
cōnstringō, cōnstringere, cōnstrīnxī, cōnstrictus, *to bind, tie up, tie on.*
mūnīmentum, -ī, n., *defense, protection.*

39 **incidentia**: *things falling, falling objects*, a neuter plural substantive.

40 **diēs**: supply **erat**.
alibī, adv., *elsewhere*.
illīc, adv., *there* (at the villa).
fax, facis, f., *torch*.

41 ***Placuit**: *It was decided*.
ex proximō: *from close up*.
aspiciō, aspicere, aspexī, aspectus, *to look at, inspect, examine*.
ecquid iam mare admitteret: *whether the sea would now allow anything* (i.e., any escape).
42 **permanēbat**: deduce from **per** + **maneō**.

43 **abiectus, -a, -um**, *thrown out, spread out*.
recubō, recubāre, *to lie, recline*.
recubāns . . . hausitque: the subject of this sentence is Pliny the Elder.
semel, adv., *once*.
semel atque iterum, *once or twice*.

44 **praenūntius, -a, -um**, *announcing in advance, heralding, warning*. Pliny means that while the villa itself was not yet on fire, the strong smell of sulfur indicated that the flames were not far away.

45 **innītor, innītī, innixus sum** + abl., *to lean on*.
servolus, -ī, m., *a little slave, young slave*.
adsurrēxit: deduce from **ad** + **surgō**.
colligō, colligere, collēgī, collēctus, *to pick up, gather, infer*.
crassus, -a, -um, *thick, dense*.
46 **cālīgō, cālīginis**, f., *darkness, murkiness* (here referring to the volcanic ash clouding the air).
spīritus, -ūs, m., *breathing*.
crassiōre cālīgine spīritū obstrūctō: *with his breathing blocked by the rather thick ashes*.
stomachus, -ī, m., *stomach; esophagus, windpipe*.
illī: *in his case*, a dative of reference.
nātūrā: *by nature, naturally*.
invalidus, -a, -um, *weak, unhealthy*.
angustus, -a, -um, *narrow*.
47 **aestuāns, aestuantis**, *hot; inflamed*.

redditus: supply **est**.
is . . . tertius: *the third from that which he had last seen*, i.e., the second day from that on which he died. Remember that the Romans counted inclusively; Pliny counts as number one the day on which his uncle died.
48 **inlaesus, -a, -um**, *unharmed*.
opertus, -a, -um, *covered*.
indūtus, -a, -um, *clothed, dressed*.
habitus, -ūs, m., *appearance*.
49 **dēfūnctus, -a, -um**, *dead*.
quiēscentī quam dēfūnctō: substantives, *a person asleep rather than a dead person*.

D. The End

Iam diēs alibī, illīc nox omnibus noctibus nigrior dēnsiorque; quam tamen facēs multae variaque lūmina solvēbant. Placuit ēgredī in lītus, et ex proximō aspicere, ecquid iam mare admitteret; quod adhūc vāstum et adversum permanēbat. Ibi super abiectum linteum recubāns semel atque iterum frīgidam aquam poposcit hausitque. Deinde flammae flammārumque praenūntius odor sulpuris aliōs in fugam vertunt, excitant illum. Innītēns servolīs duōbus adsurrēxit et statim concidit, ut ego colligō, crassiōre cālīgine spīritū obstrūctō, clausōque stomachō quī illī nātūrā invalidus et angustus et frequenter aestuāns erat. Ubi diēs redditus (is ab eō quem novissimē vīderat tertius), corpus inventum integrum, inlaesum, opertumque ut fuerat indūtus; habitus corporis quiēscentī quam dēfūnctō similior.

—Pliny, *Epistulae* VI.16 (extracts)

---

31. Why did torches and lamps need to be used during the morning? (40–41)
32. What did Pliny the Elder and the others decide to do? (41–42)
33. What was Pliny doing at this point? (42–43)
34. What caused the group to flee and Pliny the Elder to stand up? (44–45)
35. What happened after Pliny the Elder stood with the help of slaves? (45)
36. Why does Pliny the Younger think this happened? (45–47)
37. When did daylight return? (47)
38. What condition was the body in when it was found? (48–49)

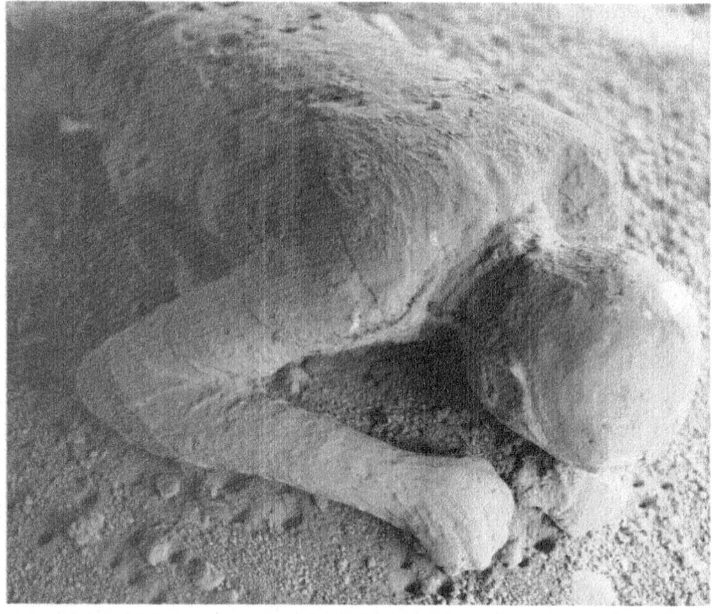

Archaeologists have discovered many hollow spaces in the ash (at Pompeii) and lava (at Herculaneum). These spaces were once occupied by the bodies of those killed in the eruption. Such voids can be filled with plaster before the surrounding material is removed, thereby creating likenesses of the victims.
Pompeii, A.D. 79, Excavation 1 November 1991

EXERCISE 76a

Read aloud and translate this portion of a letter from Pliny to Tacitus:

Pliny's Estimation of His Own Work and That of Tacitus

Posterīs an aliqua cūra nostrī, nesciō; nōs certē merēmur ut sit aliqua, nōn dīcō ingeniō (id enim superbum), sed studiō et labōre et reverentiā posterōrum. Pergāmus modo itinere īnstitūtō, quod ut paucōs in lūcem fāmamque provexit, ita multōs ē tenebrīs et silentiō protulit. Valē.

—Pliny, *Epistulae* IX.14 (extract)

posterīs . . . cūra nostrī (sit): dative of possession
nostrī: genitive of **nōs**
mereor, merērī, meritus sum, *to deserve, earn*
reverentia, -ae, f., *concern, care*
ingeniō . . . studiō . . . labōre . . . reverentiā: ablatives of cause
superbum: supply **esset**, *would be*
pergō, pergere, perrēxī, perrēctus, *to proceed, continue on*
ut . . . ita: *although . . . nevertheless* (literally, *just as . . . so)*
provehō, provehere, provexī, provectus, *to bring forward, bring out*; the subject is *it* (= **iter**)
tenebrae, tenebrārum, f. pl., *darkness, shadows*

Questions for Thought and Discussion

1. Which of Pliny the Elder's actions during the eruption of Vesuvius reflect his role as a naval commander? Which reflect his interests as a scholar? In Pliny the Elder's case, which came first, duty or intellectual curiosity? Was there any conflict between his two roles?
2. What seems to be Pliny the Younger's attitude toward his uncle? Incredulity? Respect? Apathy? Curiosity? Dismissal? Give reasons for your answer.
3. Give your own description of conditions during the eruption. Which of Pliny's two choices for survival would you have made? Why?
4. Summarize what you have learned about life during the early Empire. What was life like for members of the senatorial aristocracy? How did the institution of the Principate affect them? What was the role of freedmen such as Trimalchio in society, and how were they affected by the Principate? Base your answers on the readings in Parts IV and VI as well as on any class discussion or individual research you have done.

Appendix I: Figures of Speech

This appendix provides an alphabetical list of all figures of speech that appear in the Reading Notes in *Ecce Romani* III. The definition of each figure is followed by a reference to the page where it is explained. A general note about the importance of figures in Latin literature appears on page 27.

Alliteration: repetition of the same sound at the beginning of successive words.

Anaphora: repetition of the same word at the beginning of two or more successive clauses. (page 71)

Asyndeton: omission of connecting words such as **et** or **-que**. (page 26)

Chiasmus: contrastive, crisscross word order, where words appear in the pattern A-B-B-A. (page 99)

Diminutive: a form that indicates a small amount or small size. Diminutives can convey a variety of emotions, such as affection or contempt. (page 121)

Ellipsis: omission of a word or words that must be supplied to complete the sense; the omitted word is most often a form of **esse**. (page 89)

Enjambment: postponement of a word that completes the thought of a line of verse onto the next line. (page 260)

Hyperbaton: placement of an adjective far away from the noun it modifies. (page 133)

Hyperbole: exaggeration to create interest or emphasis. (page 111)

Litotes: expressing an idea by negating its opposite, as *not unfriendly* for *friendly*. (page 158)

Metaphor: a word used to suggest a comparison, e.g., "A wave of fear came over him" suggests that his fear was like a wave. (page 115)

Metonymy: use of one noun for another that it suggests, e.g., **Bacchus**, god of wine, for **vīnum**. (page 185)

Onomatopoeia: the sound of a word that imitates the actual sound that one hears, as in the English words "buzz" and "hiss." (page 236)

Poetic plural: use of a word in the plural which might seem more logical in the singular. (page 280)

Preterition: a figure in which the speaker says that he not going to talk about a certain topic, thereby bringing it to the attention of the audience. (page 175)

Rhetorical question: a question asked for effect, to make a point with the audience rather than to obtain real information. (page 69)

Simile: a comparison between two things expressed by using the words *like* or *as* (Latin **ut, sīcut, velut, tamquam**, or **quālis**). (page 236)

Synchysis: interlocked word order, where words appear in the order A-B-A-B. (page 103)

Synecdoche: use of a part of something to stand for the whole object. (page 213)

Transferred epithet: an adjective that agrees grammatically with one noun but more logically would describe another noun in the sentence. (page 183)

Tricolon: a series of three grammatically parallel phrases or clauses; often the third is the longest or most important, in which case it is referred to as a tricolon crescens. (page 221)

Appendix II: The Meters of Roman Poetry

Principles of Meter

The use of meter is one of the things that distinguishes poetry from prose. Meter (Greek for "measure") is a way of organizing words into units based on sound patterns; usually these units are repeated throughout the poem.

In traditional English poetry, meter is based on word stress. Read the following selection from William Blake's poem "The Tiger" aloud and notice how stressed syllables (indicated with an accent mark) alternate with unstressed ones.

Tíger, tíger, búrning bríght
Ín the fórests óf the níght

English poetry makes use of many different meters, all organized around different patterns of stressed and unstressed syllables, with a certain number of syllables per line. English poetry also often rhymes; ancient Roman poetry does not.

The earliest Roman poetry was based on word stress. Soon, however, the Romans abandoned this type of meter and adopted the meters that they found in sophisticated Greek poetry. Greek meter was based on various patterns of long and short syllables. Note the word *syllables*; we are speaking about more than just long and short vowels. Some people prefer to talk about heavy and light syllables, rather than long and short syllables, to avoid confusion with long and short vowels.

A syllable is long (or heavy) if:

- it contains a naturally long vowel (marked with a macron)
- it contains a diphthong (ae, au, eu, oe, ui)
- it is followed by two or more consonants
  - the consonants do not have to belong to the same word; in the phrase **hoc vehiculum, hoc** scans as a long syllable since it is followed by two consonants
  - **x** and **z** count as double consonants, and **h** is ignored (see below about **h**)

If none of these things applies, then the syllable is short (or light). The last syllable in a line may always be marked long, even if it would be short in other situations. Here is an example. We mark long syllables with a line – and short syllables with the symbol ˘ :

– – – ˘ ˘ – ˘ – ˘ – –
omnēs ūnius aestimēmus assis (62A:3)

The **ē** in **omnēs** and **aestimēmus** and the **ū** in **ūnius** are naturally long vowels; **ae** is a diphthong; the **o** in **omnēs** and the **a** in **assis** are followed by two consonants, making the syllables long; the final **-is** of **assis** is marked long because it is the last syllable in the line; and all other syllables are short. To *scan* a line means to mark the pattern of long and short syllables in the line, a process called *scansion*.

A Latin word has one vowel or diphthong per syllable; so if there are ten vowels or diphthongs in a line, you will have ten long or short marks if you write out the scansion (except in cases of elision; see next paragraph). Another exception involves the letter **u** after a **q**; in this case the **u** is really a w-sound, a semi-consonant, so it is not marked in scanning. Also remember that the letter **i** is sometimes a vowel and sometimes a semi-consonant (as in the Latin words **iacere** and **iānua** or in the English *yarn*). When **i** represents the y-sound it has no mark since it is not a vowel.

– ˘ ˘ – – – – ˘ ˘ – ˘ ˘ – (note absence of mark over **qu** and **I**)
quam mihi, nōn sī sē Iuppiter ipse petat (62E:2)

When a word ends in a vowel and the next word begins with a vowel or **h**, then the word-ending vowel is not pronounced. This is called *elision* ("cutting off"). This also happens when a word ends in a vowel followed by the letter **m** (**virum**, **īram**, etc.). In the following lines the symbol ‿ is used to mark the elisions; note that there is no long or short mark above an elided vowel, since that vowel is not pronounced.

– – – ˘ ˘ – ˘ – ˘ – –
Vīvāmus, mea Lesbia‿atque‿amēmus (62A:1)

– – – – – ˘ ˘ – – ˘ ˘ – –
Tōtum‿illud formōsa negō: nam nūlla venustās (62B:3)

– – – – – – ˘ ˘ – ˘ ˘ –
aeternum‿hoc sānctae foedus amīcitiae (62C:6)

Note in the last line that there is elision between **aeternum** and **hoc**, and that the **h** in **hoc** does not make the previous syllable long. When dealing with meter, you should always ignore the letter **h**. Your teacher will demonstrate how to read elisions correctly; practice following his or her example.

There is another exception to the rules about long and short syllables. If one of the letters **b**, **p**, **c**, **g**, **d**, or **t** is followed by **l** or **r**, the preceding syllable may be either long or short, as is required to make the line scan properly. In the following example, if the syllable **-go** in **ego** were treated as long, the line would not scan correctly:

– ˘ ˘ – ˘ ˘ – ˘ ˘ – – – ˘ ˘ – –
Nunc ego Triptolemī cuperem cōnsistere currū (71:1)

A final exception involves the words **es** and **est**. When either of these words is preceded by a vowel or final **-m**, that vowel is pronounced and the **e** of **es** or **est** is cut off; this is called *prodelision*. In the following example, the second and third words are pronounced "formōsast" and the first two words on the second line "rēctast:"

– ˘ ˘ – – – – – ˘ ˘ – ˘ ˘ – –
Quintia formosa‿est multis. Mihi candida, longa,

– – – ˘ ˘ – – ˘ ˘ – ˘ ˘ –
recta‿est: haec ego sic singula confiteor. (62B:1–2)

Summary of Metrical Signs

–	a long syllable	Units: dactyl	– ⏑ ⏑
⏑	a short syllable	spondee	– –
×	a syllable that may be either long or short, referred to as **anceps**		
⏕	two short syllables potentially replaced by one long		
‖	metrical pause at word-end		
/	division between feet		

The Meters

Note: this section describes four meters found in this book that are very frequent in Latin poetry: Alcaic, dactylic hexameter, elegiac couplet, and hendecasyllabic. Readings 62H, 73A, 73C, and 73D are written in meters that are less common and so are not discussed here. Your teacher may provide you with information about these meters.

Alcaic

Named after the Greek poet Alcaeus, this meter is one of the most common in the poetry of Horace. It consists of four-line stanzas, with the first two lines of each stanza having the same pattern:

× – ⏑ – – ‖ – ⏑ ⏑ – ⏑ ×
× – ⏑ – – ‖ – ⏑ ⏑ – ⏑ ×
× – ⏑ – – – ⏑ – ×
– ⏑ ⏑ – ⏑ ⏑ – ⏑ – ×

Note that the last syllable of the line, which can be either long or short, may always be marked long. (This is because the slight pause that readers often make at the end of a line has the effect of lengthening the syllable.)

– – ⏑ – – ‖ – ⏑ ⏑ – ⏑ –
Example: Nunc est bibendum, nunc pede līberō

– – ⏑ – – ‖ – ⏑ ⏑ – ⏑ –
pulsanda tellūs, nunc Saliāribus

– – ⏑ – – – ⏑ – –
ōrnāre pulvīnar deōrum

– ⏑ ⏑ – ⏑ ⏑ – ⏑ – –
tempus erat dapibus, sodālēs. (68A:1–4)

Dactylic Hexameter

A *dactyl* is a long syllable followed by two shorts; one line contains six dactyls (*hex* = six in Greek). In this meter, two short syllables may be replaced by one long syllable except in the fifth foot. A foot made up of two long syllables is called a *spondee*. The symbol ⏖ indicates the potential substitution of one long for two shorts. A slash is used to separate feet when we mark the scansion. In dactylic hexameter, there is often a pause in the middle of the third foot (between two words; often marked with a comma, semicolon, or period). This is called a *caesura* ("cutting") and is shown by a double vertical line. All epic poetry in the ancient world, such as Homer's *Iliad*, Vergil's *Aeneid*, and Ovid's *Metamorphoses*, was written in dactylic hexameter. The pattern is:

– ⏖ / – ⏖ / – ‖ ⏖ / – ⏖ / – ⏑ ⏑ / – –

	– ⏑ ⏑/– ⏑ ⏑/– –/– –/– ⏑ ⏑ /– –
Example:	Dissimulāre‿etiam spērāstī, perfide, tantum
	– ⏑ ⏑/– ⏑ ⏑/– ⏑ ⏑/– –/– ⏑ ⏑ – –
	posse nefās tacitusque meā dēcēdere terrā? (72:305–306)

Elegiac Couplet

This meter consists of pairs of lines, called *couplets*. The first line of each couplet is a dactylic hexameter (see previous entry). The second line consists of the first half of a dactylic hexameter, followed by a pause, then the same thing again. One long syllable may be substituted for two shorts only in the first half of the line. The pattern is:

– ⏖ / – ⏖ / – ‖ ⏖ / – ⏖ / – ⏑ ⏑ / – –
– ⏖ / – ⏖ / – ‖ – ⏖ / – ⏑ ⏑ / –

	– ⏑⏑/ – – / – –/ – ⏑ ⏑/– ⏑ ⏑/– –
Example:	Quīntia formosa‿est multīs. Mihi candida, longa,
	– – / – ⏑ ⏑/– ‖– ⏑ ⏑/– ⏑ ⏑/–
	recta‿est: haec ego sic singula confiteor. (62B:1–2)

Hendecasyllabic

This meter is made up of lines containing eleven syllables (*hendeka* = eleven in Greek). Although the first two syllables may be either long or short, in the poems of Catullus they are almost always long. The pattern is:

× × – ⏑ ⏑ – ⏑ – ⏑ – –

	– – – ⏑ ⏑ – ⏑ – ⏑ – –
Example:	Sōlēs occidere‿et redīre possunt (62A:4)

Forms

The following charts show the forms of typical Latin nouns, adjectives, pronouns, and verbs. As an aid in pronunciation, markings of long vowels and of accents are included.

I. Nouns

Number Case	1st Declension	2nd Declension			
	Fem.	Masc.	Masc.	Masc.	Neut.
Singular					
Nominative	puéll**a**	sérv**us**	púer	áger	bácul**um**
Genitive	puéll**ae**	sérv**ī**	púer**ī**	ágr**ī**	bácul**ī**
Dative	puéll**ae**	sérv**ō**	púer**ō**	ágr**ō**	bácul**ō**
Accusative	puéll**am**	sérv**um**	púer**um**	ágr**um**	bácul**um**
Ablative	puéll**ā**	sérv**ō**	púer**ō**	ágr**ō**	bácul**ō**
Vocative	puéll**a**	sérv**e**	púer	áger	bácul**um**
Plural					
Nominative	puéll**ae**	sérv**ī**	púer**ī**	ágr**ī**	bácul**a**
Genitive	puell**ā́rum**	serv**ṓrum**	puer**ṓrum**	agr**ṓrum**	bacul**ṓrum**
Dative	puéll**īs**	sérv**īs**	púer**īs**	ágr**īs**	bácul**īs**
Accusative	puéll**ās**	sérv**ōs**	púer**ōs**	ágr**ōs**	bácul**a**
Ablative	puéll**īs**	sérv**īs**	púer**īs**	ágr**īs**	bácul**īs**
Vocative	puéll**ae**	sérv**ī**	púer**ī**	ágr**ī**	bácul**a**

Number Case	3rd Declension			4th Declension		5th Declension	
	Masc.	Fem.	Neut.	Masc.	Neut.	Masc.	Fem.
Singular							
Nominative	páter	vōx	nṓmen	árc**us**	gén**ū**	dí**ēs**	r**ēs**
Genitive	pátr**is**	vṓc**is**	nṓmin**is**	árc**ūs**	gén**ūs**	di**ḗī**	r**éī**
Dative	pátr**ī**	vṓc**ī**	nṓmin**ī**	árc**uī**	gén**ū**	di**ḗī**	r**éī**
Accusative	pátr**em**	vṓc**em**	nṓmen	árc**um**	gén**ū**	dí**em**	r**em**
Ablative	pátr**e**	vṓc**e**	nṓmin**e**	árc**ū**	gén**ū**	dí**ē**	r**ē**
Vocative	páter	vōx	nṓmen	árc**us**	gén**ū**	dí**ēs**	r**ēs**
Plural							
Nominative	pátr**ēs**	vṓc**ēs**	nṓmin**a**	árc**ūs**	gén**ua**	dí**ēs**	r**ēs**
Genitive	pátr**um**	vṓc**um**	nṓmin**um**	árc**uum**	gén**uum**	di**ḗrum**	r**ḗrum**
Dative	pátr**ibus**	vṓc**ibus**	nōmín**ibus**	árc**ibus**	gén**ibus**	di**ḗbus**	r**ḗbus**
Accusative	pátr**ēs**	vṓc**ēs**	nṓmin**a**	árc**ūs**	gén**ua**	dí**ēs**	r**ēs**
Ablative	pátr**ibus**	vṓc**ibus**	nōmín**ibus**	árc**ibus**	gén**ibus**	di**ḗbus**	r**ḗbus**
Vocative	pátr**ēs**	vṓc**ēs**	nṓmin**a**	árc**ūs**	gén**ua**	dí**ēs**	r**ēs**

II. Adjectives

Number Case	1st and 2nd Declensions			3rd Declension		
	Masc.	Fem.	Neut.	Masc.	Fem.	Neut.
Singular						
Nominative	mágn***us***	mágn***a***	mágn***um***	ómn***is***	ómn***is***	ómn***e***
Genitive	mágn***ī***	mágn***ae***	mágn***ī***	ómn***is***	ómn***is***	ómn***is***
Dative	mágn***ō***	mágn***ae***	mágn***ō***	ómn***ī***	ómn***ī***	ómn***ī***
Accusative	mágn***um***	mágn***am***	mágn***um***	ómn***em***	ómn***em***	ómn***e***
Ablative	mágn***ō***	mágn***ā***	mágn***ō***	ómn***ī***	ómn***ī***	ómn***ī***
Vocative	mágn***e***	mágn***a***	mágn***um***	ómn***is***	ómn***is***	ómn***e***
Plural						
Nominative	mágn***ī***	mágn***ae***	mágn***a***	ómn***ēs***	ómn***ēs***	ómn***ia***
Genitive	magn***ṓrum***	magn***ā́rum***	magn***ṓrum***	ómn***ium***	ómn***ium***	ómn***ium***
Dative	mágn***īs***	mágn***īs***	mágn***īs***	ómn***ibus***	ómn***ibus***	ómn***ibus***
Accusative	mágn***ōs***	mágn***ās***	mágn***a***	ómn***ēs***	ómn***ēs***	ómn***ia***
Ablative	mágn***īs***	mágn***īs***	mágn***īs***	ómn***ibus***	ómn***ibus***	ómn***ibus***
Vocative	mágn***ī***	mágn***ae***	mágn***a***	ómn***ēs***	ómn***ēs***	ómn***ia***

III. Comparative Adjectives

Number Case	Masc.	Fem.	Neut.
Singular			
Nominative	laétior	laétior	laétius
Genitive	laetiṓr***is***	laetiṓr***is***	laetiṓr***is***
Dative	laetiṓr***ī***	laetiṓr***ī***	laetiṓr***ī***
Accusative	laetiṓr***em***	laetiṓr***em***	laétius
Ablative	laetiṓr***e***	laetiṓr***e***	laetiṓr***e***
Plural			
Nominative	laetiṓr***ēs***	laetiṓr***ēs***	laetiṓr***a***
Genitive	laetiṓr***um***	laetiṓr***um***	laetiṓr***um***
Dative	laetiṓr***ibus***	laetiṓr***ibus***	laetiṓr***ibus***
Accusative	laetiṓr***ēs***	laetiṓr***ēs***	laetiṓr***a***
Ablative	laetiṓr***ibus***	laetiṓr***ibus***	laetiṓr***ibus***

Adjectives have *positive*, *comparative*, and *superlative* forms. You can usually recognize the comparative by the letters **-ior(-)** and the superlative by ***-issimus***, ***-errimus***, or ***-illimus***:

ignā́vus, -a, -um, *lazy*	**ignā́vior, ignā́vius**	**ignāvíssimus, -a, -um**
púlcher, púlchra, púlchrum, *beautiful*	**púlchrior, púlchrius**	**pulchérrimus, -a, -um**
fácilis, -is, -e, *easy*	**facílior, facílius**	**facíllimus, -a, -um**

Some very common adjectives are irregular in the comparative and superlative:

Positive	Comparative	Superlative
bónus, -a, -um, *good*	**mélior, mélius,** *better*	**óptimus, -a, -um,** *best*
málus, -a, -um, *bad*	**péior, péius,** *worse*	**péssimus, -a, -um,** *worst*
mágnus, -a, -um, *big*	**máior, máius,** *bigger*	**máximus, -a, -um,** *biggest*
párvus, -a, -um, *small*	**mínor, mínus,** *smaller*	**mínimus, -a, -um,** *smallest*
múltus, -a, -um, *much*	**plūs,*** *more*	**plū́rimus, -a, -um,** *most, very much*
múltī, -ae, -a, *many*	**plū́rēs, plū́ra,** *more*	**plū́rimī, -ae, -a,** *most, very many*

*Note that **plūs** is not an adjective but a neuter substantive, usually found with a partitive genitive, e.g., Titus **plūs vīnī** bibit. *Titus drank* ***more (of the) wine****.*

IV. Present Participles

Number Case	Masc.	Fem.	Neut.
Singular			
Nominative	pórtāns	pórtāns	pórtāns
Genitive	portánt***is***	portánt***is***	portánt***is***
Dative	portánt***ī***	portánt***ī***	portánt***ī***
Accusative	portánt***em***	portánt***em***	pórtāns
Ablative	portánt***ī/e***	portánt***ī/e***	portánt***ī/e***
Plural			
Nominative	portánt***ēs***	portánt***ēs***	portánt***ia***
Genitive	portánt***ium***	portánt***ium***	portánt***ium***
Dative	portánt***ibus***	portánt***ibus***	portánt***ibus***
Accusative	portánt***ēs***	portánt***ēs***	portánt***ia***
Ablative	portánt***ibus***	portánt***ibus***	portánt***ibus***

V. Numbers

Case	Masc.	Fem.	Neut.	Masc.	Fem.	Neut.	Masc.	Fem.	Neut.
Nom.	ū́n**us**	ū́n**a**	ū́n**um**	dú**o**	dú**ae**	dú**o**	tr**ēs**	tr**ēs**	tr**ía**
Gen.	ūn**ī́us**	ūn**ī́us**	ūn**ī́us**	du**ṓrum**	du**ā́rum**	du**ṓrum**	tr**íum**	tr**íum**	tr**íum**
Dat.	ū́n**ī**	ū́n**ī**	ū́n**ī**	du**ṓbus**	du**ā́bus**	du**ṓbus**	tr**íbus**	tr**íbus**	tr**íbus**
Acc.	ū́n**um**	ū́n**am**	ū́n**um**	dú**ōs**	dú**ās**	dú**o**	tr**ēs**	tr**ēs**	tr**ía**
Abl.	ū́n**ō**	ū́n**ā**	ū́n**ō**	du**ṓbus**	du**ā́bus**	du**ṓbus**	tr**íbus**	tr**íbus**	tr**íbus**

	Cardinal	Ordinal
I	**ū́nus, -a, -um,** *one*	**prī́mus, -a, -um,** *first*
II	**dúo, -ae, -o,** *two*	**secúndus, -a, -um,** *second*
III	**trēs, trēs, tría,** *three*	**tértius, -a, -um,** *third*
IV	**quáttuor,** *four*	**quā́rtus, -a, -um**
V	**quī́nque,** *five*	**quī́ntus, -a, -um**
VI	**sex,** *six*	**séxtus, -a, -um**
VII	**séptem,** *seven*	**séptimus, -a, -um**
VIII	**óctō,** *eight*	**octā́vus, -a, -um**
IX	**nóvem,** *nine*	**nṓnus, -a, -um**
X	**décem,** *ten*	**décimus, -a, -um**
XI	**ū́ndecim,** *eleven*	**ūndécimus, -a, -um**
XII	**duódecim,** *twelve*	**duodécimus, -a, -um**
XIII	**trédecim,** *thirteen*	**tértius décimus, -a, -um**
XIV	**quattuórdecim,** *fourteen*	**quā́rtus décimus, -a, -um**
XV	**quī́ndecim,** *fifteen*	**quī́ntus décimus, -a, -um**
XVI	**sḗdecim,** *sixteen*	**séxtus décimus, -a, -um**
XVII	**septéndecim,** *seventeen*	**séptimus décimus, -a, -um**
XVIII	**duodēvīgíntī,** *eighteen*	**duodēvīcḗsimus, -a, -um**
XIX	**ūndēvīgíntī,** *nineteen*	**ūndēvīcḗsimus, -a, -um**
XX	**vīgíntī,** *twenty*	**vīcḗsimus, -a, -um**
L	**quīnquāgíntā,** *fifty*	**quīnquāgḗsimus, -a, -um**
C	**céntum,** *a hundred*	**centḗsimus, -a, -um**
D	**quīngéntī, -ae, -a,** *five hundred*	**quīngentḗsimus, -a, -um**
M	**mī́lle,** *a thousand*	**mīllḗsimus, -a, -um**

N.B. The cardinal numbers from **quattuor** to **centum** do not change their form to indicate case and gender.

VI. Personal Pronouns

Number Case	1st Person	2nd Person	3rd Person		
			Masc.	Fem.	Neut.
Singular					
Nominative	égo	tū	is	éa	id
Genitive	méī	túī	éius	éius	éius
Dative	míhi	tíbi	éī	éī	éī
Accusative	mē	tē	éum	éam	id
Ablative	mē	tē	éō	éā	éō
Plural					
Nominative	nōs	vōs	éī	éae	éa
Genitive	nóstrī nóstrum	véstrī véstrum	eṓrum	eā́rum	eṓrum
Dative	nṓbīs	vṓbīs	éīs	éīs	éīs
Accusative	nōs	vōs	éōs	éās	éa
Ablative	nṓbīs	vṓbīs	éīs	éīs	éīs

Note: The forms of **is, ea, id** may also serve as demonstrative adjectives.

VII. Reflexive Pronoun

	Singular	Plural
Nominative	—	—
Genitive	súī	súī
Dative	síbi	síbi
Accusative	sē	sē
Ablative	sē	sē

VIII. Relative Pronoun

Number Case	Masc.	Fem.	Neut.
Singular			
Nominative	quī	quae	quod
Genitive	cúius	cúius	cúius
Dative	cui	cui	cui
Accusative	quem	quam	quod
Ablative	quō	quā	quō
Plural			
Nominative	quī	quae	quae
Genitive	quṓrum	quā́rum	quṓrum
Dative	quíbus	quíbus	quíbus
Accusative	quōs	quās	quae
Ablative	quíbus	quíbus	quíbus

IX. Interrogative Pronoun

Number Case	Masc.	Fem.	Neut.
Singular			
Nominative	quis	quis	quid
Genitive	cúius	cúius	cúius
Dative	cui	cui	cui
Accusative	quem	quem	quid
Ablative	quō	quō	quō
Plural	Same as the plural of the relative pronoun on page 316.		

X. Indefinite Adjectives and Pronouns

Number Case	Masc.	Fem.	Neut.	Masc.	Fem.	Neut.
Singular						
Nominative	quī́dam	quaédam	quóddam	áliquī	áliqua	áliquod
Genitive	cuiúsdam	cuiúsdam	cuiúsdam	alicúius	alicúius	alicúius
Dative	cúidam	cúidam	cúidam	álicui	álicui	álicui
Accusative	quéndam	quándam	quóddam	áliquem	áliquam	áliquod
Ablative	quṓdam	quā́dam	quṓdam	áliquō	áliquā	áliquō
Plural						
Nominative	quī́dam	quaédam	quaédam	áliquī	áliquae	áliqua
Genitive	quōrúndam	quārúndam	quōrúndam	aliquṓrum	aliquā́rum	aliquṓrum
Dative	quibúsdam	quibúsdam	quibúsdam	aliquíbus	aliquíbus	aliquíbus
Accusative	quṓsdam	quā́sdam	quaédam	áliquōs	áliquās	áliqua
Ablative	quibúsdam	quibúsdam	quibúsdam	aliquíbus	aliquíbus	áliquíbus

The indefinite pronoun **quīdam, quaedam, quiddam** has the same forms as the indefinite adjective, except for **quiddam** in the neuter nominative and accusative singular. The indefinite pronoun **aliquis, aliquis, aliquid** has the regular forms of the interrogative adjective **quis, quis, quid,** as do the indefinite pronouns **quisque, quisque, quidque** and **quisquam, quisquam, quidquam (quicquam).** The indefinite pronoun and adjective **quisquis, quisquis, quidquid** also has the same forms as **quis, quis, quid,** but note that both halves of this word are declined. The indefinite pronoun and adjective **quisque, quaeque, quodque** has the same forms as the relative pronoun **quī, quae, quod** except for **quis-** in the masculine nominative singular.

XI. Demonstrative Adjectives and Pronouns

Number Case	Masc.	Fem.	Neut.	Masc.	Fem.	Neut.
Singular						
Nominative	hic	haec	hoc	ílle	ílla	íllud
Genitive	húius	húius	húius	illī́us	illī́us	illī́us
Dative	húic	húic	húic	íllī	íllī	íllī
Accusative	hunc	hanc	hoc	íllum	íllam	íllud
Ablative	hōc	hāc	hōc	íllō	íllā	íllō
Plural						
Nominative	hī	hae	haec	íllī	íllae	ílla
Genitive	hṓrum	hā́rum	hṓrum	illṓrum	illā́rum	illṓrum
Dative	hīs	hīs	hīs	íllīs	íllīs	íllīs
Accusative	hōs	hās	haec	íllōs	íllās	ílla
Ablative	hīs	hīs	hīs	íllīs	íllīs	íllīs

Number Case	Masc.	Fem.	Neut.
Singular			
Nominative	ípse	ípsa	ípsum
Genitive	ipsī́us	ipsī́us	ipsī́us
Dative	ípsī	ípsī	ípsī
Accusative	ípsum	ípsam	ípsum
Ablative	ípsō	ípsā	ípsō
Plural			
Nominative	ípsī	ípsae	ípsa
Genitive	ipsṓrum	ipsā́rum	ipsṓrum
Dative	ípsīs	ípsīs	ípsīs
Accusative	ípsós	ípsās	ípsa
Ablative	ípsīs	ípsīs	ípsīs

Number Case	Masc.	Fem.	Neut.	Masc.	Fem.	Neut.
Singular						
Nominative	is	éa	id	ī́dem	éadem	ídem
Genitive	éius	éius	éius	eiúsdem	eiúsdem	eiúsdem
Dative	éī	éī	éī	eī́dem	eī́dem	eī́dem
Accusative	éum	éam	id	eúndem	eándem	ídem
Ablative	éō	éā	éō	eṓdem	eā́dem	eṓdem
Plural						
Nominative	éī	éae	éa	eī́dem	eaédem	éadem
Genitive	eṓrum	eā́rum	eṓrum	eōrúndem	eārúndem	eōrúndem
Dative	éīs	éīs	éīs	eī́sdem	eī́sdem	eī́sdem
Accusative	éōs	éās	éa	eṓsdem	eā́sdem	éadem
Ablative	éīs	éīs	éīs	eī́sdem	eī́sdem	eī́sdem

XII. Adverbs

Latin adverbs may be formed from adjectives of the 1st and 2nd declensions by adding ***-ē*** to the base of the adjective, e.g., **strēnu*ē***, *strenuously*, from **strēnuus, -a, -um.** To form an adverb from a 3rd declension adjective, add ***-iter*** to the base of the adjective or ***-er*** to bases ending in **-nt-**, e.g., **brev*iter***, *briefly*, from **brevis, -is, -e**, and **prūdent*er***, *wisely*, from **prūdēns, prūdentis.**

láet***ē***, *happily*	laét***ius***	laet***íssimē***
fēlī́c***iter***, *luckily*	fēlī́c***ius***	fēlīc***íssimē***
celér***iter***, *quickly*	celér***ius***	celér***rimē***
prūdént***er***, *wisely*	prūdént***ius***	prūdent***íssimē***

Note the following as well:

díū, *for a long time*	diū́t***ius***	diūt***íssimē***
saépe, *often*	saép***ius***	saep***íssimē***
sḗrō, *late*	sḗr***ius***	sēr***íssimē***

Some adverbs are irregular:

béne, *well*	**mélius,** *better*	**óptimē,** *best*
mále, *badly*	**péius,** *worse*	**péssimē,** *worst*
fácile, *easily*	**facílius,** *more easily*	**facíllimē,** *most easily*
magnópere, *greatly*	**mágis,** *more*	**máximē,** *most*
paúlum, *little*	**mínus,** *less*	**mínimē,** *least*
múltum, *much*	**plūs,** *more*	**plū́rimum,** *most*

XIII. Regular Verbs Active: Infinitive, Imperative, Indicative

		1st Conjugation	2nd Conjugation	3rd Conjugation		4th Conjugation
	Infinitive	portā́***re***	movḗ***re***	mítt***ere***	iác***ere*** (-iō)	audī́***re***
	Imperative	pórt***ā***	móv***ē***	mítt***e***	iác***e***	aúd***ī***
		portā́***te***	movḗ***te***	mítt***ite***	iác***ite***	audī́***te***
Present	Sing. 1	pórt***ō***	móve***ō***	mítt***ō***	iáci***ō***	aúdi***ō***
	2	pórtā***s***	móvē***s***	mítti***s***	iáci***s***	aúdī***s***
	3	pórta***t***	móve***t***	mítti***t***	iáci***t***	aúdi***t***
	Pl. 1	portā́***mus***	movḗ***mus***	mítti***mus***	iáci***mus***	audī́***mus***
	2	portā́***tis***	movḗ***tis***	mítti***tis***	iáci***tis***	audī́***tis***
	3	pórta***nt***	móve***nt***	míttu***nt***	iáciu***nt***	aúdiu***nt***
Imperfect	Sing. 1	portā́***bam***	movḗ***bam***	mittḗ***bam***	iaciḗ***bam***	audiḗ***bam***
	2	portā́***bās***	movḗ***bās***	mittḗ***bās***	iaciḗ***bās***	audiḗ***bās***
	3	portā́***bat***	movḗ***bat***	mittḗ***bat***	iaciḗ***bat***	audiḗ***bat***
	Pl. 1	portā***bā́mus***	movē***bā́mus***	mittē***bā́mus***	iaciē***bā́mus***	audiē***bā́mus***
	2	portā***bā́tis***	movē***bā́tis***	mittē***bā́tis***	iaciē***bā́tis***	audiē***bā́tis***
	3	portā́***bant***	movḗ***bant***	mittḗ***bant***	iaciḗ***bant***	audiḗ***bant***
Future	Sing. 1	portā́***bō***	movḗ***bō***	mítt***am***	iáci***am***	aúdi***am***
	2	portā́***bis***	movḗ***bis***	mítt***ēs***	iáci***ēs***	aúdi***ēs***
	3	portā́***bit***	movḗ***bit***	mítt***et***	iáci***et***	aúdi***et***
	Pl. 1	portā́***bimus***	movḗ***bimus***	mitt***ḗmus***	iaci***ḗmus***	audi***ḗmus***
	2	portā́***bitis***	movḗ***bitis***	mitt***ḗtis***	iaci***ḗtis***	audi***ḗtis***
	3	portā́***bunt***	movḗ***bunt***	mítt***ent***	iáci***ent***	aúdi***ent***
Perfect	Sing. 1	portā́v***ī***	mṓv***ī***	mī́s***ī***	iḗc***ī***	audī́v***ī***
	2	portav***ístī***	móv***ístī***	mīs***ístī***	iēc***ístī***	audīv***ístī***
	3	portā́v***it***	mṓv***it***	mī́s***it***	iḗc***it***	audī́v***it***
	Pl. 1	portā́v***imus***	mṓv***imus***	mī́s***imus***	iḗc***imus***	audī́v***imus***
	2	portāv***ístis***	mōv***ístis***	mīs***ístis***	iēc***ístis***	audīv***ístis***
	3	portāv***ḗrunt***	mōv***ḗrunt***	mīs***ḗrunt***	iēc***ḗrunt***	audīv***ḗrunt***
Pluperfect	Sing. 1	portā́v***eram***	mṓv***eram***	mī́s***eram***	iḗc***eram***	audī́v***eram***
	2	portā́v***erās***	mṓv***erās***	mī́s***erās***	iḗc***erās***	audī́v***erās***
	3	portā́v***erat***	mṓv***erat***	mī́s***erat***	iḗc***erat***	audī́v***erat***
	Pl. 1	portāv***erā́mus***	mōv***erā́mus***	mīs***erā́mus***	iēc***erā́mus***	audīv***erā́mus***
	2	portāv***erā́tis***	móv***erā́tis***	mīs***erā́tis***	iēc***erā́tis***	audīv***erā́tis***
	3	portā́v***erant***	mṓv***erant***	mī́s***erant***	iḗc***erant***	audī́v***erant***
Future Perfect	Sing. 1	portā́v***erō***	mṓv***erō***	mī́s***erō***	iḗc***erō***	audī́v***erō***
	2	portā́v***eris***	mṓv***eris***	mī́s***eris***	iḗc***eris***	audī́v***eris***
	3	portā́v***erit***	mṓv***erit***	mī́s***erit***	iḗc***erit***	audī́v***erit***
	Pl. 1	portāv***érimus***	mōv***érimus***	mīs***érimus***	iēc***érimus***	audīv***érimus***
	2	portāv***éritis***	mōv***éritis***	mīs***éritis***	iēc***éritis***	audīv***éritis***
	3	portā́v***erint***	mṓv***erint***	mī́s***erint***	iḗc***erint***	audī́v***erint***

XIV. Regular Verbs Passive: Infinitive, Imperative, Indicative

		1st Conjugation	2nd Conjugation	3rd Conjugation		4th Conjugation
	Infinitive	port***ā́rī***	mov***ḗrī***	mítt***ī***	iác***ī***	aud***ī́rī***
	Imperative	port***ā́re*** port***ā́minī***	mov***ḗre*** mov***ḗminī***	mítt***ere*** mitt***íminī***	iác***ere*** iac***íminī***	aud***ī́re*** aud***ī́minī***
Present	Sing. 1 2 3	pórto***r*** portā́***ris*** portā́***tur***	móveo***r*** movḗ***ris*** movḗ***tur***	mítto***r*** mítte***ris*** mítti***tur***	iácio***r*** iáce***ris*** iáci***tur***	aúdio***r*** audī́***ris*** audī́***tur***
	Pl. 1 2 3	portā́***mur*** portā́***minī*** portá***ntur***	movḗ***mur*** movḗ***minī*** mové***ntur***	mítti***mur*** mittí***minī*** mittú***ntur***	iáci***mur*** iací***minī*** iaci***úntur***	audī́***mur*** audī́***minī*** audi***úntur***
Imperfect	Sing. 1 2 3	portā́***bar*** portā***bā́ris*** portā***bā́tur***	movḗ***bar*** movē***bā́ris*** movē***bā́tur***	mittḗ***bar*** mittē***bā́ris*** mittē***bā́tur***	iaciḗ***bar*** iaciē***bā́ris*** iaciē***bā́tur***	audiḗ***bar*** audiē***bā́ris*** audiē***bā́tur***
	Pl. 1 2 3	portā***bā́mur*** portā***bā́minī*** portā***bántur***	movē***bā́mur*** movē***bā́minī*** movē***bántur***	mittē***bā́mur*** mittē***bā́minī*** mittē***bántur***	iaciē***bā́mur*** iaciē***bā́minī*** iaciē***bántur***	audiē***bā́mur*** audiē***bā́minī*** audiē***bántur***
Future	Sing. 1 2 3	portā́***bor*** portā́***beris*** portā́***bitur***	movḗ***bor*** movḗ***beris*** movḗ***bitur***	mítt***ar*** mitt***ḗris*** mitt***ḗtur***	iáci***ar*** iaci***ḗris*** iaci***ḗtur***	aúdi***ar*** audi***ḗris*** audi***ḗtur***
	Pl. 1 2 3	portā́***bimur*** portā***bíminī*** portā***búntur***	movḗ***bimur*** movē***bíminī*** movē***búntur***	mitt***ḗmur*** mitt***ḗminī*** mitt***éntur***	iaci***ḗmur*** iaci***ḗminī*** iaci***éntur***	audi***ḗmur*** audi***ḗminī*** audi***éntur***

	Perfect Passive		Pluperfect Passive		Future Perfect Passive	
Sing. 1 2 3	portā́tus, -a portā́tus, -a portā́tus, -a, -um	sum es est	portā́tus, -a portā́tus, -a portā́tus, -a, -um	éram érās érat	portā́tus, -a portā́tus, -a portā́tus, -a, -um	érō éris érit
Pl. 1 2 3	portā́tī, -ae portā́tī, -ae portā́tī, -ae, -a	súmus éstis sunt	portā́tī, -ae portā́tī, -ae portā́tī, -ae, -a	erā́mus erā́tis érant	portā́tī, -ae portā́tī, -ae portā́tī, -ae, -a	érimus éritis érunt

XV. Regular Verbs Active: Subjunctive

		1st Conjugation	2nd Conjugation	3rd Conjugation		4th Conjugation
Present	Sing. 1	pórt***em***	móve***am***	mítt***am***	iáci***am***	aúdi***am***
	2	pórt***ēs***	móve***ās***	mítt***ās***	iáci***ās***	aúdi***ās***
	3	pórt***et***	móve***at***	mítt***at***	iáci***at***	aúdi***at***
	Pl. 1	port***ḗmus***	move***ā́mus***	mitt***ā́mus***	iaci***ā́mus***	audi***ā́mus***
	2	port***ḗtis***	move***ā́tis***	mitt***ā́tis***	iaci***ā́tis***	audi***ā́tis***
	3	pórt***ent***	móve***ant***	mítt***ant***	iáci***ant***	aúdi***ant***
Imperfect	Sing. 1	portā́re***m***	movḗre***m***	míttere***m***	iácere***m***	audī́re***m***
	2	portā́rē***s***	movḗrē***s***	mítterē***s***	iácerē***s***	audī́rē***s***
	3	portā́re***t***	movḗre***t***	míttere***t***	iácere***t***	audī́re***t***
	Pl. 1	portārḗ***mus***	movērḗ***mus***	mitterḗ***mus***	iacerḗ***mus***	audīrḗ***mus***
	2	portārḗ***tis***	movērḗ***tis***	mitterḗ***tis***	iacerḗ***tis***	audīrḗ***tis***
	3	portā́re***nt***	movḗre***nt***	mittere***nt***	iácere***nt***	audī́re***nt***
Perfect	Sing. 1	portā́v***erim***	mṓv***erim***	mī́s***erim***	iḗc***erim***	audī́v***erim***
	2	portā́v***eris***	mṓv***eris***	mī́s***eris***	iḗc***eris***	audī́v***eris***
	3	portā́v***erit***	mṓv***erit***	mī́s***erit***	iḗc***erit***	audī́v***erit***
	Pl. 1	portāv***érimus***	mōv***érimus***	mīs***érimus***	iēc***érimus***	audīv***érimus***
	2	portāv***éritis***	mōv***éritis***	mīs***éritis***	iēc***éritis***	audīv***éritis***
	3	portā́v***erint***	mṓv***erint***	mī́s***erint***	iḗc***erint***	audī́v***erint***
Pluperfect	Sing. 1	portāvísse***m***	mōvísse***m***	mīsísse***m***	iēcísse***m***	audīvísse***m***
	2	portāvíssē***s***	mōvíssē***s***	mīsíssē***s***	iēcíssē***s***	audīvíssē***s***
	3	portāvísse***t***	mōvísse***t***	mīsísse***t***	iēcísse***t***	audīvísse***t***
	Pl. 1	portāvissḗ***mus***	mōvissḗ***mus***	mīsissḗ***mus***	iēcissḗ***mus***	audīvissḗ***mus***
	2	portāvissḗ***tis***	mōvissḗ***tis***	mīsissḗ***tis***	iēcissḗ***tis***	audīvissḗ***tis***
	3	portāvísse***nt***	mōvísse***nt***	mīsísse***nt***	iēcísse***nt***	audīvísse***nt***

XVI. Regular Verbs Passive: Subjunctive

		1st Conjugation	2nd Conjugation	3rd Conjugation		4th Conjugation
Present	Sing. 1	pórt***er***	móve***ar***	mítt***ar***	iáci***ar***	aúdi***ar***
	2	port***ḗris***	move***ā́ris***	mitt***ā́ris***	iaci***ā́ris***	audi***ā́ris***
	3	port***ḗtur***	move***ā́tur***	mitt***ā́tur***	iaci***ā́tur***	audi***ā́tur***
	Pl. 1	port***ḗmur***	move***ā́mur***	mitt***ā́mur***	iaci***ā́mur***	audi***ā́mur***
	2	port***ḗminī***	move***ā́minī***	mitt***ā́minī***	iaci***ā́minī***	audi***ā́minī***
	3	port***éntur***	move***ántur***	mitt***ántur***	iaci***ántur***	audi***ántur***
Imperfect	Sing. 1	portā́re***r***	movḗre***r***	míttere***r***	iácere***r***	audī́re***r***
	2	portārḗ***ris***	movērḗ***ris***	mitterḗ***ris***	iacerḗ***ris***	audīrḗ***ris***
	3	portārḗ***tur***	movērḗ***tur***	mitterḗ***tur***	iacerḗ***tur***	audīrḗ***tur***
	Pl. 1	portārḗ***mur***	movērḗ***mur***	mitterḗ***mur***	iacerḗ***mur***	audīrḗ***mur***
	2	portārḗ***minī***	movērḗ***minī***	mitterḗ***minī***	iacerḗ***minī***	audīrḗ***minī***
	3	portāré***ntur***	movēré***ntur***	mitteré***ntur***	iaceré***ntur***	audīré***ntur***
Perfect	1	portā́tus sim etc.	mṓtus sim etc.	míssus sim etc.	iáctus sim etc.	audī́tus sim etc.
Pluperfect	1	portā́tus éssem etc.	mṓtus éssem etc.	míssus éssem etc.	iáctus éssem etc.	audī́tus éssem etc.

XVII. Deponent Verbs: Infinitive, Imperative, Indicative

		1st Conjugation	2nd Conjugation	3rd Conjugation		4th Conjugation
Present Infinitive		cōn***ā́rī***	ver***ḗrī***	lóqu***ī***	régred***ī***	exper***ī́rī***
Imperative		cōn***ā́re*** cōn***ā́minī***	ver***ḗre*** ver***ḗminī***	lóqu***ere*** loqu***íminī***	regréd***ere*** regred***íminī***	exper***ī́re*** exper***ī́minī***
Present	**Sing. 1 2 3**	cṓno***r*** cōnā́***ris*** cōnā́***tur***	véreo***r*** verḗ***ris*** verḗ***tur***	lóquo***r*** lóque***ris*** lóqui***tur***	regrédio***r*** regréde***ris*** regrédi***tur***	expério***r*** experī́***ris*** experī́***tur***
	Pl. 1 2 3	cōnā́***mur*** cōnā́***minī*** cōná***ntur***	verḗ***mur*** verḗ***minī*** veré***ntur***	lóqui***mur*** loquí***minī*** loquú***ntur***	regrédi***mur*** regredí***minī*** regrediú***ntur***	experī́***mur*** experī́***minī*** experiú***ntur***
Imperfect	**Sing. 1 2 3**	cōnā́***bar*** cōnā***bā́ris*** cōnā***bā́tur***	verḗ***bar*** verē***bā́ris*** verē***bā́tur***	loquḗ***bar*** loquē***bā́ris*** loquē***bā́tur***	regrediḗ***bar*** regrediē***bā́ris*** regrediē***bā́tur***	experiḗ***bar*** experiē***bā́ris*** experiē***bā́tur***
Future	**Sing. 1 2 3**	cōnā́***bor*** cōnā́***beris*** cōnā́***bitur***	verḗ***bor*** verḗ***beris*** verḗ***bitur***	lóqua***r*** loquḗ***ris*** loquḗ***tur***	regrédia***r*** regrediḗ***ris*** regrediḗ***tur***	expéria***r*** experiḗ***ris*** experiḗ***tur***
Perfect	**1**	cōnā́tus sum	véritus sum	locū́tus sum	regréssus sum	expértus sum
Pluperfect	**1**	cōnā́tus éram	véritus éram	locū́tus éram	regréssus éram	expértus éram
Future Perfect	**1**	cōnā́tus érō	véritus érō	locū́tus érō	regréssus érō	expértus érō

XVIII. Deponent Verbs: Subjunctive

		1st Conjugation	2nd Conjugation	3rd Conjugation		4th Conjugation
Present	**Sing. 1 2 3**	cṓn***er*** cōn***ḗris*** cōn***ḗtur***	vére***ar*** vere***ā́ris*** vere***ā́tur***	lóqu***ar*** loqu***ā́ris*** loqu***ā́tur***	regrédi***ar*** regredi***ā́ris*** regredi***ā́tur***	expéri***ar*** experi***ā́ris*** experi***ā́tur***
	Pl. 1 2 3	cōn***ḗmur*** cōn***ḗminī*** cōn***éntur***	vere***ā́mur*** vere***ā́minī*** vere***ántur***	loqu***ā́mur*** loqu***ā́minī*** loqu***ántur***	regredi***ā́mur*** regredi***ā́minī*** regredi***ántur***	experi***ā́mur*** experi***ā́minī*** experi***ántur***
Imperfect	**Sing. 1 2 3**	cōnā́re***r*** cōnārḗ***ris*** cōnārḗ***tur***	verḗre***r*** verērḗ***ris*** verērḗ***tur***	lóquere***r*** loquerḗ***ris*** loquerḗ***tur***	regrēdere***r*** regrederḗ***ris*** regrederḗ***tur***	experī́re***r*** experīrḗ***ris*** experīrḗ***tur***
	Pl. 1 2 3	cōnārḗ***mur*** cōnārḗ***minī*** cōnāré***ntur***	verērḗ***mur*** verērḗ***minī*** verēré***ntur***	loquerḗ***mur*** loquerḗ***minī*** loqueré***ntur***	regrederḗ***mur*** regrederḗ***minī*** regrederé***ntur***	experīrḗ***mur*** experīrḗ***minī*** experīré***ntur***
Perfect	**1**	cōnā́tus sim etc.	véritus sim etc.	locū́tus sim etc.	regréssus sim etc.	expértus sim etc.
Pluperfect	**1**	cōnā́tus éssem etc.	véritus éssem etc.	locū́tus éssem etc.	regréssus éssem etc.	expértus éssem etc.

XIX. Irregular Verbs: Infinitive, Imperative, Indicative

	Infinitive	ésse	pósse	vélle	nṓlle	mā́lle
	Imperative	es	—	—	nṓl***ī***	—
		és***te***	—	—	nōl***ī́te***	—
Present	**Sing. 1**	su***m***	pós***sum***	vól***ō***	nṓl***ō***	mā́l***ō***
	2	e***s***	pót***es***	vīs	nōn vīs	mā́vīs
	3	es***t***	pót***est***	vul***t***	nōn vul***t***	mā́vul***t***
	Pl. 1	sú***mus***	pós***sumus***	vólu***mus***	nṓlu***mus***	mā́lu***mus***
	2	és***tis***	pot***éstis***	vúl***tis***	nōn vúl***tis***	māvúl***tis***
	3	su***nt***	pós***sunt***	vólu***nt***	nṓlu***nt***	mā́lu***nt***
Imperfect	**Sing. 1**	éra***m***	póte***ram***	volḗ***bam***	nōlḗ***bam***	mālḗ***bam***
	2	érā***s***	póte***rās***	volḗ***bās***	nōlḗ***bās***	mālḗ***bās***
	3	éra***t***	póte***rat***	volḗ***bat***	nōlḗ***bat***	mālḗ***bat***
	Pl. 1	erā́***mus***	pote***rā́mus***	volē***bā́mus***	nōlē***bā́mus***	mālē***bā́mus***
	2	erā́***tis***	pote***rā́tis***	volē***bā́tis***	nōlē***bā́tis***	mālē***bā́tis***
	3	éra***nt***	póte***rant***	volḗ***bant***	nōlḗ***bant***	mā́lḗ***bant***
Future	**Sing. 1**	ér***ō***	póte***rō***	vól***am***	nṓl***am***	mā́l***am***
	2	éri***s***	póte***ris***	vól***ēs***	nṓl***ēs***	mā́l***ēs***
	3	éri***t***	póte***rit***	vól***et***	nṓl***et***	mā́l***et***
	Pl. 1	éri***mus***	poté***rimus***	vol***ḗmus***	nōl***ḗmus***	māl***ḗmus***
	2	éri***tis***	poté***ritis***	vol***ḗtis***	nōl***ḗtis***	māl***ḗtis***
	3	éru***nt***	póte***runt***	vól***ent***	nṓl***ent***	mā́l***ent***
Perfect	**Sing. 1**	fú***ī***	pótu***ī***	vólu***ī***	nṓlu***ī***	mā́lu***ī***
	2	fu***ístī***	potu***ístī***	volu***ístī***	nōlu***ístī***	mālu***ístī***
	3	fú***it***	pótu***it***	vólu***it***	nṓlu***it***	mā́lu***it***
	Pl. 1	fú***imus***	potú***imus***	volú***imus***	nōlú***imus***	mālú***imus***
	2	fu***ístis***	potu***ístis***	volu***ístis***	nōlu***ístis***	mālu***ístis***
	3	fu***ḗrunt***	potu***ḗrunt***	volu***ḗrunt***	nōlu***ḗrunt***	mālu***ḗrunt***
Pluperfect	**Sing. 1**	fú***eram***	potú***eram***	volú***eram***	nōlú***eram***	mālú***eram***
	2	fú***erās***	potú***erās***	volú***erās***	nōlú***erās***	mālú***erās***
	3	fú***erat***	potú***erat***	volú***erat***	nōlú***erat***	mālú***erat***
	Pl. 1	fu***erā́mus***	potu***erā́mus***	volu***erā́mus***	nōlu***erā́mus***	mālu***erā́mus***
	2	fu***erā́tis***	potu***erā́tis***	volu***erā́tis***	nōlu***erā́tis***	mālu***erā́tis***
	3	fú***erant***	potú***erant***	volú***erant***	nōlú***erant***	mālú***erant***
Future Perfect	**Sing. 1**	fú***erō***	potú***erō***	volú***erō***	nōlú***erō***	mālú***erō***
	2	fú***eris***	potú***eris***	volú***eris***	nōlú***eris***	mālú***eris***
	3	fú***erit***	potú***erit***	volú***erit***	nōlú***erit***	mālú***erit***
	Pl. 1	fu***érimus***	potu***érimus***	volu***érimus***	nōlu***érimus***	mālu***érimus***
	2	fu***éritis***	potu***éritis***	volu***éritis***	nōlu***éritis***	mālu***éritis***
	3	fú***erint***	potú***erint***	volú***erint***	nōlú***erint***	mālú***erint***

	Infinitive	férre	férrī	fíerī	ī́re	
	Imperative	fer fér***te***	férre ferí***minī***	— —	ī ī́***te***	
Present	**Sing. 1** **2** **3**	fér***ō*** fer***s*** fer***t***	fér***or*** fér***ris*** fér***tur***	fī́***ō*** fī***s*** fi***t***	é***ō*** ī***s*** i***t***	
	Pl. 1 **2** **3**	féri***mus*** fér***tis*** féru***nt***	féri***mur*** ferí***minī*** ferú***ntur***	fī́***mus*** fī́***tis*** fī́***unt***	ī́***mus*** ī́***tis*** éu***nt***	
Imperfect	**Sing. 1** **2** **3**	ferḗ***bam*** ferḗ***bās*** ferḗ***bat***	ferḗ***bar*** ferē***bā́ris*** ferē***bā́tur***	fīḗ***bam*** fīḗ***bās*** fīe***bat***	ī́***bam*** ī́***bās*** ī́***bat***	
	Pl. 1 **2** **3**	ferē***bā́mus*** ferē***bā́tis*** ferḗ***bant***	ferē***bā́mur*** ferē***bā́mini*** ferē***bántur***	fīē***bā́mus*** fīē***bā́tis*** fīḗ***bant***	ī***bā́mus*** ī***bā́tis*** ī́***bant***	
Future	**Sing. 1** **2** **3**	fér***am*** fér***ēs*** fér***et***	fér***ar*** fer***ḗris*** fer***ḗtur***	fī́***am*** fī́***ēs*** fī́***et***	ī́***bō*** ī́***bis*** ī́***bit***	
	Pl. 1 **2** **3**	fer***ḗmus*** fer***ḗtis*** fér***ent***	fer***ḗmur*** fer***ḗminī*** fer***éntur***	fī***ḗmus*** fī***ḗtis*** fī́***ent***	ī́***bimus*** ī́***bitis*** ī́***bunt***	
Perfect	**Sing. 1** **2** **3**	túl***ī*** tul***ístī*** túl***it***	lā́tus sum lā́tus es lā́tus est	fáctus sum fáctus es fáctus est	ī́v***ī*** īv***ístī*** ī́v***it***	or, more usually ***íī*** i***ístī*** > ī́stī í***it***
	Pl. 1 **2** **3**	túl***imus*** tul***ístis*** tul***ḗrunt***	lā́tī súmus lā́tī éstis lā́tī sunt	fáctī súmus fáctī éstis fáctī sunt	ī́v***imus*** īv***ístis*** īv***ḗrunt***	í***imus*** i***ístis*** > ī́stis i***ḗrunt***
Pluperfect	**Sing. 1** **2** **3**	túl***eram*** túl***erās*** túl***erat***	lā́tus éram lā́tus érās lā́tus érat	fáctus éram fáctus érās fáctus érāt	ī́v***eram*** ī́v***erās*** ī́v***erat***	í***eram*** í***erās*** í***erat***
	Pl. 1 **2** **3**	tul***erā́mus*** tul***erā́tis*** túl***erant***	lā́tī erā́mus lā́tī erā́tis lā́tī érant	fáctī erā́mus fáctī erā́tis fáctī érant	īv***erā́mus*** īv***erā́tis*** ī́v***erant***	i***erā́mus*** i***erā́tis*** í***erant***
Future Perfect	**Sing. 1** **2** **3**	túl***erō*** túl***eris*** túl***erit***	lā́tus érō lā́tus éris lā́tus érit	fáctus érō fáctus éris fáctus érit	ī́v***erō*** ī́v***eris*** ī́v***erit***	í***erō*** í***eris*** í***erit***
	Pl. 1 **2** **3**	tul***érimus*** tul***éritis*** túl***erint***	lā́tī érimus lā́tī éritis lā́tī érunt	fáctī érimus fáctī éritis fáctī érunt	īv***érimus*** īv***éritis*** ī́v***erint***	i***érimus*** i***éritis*** í***erint***

XXI. Irregular Verbs: Subjunctive

Present	Sing.	1	s***im***	póss***im***	vél***im***	nṓl***im***	mā́l***im***
		2	s***īs***	póss***īs***	vél***īs***	nṓl***īs***	mā́l***īs***
		3	s***it***	póss***it***	vél***it***	nṓl***it***	mā́l***it***
	Pl.	1	s***ī́mus***	poss***ī́mus***	vel***ī́mus***	nōl***ī́mus***	māl***ī́mus***
		2	s***ī́tis***	poss***ī́tis***	vel***ī́tis***	nōl***ī́tis***	māl***ī́tis***
		3	s***int***	póss***int***	vél***int***	nōl***int***	mā́l***int***
Imperfect	Sing.	1	ésse***m***	pósse***m***	vélle***m***	nṓlle***m***	mā́lle***m***
		2	éssē***s***	póssē***s***	véllē***s***	nṓllē***s***	mā́llē***s***
		3	ésse***t***	pósse***t***	vélle***t***	nṓlle***t***	mā́lle***t***
	Pl.	1	essḗ***mus***	possḗ***mus***	vellḗ***mus***	nōllḗ***mus***	māllḗ***mus***
		2	essḗ***tis***	possḗ***tis***	vellḗ***tis***	nōllḗ***tis***	māllḗ***tis***
		3	ésse***nt***	pósse***nt***	vélle***nt***	nṓlle***nt***	mā́lle***nt***
Perfect	Sing.	1	fú***erim***	potú***erim***	volú***erim***	nōlú***erim***	mālú***erim***
		2	fú***eris***	potú***eris***	volú***eris***	nōlú***eris***	mālú***eris***
		3	fú***erit***	potú***erit***	volú***erit***	nōlú***erit***	mālú***erit***
	Pl.	1	fu***érimus***	potu***érimus***	volu***érimus***	nōlu***érimus***	mālu***érimus***
		2	fu***éritis***	potu***éritis***	volu***éritis***	nōlu***éritis***	mālu***éritis***
		3	fú***erint***	potú***erint***	volú***erint***	nōlú***erint***	mālú***erint***
Pluperfect	Sing.	1	fuísse***m***	potuísse***m***	voluísse***m***	nōluísse***m***	māluísse***m***
		2	fuíssē***s***	potuíssē***s***	voluíssē***s***	nōluíssē***s***	māluíssē***s***
		3	fuísse***t***	potuísse***t***	voluísse***t***	nōluísse***t***	māluísse***t***
	Pl.	1	fuissḗ***mus***	potuissḗ***mus***	voluissḗ***mus***	nōluissḗ***mus***	māluissḗ***mus***
		2	fuissḗ***tis***	potuissḗ***tis***	voluissḗ***tis***	nōluissḗ***tis***	māluissḗ***tis***
		3	fuísse***nt***	potuísse***nt***	voluísse***nt***	nōluísse***nt***	māluísse***nt***

XXI. Irregular Verbs: Subjunctive (continued)

Present	Sing. 1 2 3	fér***am*** fér***ās*** fér***at***	fér***ar*** fer***ā́ris*** fer***ā́tur***	fī́***am*** fī́***ās*** fī́***at***	é***am*** é***ās*** é***at***
	Pl. 1 2 3	fer***ā́mus*** fer***ā́tis*** fér***ant***	fer***ā́mur*** fer***ā́minī*** fer***ántur***	fī***ā́mus*** fī***ā́tis*** fī́***ant***	e***ā́mus*** e***ā́tis*** é***ant***
Imperfect	Sing. 1 2 3	férre***m*** férrē***s*** férre***t***	férre***r*** ferrḗ***ris*** ferrḗ***tur***	fíere***m*** fíerē***s*** fíere***t***	ī́re***m*** ī́rē***s*** ī́re***t***
	Pl. 1 2 3	ferrḗ***mus*** ferrḗ***tis*** férre***nt***	ferrḗ***mur*** ferrḗ***minī*** ferré***ntur***	fierḗ***mus*** fierḗ***tis*** fíere***nt***	īrḗ***mus*** īrḗ***tis*** ī́re***nt***
Perfect	Sing. 1 2 3	túl***erim*** túl***eris*** túl***erit***	lā́tus sim lā́tus sīs lā́tus sit	fáctus sim fáctus sīs fáctus sit	í***erim*** í***eris*** í***erit***
	Pl. 1 2 3	tul***érimus*** tul***éritis*** túl***erint***	lā́tī sī́mus lā́tī sī́tis lā́tī sint	fáctī sī́mus fáctī sī́tis fáctī sint	i***érimus*** i***éritis*** í***erint***
Pluperfect	Sing. 1 2 3	tulísse***m*** tulíssē***s*** tulísse***t***	lā́tus éssem lā́tus éssēs lā́tus ésset	fáctus éssem fáctus éssēs fáctus ésset	ī́sse***m*** ī́ssē***s*** ī́sse***t***
	Pl. 1 2 3	tulissḗ***mus*** tulissḗ***tis*** tulísse***nt***	lā́tī essḗmus lā́tī essḗtis lā́tī éssent	fáctī essḗmus fáctī essḗtis fáctī éssent	īssḗ***mus*** īssḗ***tis*** ī́sse***nt***

Note: the perfect subjunctive of **eō** may be **ierim,** etc., as above, or **īverim.** The pluperfect subjunctive of **eō** may be **īssem,** etc., as above, or **īvissem.**

XXII. Participles of Non-deponent Verbs

		Active	Passive
Present	1 2 3 -iō 4	pórtāns, portántis móvēns, movéntis míttēns, mitténtis iáciēns, iaciéntis aúdiēns, audiéntis	
Perfect	1 2 3 -iō 4		portā́tus, -a, -um mṓtus, -a, -um míssus, -a, -um iáctus, -a, -um audī́tus, -a, -um
Future	1 2 3 -iō 4	portātū́rus, -a, -um mōtū́rus, -a, -um missū́rus, -a, -um iactū́rus, -a, -um audítū́rus, -a, -um	portándus, -a, -um movéndus, -a, -um mitténdus, -a, -um iaciéndus, -a, -um audiéndus, -a, -um

Note: the future passive participle is also known as the gerundive.

XXIII. Participles of Deponent Verbs

		Active	Passive
Present Participle	1 2 3 -iō 4	cṓnāns, cōnántis vérēns, veréntis lóquēns, loquéntis ēgrédiēns, ēgrediéntis expériēns, experiéntis	
Perfect Participle	1 2 3 -iō 4	cōnā́tus, -a, -um véritus, -a, -um locū́tus, -a, -um ēgréssus, -a, -um expértus, -a, -um	
Future Participle	1 2 3 -iō 4	cōnātū́rus, -a, -um veritū́rus, -a, -um locūtū́rus, -a, -um ēgressū́rus, -a, -um expertū́rus, -a, -um	cōnándus, -a, -um veréndus, -a, -um loquéndus, -a, -um ēgrediéndus, -a, -um experiéndus, -a, -um

XXIV. Infinitives of Non-deponent Verbs

		Active	Passive
Present	1	portā́re	portā́rī
	2	mōvḗre	mōvḗrī
	3	míttere	míttī
	-iō	iácere	iácī
	4	audī́re	audī́rī
Perfect	1	portāvísse	portā́tus, -a, -um ésse
	2	mōvísse	mṓtus, -a, -um ésse
	3	mīsísse	míssus, -a, -um ésse
	-iō	iēcísse	iáctus, -a, -um ésse
	4	audīvísse	audī́tus, -a, -um ésse
Future	1	portātū́rus, -a, -um ésse	
	2	mōtū́rus, -a, -um ésse	
	3	missū́rus, -a, -um ésse	
	-iō	iactū́rus, -a, -um ésse	
	4	audītū́rus, -a, -um ésse	

XXV. Infinitives of Deponent Verbs

Present	1	cōnā́rī
	2	verḗrī
	3	lóquī
	-iō	ḗgredī
	4	experī́rī
Perfect	1	cōnā́tus, -a, -um ésse
	2	véritus, -a, -um ésse
	3	locū́tus, -a, -um ésse
	-iō	ēgréssus, -a, -um ésse
	4	expértus, -a, -um ésse
Future	1	cōnātū́rus, -a, -um ésse
	2	veritū́rus, -a, -um ésse
	3	locūtū́rus, -a, -um ésse
	-iō	ēgressū́rus, -a, -um ésse
	4	expertū́rus, -a, -um ésse

XXVI. Gerunds of Non-deponent Verbs

Case Singular	1st Conjugation	2nd Conjugation	3rd Conjugation	3rd *-iō* Conjugation	4th Conjugation
Genitive	portá***ndī***	movέ***ndī***	mitté***ndī***	iacié***ndī***	audié***ndī***
Dative	portá***ndō***	movέ***ndō***	mitté***ndō***	iacié***ndō***	audié***ndō***
Accusative	portá***ndum***	movέ***ndum***	mitté***ndum***	iacié***ndum***	audié***ndum***
Ablative	portá***ndō***	movέ***ndō***	mitté***ndō***	iacié***ndō***	audié***ndō***

XXVII. Gerunds of Deponent Verbs

Case Singular	1st Conjugation	2nd Conjugation	3rd Conjugation	3rd *-iō* Conjugation	4th Conjugation
Genitive	cōná***ndī***	veré***ndī***	loqué***ndī***	ēgredié***ndī***	experié***ndī***
Dative	cōná***ndō***	veré***ndō***	loqué***ndō***	ēgredié***ndō***	experié***ndō***
Accusative	cōná***ndum***	veré***ndum***	loqué***ndum***	ēgredié***ndum***	experié***ndum***
Ablative	cōná***ndō***	veré***ndō***	loqué***ndō***	ēgredié***ndō***	experié***ndō***

Note: gerunds have only singular forms and are not used in the nominative case.

LATIN TO ENGLISH VOCABULARY

This list includes all basic words that do not appear in the running vocabularies. It also includes all mastery words, those that appear in the running vocabularies with asterisks, since these words are usually not repeated in the running vocabularies when they reappear in the readings. Numbers in parentheses at the end of entries refer to the chapters in all the *Ecce Romani* student books in which the words appear in the running vocabulary, in a Building the Meaning section, or in a Reading Note. However, this list includes only words used in Book III; for a cumulative list of words introduced in Books I and II, see the Latin to English Vocabulary at the end of Book II.

A

ā, ab, prep. + abl., *from, away from, by* (13, 29, 31)
abdō, abdidere, abdidī, abditus, *to hide, put away; to devote oneself completely to* (63A)
abeō, abīre, abiī or **abīvī, abitūrus**, irreg., *to go away* (3, 9)
***absēns, absentis**, *absent* (55d)
absentia, -ae, f., *absence*
absolvō, absolvere, absolvī, absolūtus, *to set free, acquit* (65E)
absum, abesse, āfuī, āfutūrus, irreg., *to be away, be absent, be distant* (11, 25)
***ac**, conj., *and* (30, 55D)
accēdō, accēdere, accessī, accessūrus, *to approach, draw near, come toward* (63C, 76B)
accidit, accidere, accidit, *it happens* (14, 26)
accipiō, accipere, accēpī, acceptus, *to receive, get* (31)
accurrō, accurrere, accurrī, accursūrus, *to run toward, run up to* (29)
***ācer, ācris, ācre**, *fierce, sharp, eager, keen* (60A)
ācriter, adv., *fiercely* (48)
aciēs, -ēī, f., *battle line* (55C)
ad, prep. + acc., *to, toward, at, near* (2, 9); + gerund(ive), *to, in order to* (64)
***adeō**, adv., *so much, to such an extent* (50, 57b)
adeō, adīre, adiī, aditus, irreg., *to come to, approach*
adferō, see **afferō**
***adhūc**, adv., *still, as yet* (5, 13, 55C)
adiciō, adicere, adiēcī, adiectus, *to add* (56B)
adigō, adigere, adēgī, adāctus, *to drive toward* (60B)
adimō, adimere, adēmī, adēmptus + dat., *to take away (from)* (35)
administrō, -āre, -āvī, -ātus, *to administer, govern* (56b, 57B)
admittō, admittere, admīsī, admissus, *to let in, allow* (56B)
***admoneō, admonēre, admonuī, admonitus**, *to remind, advise* (67D)
***admoveō, admovēre, admōvī, admōtus**, *to move toward, apply to, advance to; to touch* (70A)
adolēscentia, -ae, f., *youth, adolescence*
***admoveō, admovēre, admōvī, admōtus**, *to move toward, bring to* (22, 70A)
adoptō, -āre, -āvī, -ātus, *to adopt* (56A)
adorior, adorīrī, adortus sum, *to attack* (42)
adsequor, adsequī, adsecūtus sum, *to follow* (75B)
adsum, adesse, adfuī, adfutūrus, irreg., *to be present* (26)
adsurgō, adsurgere, adsurrēxī, adsurrēctūrus, *to stand up* (76D)
adulēscēns, adulēscentis, m., *young man, youth* (36)
adversārius, -ī, m., *adversary*
adversum or **adversus**, prep. + acc., *against* (55B)
***adversus, -a, -um**, *opposite, turned toward, facing; unfavorable, bad* (63B)
***aedēs, aedis**, gen. pl., **aedium**, f., *building, temple;* pl., *house* (69B)
aedificō, -āre, -āvī, -ātus, *to build* (24)
aeger, aegra, aegrum, *ill* (39)
aegrōtō, -āre, -āvī, -ātūrus, *to be ill* (39)
Aegyptus, -ī, f., *Egypt* (55C)
aequō, -āre, -āvī, -ātus, *to make equal* (57A)
***aequor, aequoris**, n., *flat surface; sea* (54, 72A)
***aequus, -a, -um**, *fair, equal* (63B)
āēr, āeris, m., *air* (74D)
aestus, -ūs, m., *heat* (24, 25)
***aetās, aetātis**, f., *age, time of life* (55C)
aeternus, -a, -um, *eternal*
afferō, afferre, attulī, allātus, irreg., *to bring in, carry to* (29, 32)

afficiō, afficere, affēcī, affectus, *to weaken, debilitate* (61A)
afflīgō, afflīgere, afflīxī, afflīctus, *to strike down* (66C)
ager, agrī, m., *field, territory, land* (2)
aggredior, aggredī, aggressus sum, *to attack* (55A)
***agmen, agminis**, n., *line of march, column, group* (64A)
agrestis, -is, gen. pl., **agrestium**, m., *farmer, peasant* (76C)
agō, agere, ēgī, āctus, *to do, drive* (8, 14, 23, 52)
grātiās agere + dat., *to thank* (26, 51)
***aiō**, defective verb used mainly in pres. and imperf. indic., *to affirm, say* (50, 58B)
āla, -ae, f., *wing* (74D)
***aliquī, aliqua, aliquod**, *some (or other), any* (38, 55B)
***aliquis, aliquis, aliquid**, *someone, something, anyone, anything* (25, 51, 58B, 65)
nē quis (quis = aliquis), *that no one* (52, 65)
sī quis (quis = aliquis), *if anyone* (51, 65)
alius, alia, aliud, *another, other* (10)
aliī... aliī, *some...others* (9)
alter, altera, alterum, *the other, the other (of two), the second* (1)
***altus, -a, -um**, *high, deep* (38, 72A)
altum, -ī, n., *the deep, the sea*
amāns, amantis, m., *lover* (62E)
ambūrō, ambūrere, ambussī, ambustus, *to burn up* (64C)
ambō, ambae, ambō, *both* (46)
āmēns, āmentis, *mad, insane, mindless* (66A)
amīca, -ae, f., *girlfriend*
amīcus, -ī, m., *friend* (3)
***amīcitia, -ae**, f., *friendship* (55C)
***āmittō, āmittere, āmīsī, āmissus**, *to lose* (56A)
amō, -āre, -āvī, -ātus, *to like, love* (4)
***amor, amōris**, m., *love* (34, 57B)
ampliō, -āre, -āvī, -ātus, *to enlarge, increase* (69D)
amplitūdō, amplitūdinis, f., *size* (76C)
***amplius**, adv., *more* (55D)
amplus, -a, -um, *ample*
***an**, conj., *whether, or* (51, 63A)
ancilla, -ae, f., *slave-woman* (6)
angō, angere, *to distress, trouble* (75A)
angustus, -a, -um, *narrow* (76D)
***anima, -ae**, f., *breath of life, soul; darling* (33, 66A)
animadvertō, animadvertere, animadvertī, animadversus, *to notice* (39)
animal, animālis, n., *animal*
animus, -ī, m., *mind, spirit, heart* (16)
annus, -ī, m., *year* (38)
ante, prep. + acc., *before, in front of* (36, 39)
anteā, adv., *before, previously* (20)
***anteferō, anteferre, antetulī, antelātus**, *to put ahead, prefer* (60B)
***antīquus, -a, -um**, *ancient* (26, 58A)
ānulus, -ī, m., *ring* (50)
Apollō, Apollinis, m., *Apollo* (god of the sun, medicine, and poetry)
appāreō, -ēre, -uī, -itūrus, *to appear* (15, 18)
apparō, -āre, -āvī, -ātus, *to prepare, make ready, plan* (65B)
***appellō, -āre, -āvī, -ātus**, *to call by name, name* (21, 55A)
appropinquō, -āre, -āvī, -ātūrus + dat., *to approach, draw near to* (4, 22)
***apud**, prep. + acc., *at the house of, near, at, with, among* (16, 55B)
aqua, -ae, f., *water, aqueduct* (6)
āra, -ae, f., *altar* (53)
***arbitror, arbitrārī, arbitrātus**, *to think* (59A)
arbor, arboris, f., *tree* (1)
***ardeō, ardēre, arsī**, *to burn, blaze* (53, 62b)
ārea, -ae, f., *open space, courtyard* (11)
arma, -ōrum, n. pl., *arms, weapons* (39)
ars, artis, f., *skill, art* (14)
***artus, -ūs**, m., *limb* (71B)
***arvum, -ī**, n., *field, land* (72A)
ascendō, ascendere, ascendī, ascēnsus, *to climb up* (4, 22)
Asia, -ae, f., *Asia* (Roman province in western Asia Minor) (38)
***asper, aspera, asperum**, *harsh, rough* (68)
***aspiciō, aspicere, aspexī, aspectus**, *to look at, see, examine* (71A)
astrum, -ī, n., *star* (72B)
***at**, conj., *but* (60A)
***āter, ātra, ātrum**, *black* (68)
atque, conj., *and, also* (22)
ātrium, -ī, n., *atrium* (main room of a Roman house) (26)
attentē, adv., *attentively, closely* (20)
attonitus, -a, -um, *astonished* (24)
***auctor, auctōris**, m., *creator, founder, person responsible; author* (66D)
***auctōritās, auctōritātis**, f., *influence, prestige; authority* (69B)
audāx, audācis, *bold, daring, reckless* (36)
***audeō, audēre, ausus sum**, semi-deponent + infin., *to dare* (40, 59D)
audiō, -īre, -īvī, -ītus, *to hear, listen to* (4)
auferō, auferre, abstulī, ablātus, irreg., *to carry away, take away* (29, 32)
augeō, augēre, auxī, auctus, *to increase, enlarge*

*aura, -ae, f., *breeze* (71A)
*aureus, -a, -um, *golden, of gold* (25, 69B)
aureus, -ī, m., *aureus* (gold coin) (75C)
*auris, auris, f., *ear* (72B)
*aurum, -ī, n., *gold* (21, 67B)
aut, conj., *or* (26)
aut...aut, conj., *either...or* (26)
autem, conj., *however, moreover* (31)
autumnus, -ī, m., *autumn, fall*
auxilium, -ī, n., *help, aid* (5, 15)
auxilia, -ōrum, n. pl., *auxiliary troops; reinforcements* (55C)
āvertō, āvertere, āvertī, aversus, *to turn aside* (60D)
avis, avis, gen. pl., **avium**, m./f., *bird* (50, 74D)

B

baculum, -ī, n., *stick* (10, 15)
barbaricus, -a, -um, *barbarian, foreign* (57B)
***barbarus, -a, -um**, *barbarian, foreign* (55C)
basilica, -ae, f., *courthouse, basilica* (64C)
bāsium, -ī, n., *kiss* (62A)
***beātus, -a, -um**, *happy, joyful, contented* (62J)
***bellum, -ī**, n., *war* (39, 55A)
bellum commovēre, *to begin war, undertake war*
bellum gerere, *to wage war* (56A)
bellum īnferre + dat., *to make war upon* (55A)
***bellus, -a, -um**, *pretty, attractive* (62H)
***beneficium, -ī**, n., *kindness* (67D)
***benevolentia, -ae**, f., *kindness, goodwill* (63A)
bēstia, -ae, f., *beast, animal* (49)
bibō, bibere, bibī, *to drink* (31)
***bis**, adv., *twice* (55A)
bonus, -a, -um, *good* (12, 34)
bona, -ōrum, n. pl., *goods, possessions* (26, 65E)
***bracchium, -ī**, n., *arm* (73D)
brevis, -is, -e, *short, brief* (2, 34)

C

cadō, cadere, cecidī, cāsūrus, *to fall* (3, 22)
***caedēs, caedis**, gen. pl., **caedium**, f., *murder, killing* (59A)
***caedō, caedere, cecīdī, caesus**, *to cut, beat, cut down, kill* (57B)
caelum, -ī, n., *sky, heaven* (17)
***calamitās, calamitātis**, f., *disaster* (55B)
calidus, -a, -um, *warm, hot* (5)
campus, -ī, m., *field, plain* (41)
***candidus, -a, -um, white**, *white, bright, fair-skinned* (62B)
candidātus, -ī, m., *candidate*
capiō, capere, cēpī, captus, *to take, capture* (21)
captīvus, -a, -um, *captive, captured* (26)
***captō, -āre, -āvī, -ātus**, *to catch at eagerly, try to catch, keep catching* (74D)
***careō, carēre, caruī, caritūrus**, *to be without, be free from, need, lack* (63B)
caput, capitis, n., *head* (25)
carcer, carceris, m., *prison* (55A)
***carpō, carpere, carpsī, carptus**, *to pick, pluck, seize* (73C)
Carthāgō, Carthāginis, f., *Carthage* (city in North Africa) (39)
***cārus, -a, -um**, *dear, beloved* (53, 66A)
casa, -ae, f., *hut* (42)
***castra, -ōrum**, n. pl., *camp*, (55C, 60A)
***cāsus, -ūs**, m., *falling; chance, misfortune, mishap, accident* (60B)
cāsū, *by chance, accidentally* (32)
catella, -ae, f., *pupppy* (75A)
causa, -ae, f., *reason, cause; case* (25, 65B)
gen. + **causā**, *for the sake of, as* (52, 64)
caveō, cavēre, cāvī, cautus, *to be careful, watch out for, beware* (4, 13, 23)
***cēdō, cēdere, cessī, cessūrus** + dat., *to yield to, go, move* (67A)
celer, celeris, celere, *swift, quick* (34)
celeriter, adv., *quickly* (8, 13, 35)
celeritās, celeritātis, f., *speed* (29)
cēlō, -āre, -āvī, -ātus, *to hide, conceal* (11)
cēna, -ae, f., *dinner* (19)
cēnō, -āre, -āvī, -ātus, *to dine, eat dinner, eat* (19)
***cēnseō, cēnsēre, cēnsuī, cēnsus**, *to be of the opinion, think* (66C)
centēnī, -ae, -a, *a hundred each* (55A)
centiēs, adv., *a hundred times* (75C)
centum, *a hundred* (15, 38)
***centuriō, centuriōnis**, m., *centurion, commander of a century* (unit of about 80 men) (60A)
cēra, -ae, f., *wax* (74D)
cernō, cernere, crēvī, crētus, *to discern, see, understand* (75B)
certāmen, certāminis, n., *contest, rivalry* (60E)
certus, -a, -um, *certain* (35)
certē, adv., *certainly, surely, at least* (19, 35)
certior fierī, *to be made more certain, to be informed* 70C
cēterī, -ae, -a, *the rest, the others, the remainder* (33)
cibus, -ī, m., *food* (6)

cingō, cingere, cīnxī, cīnctus, *to surround; to equip, strap on* (64A)
***cinis, cineris**, m., *ash* (75A)
***circā**, prep. + acc., *around, about* (64A)
circuitus, -ūs, m., *circuit, circumference, perimeter* (55A)
***citus, -a, -um**, *swift* (68)
cito, adv., *quickly, soon* (75A)
cīvicus, -a, -um, *civic, civil* (69B)
***cīvīlis, -is, -e**, *polite, civil* (55B)
cīvis, cīvis, gen. pl., **cīvium**, m./f., *citizen* (13)
***cīvitās, cīvitātis**, f., *state; city* (56A)
clāmō, -āre, -āvī, -ātūrus, *to shout* (3)
clāmor, clāmōris, m., *shout, shouting* (5)
***clārus, -a, -um**, *bright; well-known, distinguished* (53, 55A)
***classis, classis**, gen. pl., **classium**, f., *fleet* (58A)
claudō, claudere, clausī, clausus, *to shut, close* (26)
***clēmentia, -ae**, f., *mercy, clemency* (67D)
cōdex, cōdicis, m., *ledger* (64C)
coemō, coemere, coēmī, coēmptus, *to buy up* (75C)
***coepī, coepisse, coeptus** (perfect system only), *to begin* (38, 55B)
cōgitātiō, cōgitātiōnis, f., *thinking, rational ability, idea; contemplation, regard.* (63C)
cōgitō, -āre, -āvī, -ātus, *to think, consider* (21)
cognōscō, cognōscere, cognōvī, cognitus, *to find out, learn, hear of; to get to know, become acquainted with* (43)
***cōgō, cōgere, coēgī, coāctus**, *to compel, force* (49, 56B)
***cohors, cohortis**, f., *cohort* (one tenth of a legion); *staff, retinue* (of a governor) (58B)
collābor, collābī, collāpsus sum, *to collapse* (34, 37)
collēga, -ae, m., *colleague, partner* (69B)
colligō, colligere, collēgī, collectus, *to gather, collect*
collis, collis, gen. pl., **collium**, m., *hill* (35)
collocō, -āre, -āvī, -ātus, *to locate, set up* (65A)
***colō, colere, coluī, cultus**, *to cultivate, tend; to worship, revere* (23, 61B)
color, colōris, m., *color* (70C)
***comes, comitis**, m., *companion, comrade* (39, 59D)
comitātus, -ūs, m., *company, retinue* (65B)
comitia, -ōrum, n. pl., *comitia* (assembly of the people) (65)
commemorō, -āre, -āvī, -ātus, *to remember, recall* (54)
committō, committere, commīsī, commissus, *to bring together, entrust* (48, 55D)
commoveō, commovēre, commōvī, commōtus, *to move, upset; to start, stir up* (29, 30, 56A)
bellum commovēre, *to begin war, undertake war*
***commūnis, -is, -e**, *common, joint* (45, 57A)
***commūnicō, -āre, -āvī, -ātus**, *to unite, link, join* (61D)
***comparō, -āre, -āvī, -ātus**, *to get ready, prepare* (32, 65B)
comperiō, comperīre, comperī, compertus, *to find out, discover* (59B, 61D)
***competītor, competītōris**, m., *political rival* (59C)
complector, complectī, complexus sum, *to embrace* (76B)
compleō, complēre, complēvī, complētus, *to fill (up)*
***complūrēs, -ēs, -a**, *several* (32, 60B)
***compōnō, compōnere, composuī, compositus**, *to compose, put together, arrange; to settle* (53, 55D)
***comprehendō, comprehendere, comprendī, comprehēnsus**, *to seize, catch* (60A)
concēdō, concēdere, concessī, concessus, *to grant, concede* (63B)
***concidō, concidere, concidī**, *to fall down* (14, 60B)
concurrō, concurrere, concurrī, concursūrus, *to run together, rush up, charge* (34)
condemnō, -āre, -āvī, -ātus, *to condemn, find guilty* (49)
condiciō, condiciōnis, f., *condition, circumstance, arrangement* 70C
***condō, condere, condidī, conditus**, *to establish, found* (36, 55A)
***cōnferō, cōnferre, contulī, collātus**, irreg., *to bring together, collect; to confer, bestow* (54, 59A)
sē cōnferre, *to take oneself, go, flee* (66B)
***cōnficiō, cōnficere, cōnfēcī, cōnfectus**, *to accomplish, finish, finish off; overwhelm* (30, 57A)
cōnfīdō, cōnfīdere, cōnfīsus sum + dat., *to give trust (to), trust completely, believe in* (26, 66D)
cōnfirmō, -āre, -āvī, -ātus, *to strengthen, support, assert, encourage* (59B)
confiteor, confitērī, confessus sum, *to admit, confess* (63D)
cōnfodiō, cōnfodere, cōnfōdī, cōnfossus, *to dig up; stab*
cōnfugiō, cōnfugere, cōnfūgī, *to flee, run away* (44)
congregō, -āre, -āvī, -ātus, *to bring together, assemble, flock* (55B)
coniciō, conicere, coniēcī, coniectus, *to throw, throw together, hurl* (21, 48, 60B)
***coniungō, coniungere, coniūnxī, coniūnctus**, *to join together, link* (59C)
***coniūnx, coniugis**, m./f., *husband, wife, spouse* (26, 70C)

***coniūrātiō, coniūrātiōnis**, f., *conspiracy* (59A)
***coniūrō, -āre, -āvī, -ātūrus**, *to plot, make a conspiracy, conspire* (55A)
cōnor, -ārī, -ātus sum, *to try* (36, 37)
cōnscrībō, cōnscrībere, cōnscrīpsī, cōnscrīptus, *to enlist, recruit* (55)
cōnsēnsus, -ūs, m., *agreement* (49, 69B)
***cōnservō, -āre, -āvī, -ātus**, *to protect, guard, save* (63c)
cōnsīderō, -āre, -āvī, -ātus, *to consider, think about, make plans* (66A)
***cōnsilium, -ī**, n., *plan, counsel, advice* (45)
cōnsilium capere, *to adopt a plan* (45)
***cōnsistō, cōnsistere, cōnstitī**, *to halt, stop; to stand fast, make a stand* (48, 71A)
cōnsōlor, -ārī, -ātus sum, *to console, comfort* (76B)
cōnspiciō, cōnspicere, cōnspexī, cōnspectus, *to catch sight of, notice* (4, 21)
cōnspectus, cōnspectūs, m., *sight, view*
***cōnstat, cōnstāre**, *it is agreed* (47, 55f)
***cōnstituō, cōnstituere, cōnstituī, cōnstitūtus**, *to decide, determine* (23, 58A)
cōnsuētūdō, cōnsuētūdinis, f., *custom, habit, practice* (55D)
***cōnsul, cōnsulis**, m., *consul* (one of two chief officials in Roman government) (36, 55A)
***cōnsulāris, -is, -e**, *belonging to a consul, consular;* as noun, *ex-consul* (55C)
***cōnsulātus, -ūs**, m., *consulship, office of consul* (55B)
cōnsultō, -āre, -āvī, -ātus, *to consult* (76C)
***cōnsultum, -ī**, n., *decree, decision, edict* (52, 69B)
Senātūs cōnsultum, *decree of the Senate*
cōnsūmō, cōnsūmere, cōnsūmpsī, cōnsūmptus, *to use up, destroy*
contactus, -ūs, m., *touch*
contendō, contendere, contendī, contentus, *to hurry, exert, strive*
contentiō, contentiōnis, f., *disagreement, rivalry*
contineō, continēre, continuī, contentus, *to hold together, contain, enclose* (47)
***contingō, contingere, contigī, contactus**, *to touch, reach, make contact with; to befall, happen to* (60B, 67A)
contiō, contiōnis, f., *public meeting, assembly* (64C)
***contrā**, prep. + acc., *opposite, facing, against* (34, 55B)
contrādīcō, contrādīcere, contrādīxī, contrādictus, *to speak out against, oppose* (55B)
contrahō, contrahere, contrāxī, contractus, *to contract, get* (75A)
contrārius, -a, -um, *opposing, contrary* (76B)
controversia, -ae, f., *strife, controversy* (66e)
convalēscō, convalēscere, convaluī, *to grow stronger, get well* (42)
conveniō, convenīre, convēnī, conventūrus, *to come together, meeet, assemble, gather* (43)
convertō, convertere, convertī, conversus, *to turn around*
convīva, -ae, m., *guest* (at a banquet) (31)
convīvium, -ī, n., *feast, banquet* (34)
convocō, -āre, -āvī, -ātus, *to call together, assemble* (12)
***cōpia, -ae**, f., *abundance, supply*; pl., *resources, troops* (55C)
***cor, cordis**, n., *heart* (61D)
cornū, -ūs, n., *horn; wing of an army, end of a battle line* (55C)
***corōna, -ae**, f., *garland, wreath, crown* (34, 69B)
corpus, corporis, n., *body* (21)
cotīdiē, adv., *daily, every day* (37)
crēber, crēbra, crēbrum, *thick, crowded, frequent* (76C)
crēdō, crēdere, crēdidī, crēditus + dat., *to trust, believe* (35)
***cremō, -āre, -āvī, -ātus**, *to cremate, burn* (61D)
creō, -āre, -āvī, -ātus, *to appoint, create, elect, choose* (34, 54)
***crēscō, crēscere, crēvī, crētūrus**, *to increase, grow, enlarge* (63B)
crīmen, crīminis, n., *charge, accusation; crime* (65D)
***crūdēlis, -is, -e**, *cruel* (40, 62K)
crūdēlitās, crūdēlitātis, f., *cruelty*
cubiculum, -ī, n., *room, bedroom* (8, 15)
culpa, -ae, f., *fault, blame* (14)
***cultus, -ūs**, m., *attention, worship; care (of one's person); culture* (61D)
cum, prep. + abl., *with* (12)
cum, conj., *when, whenever, after, since, because, although* (22, 40)
cūnctī, -ae, -a, *all* (14)
cupidus, -a, -um + gen., *desirous of, wanting, greedy for* (64)
cupiō, cupere, cupīvī, cupītus, *to desire, want* (40)
cūr, adv., *why* (1)
cūra, -ae, f., *care, anxiety, concern* (34, 48)
Cūria, -ae, f., *Senate House* (23)
cūrō, -āre, -āvī, -ātus, *to look after, take care of, attend to* (6)
currō, currere, cucurrī, cursūrus, *to run* (2, 23)
***cursus, -ūs**, m., *a running, course, voyage* (72D)
custōdia, -ae, f., *guard, protection, custody*
custōs, custōdis, m., *guard* (26, 44)

D

***damnō, -āre, -āvī, -ātus,** *to condemn* (58A)
dē, prep. + abl., *down from; concerning, about* (16, 53)
dēbeō, -ēre, -uī, -itus, *to owe; + infin., ought, should* (26)
***dēcēdō, dēcēdere, dēcessī, decessūrus,** *to leave, depart from; to die* (60A, 61D)
decem, *ten* (15, 38)
dēcernō, dēcernere, dēcrēvī, dēcrētus, *to decide, assign* (55A)
***dēcrētum, -ī,** n., *decree* (55A)
decuriō, decuriōnis, m., *town councilman* (64A)
dēdō, dēdere, dēdidī, dēditus, *to give up, surrender; to devote to, dedicate to, commit to*
***dēdūcō, dēdūcere, dēdūxī, dēductus,** *to lead, lead down* (68)
***dēfendō, dēfendere, dēfendī, dēfēnsus,** *to defend* (35, 56A)
***dēferō, dēferre, dētulī, dēlātus,** irreg., *to carry down, offer, confer* (55B)
dēfessus, -a, -um, *tired, weary* (2)
***dēficiō, dēficere, dēfēcī, dēfēctus,** *to be lacking, fail* (61A)
***deinde,** also spelled **dein,** adv., *then, next* (8, 13, 62A, 65B)
dēleō, dēlēre, dēlēvī, dēlētus, *to destroy* (38)
***dēlīberō, -āre, -āvī, -ātus,** *to weigh carefully, consider* (68)
***dēligō, dēligere, dēlēgī, dēlēctus,** *to choose* (59B, 67C)
***dēmēns, dēmentis,** *mad, insane, mindless* (68)
dēmittō, dēmittere, dēmīsī, dēmissus, *to send down*
dēnārius, -ī, m., *denarius* (silver coin) (31)
***dēnique,** adv., *finally, at last* (58A)
dēnsus, -a, -um, *thick, dense*
dēpellō, dēpellere, dēpulī, dēpulsus, *to drive away* (61B)
dēnsus, -a, -um, *dense, thick* (76D)
***dēserō, dēserere, dēseruī, dēsertus,** *to desert, abandon* (72A)
dēsīderō, -āre, -āvī, -ātus, *to long for, miss* (26)
***dēsignō, -āre, -āvī, -ātus,** *to mark, indicate, designate* (59A)
***dēsinō, dēsinere, dēsiī, dēsitus,** *to stop, cease from* (62H)
dēstruō, dēstruere, dētrūxī, dēstrūctus, *to destroy* (72A)
dēsum, dēesse, dēfuī, dēfutūrus + dat., irreg., *to be lacking, wanting*
dētrahō, dētrahere, dētrāxī, dētractus, *to remove, take away* (63D)
dētrīmentum, -ī, n., *damage, harm* (69A)
deus, -ī, nom. pl., **dī,** m., *god* (35, 39)
Dī immortālēs! *Immortal Gods! Good heavens!* (33)
dēvorō, -āre, -āvī, -ātus, *to devour, swallow* (20)
***dexter, dextra, dextrum,** *right* (the direction) (53, 55C)
  dextra, -ae, f., *right hand* (53)
dīcō, dīcere, dīxī, dictus, *to say, tell* (20, 21)
***dictātor, dictātōris,** m., *dictator* (55B)
diēs, diēī, m., *day* (5, 13, 25)
differō, differre, distulī, dīlātus, irreg., *to carry in different directions, spread; to differ, be different from* (60A, 61C)
difficilis, -is, -e, *difficult* (34)
digitus, -ī, m., *finger* (43)
dignitās, dignitātis, f., *good name, reputation* (66D)
dīligenter, adv., *carefully, attentively* (19)
***dīligō, dīligere, dīlēxī, dīlēctus,** *to love, have special regard for, cherish* (54, 61D)
***dīmicō, -āre, -āvī, -ātūrus,** *to fight, struggle* (55B)
***dīmittō, dīmittere, dīmīsī, dīmissus,** *to send away, let go* (51, 55B)
***dīripiō, dīripere, dīripuī, dīreptus,** *to lay waste, plunder, ransack* (55C)
discēdō, discēdere, discessī, discessūrus, *to go away, depart, leave* (9, 22)
discrīmen, discrīminis, n., *crisis, danger* (76A)
distribuō, distribuere, distribuī, distribūtus, *to distribute, hand out* (59B)
diū, adv., *for a long time* (15, 35)
  diūtius, adv., *longer*
dīves, dīvitis, *rich* (42)
dīvidō, dīvidere, dīvīsī, dīvīsus, *to divide, separate* (56A)
***dīvitiae, -ārum,** f. pl., *wealth, riches* (48, 63A)
***dīvus, -a, -um,** *divine, deified*; as substantive, *a god* (57B)
dō, dare, dedī, datus, *to give* (21)
doceō, docēre, docuī, doctus, *to teach* (6, 21)
doctrīna, -ae, f., *study, formal instruction; study of literature* (63A)
doleō, -ēre, -uī, -itūrus, *to be sad, grieve* (18, 49)
***dolor, dolōris,** m., *pain, grief, sadness* (38, 63B)
domesticus, -a, -um, *domestic*
dominātiō, dominātiōnis, f., *control, power, mastery* (69A)
dominus, -ī, m., *master, overlord* (11)
domus, -ūs, f., *home* (23, 25, 39)
***dōnec,** conj. + indicative, *while, as long as;* + subjunctive, *until* (73B)
dōnō, -āre, -āvī, -ātus, *to give* (34, 54)

dōnum, -ī, n., *gift* (46)
dormiō, -īre, -īvī, -ītūrus, *to sleep* (4)
***dubitō, -āre, -āvī, -ātus**, *to doubt, hesitate* (59D)
dūcō, dūcere, dūxī, ductus, *to lead* (7, 19, 20)
***dulcis, -is, -e**, *sweet* (63B)
dum, conj., *while, as long as* (1)
duo, duae, duo, *two* (15, 38)
duodēvīgintī, *eighteen* (38, 70B)
***dux, ducis**, m., *leader, general* (55B)

E

ē, ex, prep. + abl., *from, out of* (2, 5, 9)
ēbrius, -a, -um, *drunk* (34)
ecce, interj., *look, look at* (1)
ēdūcō, ēdūcere, ēdūxī, ēductus, *to lead out, withdraw* (46)
efferō, efferre, extulī, ēlātus, irreg., *to carry out* (30)
effigiēs, effigieī, f., *representation, effigy, portrait* (63E)
effugiō, effugere, effūgī, *to flee, run away, escape* (11, 21, 29)
ego, *I* (5, 27)
ēgredior, ēgredī, ēgressus sum, *to go out* (37, 39)
ēheu, *alas* (7)
ēiciō, ēicere, ēiēcī, ēiectus, *to throw out* (30)
emō, emere, ēmī, ēmptus, *to buy* (21, 31)
ēmoveō, ēmovēre, ēmōvī, ēmōtus, *to move (from)* (76C)
enim, conj., *for, because* (20)
ēnsis, ēnsis, gen. pl., **ēnsium**, m. *sword* (68)
ēnumerō, -āre, -āvī, -ātus, *to count, enumerate* (72B)
***eō**, adv., *there, to that place* (23, 58B)
eō, īre, iī or **īvī, itūrus**, irreg., *to go* (7, 17, 19, 20, 21)
epistula, -ae, f., *letter* (7)
epulum, -ī, n., *banquet, feast* (75B)
***eques, equitis**, m., *knight, horseman, member of the equestrian order* (55C)
***equidem**, adv., *certainly, surely* (63C)
equus, -ī, m., *horse* (10)
***ergō**, conj., *therefore, so* (55D)
***ēripiō, ēripere, ēripuī, ēreptus**, *to snatch away, rescue* (29, 62K)
ērudītus, -a, -um, *learned, scholarly* (37)
et, conj., *and, also, too* (1)
etiam, adv., *also, even* (1, 6, 13)
  etiam sī, *even if, although* (37, 64)
etsī, conj., *even if, although* (62F, 66D)
ēvādō, ēvādere, ēvāsī, ēvāsus, *to escape* (42)
ēvenit, ēvenīre, ēvēnit, *it happens, it turns out* (55D)
ēventus, -ūs, m., *outcome, result* (60B)
ēvocō, -āre, -āvī, -ātus, *to call out, summon*
exanimātus, -a, -um, *struck senseless, paralyzed* (49, 60D)
excellēns, excellentis, *outstanding, eminent, distinguished*
excīdō, excīdere, excīdī, excīsus, *to cut out, exterminate* (69C)
excipiō, excipere, excēpī, exceptus, *to take away, receive, withstand* (5, 16, 22)
excitō, -āre, -āvī, -ātus, *to rouse, wake up* (8)
exclūdō, exclūdere, exclūsī, exclūsus, *to exclude, keep out* (59B)
excruciō, -āre, -āvī, -ātus, *to torture, torment* (61D)
exemplar, exemplāris, n., *copy* (75A)
exemplum, -ī, n., *model, example, precedent* (63C)
exeō, exīre, exiī or **exīvī, exitūrus**, irreg., *to go out, leave* (5, 23, 44)
***exercitus, -ūs**, m., *army* (55B)
exiguus, -a, -um, *brief, slight, insignificant* (63D)
exilium, -ī, n., *exile* (59D)
***exitium, -ī**, n., *destruction, ruin* (59B)
exitus, -ūs, m., *exit* (76C)
expellō, expellere, expulī, expulsus, *to drive out, expel* (39)
expetō, expetere, expetīvī, expetītus, *to seek out, strive for*
explicō, -āre, -āvī, -ātus, *to explain* (19, 66B)
exsilium, -ī, n., *exile* (65E)
exspectō, -āre, -āvī, -ātus, *to look out for, wait for* (15)
exprimō, exprimere, expressī, expressus, *to make, produce; to portray, express* (63C)
exstinguō, exstinguere, exstīnxī, exstīnctus, *to put out, exstinguish* (30)
externus, -a, -um, *foreign, outside* (69C)
extrahō, extrahere, extrāxī, extractus, *to drag out, drag away* (14, 21)
extrēmus, -a, -um, *last, final, terminal* (63E)
exul, exulis, m. or f., *exiled person, exile* (67B)

F

fābula, -ae, f., *story* (20)
facile, adv., *easily* (35)
facinus, facinoris, n., *villainy, crime, foul deed* (65A)
faciō, facere, fēcī, factus, *to make, do* (1, 23); when completed by subjunctive clause, *bring it about that, see to it that* (62C)
  iter facere, *to make a journey, travel* (13)

factiō, factiōnis, f., *gang, political faction* (27, 69A)
***factum, -ī**, n., *deed, act* (62J, 64C)
facultās, facultātis, f., *ability, skill; opportunity, chance, occasion* (63B, 60D)
***fāma, -ae**, f., *fame, reputation; rumor* (58B)
***famēs, famis**, f., *hunger, starvation, famine* (56B)
***familia, -ae**, f., *family, household* (51)
***familiāris, familiāris**, gen. pl., **familiārium**, m./f., *close friend* (54, 64A)
***fās**, indeclinable, n., *right, proper* (72B)
***fātālis, -is, -e**, *given by fate, destined; fatal, destructive* (68)
***fateor, fatērī, fassus sum**, *to admit, confess* (67D)
fātum, -ī, n., *destiny, fate* (39)
faveō, favēre, fāvī, fautūrus + dat., *to give favor (to), favor, support* (27)
***fax, facis**, f., *torch* (73D)
fēlīx, fēlīcis, *lucky, happy, fortunate* (34)
  fēlīciter, adv., *happily* (35)
fēmina, -ae, f., *woman* (3)
fēmineus, -a, -um, *of a woman, woman's*
***ferē**, adv., *almost, approximately* (46, 55A)
ferō, ferre, tulī, lātus, irreg., *to bring, carry, bear* (5, 12, 17, 21)
***ferrum, -ī**, n., *iron, object made of iron, sword* (59B)
festīnō, -āre, -āvī, -ātūrus, *to hurry* (9)
fidēlis, -is, -e, *faithful, loyal* (31, 34)
***fidēs, fideī**, f., *faith, reliability, trust, loyalty* (52, 62D)
***fīdus, -a, -um**, *loyal, faithful* (57A)
fīgō, fīgere, fīxī, fīxus, *to fasten, attach*
fīlia, -ae, f., *daughter* (11)
fīlius, -ī, m., *son* (11)
***fingō, fingere, fīnxī, fictus**, *to imagine, think* (72B)
fīniō, -īre, -īvī, -ītus, *to finish* (21)
fīnis, fīnis, gen pl., **fīnium**, m., *end, limit, boundary*, pl., *territory* (29)
fīnitimus, -a, -um, *neighboring, having the same boundary* (69C)
fīō, fierī, factus sum, irreg., *to become, be made, happen* (34)
firmō, -āre, -āvī, -ātus, *to strengthen* (59B)
flagrō, -āre, -āvī, -ātus, *to burn, blaze* (64C)
flāmen, flāminis, m., *priest* (64A)
***flamma, -ae**, f., *flame, fire* (29, 60A)
***flectō, flectere, flexī, flexus** *to bend, change* (72C)
***fleō, flēre, flēvī, flētus**, *to weep, cry* (53, 73A)
***flūmen, flūminis**, n., *river* (55A)
flōreō, flōrēre, flōruī, *to flourish, prosper* (57A)
***foedus, foederis**, n., *pact, treaty, alliance* (62C)
***fōns, fontis**, f., *spring, fountain, source* (69D)
***for, fārī, fātus sum**, *to to say, speak* (72B)
fore, = **futūrus esse** (see **sum**) (55, 62C)
fōrma, -ae, f., *shape, form*
fortasse, adv., *perhaps* (15)
***fors, fortis**, f., *chance, luck, fortune* (58B)
***forte**, adv., *by chance* (33, 64B)
fortis, -is, -e, *brave, strong* (18)
  fortiter, adv., *bravely* (35)
***fortūna, -ae**, f., *fortune, good luck, prosperity; possessions, property* (54, 55B)
***forum, -ī**, n., *forum* (center of a Roman town) (25, 55b)
fragilis, -is, -e, *fragile* (63C)
***frangō, frangere, frēgī, frāctus**, *to break, shatter, wreck* (a ship) (54, 70B)
frāter, frātris, m., *brother* (11)
frequēns, frequentis, *closely packed, crowded, thronged* (76A)
  frequenter, adv., *frequently*
frīgidus, -a, -um, *cool, cold* (5)
***frūctus, -ūs**, m., *fruit; benefit, advantage, profit, income* (61D)
frūgālitās, frūgālitātis, f., *frugality, economy* (75C)
***fruor, fruī, frūctus sum** + abl., *to enjoy, have benefit of* (61RN)
frūstrā, adv., *in vain* (14)
***fuga, -ae**, f., *flight, escape; exile* (58B, 67B)
fugiō, fugere, fūgī, fugitūrus, *to flee, run away* (18, 25)
fugitīvus, -ī, m., *fugitive, deserter*
***fugō, -āre, -āvī, -ātus**, *to put to flight* (55B)
fulvus, -a, -um, *tawny, yellow*
fūmus, -ī, m., *smoke* (29)
funditor, funditōris, m., *slinger*
***fundō, fundere, fūdī, fūsus**, *to pour out, shed* (55C)
fundus, -ī, m., *farm, estate* (39, 60A)
fungor, fungī, fūnctus sum + abl., *to carry out, perform* (61 RN, 63B)
***fūnus, fūneris**, n., *funeral* (53, 61D)
furēns, furentis, *raging*
***furor, furōris**, m., *frenzy, madness* (48, 59A)
***fūrtum, -ī**, n., *theft, fraud* (61A)

G

Gallia, -ae, f., *Gaul* (modern France, Belgium, and northern Italy) (55A)
***Gallī, -ōrum**, m. pl., *Gauls, people of Gaul* (55b)
gaudeō, gaudēre, gavīsus sum, *to be glad, rejoice* (14, 40)

***gēns, gentis**, gen. pl., **gentium**, f., *family, clan*; pl., *peoples* (50, 54, 59B)
***genus, generis**, n., *type, class, race, family* (39, 55A)
***gerō, gerere, gessī, gestus**, *to carry on, perform, do, manage; to wear* (clothing) (10, 55d, 69C)
rēs gestae, *deeds, accomplishments* (69)
gladiātor, gladiātōris, m., *gladiator* (47)
gladius, -ī, m., *sword* (21, 26)
glaeba, -ae, f., *lump of earth, clod* (74A)
glōria, -ae, f., *fame, glory* (27)
grandis, -is, -e, *great, huge, considerable* (56A)
***grātia, -ae**, f., *favor, influence* (26, 66D)
gen. + **grātiā**, *for the sake of* (63)
***grātiās agere** + dat., *to thank* (26, 51, 62L)
grātulor, -ārī, -ātus sum + dat., *to congratulate* (50)
***grātus, -a, -um** + dat., *pleasing to, appropriate for* (61A)
gravis, -is, -e, *heavy, serious* (35)
gubernō, -āre, -āvī, -ātus, *to govern, rule* (64)
gustō, -āre, *to taste, enjoy* (75A)

H

habeō, -ēre, -uī, -itus, *to have, hold* (10, 20, 26)
habitō, -āre, -āvī, -ātus, *to live, dwell* (1)
haereō, haerēre, haesī, haesūrus, *to stick* (14)
***hauriō, haurīre, hausī, hausus**, *to drink, draw* (34, 72B)
***hērēs, hērēdis**, m., *heir* (55D)
***heu**, interjection, *alas* (62K)
hīc, adv., *here* (9, 13, 54)
hic, haec, hoc, *this*, pl., *these* (18, 19, 20, 25, 26, 31)
***hiems, hiemis**, f., *winter* (39, 71A)
hilaris, -is, -e, *cheerful* (54)
hodiē, adv., *today* (2, 13)
homō, hominis, m., *man, fellow* (18)
honestās, honestātis, f., *esteem, admiration, respect, honor* (63C)
***honestus, -a, -um**, *respectable, honorable* (58A)
***honor, honōris**, m., *honor, political office* (IX, 55D)
honōrificus, -a, -um, *bestowing honor, honorary*
honōrō, -āre, -āvī, -ātus, *to honor*
hōra, -ae, f., *hour* (9)
horribilis, -is, -e, *horrible* (59C)
horridus, -a, -um, *horrible, dreadful*
***hortor, -ārī, -ātus sum**, *to encourage, urge* (51, 53, 59D)
hospes, hospitis, m., *guest, host* (16)
hospitium, -ī, n., *lodging, accomodation* (75A)
***hostis, hostis**, gen. pl., **hostium**, m., *enemy* (55D)
hūc, adv., *here, to this place* (36)
hūc illūc, adv., *here and there, this way and that* (23)
hūmānus, -a, -um, *human* (48)
***humus, -ī**, f., *earth, ground* (67D)
humī, *on the ground* (27, 67D)

I

iaceō, iacēre, iacuī, *to lie, be lying down* (26)
***iactō, -āre, -āvī, -ātus**, *to toss around* (59A)
iam, adv., *now, already* (1, 8, 13)
iānua, -ae, f., *door* (9)
ibi, adv., *there, in that place* (5, 13)
īdem, eadem, idem, *the same* (3, 31)
ideō, adv., *for this reason, therefore* (75A)
***idōneus, -a, -um** + dat., *fit, suitable* (63a)
***igitur**, conj., *therefore* (4, 56A)
***ignis, ignis**, gen. pl., **ignium**, m., *fire* (32, 60A)
ignōrō, -āre, -āvī, -ātus, *to be ignorant of, be unaware of* (40)
***ignōtus, -a, -um**, *unknown* (71A)
ille, illa, illud, *that*, pl., *those* (11, 15, 16, 20, 22, 25, 26, 31)
illūc, adv., *there, to that place* (23)
***imāgō, imāginis**, f., *likeness, image; ghost* (54, 72B)
imitor, -ārī, -ātus sum, *to imitate*
***immānis, -is, -e**, *huge, immense, extensive* (49, 55A)
***immittō, immittere, immīsī, immissus**, *to send in, throw into* (49, 60B)
***immō**, adv., *rather, on the contrary* (31, 59A)
***immortālis, -is, -e**, *immortal* (27, 59B)
immōtus, -a, -um, *unmoving, motionless*
immurmurō, -āre, -āvī, -ātus, *to whisper into*
***impedīmenta, -ōrum**, n. pl., *military equipment, supplies, baggage* (60B)
impediō, impedīre, impedīvī, impedītus, *to stop, hinder, prevent* (11, 60B)
impēnsa, -ae, f., *expense, cost* (69A)
imperātor, imperātōris, m., *commander; emperor* (49, 59B, 66C)
***imperium, -ī**, n., *power, right to command soldiers; empire* (56B)
***imperō, -āre, -āvī, -ātus** + dat., *to order; to impose, levy something* (acc.) *upon someone* (dat.) (51, 55A)
***impetus, -ūs**, m., *attack* (49, 58B)
impōnō, impōnere, imposuī, impositus, *to place something* (acc.) *upon something* (dat.) (54, 74A)
***impotēns, impotentis**, *lacking power (over self), lacking self-control* (62H)
in, prep. + abl., *in, on, among* (1, 9, 28)
in, prep. + acc., *into, toward, against* (3, 9)

incendium, -ī, n., *fire* (30)
incendō, incendere, incendī, incēnsus, *to burn, set on fire* (38)
***incidō, incidere, incidī, incāsūrus**, *to fall, fall into, occur, turn up* (54, 67A)
***incipiō, incipere, incēpī, inceptus**, *to begin, undertake* (49, 72A)
incitō, -āre, -āvī, -ātus, *to spur on, arouse, stir up* (10)
incolumis, -is, -e, *unhurt, safe and sound* (14)
incrēscō, incrēscere, incrēvī, incrētūrus, *to grow, increase* (75A)
***inde**, adv., *from there, then, in consequence of that* (38, 40, 55B)
indicō, -āre, -āvī, -ātus, *to point out, make known* (76A)
indulgentia, -ae, f., *indulgence, kindness* (75A)
īnfāns, īnfantis, *unable to speak*; as noun, *infant, young child* (30, 70C)
īnferō, īnferre, intulī, illātus, irreg., *to bring in, carry on, inflict on* (39, 55A)
īnfestus, -a, -um, *hostile, prepared for attack* (59C)
īnfīnītus, -a, -um, *countless* (56A)
ingemēscō, ingemēscere, ingemuī, ingemitus, *to sigh over, groan over* 70C
***ingenium, -ī**, n., *talent, genius* (55A, 63E)
ingēns, ingentis, *huge, big, long* (22)
ingredior, ingredī, ingressus sum, *to go in, go against, attack* (37)
***inimīcus, -ī**, m., *rival, personal enemy* (60B)
***initium -ī**, n., *beginning* (57A)
***iniūria, -ae**, f., *injury, injustice, wrong* (55B)
iniūstus, -a, -um, *unfair, unjust*
inquit, *(he / she) says, said* (7)
***īnscius, -a, -um**, *not knowing, ignorant* (45, 65E)
īnscrīptiō, īnscrīptiōnis, f., *inscription* (69B)
īnsidiae, -ārum, f. pl., *ambush, treachery* (65A)
īnsidiātor, īnsidiātōris, m., *someone in ambush, waylayer* (65B)
īnsolenter, adv., *arrogantly* (55D)
īnsomnia, -ae, f., *insomia, lack of sleep*
īnspiciō, īnspicere, īnspexī, īnspectus, *to look at, examine* (21)
īnstabilis, -is, -is, *unstable*
***īnstituō, īnstituere, īnstituī, īnstitūtus**, *to establish, set up, organize* (61A)
īnstitūtum, -ī, n., *institution, undertaking* (61C)
***īnstō, īnstāre, īnstitī**, *to press on, attack* (56B)
***īnstruō, īnstruere, īnstrūxī, īnstrūctus**, *to prepare, arrange, draw up* (58B)
īnsula, -ae, f., *island* (30)
***integer, integra, integrum**, *whole, complete, unhurt, intact* (55C)
***intellegō, intellegere, intellēxī, intellēctus**, *to understand, realize* (49, 55f)
inter, prep. + acc., *between, among* (33)
interclūdō, interclūdere, interclūsī, interclūsus, *to shut off, cut off* (66A)
intereā, adv., *meanwhile* (10, 13)
***interficiō, interficere, interfēcī, interfectus**, *to kill* (55A)
***interim**, adv., *meanwhile* (65A)
intermittō, intermittere, intermīsī, intermissus, *to separate, interrupt, discontinue* (60B)
interrogō, -āre, -āvī, -ātus, *to ask, question* (53)
interrumpō, interrumpere, interrūpī, interruptus, *to interrupt, break off*
intrā, prep. + acc., *inside, within* (22)
intrō, -āre, -āvī, -ātūrus, *to enter, go into* (8, 19)
introeō, introīre, introiī, introitus, irreg., *to enter, go in* (60B)
***intueor, intuērī, intuitus sum**, *to gaze at, look upon, contemplate* (55C)
inveniō, invenīre, invēnī, inventus, *to come upon, find, discover* (12, 21)
inventor, inventōris, m., *inventor, discoverer*
invictus, -a, -um, *unconquered* (57A)
***invideō, invidēre, invīdī, invīsus**, *to look askance at, begrudge, envy, hate* (62A)
***invidia, -ae**, f., *hatred, ill-will* (64C)
invīsus, -a, -um, *hateful*
invītō, -āre, -āvī, -ātus, *to invite* (28, 32, 51)
iocus, -ī, m., *joke, funny story* (16)
Iovis, see **Iuppiter**
ipse, ipsa, ipsum, *himself, herself, itself*, pl., *themselves* (6, 10, 29, 31)
īra, -ae, f., *anger* (11)
īrātus, -a, -um, *angry* (3, 33)
***irrumpō, irrumpere, irrūpī, irruptus**, *to burst in, break in* (33, 56B)
is, ea, id, *he, she it; this, that* (27, 31)
***iste, ista, istud**, *that* (used to show contempt) (59A, 66B)
ita, adv., *thus, so, in this way, in such a way* (3, 13, 21, 50)
Italia, -ae, f., *Italy* (1)
***itaque**, adv., *and so, therefore* (16, 58B)
item, adv., *likewise, also* (64C)
iter, itineris, n., *journey, route, road* (10, 13, 15)
  iter facere, *to make a journey, travel* (13)
iterum, adv., *again, a second time* (8, 13)

iubeō, iubēre, iussī, iussus, *to order* (10, 19, 21)
***iūcundus, -a, -um,** *pleasant* (54, 62C)
***iūdex, iūdicis,** m., *judge, juror; governor* (56B, 58B)
***iūdicium, -ī,** n., *judgment* (58A)
***iūdicō, -āre, -āvī, -ātus,** *to judge, ascertain* (55D)
***iugum, -ī,** n., *yoke; mountain ridge* (73D)
iungō, iungere, iūnxī, iūnctus, *to join, attach*
Iūnō, Iūnōnis, f., *Juno* (queen of the gods)
Iuppiter, Iovis, m., *Jupiter, Jove* (king of the gods)
iūrō, -āre, -āvī, -ātus, *to swear an oath* (69A)
iussū, *by the order* (59A, 65E)
iūstitia, -ae, f., *justice* (69B)
***iūstus, -a, -um,** *fair, just, well-deserved* (56B)
***iuvenis, iuvenis,** m., *young man* (50, 70A)
***iuvō, iuvāre, iūvī, iūtus,** *to help* (55f)

K

Kalendae, -ārum, f. pl., *the Kalends* (first day in the month) (36)

L

***lābor, lābī, lāpsus sum,** *to slip, fall; fall away, fail* (44, 53)
***labor, labōris,** m., *work, labor, struggle* (24, 48, 58B)
labōrō, -āre, -āvī, -ātus, *to work; to suffer, be in distress* (3)
***lacrima, -ae,** f., *tear, weeping* (45, 72A)
lacrimō, -āre, -āvī, -ātus, *to weep, cry* (9)
laedō, laedere, laesī, laesus, *to harm, injure* (46)
laetus, -a, -um, *happy, glad* (1)
lamentātiō, lamentātiōnis, f., *lamentation, weeping* (64C)
lāmentum, -ī, n., *lament*
***lapis, lapidis,** m., *stone, rock* (25, 60B)
***lateō, -ēre, -uī,** *to lie in hiding, hide* (49, 64B)
lātus, see **ferō**
lātus, -a, -um, *wide, broad, extensive* (76C)
laudō, -āre, -āvī, -ātus, *to praise* (18)
laus, laudis, f., *praise, applause, commendation*
lavō, lavāre, lāvī, lautus or **lōtus,** *to wash, bathe* (20, 54)
lectīca, -ae, f., *litter* (23)
lectus, -ī, m., *bed, couch, litter, bier* (19)
lēgātus, -ī, m., *envoy, ambassador; second-in-command of an army* (18)
***legiō, legiōnis,** f., *legion* (a military unit) (55A)
lēgitimus, -a, -um, *lawful, legal, legitimate* 69A
legō, legere, lēgī, lēctus, *to read* (1, 24)
lentē, adv., *slowly* (2, 13)
lentus, -a, -um, slow (35)
lepus, leporis, *hare* (31)
***levis, -is, -e,** *light* (54, 62F)
lēx, lēgis, f., *law*
libenter, adv., *gladly* (36)
liber, librī, m., *book* (24)
līber, lībera, līberum, *free* (75A)
līberī, -ōrum, m. pl., *children* (10, 11)
līberō, -āre, -āvī, -ātus, *to set free* (49, 58A)
līberta, -ae, f., *freedwoman*
lībertās, lībertātis, f., *freedom* (21, 55D)
lībertus, -ī, m., *freedman, ex-slave* (29)
librārius, -ī, m., *secretary, clerk* (64C)
licet, licēre, licuit + dat., *it is allowed* (20, 24)
liquidus, -a, -um, *liquid, flowing*
litterae, -ārum, f. pl., *letter, epistle; literature* (39)
***lītus, lītoris,** n., *shore* (39, 72C)
locus, -ī, m., n. in pl., *place* (33)
longus, -a, -um, *long, tall* (15)
  longē, adv., *far, far away* (35)
  longē lātēque, adv., *far and wide*
loquor, loquī, locūtus sum, *to speak, talk* (37, 70A)
lūdō, lūdere, lūsī, lūsūrus, *to play* (16)
***lūmen, lūminis,** n., *light, illumination; lamp;* pl., *eyes* (72B)
lūx, lūcis, f., *light, daylight* (21)

M

magis, adv., *more, rather* (34, 35)
magistrātus, -ūs, m., *official, magistrate; office, magistracy* (69C)
magnificus, -a, -um, *grand, splendid, magnificent*
magnitūdō, magnitūdinis, f., *size, large size; strength* (60A)
magnopere, adv., *greatly, seriously* (31, 35)
magnus, -a, -um, *big, great, large* (4, 34)
maior, maior, maius, gen., **maiōris,** *bigger* (34)
  maiōrēs, maiōrum, m. pl., *ancestors* (54, 69C)
male, adv., *badly* (35)
mālō, mālle, māluī, *to prefer* (47)
malus, -a, -um, *bad, evil* (21, 34)
  malum, -ī, n., *bad thing, evil, disaster* (76A)
mandātum, -ī, n., *order, instruction* (22)
mandō, -āre, -āvī, -ātus, *to entrust, hand over* (75A)
maneō, manēre, mānsī, mānsūrus, *to remain, stay, wait* (9, 20, 23)
manus, -ūs., f., *hand; band, group* (18, 25)
  manū mittere, *to send from one's power, set free, manumit* (75A)

mare, maris, gen. pl., **marium**, n., *sea* (38)
marītus, -ī, m., *husband* (53)
māter, mātris, f., *mother* (6, 11)
mātrimōnium, -ī, n., *marriage* (50)
mātūrēscō, mātūrēscere, mātūruī, *to mature*
mātrōna, -ae, f., *married woman* (52)
maximus, -a, -um, *biggest, greatest, largest* (23, 24)
maximē, adv., *most, very much, very* (35, 35)
medius, -a, -um, *mid-, middle of* (20)
mehercule or **mehercules**, *by Hercules* (18)
melior, melior, melius, gen. **meliōris**, *better* (19, 34)
***membrum, -ī**, n., *limb* (58B)
meminī, meminisse (perfect system only) + gen., *to be mindful of, remember* (72 RN)
***memor, memoris**, *remembering, mindful, unforgetting* (39, 71A)
memoria, -ae, f., *memory* (30)
memoriā tenēre, *to remember* (37)
***mēns, mentis**, f., *mind* (62H)
mēnsa, -ae, f., *table* (29)
mēnsis, mēnsis, m., *month* (38)
mentiō, mentiōnis, f., *a speaking of, mention*
***mereō, merēre, meruī, meritus**, sometimes deponent, *to deserve, earn* (66D)
merīdiēs, -ēī, m., *noon, midday* (46)
meritum, -ī, n., *good deed, merit, honor* (54, 69B)
***merus, -a, -um**, *pure, undiluted* (34, 73B)
merum, -ī, n., *undiluted wine* (34)
***metuō, metuere, metuī, metūtus**, *to fear, be afraid of* (66A)
***metus, -ūs**, m., *fear* (26, 59B, 66)
meus, -a, -um, *my, mine* (7)
mī, masc. vocative sing. of **meus**
***mī**, = **mihi** (see **ego**)
mīles, mīlitis, m., *soldier* (20)
***mīlitia, -ae**, f., *military service* (61C)
mīlle, *a thousand* (15, 38)
mīlia, mīlium, n. pl., *thousands* (48)
mīlle passūs, *a thousand paces, a mile*
mīlia passuum, *miles* (55A)
Milōniānus, -ī, m., *follower of Milo* (64B)
minimus, -a, -um, *very small, smallest* (34)
minor, -ārī, -ātus sum, *to threaten* (65A)
minor, minor, minus, gen., **minōris**, *smaller, lesser* (34)
minuō, minuere, minuī, minūtus, *to lessen, reduce, decrease, diminish* (31)
mīror, -ārī, -ātus sum, *to wonder, be amazed at* (49)
misceō, miscēre, miscuī, mixtus, *to mix* (34)
miser, misera, miserum, *unhappy, miserable, wretched* (9)
***misereor, -ērī, -itus sum** + gen., *to pity, feel sorry for* (72A)
miseret, miserēre, miseruit, *it makes one* (acc.) *feel sorry for something* (gen.) (72 RN)
mittō, mittere, mīsī, missus, *to send, let go* (9, 20)
manū mittere, *to send from one's power, set free, manumit* (75A)
moderātus, -a, -um, *restrained, controlled* (57A)
***modestus, -a, -um**, *modest* (66A)
***modo**, adv., *only; just now, recently* (18, 74B)
***modus, -ī**, m., *way, method* (34)
***moenia, moenium**, n. pl., *walls* (39, 72A)
molestus, -a, -um, *troublesome, annoying* (4)
***mollis, -is, -e**, *soft, gentle* (54, 68)
moneō, -ēre, -uī, -itus, *to advise, warn* (39, 51)
mōns, montis, gen. pl., **montium**, m., *mountain, hill* (24)
mōnstrum, -ī, n., *wonder, portent, monster*
***monumentum -ī**, n., *monument, tomb* (54, 58A)
mora, -ae, f., *delay* (76C)
morbus, -ī, m., *disease, illness* (54)
morior, morī, mortuus sum, *to die* (39, 45)
moror, morārī, morātus sum, *to delay, remain, stay* (36, 37)
mors, mortis, gen. pl., **mortium**, f., *death* (21)
mortuus, -a, -um, *dead* (16)
***mōs, mōris**, m., *custom, habit*; pl., *character* (52, 59A)
moveō, movēre, mōvī, mōtus, *to move, remove* (14, 24)
mox, adv., *soon* (6, 13)
***mulier, mulieris**, f., *woman* (27, 62D)
***multitūdō, multitūdinis**, f., *large number; crowd, mob* (23)
multus, -a, -um, *much*; pl., *many* (31, 34)
multō, adv., *greatly, by much, very* (47)
mūnicipium, -ī, n., *town* (64A)
mūnītiō, mūnītiōnis, f., *fortification* (60C)
***mūnus, mūneris**, n., *gift; duty, obligation, gladiatorial show* (47, 54, 57B, 61C)
mūrus, -ī, m, *wall* (23)
***mūtō, -āre, -āvī, -ātus**, *to change, transform* (55B)
mūtuus, -a, -um, *reciprocal, mutual* (49, 63B)

N

nam, conj., *for* (8)
nārrō, nārrāre, nārrāvī, nārrātus, *to tell (a story)* (20)

*__nāscor, nāscī, nātus sum__, *to be born* (39, 55D)
__nātālis, -is, -e__, *of/belonging to birth* (46)
__nātūra, -ae__, f., *nature* (IX)
__nātūrā__, *by nature, naturally* (76D)
*__nātus, -ī__, m., *son* (54, 74E)
__nāvālis, -is, -e__, *naval* (56B)
__nāvigō, -āre, -āvī, -ātus__, *to sail* (38)
__nāvis, nāvis__, gen. pl., __nāvium__, f., *ship* (38)
__-ne__ (indicates a question) (3)
__nē__, conj. + subjunctive, *not to, so that . . . not, to prevent, to avoid* (51, 53, 57, 75); introducing clause of fearing, *that* (66)
__nē...quidem__, adv., *not even* (34, 63C)
__nec__, conj., *and...not, but...not, nor* (45)
__nec...nec__, *neither...nor*
__necessārius, -a, -um__, *necessary* (65A)
__necesse__, adv. or indecl. adj., *necessary* (6, 13, 52)
__necessitās, necessitātis__, f., *necessity* (75A)
__necō, -āre, -āvī, -ātus__, *to kill* (20)
*__nefās__, n., indeclinable, *sinful, improper* (68)
*__negō, -āre, -āvī, -ātus__, *to say no, deny, refuse* (62B)
__nēmō, nēminis__, m./f., *no one* (9)
__nepōs, nepōtis__, m., *grandson, nephew* (55D)
__Neptūnus, -ī__, m., *Neptune* (god of the sea) (75C)
__neque__, conj., *and...not* (6)
__neque...neque__, *neither...nor* (5)
__nesciō, -īre, -īvī, -ītus__, *to be ignorant, not to know* (9)
__niger, nigra, nigrum__, *black* (33)
__nihil__, *nothing* (3)
__nihilō amplius__, adv., *nothing more* (69B)
__nimium__, adv., *too, too much, excessively* (59B)
__nisi__, conj., *unless, if . . not, except* (18, 26, 75)
*__nōbilis, -is, -e__, *of noble birth, known* (50, 55A)
*__nōbilitās, nōbilitātis__, f., *nobility, senatorial class* (55B)
__noceō, -ēre, -uī, -itūrus__ + dat., *to do harm (to), harm* (26)
__nocturnus, -a, -um__, *occurring at night* (22)
__nōlō, nōlle, nōluī__, irreg., *to be unwilling, not to wish, refuse* (5, 17, 21)
__nōlī / nōlīte__ + infin., *don't...!* (9, 75)
__nōmen, nōminis__, n., *name* (1, 15)
__nōminō, -āre, -āvī, -ātus__, *to name, call by name, speak of* (54)
__nōn__, adv., *not, no* (2, 13)
__nōndum__, adv., *not yet* (6, 13)
__nōnnūllī, -ae, -a__, *some, several* (51)
__nōnus, -a, -um__, *ninth* (16, 38, 64A)
__nōs__, *we, us* (8, 27)
*__nōscō, nōscere, nōvī, nōtus__, *to find out, get to know, ascertain* (62F, 75D)
__noster, nostra, nostrum__, *our* (14, 27)
__nostrī, nostrōrum__, m. pl., *our (men), our (soldiers)*
*__notō, -āre, -āvī, -ātus__, *to mark, mark out* (59A)
*__nōtus, -a, -um__, *known, well-known* (31, 64A)
__novem__, *nine* (15, 38)
__novus, -a, -um__, *new* (16)
__nox, noctis__, gen. pl., __noctium__, f., *night* (11)
*__nūbō, nūbere, nūpsī, nūptūrus__ + dat., *to marry* (62E)
__nūdus, -a, -um__, *naked, bare* (64C)
__nūllus, -a, -um__, *no, none* (9)
__num__, adv., *surely...not...?* (introduces a question that expects the answer "no") (46)
*__nūmen, nūminis__, n., *divine power, divine will, divinity, god* (61A)
__numerus, -ī__, m., *number* (11)
__nummus, -ī__, m., *coin* (75B)
__numquam__, adv., *never* (20)
__nunc__, adv., *now* (6, 13)
__nūntius, -ī__, m., *messenger; message* (7)
*__nusquam__, adv., *nowhere* (39, 72C)

O

__ō__ (used with vocative and in exclamations) (9)
*__ob__, prep. + acc., *on account of, because of* (39, 61A)
*__obeō, obīre, obiī__ or __obīvī, obitūrus__, irreg., *to go to, appear at; to take on, undertake, pursue; to die* (57A, 65A)
*__oblīvīscor, oblīvīscī, oblītus sum__ + gen., *to forget* (62b, RN 72)
__obsecrō, -āre, -āvī, -ātus__, *to beseech, beg* (40, 51)
__observō, -āre, -āvī, -ātus__, *to watch, pay attention to, obey* (6, 50)
__obses, obsidis__, m., *hostage* (55A)
__obtineō, obtinēre, obtinuī, obtentus__, *to hold, possess* (57A)
__obviam__, adv., *in the way, on the way* (65B)
__occīdō, occīdere, occīdī, occīsus__, *to kill* (45)
__occupō, -āre, -āvī, -ātus__, *to seize, take over* (56A)
*__occurrō, occurrere, occurrī, occursūrus__ + dat., *to meet* (24, 64A)
__octō__, *eight* (15, 38)
__oculus, -ī__, m., *eye* (26)
*__ōdī, ōdisse__, *to hate* (62G)
__odor, odōris__, m., *smell, odor* (73A)
__offēnsa, -ae__, f., *offense; resentment, unhappiness, hatred*
__offerō, offerre, obtulī, oblātus__, *to offer, provide*

officium, -ī, n., *duty, job* (51)
***ōlim**, adv., *once (upon a time); at some time, someday* (18, 56B)
Olympus, -ī, m., *Mt. Olympus* (home of the gods)
***omnīnō**, adv., *altogether* (58B)
omnis, -is, -e, *all, the whole, every, each* (6, 18)
onus, oneris, n., *load, burden* (15)
***opera, -ae**, f., *work, task, undertaking* (56A)
operam dare, *to make effort, pay attention*
***operiō, operīre, operuī, opertus**, *to cover, hide* (53, 72B)
operō, -āre, -āvī, -ātus, *to operate*
***oportet, oportēre, oportuit**, *it is fitting; ought* (50, 52, 58B)
oppidum, -ī, n., *town, stronghold* (39, 57A)
oppōnō, oppōnere, opposuī, oppositus, *to oppose, stand in the way of*
opprimō, opprimere, oppressī, oppressus, *to overwhelm* (30)
***ops, opis**, f., *power; riches; aid, help* (63B)
optimus, -a, -um, *best, very good, excellent* (20, 31, 34)
***optō, -āre, -āvī, -ātus**, *to wish* (54, 56B)
***opus, operis**, n., *work, effort* (61B)
***ōra, -ae**, f., *shore* (68)
ōrātiō, ōrātiōnis, f., *oration, speech* (26, 65)
ōrātiōnem habēre, idiom, *to deliver a speech* (26)
***ōrātor, ōrātōris**, m., *orator, speaker* (22, 55A)
***orbis, orbis**, gen. pl., **orbium**, m., *circle*
orbis terrārum, idiom, *the world* (55C)
***ōrdō, ōrdinis**, m., *order, rank, class* (60B)
Oriēns, Orientis, m., *the East* (55C)
***orior, orīrī, ortus sum**, *to rise, arise, come* or *derive from* (45, 64B)
ōrnō, -āre, -āvī, -ātus, *decorate, equip* (53)
ōrō, -āre, -āvī, -ātus, *to beg, ask* (51)
***ōs, ōris**, n., *mouth, face, expression* (38, 59A)
os, ossis, n., *bone* (54)
***ostendō, ostendere, ostendī, ostentus**, *to show, point out* (48, 64C)
ōtiōsus, -a, -um, *restful, at leisure, idle, easy* (63E)
ōtium, -ī, n., *leisure time* (63A)

P

paene, adv., *almost* (30)
paenitet, paenitēre, paenituit, *it causes one* (acc.) *to regret something* (gen.), *it makes one* (acc.) *be sorry for something* (gen.) (72 RN)
pallēscō, pallēscere, palluī, *to become pale, grow yellow, be yellow* (74A)
***parcō, parcere, pepercī** + dat., *to spare* (49, 73D)
parēns, parentis, m./f., *parent* (11)
pāreō, pārēre, pāruī, pāritūrus + dat., *to obey* (39)
pariēs, pariētis, m. *wall* (30)
***pariō, parere, peperī, partus**, *to bear, give birth to* (60A)
parō, -āre, -āvī, -ātus, *to prepare* (5, 20)
pars, partis, gen. pl., **partium**, f., *part, direction*; pl., *faction* (13)
partim, adv., *partly, some* (58A)
parvulus, -a, -um, *little, small* (26)
parvus, -a, -um, *small, little* (30, 34)
***pateō, patēre, patuī**, *to be open, be accessible* (55A)
pater, patris, m., *father* (6, 11)
paternus, -a, -um, *inherited from one's father, belonging to one's family, ancestral* (75D)
patientia, -ae, f., *patience, endurance, forbearance* (59A)
patior, patī, passus sum, *to suffer, endure, allow* (38, 59B)
***patria, -ae**, f., *fatherland, country, native land* (55A)
***patrius, -a, -um**, *father's, ancestral* (58B)
***patrōnus, -ī**, m., *patron* (25, 62L)
paucī, -ae, -a, *few* (34)
paulātim, adv., *gradually, little by little* (34)
paulisper, adv., *for a short time* (20)
***paulum**, adv., *little* (35)
***paulum, -ī**, n., *a small amount, a little* (37, 59B)
***paulō**, *by a little, slightly* (58A)
***pāx, pācis**, f., *peace* (56A)
pedes, peditis, m., *foot-soldier, infantryman* (55C)
penitus, adv., *thoroughly, completely* (57A)
***penna, -ae**, f., *feather; wing* (71A)
per, prep. + acc., *through, along* (6, 9)
***percutiō, percutere, percussī, percussus**, *to strike* (35, 60B)
***perdō, perdere, perdidī, perditus**, *to ruin, ravage, destroy* (45, 58A)
perdūcō, perdūcere, perdūxī, perductus, *to bring through, bring to; to extend, prolong* (62C)
***pereō, perīre, periī**, or **perīvī, peritūrus**, irreg., *to die, perish* (56A)
perficiō, perficere, perfēcī, perfectus, *to complete, finish* (63D)
perfidus, -a, -um, *treacherous*; as noun, *traitor* (72A)
perīculōsus, -a, -um, *dangerous* (17)
perīculum, -ī, n., *danger* (14, 15)
permaneō, permanēre, permansī, permansūrus, *to remain, stay* (76D)

permittō, permittere, permīsī, permissus, *to allow*
permultus, -a, -um, *very many*
***perpetuus, -a, -um**, *continuous, eternal, lasting* (60B)
***persequor, persequī, persecūtus sum**, *to follow, pursue* (55D)
persuādeō, persuādēre, persuāsī, persuāsus, *to make something* (acc.) *agreeable to someone* (dat.), *to persuade someone of something; to persuade someone* (dat.) (36, 51)
perterritus, -a, -um, *frightened* (5)
perturbātus, -a, -um, *confused, upset* (50)
perveniō, pervenīre, pervēnī, perventūrus, *to come through to, arrive at, reach* (25)
pervigilō, -āre, -āvī, -ātūrus, *to stay awake all night* (76C)
pēs, pedis, m., *foot* (13)
pessimus, -a, -um, *worst* (34)
***pestis, pestis**, f., *plague, disease, death* (59A)
petō, petere, petīvī, petītus, *to look for, seek, head for, aim at, attack* (5, 21)
philosophus, -ī, m., *philosopher* (75B)
***pietās, pietātis**, f., *devotion* (to duty) (67A)
pīlum, -ī, n., *spear, javelin* (60D)
***pius, -a, -um**, *dutiful* (72C)
placeō, -ēre, -uī + dat., *to please* (34, 52)
***plēbs, plēbis**, f., *plebeians, common people* (64A)
plēnus, -a, -um, *full* (11)
plūrimus, -a, -um, *most, very much* (34)
plūs, plūris, n., *more* (34)
poena, -ae, f., *punishment, penalty* (40)
poēta, -ae, m., *poet* (25)
***polliceor, pollicērī, pollicitus sum**, *to promise* (45, 59B)
pōnō, pōnere, posuī, positus, *to put, place* (10, 21)
pōns, pontis, gen. pl., **pontium**, m., *bridge* (23)
***populus, -ī**, m., *people* (47, 55B)
porta, -ae, f., *gateway* (11)
***poscō, poscere, poposcī**, *to demand, ask for* (34, 55B)
possessiō, possessiōnis, f., *possession*
possum, posse, potuī, irreg., *to be able; can* (5, 14, 21)
post, prep. + acc., *after* (20)
***posteā**, adv., *later on, afterwards* (33, 55A)
posterus, -a, -um, *next, following* (52)
  posterī, -ōrum, m. pl., *posterity, future generations*
postis, postis, gen. pl., **postium**, m., *door-post* (25)
postquam, conj., *after* (20)
***postrēmus, -a, -um**, *last, final* (55C)
  postrēmō, adv., *finally, at last, in the end* (46)
***potēns, potentis**, *powerful* (57a, 73A)
***potestās, potestātis**, f., *power, control; ability* (61D)
***potior, potīrī, potītus sum** + gen. or abl., *to get possession of, get control of, obtain* (55D)
praeceptum, -ī, n., *instruction, principle* (63C)
praecipuus, -a, -um, *notable, outstanding, remarkable* (55D)
praeclārus, -a, -um, *distinguished, famous* (13)
praedīcō, praedīcere, praedīxī, praedictus, *to set forth, relate, assert* (59B)
praedō, praedōnis, m., *robber, thief* (26)
praeferō, praeferre, praetulī, praelātus, irreg., *to carry in front, give precedence to, prefer* (37)
praemittō, praemittere, praemīsī, praemissus, *to send ahead* (66D)
praepōnō, praepōnere, praeposuī, praepositus, *to put someone* (acc.) *in charge of something* (dat.) (56B, 63A)
***praesēns, praesentis**, *present, at hand, immediate; resolute* (65D)
***praesentia, -ae**, f., *presence* (60A)
praesidium, -ī, n., *defense, protection, garrison* (59A)
***praestō, praestāre, praestitī, praestitus**, *to stand out, surpass; to bestow* (55D)
praeter, prep. + acc., *except* (21, 69D)
***praetereā**, adv., *besides, too, moreover* (15, 55C)
***praetereō, praeterīre, praeteriī** or **praeterīvī, praeteritūrus**, irreg., *to go past* (15, 66D)
praetermittō, praetermittere, praetermīsī, praetermissus, *to pass over, neglect, omit* (69D)
praetextātus, -a, -um, *wearing the* ***toga praetexta*** (52)
***praetor, praetōris**, m., *praetor, judge* (58A)
precor, -ārī, -ātus sum, *to pray, pray for* (71A)
***premō, premere, pressī, pressus**, *to press, press upon* (60A)
pretium, -ī, n., *price* (31, 62K)
prīdiē, adv., *on the day before* (36)
prīmus, -a, -um, *first* (21, 38)
  prīmō, adv., *first, at first* (40)
  prīmum, adv., *first, at first* (23)
  in prīmīs, *in particular* (66D)
prīnceps, prīncipis, m., *leader, leading citizen; emperor* (7)
prīncipātus, -ūs, m., *principate, imperial rule* (57A)
prīstinus, -a, -um, *previous, former* (66C)
priusquam, conj., *before* (69C)
prīvātus, -a, -um, *private, personal* (59C)
prīvignus, -ī, m., *stepson* (57B)
***prō**, prep. + abl., *before, on behalf of* (55b)

probō, -āre, -āvī, -ātus, *to prove, demonstrate, establish* (60C)
prōcēdō, prōcēdere, prōcessī, prōcessūrus, *to go forward, come forth* (33)
prōclāmō, -āre, -āvī, -ātus, *to speak out, proclaim*
prōcōnsul, prōcōnsulis, m., *official acting on behalf of a consul, proconsul, governor* (66C)
procul, adv., *in the distance, far off* (15)
prōcurrō, procurrere, pro(cu)currī, procursūrus, *to run forth, rush out*
*__prōdō, prōdere, prōdidī, prōditus__, *to hand down, transmit; to hand over, betray; to nominate, appoint* (61C)
prōdūcō, prōdūcere, prōdūxī, prōductus, *to lead forth, bring forth*
*__proelium, -ī__, n., *battle* (55A)
proferō, proferre, protulī, prolātus, irreg., *to carry forward, continue* (52)
proficīscor, proficīscī, profectus sum, *to set out* (36, 37)
*__prohibeō, -ēre, -uī, -itus__, *to prohibit, forbid, prevent* (65D)
prōmittō, prōmittere, prōmīsī, prōmissus, *to promise* (9)
prope, adv., *near, nearby* (45)
prope, prep. + acc., *near* (5, 9)
propellō, propellere, propūlī, propulsus, *to drive forward*
*__properō, -āre, -āvī, -ātus__, *to hurry, hasten* (66D)
*__propinquus, -ī__, m., *relative* (50, 61D)
prōponō, prōponere, prōposuī, prōpositus, *to set forward or forth* (63C)
prōpraetor, prōpraetōris, m., *official acting for a praetor, propraetor, governor* (57B)
propter, prep. + acc., *because of* (26)
*__prosperus, -a, -um__, *prosperous, successful, favorable* (56B)
prōvideō, prōvidēre, prōvīdī, prōvīsus, *to foresee, expect* (69A)
*__prōvincia, -ae__, f., *conquered territory, province* (56b)
*__proximus, -a, -um__, *nearest, next; most recent, last* (33, 59A)
prūdēns, prūdentis, *wise, sensible* (34)
prūdentia, -ae, f., *good sense, wisdom, discretion, skill* (52)
*__pūblicus, -a, -um__, *public* (51, 58A)
pūblicē, adv., *publicly* (59C)
pudet, pudēre, puduit, *it causes one* (acc.) *to be ashamed of something* (gen.) (63A)
*__pudor, pudōris__, m., *sense of honor, sense of shame* (70B)
puer, -ī, m., *boy, youth, slave* (3)
puerīlis, -is, -e, *boyish, youthful* (61C)
pugna, -ae, f., *fight, battle* (48)
*__pugnō, -āre, -āvī, -ātūrus__, *to fight* (48, 55C)
pulcher, pulchra, pulchrum, *beautiful, handsome* (28)
pūmex, pūmicis, m., *pumice stone* (76B)
pūniō, -īre, -īvī, -ītus, *to punish* (21)
pūrgō, -āre, -āvī, -ātus, *to clean* (8)
pūrus, -a, -um, *pure, clean*
purpureus, -a, -um, *dark red, purple*
putō, -āre, -āvī, -ātus, *to think* (46)

Q

quādrāgintā, *forty* (55C)
quaerō, quaerere, quaesīvī, quaesītus, *to seek, look for, ask for* (30)
quaestor, quaestōris, m., *quaestor, magistrate in charge of the state treasury*
quālis, -is, -e, *what sort of* (4)
quam...! adv., *how...!, what a...!* (13, 29, 36)
quam...? adv., *how...?* (36)
quam, adv., *than, as* (34, 36)
quam, adv. + superlative adj. or adv., *as...as possible* (35, 36)
quamquam, conj., *although* (11)
quantus, -a, -um, *how big, how much* (41, 58A)
*__quārē__, adv., *for what reason?, why?; for this reason, therefore* (55D, 62F)
quārtus, -a, -um, *fourth* (38)
*__quasi__, adv., *as if, just as, as* (49, 56A)
quattuor, *four* (15, 38)
-que, enclitic conj., *and* (36)
quemadmodum, *in what way, as* (75A)
quī, quae, quod, *who, which, that* (1, 3, 14, 28, 29, 36); after a period or semicolon, *he, she, it, this* (44)
quia, conj., *because, since, that* (55B)
quīdam, quaedam, quoddam, *a certain*, pl., *some* (10, 29, 69)
quidem, adv., *indeed* (31)
nē...quidem, *not even*
quiēs, quiētis, f., *rest, sleep* (23)
quiēscō, quiēscere, quiēvī, quiētūrus, *to rest, sleep* (13, 23)
quiētus, -a, -um, *quiet, at rest* (66a)
*__quīn__, conj. + subjunctive, *that...not, (but) that, who...not* (58B)
quīnquāgintā, *fifty* (57A)
quīnque, *five* (15, 38)
quis...? quid...? who...? what...? (1, 4, 29)
quis, nē (see **aliquis**) (52, 69)
quis, sī (see **aliquis**) (51, 69)

*__quisquam, quisquam, quidquam__ (or __quicquam__), *anyone, anything* (58B, 69)
*__quisque, quaeque, quidque__ or __quicque__, *each, each person, each one* (58A, 69)
*__quisquis, quisquis, quidquid__, *whoever, whatever* (65, 69)
quō...? adv., *where...to?* (4)
quō, adv., *there, to that place* (43)
quoad, conj., *until* (65B)
quod, conj., *because;* with verbs of feeling, *that* (1, 11, 13, 29)
quōmodo, adv., *in what way, how* (12)
*__quondam__, adv., *once, formerly* (55C, 59D)
*__quoniam__, conj., *since, because* (42)
quoque, adv., *also* (2, 13)
quot, indecl. adj., *as many, how many* (15, 38)

R

raeda, -ae, f., *carriage* (10)
raedārius, -ī, m., *coachman, driver* (10)
rapidus, -a, -um, *rapid, swift, rushing*
rārus, -a, -um, *rare*
ratiō, ratiōnis, f., *account, reckoning* (61D)
*__recēdō, recēdere, recessī, recessūrus__, *to go back, go away, retreat* (56B)
*__recipiō, recipere, recēpī, receptus__, *to receive, accept, recapture* (54, 57B)
*__sē recipere__, *to return, take oneself back, withdraw, retreat* (60B)
recitō, -āre, -āvī, -ātus, *to read aloud, recite* (29)
recognōscō, recognōscere, recognōvī, recognitus, *to recognize* (66C)
recēdō, recēdere, recessī, recessūrus, *to withdraw, move back* (60B)
rēctus, -a, -um, *right, proper, correct, straight, upright* (35)
rēctē, adv., *rightly, properly, correctly* (31, 35)
recurrō, recurrere, recurrī, recursūrus, *to run back, return* (65C)
reddō, reddere, reddidī, redditus, *to give back, return* (29)
redeō, redīre, rediī or **redīvī, reditūrus**, irreg., *to return, go back* (7, 23)
reditus, -ūs, m., *return*
redūcō, redūcere, redūxī, reductus, *to lead back, bring back*
*__referō, referre, rettulī, relātus__, irreg., *to bring back, bring back again, report* (46, XI, 58B)
reficiō, reficere, refēcī, refectus, *to remake, repair, rebuild; to restore, revive* (32, 63A, 69D)
*__rēgīna, -ae__, f., *queen* (38, 56B)
regiō, regiōnis, f., *region* (XVII)
rēgnō, -āre, -āvī, -ātus, *to rule, reign over* (56B)
rēgnum, -ī, n., *kingdom, realm* (32, 57B)
*__regō, regere, rēxī, rēctus__, *to rule* (57b)
regredior, regredī, regressus sum, *to go back, return* (36)
*__reiciō, reicere, reiēcī, reiectus__, *to throw back, throw off; drive back* (65C)
relaxō, -āre, -āvī, -ātus, *to relax, relieve tension*
*__religiō, religiōnis__, f., *religion, strict observance of religious ritual* (58A)
religiōsus, -a, -um, *holy* (58B)
relinquō, relinquere, relīquī, relictus, *to leave behind, abandon* (16, 21)
*__reliquus, -a, -um__, *the rest, the remaining, other* (59D)
remaneō, remanēre, remānsī, *to remain* (56A)
remittō, remittere, remīsī, remissus, *to send back* (62I)
renovō, -āre, -āvī, -ātus, *to renew* (38)
reparō, -āre, -āvī, -ātus, *to restore, renew, make good; restart, begin again* (55D)
repellō, repellere, reppulī, repulsus, *to drive off, drive back* (5, 40)
*__repente__, *suddenly, unexpectedly* (58B)
*__reperiō, reperīre, repperī, repertus__, *to find* (59B)
repetō, repetere, repetīvī, repetītus, *to try again, seek again, repeat* (43)
repōnō, repōnere, reposuī, repositus, *to put back, replace*
repudiō, -āre, -āvī, -ātus, *to reject, divorce* (56B)
requiēscō, requiēscere, requiēvī, requiētūrus, *to rest*
rēs, reī, f., *thing, event, matter, situation, affair* (19, 25)
rēs gestae, *deeds, accomplishments* (69)
*__rēs pūblica__, *state, government* (55D)
rē vērā, adv., *really, actually* (49, 55f, 65D)
reservō, -āre, -āvī, -ātus, *to reserve, keep*
resistō, resistere, restitī + dat., *to resist, stand up to* (42, ?RN)
*__respiciō, respicere, respexī, respectus__, *to look behind, look back at* (60B)
respondeō, respondēre, respondī, respōnsūrus, *to answer, reply* (5, 21)
retineō, retinēre, retinuī, retentus, *to keep, retain*
revertor, revertī, reversus sum, *to turn back, return* (64B)
revocō, -āre, -āvī, -ātus, *call back, bring back* (70C)

***rēx, rēgis**, m., *king* (36, 55C)
Rhēnus, -ī, m., *the Rhine River* (57A)
rīpa, -ae, f., *river bank* (57B)
rīte, adv., *properly* (53)
rīvus, -ī, m., *stream, river; channel of aqueduct* (5, 69D)
rogō, -āre, -āvī, -ātus, *to ask* (12, 51)
Rōma, -ae, f., *Rome* (7)
Rōmānus, -a, -um, *Roman* (1)
rosa, -ae, f., *rose* (34)
***rōstrum, -ī**, n., *beak* (of a ship); n. pl., *speaker's platform* (64C)
ruīna, -ae, f., *collapse, ruin, destruction* (38)
rūrsus, adv., *again* (36)
rūs, rūris, n., *country* (as opposed to city) (39, 64B)
rūsticus, -a, -um, *of the country, rustic*

S

***sacer, sacra, sacrum**, *sacred, holy* (72D)
sacerdōs, sacerdōtis, m., *priest* (69C)
sacrificium, -ī, n., *sacrifice*
saepe, adv., *often* (2, 13, 35)
saevus, -a, -um, *savage, cruel* (39)
salūs, salūtis, f., *good health, safety; greetings* (36)
salūtō, -āre, -āvī, -ātus, *to greet, welcome* (7)
sānctitās, sānctitātis, f., *purity, virtue*
***sānctus, -a, -um**, *hallowed, sacred* (58A)
***sānē**, adv., *certainly; exceedingly, extremely* (36, 58B)
sanguis, sanguinis, m., *blood* (33)
sapiēns, sapientis, *wise man; philosopher* (63C)
satis, adv., *enough* (23)
scelestus, -a, -um, *wicked* (10, 62H)
scelus, sceleris, n., *crime* (41)
***scīlicet**, adv., *obviously, of course, no doubt* (sometimes ironic) (57B)
sciō, scīre, scīvī, scītus, *to know* (16, 49)
scrībō, scrībere, scrīpsī, scrīptus, *to write* (1, 24)
sē, *himself, herself, itself, themselves* (11)
secundus, -a, -um, *second, next, following; favorable* (9, 38)
secus, adv., *otherwise, not so* (65C)
sed, conj., *but* (2)
sedeō, sedēre, sēdī, sessūrus, *to sit* (1, 21)
***semel**, adv., *once; at some time* (62A)
sēmis, sēmissis, m., *one-half*
semper, adv., *always* (4, 13)
senātor, senātōris, m., *senator* (7)
senātus, -ūs, m., *Senate* (25, 55B)
senex, senis, m., *old man* (43)
sēnsus, -ūs, m., *ability to perceive or feel, perception, sense* (63E)
***sententia, -ae**, f., *feeling, opinion; motion* (59B)
sentiō, sentīre, sēnsī, sēnsus, *to feel, notice, realize* (45, 49)
***sepeliō, sepelīre, sepelīvī, sepultus**, *to bury* (39, 57A)
September, Septembris, Septembre, *September* (36)
septimus, -a, -um, *seventh* (13, 38, 76A)
septingentēsimus, -a, um, *690th* (55D)
septuāgēsimus, -a, -um, *69th* (57A)
***sepulcrum, -ī**, n., *tomb* (22, 74F)
sequor, sequī, secūtus sum, *to follow* (36, 37)
serēnus, -a, -um, *clear, bright; tranquil, calm* (50)
***sermō, sermōnis**, m., *speech, conversation* (67C)
serpēns, serpentis, m., *viper, serpent*
***servīlis, -is, -e**, *relating to a slave, servile* (58A)
servō, -āre, -āvī, -ātus, *to save, preserve, protect, keep, guard* (26, 30)
servus, -ī, m., *slave* (3)
***sēsē**, alternate form of **sē** (58B)
sēstertius, -ī, gen. pl., **sēstertium**, *sesterce* (small silver coin, worth one-quarter of a denarius) (75B)
sex, *six* (15, 38)
sexāgintā, *sixty*
sextus, -a, -um, *sixth* (37, 38)
sī, conj., *if* (5, 75)
sīc, adv., *thus, in this way, so* (38, 39, 50)
sicilia, -ae, f., *sicily*
***sīcut** or **sīcutī**, conj., *just as* (57B)
signum, -ī, n., *sign, signal; military standard* or *insignia; image, statue.* (27, 57B, 58B)
silentium, -ī, n., *silence* (15)
silva, –ae, f., *woods, forest* (5)
similis, -is, -e + dat., *similar (to), like* (34, 50)
simul, adv., *together, at the same time* (9, 13)
***simulācrum, -ī**, n., *image, figure, effigy* (58B)
sīn (sī + nē), conj., *but if, on the other hand* (59D, 66A)
sincērus, -a, -um, *sincere*
sine, prep. + abl., *without* (26)
***singulī, -ae, -a**, *one at a time, individually, separately* (62B)
sinister, sinistra, sinistrum, *left, on the left* (50)
***sinō, sinere, sīvī, situs**, *to allow* (34, 59B)
***sīve...sīve**, *whether...or* (71A)
***socius, -ī**, m., *comrade, friend, ally* (55A)
***sodālis, sodālis**, gen. pl., **sodālium**, m., *comrade, friend* (62I)
sōlācium, -ī, n., *comfort, consolation, relief* (64B)
***sōl, sōlis**, m., *sun* (50)
soleō, solēre, solitus sum + infin., *to be accustomed (to), be in the habit of* (10, 40)

sollicitus, -a, -um, *anxious, worried* (4)
sōlus, -a, -um, *alone* (3)
sōlum, adv., *alone, only*
***solvō, solvere, solvī, solūtus**, *to release, untie; pay* (a debt) (54, 72D)
somnus, -ī, m., *sleep* (21)
soror, sorōris, f., *sister* (11)
***sors, sortis**, f., *lot; prophecy; oracle* (72B)
spargō, spargere, sparsī, sparsus, *to scatter, sow* (63E)
***spatium, -ī**, n., *space; distance, extent, length* (60B)
spectō, -āre, -āvī, -ātus, *to watch, look at* (7)
spērō, -āre, -āvī, -ātus, *to hope* (47)
***spēs, speī**, f., *hope* (73C)
***spīritus, -ūs**, m., *breath, breath of life, spirit* (67D)
splendidus, -a, -um, *brilliant, splendid*
***sponte**, *of one's own accord, voluntarily* (59D)
statim, adv., *immediately* (5, 13)
statua, -ae, f., *statue* (3)
statuō, statuere, statuī, status, *to establish, build*
stīpendium, -ī, n., *tax, tribute* (55A)
stō, stāre, stetī, statūrus, *to stand* (10, 22)
strangulō, -āre, -āvī, -ātus, *to strangle, choke*
stringō, stringere, strīnxī, strictus, *to draw* (a sword) (26)
***studeō, studēre, studuī** + dat., *to be eager, be enthusiastic, favor, support; to study* (39, 64C)
studiōsus, -a, -um, *eager* (76A)
studiōsē, adv., *earnestly, eagerly* (63E)
***studium, -ī**, n., *enthusiasm, zeal, support; study* (41, 66C)
stultitia, -ae, f., *foolishness*
***suāvis, -is, -e**, *sweet* (34, 66A)
sub, prep. + abl., *under, beneath, at the foot of* (1, 9)
subeō, subīre, subiī, subitus, irreg., *to go under, undergo, endure, occur* (64B)
subitō, adv., *suddenly* (3, 13)
***subsequor, subsequī, subsecūtus sum**, *to follow (up)* (44, 60B)
succendō, succendere, succendī, succēnsus, *to burn, set on fire* (60B)
succurrō, succurrere, succurrī, succursūrus + dat., *to help, come to the aid of* (60B)
sulpur, sulpuris, n., *sulphur* (76D)
sum, esse, fuī, futūrus, irreg., *to be* (1, 14, 20, 21)
summoveō, summovēre, summōvī, summōtus, *to drive off, remove* (57B)
summus, -a, -um, *greatest, very great; highest; the top of...* (35)
ad summam, *on the whole; in short*
sūmō, sūmere, sūmpsī, sūmptus, *to take, take up* (22, 51)
***super**, prep. + acc., *over, above* (53, 69B)
superbus, -a, -um, *proud, arrogant* (48)
***superior, superior, superius**, gen., **superiōris**, *higher, previous, earlier* (59A, 65C)
superō, -āre, -āvī, -ātus, *to overcome, defeat* (42)
superstitiō, superstitiōnis, f., *superstition*
supersum, superesse, superfuī, irreg., *to be left, remain, survive*
***supplicium, -ī**, n., *punishment, capital punishment, execution* (61A)
suprā, prep. + acc., *above, over* (23)
surgō, surgere, surrēxī, surrectūrus, *to get up, rise* (6, 21)
surripiō, surripere, surripuī, surreptus, *to steal* (44)
suscipiō, suscipere, suscēpī, susceptus, *to undertake, support, receive under one's protection* (56A)
suspiciō, suspiciōnis, f., *suspicion*
***sustineō, sustinēre, sustinuī, sustentus**, *to sustain, endure, withstand, hold out* (61C)
sustulī, see **tollō**
suus, -a, -um, *his, her, one's, its, their (own)* (9, 27)

T

taberna, -ae, f., *shop, inn* (25)
tābula, -ae, f., *tablet* (51)
tacitus, -a, -um, *quiet, silent* (9)
taedet, taedēre, taesum est, *it bores, makes one* (acc.) *tired of something* (gen.) (16, 50, 52, 72 RN)
***tālis, -is, -e**, *such, of this kind* (23, 50, 65D)
tam, adv., *so* (30, 50)
tamen, adv., *however, nevertheless* (6, 13)
***tamquam**, conj., *just as if, as* (33, 75A)
tandem, adv., *at last, at length, finally* (2, 13)
***tangō, tangere, tetigī, tāctus**, *to touch* (54, 71B)
tantus, -a, -um, *so great, such a big, so much* (24, 50)
***tantum** adv., *only; so much, to such an extent* (15, 50, 55B)
tantus...quantus, *as much as* (62C)
tardus, -a, -um, *slow* (15)
tardē, adv., *slowly*
***tēctum, -ī**, n., *roof;* pl., *house* (59D)
***tegō, tegere, texī, tēctus**, *to cover* (60A)
***tellūs, tellūris**, f., *ground* (68)
***tēlum, -ī**, n., *weapon, spear* (58B, 65C)
templum, -ī, n., *temple* (40)
temptō, -āre, -āvī, -ātus, *to try, attempt* (9)
tempus, temporis, n., *time* (2, 8, 12, 15)

tenebrae, -ārum, f. pl., *darkness, shadows; obscurity* (63C, 76C)
teneō, tenēre, tenuī, tentus, *to hold* (9, 25)
memoriā tenēre, *to remember* (37)
***tener, tenera, tenerum**, *tender, young* (70A)
tergum, -ī, n., *back* (35)
terra, -ae, f., *earth, land* (26, 38)
terreō, terrēre, terruī, territus, *to frighten, terrify* (4)
tertius, -a, -um, *third* (25, 36, 38)
***testāmentum, -ī**, n., *will, testament* (IX, 55D)
testor, -ārī, -ātus sum, *to bear witness to, give evidence of* (69B)
theātrum, -ī, n., *theater* (55f)
tigris, tigris, gen. pl., **tigrium**, f., *tiger*
timeō, -ēre, -uī, *to fear, be afraid* (5)
timor, timōris, m., *fear, anxiety* (35)
***tollō, tollere, sustulī, sublātus**, irreg., *to lift, raise, pick up* (48, 58B)
tormentum, -ī, n., *torment, torture*
tot, indecl. adj., *so many* (48)
totiēns, adv., *so often, so many times* (63D)
tōtus, -a, -um, *all, the whole, the entire* (21)
trādō, trādere, trādidī, trāditus, *to hand over, surrender; pass on (information), report* (7, 22)
trādūcō, trādūcere, trādūxī, trāductus, *to lead across*
trahō, trahere, trāxī, tractus, *to drag, pull* (6, 12, 25)
trāiciō, trāicere, trāiēci, trāiectus, *to pierce, penetrate* (60D)
tranquillus, -a, -um, *tranquil, peaceful, calm* (63E)
trāns, prep. + acc., *across* (39)
***trānseō, trānsīre, trānsiī, trānsitus**, irreg., *to go across, go over; to desert* (55B)
***trānsferō, trānsferre, trānstulī, trānslātus**, irreg., *to carry over, carry across, transport* (57B)
trānsfīgō, trānsfīgere, trānsfīxī, trānsfixus, *to pierce through* (60B)
trānsportō, -āre, -āvī, -ātus, *to carry across*
trecentiēs, adv., *three hundred times* (75B)
tremō, tremere, tremuī, *to tremble*
tremor, tremōris, m., *tremor* (76C)
tremulus, -a, -um, *trembling*
trepidāns, trepidantis, *in a panic, frightened* (52)
trēs, trēs, tria, *three* (13, 15, 38)
***tribuō, tribuere, tribuī, tribūtus**, *to allot, grant, devote* (63B)
triciēs, *30 times* (55A)
trīclīnium, -ī, n., *dining room* (31)
triumphālis, -is, -e, *of victory, triumphal*
***triumphus, -ī**, m., *triumph, victory parade* (56B)
Troiānus, -a, -um, *Trojan, from Troy*
trucidō, -āre, -āvī, -ātus, *to murder* (59B, 69A)
tū, *you* (sing.) (4, 27)
tulī, see **ferō**
tum, adv., *at that moment, then* (4, 13)
tumultus, -ūs, m., *uproar, din, commotion* (25)
***tunc**, adv., *then, at that moment* (75C)
turbō, -āre, -āvī, -ātus, *to upset*
***turpis, -is, -e**, *disgraceful, improper* (61C)
turris, -is, f., *tower; wooden tower on wheels* (60A)
***tūtus, -a, -um**, *safe* (55d)
tuus, -a, -um, *your* (sing.) (9, 27)
tyrannicus, -a, -um, *pertaining to a tyrant, tyrannical* (55D)
tyrannus, -ī, m., *tyrant* (72A)

U

ubi, adv., conj., *where, when* (1, 5, 13)
ulcīscor, ulcīscī, ultus sum, *to take revenge on, punish* (69A)
***ūllus, -a, -um**, *any* (57A)
***ultrā**, prep. + acc., *beyond* (57B)
***ultimus, -a, -um**, *last, least, farthest* (36, 64A)
umbra, -ae, f., *shadow, shade, ghost* (31, 33)
umquam, adv., *ever* (31)
***ūnā**, adv., *together, along with* (33, 61D)
***unda, -ae**, f., *wave; water* (72C)
***unde...?**, adv., *from where...?* (12, 64B)
ūndecimus, -a, -um, *eleventh* (17, 38)
ūndēvīgintī, *nineteen* (38, 69A)
unguentum, -ī, n., *ointment, oil, perfume* (34, 43)
unguō, unguere, ūnxī, ūnctus, *to anoint, smear (with oil)* (43)
***ūniversus, -a, -um**, *the whole of, the entire* (48, 55B)
ūnus, -a, -um, *one, single* (15, 38)
urbs, urbis, gen. pl., **urbium**, f., *city* (7)
urna, -ae, f., *pot, urn, vase* (75B)
***usque ad** + acc., up *to, as far as* (55A)
ut, conj. + indicative, *as, how, when; whether;* + subjunctive, *so that, that, in order to;* introducing clause of fearing, *that...not* (16, 50, 53, 54, 55, 66, 75)
***uter, utra, utrum**, *which, which one (of two)* (60B)
***uterque, utraque, utrumque**, *each* (of two), *both* (45, 60B)
ūtilis, -is, -e, *useful* (37, 59D)

*ūtor, ūtī, ūsus sum + abl., *to use, employ, take advantage of* (60a)
uxor, uxōris, f., *wife* (11)

V

***vacuus, -a, -um**, *empty* (55B)
vadum, -ī, n., *shallow water*
vagor, -ārī, -ātus sum, *to wander* (76C)
valdē, adv., *very, very much, exceedingly* (19)
***valeō, valēre, valuī, valitūrus**, *to be strong, be well, fare well* (40)
valē / valēte, *goodbye* (9)
valētūdō, valētūdinis, f., *health, good health, sickness* (39)
vāllum, -ī, n., *rampart* (60A)
varietās, varietātis, f., *diversity, difference, variety*
varius, -a, -um, *different, varied, diverse* (43, 53)
vastus, -a, -um, *huge, immense, vast*
***-ve**, enclitic conj., *or* (34, 62J)
vehementer, adv., *very much, violently, greatly* (19)
vehiculum, -ī, n., *vehicle* (13, 15)
***vehō, vehere, vexī, vectus**, *to carry, convey;* pass., *to travel* (54, 64A)
vel, conj., *or* (37)
vēlum, -ī, n., *sail* (75B)
***velut**, conj., *as, even as, just as* (58B)
vēndō, vēndere, vēndidī, vēnditus, *to sell* (28)
venēnum, -ī, n., *poison, venom* (56B)
venia, -ae, f., *pardon, forgiveness* (69C)
veniō, venīre, vēnī, ventūrus, *to come* (7, 20)
***ventus, -ī**, m., *wind* (42, 60A)
verbum, -ī, n., *word* (39)
***vereor, -ērī, -itus sum**, *to be afraid, fear* (37)
***versor, -ārī, -ātus sum**, *to stay, be situated; be engaged in* (59B, 63E)
vertō, vertere, vertī, versus, *to turn; to change* (16)
vērum, -ī, n., *truth*
***vērus, -a, -um**, *true, real* (40)
vērō, adv., *truly, really, indeed* (31)
vērum, adv., *truly* (75A)
vēscor, vēscī + abl., *to feed (on)* (49, 61 RN)
vester, vestra, vestrum, *your* (pl.) (22, 27)
vestīmenta, -ōrum, n. pl., *clothes* (33)
Vesuvius, -ī, m., *Vesuvius* (volcano near the Bay of Naples)
vetō, vetāre, vetuī, vetitus, *to forbid, prohibit* (26)
***vetus, veteris**, *old* (34, 73B)
vexō, -āre, -āvī, -ātus, *to annoy, bother* (4)
via, -ae, f., *road, way* (10)
vīcīnus, -a, -um, *neighboring, nearby* (1)
victima, -ae, f., *victim, sacrifice*
***victor, victōris**, m., *conqueror, victor* (27, 55B)
victōria, -ae, f., *victory* (60A)
videō, vidēre, vīdī, vīsus, *to see* (4, 21, 49)
videor, vidērī, vīsus sum, *to seem* (21)
vigilia, -ae, f., *wakefulness, sleepless night* (63D)
vigilō, -āre, -āvī, -ātūrus, *to stay awake, be watchful* (19)
vīgintī, *twenty* (36, 38)
vīlla, -ae, f., *country house, estate* (1)
vincō, vincere, vīcī, victus, *to conquer, overcome, defeat* (27)
***vindicō, -āre, -āvī, -ātus**, *to support, champion; to claim as free, liberate; to avenge, get revenge for* (56A, 67A, 69A)
vīnum, -ī, n., *wine* (25)
vir, virī, m., *man; husband* (3, 11, 67C)
virgō, virginis, f., *maiden, young girl* (45)
Virgō Vestālis, *Vestal Virgin* (one of six priestesses of Vesta) (69, 75)
***virtūs, virtūtis**, f., *courage, determination; character, virtue, merit* (60B)
***vīs**, acc., **vim**, abl., **vī**, f., *force, violence; amount;* pl. **vīrēs**, *strength, violence* (58B, 61B)
vīsitō, -āre, -āvī, -ātus, *to visit* (23)
***vīta, -ae**, f., *life* (54, 59D)
vītō, -āre, -āvī, -ātus, *to avoid* (13)
***vīvō, vīvere, vīxī, vīctūrus**, *to live, be alive* (39, 57A)
***vīvus, -a, -um**, *alive, living* (61A)
***vix**, adv., *scarcely, with difficulty, only just* (24, 68)
***vocō, -āre, -āvī, -ātus**, *to call* (16, 59D)
volō, -āre, -āvī, -ātūrus, *to fly* (74E)
volō, velle, voluī, irreg., *to wish, want* (5, 17, 20, 21)
voluntās, voluntātis, f., *will, willingness, consent* (55D)
***voluptās, voluptātis**, f., *pleasure, delight* (48, 63A)
vōs, *you* (pl.) (8, 27)
vōtīvus, -a, -um, *votive* (73A)
vōx, vōcis, f., *voice* (4)
***vulgus, -ī**, n., *common people, mob, rabble* (62F)
vulnerō, -āre, -āvī, -ātus, *to wound* (33)
***vulnus, vulneris**, n., *wound* (35, 55D)
***vultus, -ūs**, m., *face, countenance, expression* (45, 59A)

INDEX OF GRAMMAR

Index of Cultural Information

Latin terms are given in **boldface**; page numbers in **boldface** refer to illustrations. References are given to appearances in the Latin text, not the facing notes.

CREDITS

The publisher gratefully acknowledges the contributions of the agencies, institutions, and photographers listed below:

Chapter 55
(p. 2) Bust, Julius Caesar, © Robert Harding Picture Library Ltd/ Alamy

(p. 13) *Cicero Accusing Catiline of Conspiracy in the Senate* (October 21, 63 B.C.), © SuperStock, Inc./SuperStock

(p. 19) *Julius Caesar Crossing the Rubicon*, Musée Condé, Chantilly, France / The Bridgeman Art Library

(p. 25) *Caesar*, Adolphe Vyon (1817–1893), Giraudon/Art Resource, NY

(p. 29) *Death of Julius Caesar*, Vincenzo Camuccini, Scala/Art Resource, NY

(p. 34) *Left*: Coin issued by Caesar, Courtesy of the American Numismatic Society

(p. 34) *Right*: Coin issued to commemorate Caesar's murder, © The Trustees of the British Museum

Chapter 56
(p. 37) *Left*: Aureus issued in 39 B.C. (Octavian), Courtesy of the American Numismatic Society

(p. 37) *Right*: Aureus issued in 39 B.C. (Antony), Courtesy of the American Numismatic Society

(p. 38) Reconstruction, Forum of Augustus and the Temple of Mars Ultor, first century A.D., I. Gismondi, © Alinari/Art Resource

(p. 39) Forum of Augustus, Podium of the Temple of Mars, © Adam Eastland/Alamy

(p. 40) *Left*: Coin issued in 39 B.C. (Antony), Bildarchiv Preussischer Kulturbesitz/Art Resource, NY

(p. 40) *Right*: Coin issued in 39 B.C. (Octavia), Bildarchiv Preussischer Kulturbesitz/Art Resource, NY

(p. 41) *Middle:* Coin issued after conquest of Armenia by Antony in 34 B.C. (Antony), Courtesy of the American Numismatic Society

(p. 41) *Right*: Coin issued after conquest of Armenia by Antony in 34 B.C. (Cleopatra), (Courtesy of the American Numismatic Society

(p. 41) *Left*: *Middle:* Coin issued after conquest of Armenia by Antony in 34 B.C. (King Orodes II), Courtesy of the American Numismatic Society

(p. 43) *The Battle of Actium*, Lorenzo A. Castro (active circa 1664–1700), © National Maritime Museum, London

(p. 45) *Left*: Obverse of coin of Augustus, Courtesy of the American Numismatic Society

(p. 45) *Right*: Verso of coin of Augustus, Courtesy of the American Numismatic Society

(p. 49) Courtesy of the American Numismatic Society

Chapter 58
(p. 52) © AAA Collection

(p. 59) © Scala/Art Resource, NY

(p. 63) Temple of Hercules, Agrigento, Sicily, © Eric Renard/iStockphoto.com

(p. 65) Vase, Greece, approx. sixth century B.C., RMN-Grand Palais/Art Resource

Chapter 59
(p. 71) Bust, Marcus Tullius Cicero, © Alinari/Art Resource, NY

(p. 75) Roman mosaic showing an orator, © Erich Lessing/Art Resource, NY

(p. 77) Medal depicting Jupiter, France, Napoleonic era, Private Collection

(p. 80) Statuette, Roman legionary, second to first century, B.C., © Vanni/Art Resource, NY

(p. 81) Plaster mold of the Column of Trajan, 1860, © Alinari Archives/The Image Works

(p. 82) Roman army camp plan from LATIN TWO YEARS, REVIEW TEXT by Charles I. Freundlich, © 1966. Image used by permission from Perfection Learning. All rights reserved.

Chapter 60
(p. 84) Roman bullet, © Claudia Karabaic Sargent

(p. 87) Funditor, Bas-relief frieze, Iberfoto/SuperStock

(p. 89) Roman relief showing a Roman legionary fighting, early second century A.D., © Erich Lessing/Art Resource, NY

(P.91) Bust, Gaius Julius Caesar, Scala/Art Resource, NY

(p. 93) Roman copy of Greek statue depicting a dying Gaul, © Araldo De Luca

Chapter 61

(p. 100) Gold torque, first century B.C.–first century A.D., © Erich Lessing/Art Resource, NY

(p. 101) *Top*: Gallo-Roman relief, © Musée Carnavalet/Roger-Viollet/The Image Works

(p. 101) *Bottom*: Romano-Celtic bust of Minerva, first century A.D., © Bill Blank

(p. 103) *Left*: Coin, Rome, 48 B.C., Courtesy of the American Numismatic Society

(p. 103) *Right*: Coin, Rome, 48 B.C., Courtesy of the American Numismatic Society

(p. 108) A centurion's epitaph, Rome, 9 A.D., © akg-images

Chapter 62

(p. 114) Relief, Roman altar, first century B.C., Cameraphoto Arte, Venice/Art Resource, NY

(p. 119) Roman curse tablet, circa 150–275 A.D., © The British Museum and the Centre for the Study of Ancient Documents

(p. 121) Roman banquet, as depicted in a Pompeian fresco, Erich Lessing/Art Resource, NY

Chapter 63

(p. 127) Sarcophagus of Lucius Cornelius Scipio Barbatus, circa 200 B.C., Pirozzi/akg-images

(p. 129) Painting from a French manuscript, illuminated by Martin de Braga, Erich Lessing/Art Resource, NY

(p. 138) Fresco of warships, Pompeii, first century, A.D., © Scala/Art Resource, NY

(p. 142) The Appian Way, © Ron Palma

Chapter 64

(p. 143) Funerary stele of a gladiator, Ephesus, Turkey, 300–27 B.C., Erich Lessing/Art Resource, NY

(p. 145) Lithograph by Comeleran in José Coroleu's "Las supersticiones de la humanidad," 1891, © Mary Evans Picture Library/The Image Works

(p. 149) Senate House, Rome, © akg-images/Tristan Lafranchis

Chapter 65

(p. 153) Tomb relief, Virunum, akg-images/Bildarchiv Steffens

(p. 155) Tombstone of a Roman cavalryman, first century A.D., C.M. Dixon/Ancient Art & Architecture Collection Ltd.

(p. 157) Sarcophagus, Aquileia, Italy, © Alinari/Art Resource

(p. 158) Coin from the Roman Republic, Courtesy of the American Numismatic Society

Chapter 66

(p. 167) Bust, Marcus Tullius Cicero, first century B.C., Bildarchiv Preussischer Kulturbesitz/Art Resource, NY

(p. 168) Fresco, Naples, first century, A.D., © Erich Lessing/Art Resource, NY

(p. 169) Bust of Pompey, first half of first century B.C., Bildarchiv Preussischer Kulturbesitz/Art Resource, NY

Chapter 67

(p. 175) Roman relief, first to second century A.D., Scala/Art Resource, NY

(p. 177) Depiction of a Roman couple, circa 230 A.D., Erich Lessing/Art Resource, NY

Chapter 68

(p. 185) Outer Wall of the Hathor Temple, Egypt, 47–30 B.C., Erich Lessing/Art Resource, NY

(p. 187) Bust of Cleopatra, Bildarchiv Preussischer Kulturbesitz/Art Resource, NY

Chapter 69

(p. 188) Statue, Augustus, © Araldo de Luca

(p. 190) *Left:* The Ara Pacis, Scala/Art Resource, NY

(p. 190) *Right:* Goddess Pax from the Ara Pacis, © Frédéric-Auguste Bartholdi/AA World Travel/Topfoto/The Image Works

(p. 191) Marble bust, © Araldo De Luca

(p. 193) Portion of the *Res gestae*, © Ron Palma

(p. 195) Temple of Rome and Augustus in Ankara, Turkey, © Valery Shanin/iStockphoto

(p. 197) *Left:* Obverse of coin of Augustus, Courtesy of the American Numismatic Society

(p. 197) *Right:* Reverse of coin of Augustus, Courtesy of the American Numismatic Society

(p. 201) Coin depicting the shrine of Janus, Courtesy of the American Numismatic Society

(p. 203) *Right:* Obverse of coin showing Augustus, Courtesy of the American Numismatic Society

(p. 203) *Left:* Reverse of coin showing Gaius and Lucius, grandsons and adopted sons of Augustus, Courtesy of the American Numismatic Society

Chapter 70

(p. 205) Julia, daughter of Augustus, © Alinari Archives/The Image Works

(p. 213) Greek vase painting, 490–480 B.C., © Leemage / Universal Images Group Universal Images Group/Newscom

Chapter 72
(p. 218) Roman mosaic from Tunisia, early third century A.D., © Erich Lessing/Art Resource, NY

(p. 225) The Roman Vergil manuscript, from the *Aeneid*, fifth century A.D., The Print Collector/Alamy

(p. 231) Aeneas takes leave of Dido, c.1630 (oil on canvas), Guido Reni (1575–1642/ Gemäldegalerie Alte Meister, Kassel, Germany, © Museumslandschaft Hessen Kassel/ The Bridgeman Art Library International

(p. 233) Relief, circa 180 B.C., © Erich Lessing/Art Resource, NY

(p. 237) Painting of a scene from the *Aeneid*, DeAgostini / SuperStock

Chapter 73
(p. 245) Votive tablet, circa 100–200 A.D., HIP/Art Resource, NY

(p. 247) Mt. Soracte, Lazio, Italy, © Marco Scataglini

(p. 249) The remains of Horace's Sabine farm, © David Perry

(p. 255) *Mars and Rhea Silvia*, Peter Paul Rubens (1577–1640), akg-images

(p. 257) Painting of a lekythos, Peter Connolly (1936–), © akg-images/Peter Connolly

Chapter 74
(p. 263) Detail from a mosaic, Pompeii, first century B.C., Museo Archeologico Nazionale, Naples, Italy, Index/The Bridgeman Art Library International

(p. 269) Mosaic, second century A.D., © De Agostini/Getty Images

(p. 271) *Judgment of King Midas*, Jacopo da Empoli (1554–1640), Scala/Art Resource, NY

(p. 273) Minoan palace ruins, Gnossos, Crete, © SuperStock

(p. 275) Depiction of Daedalus making wings, from *Thesaurus Graecarum Antiquitatum*, Jakob Gronovius, 1645–1716, © Charles Walker/Topfoto/The Image Works

(p. 281) *Landscape with the Fall of Icarus*, Peter Brueghel the Elder (1525–1569), © Bridgeman Art Library, London/SuperStock

(p. 284) Relief from the tomb of Quintus Haterius Tychicus, © Araldo De Luca

(p. 286) Fresco of Roman banquet, Pompeii, © Erich Lessing/Art Resource, NY

Chapter 75
(p. 291) Tomb relief of the Publius Gessius family, Photograph © 2008 Museum of Fine Arts, Boston

Chapter 76
(p. 297) Italian umbrella pine, © Patrick Morand/iStockphoto

(p. 299) *The Eruption of Vesuvius*, Jean-Baptiste Genillion (1750–1829), Réunion des Musées Nationaux/Art Resource, NY

(p. 305) Excavation of Pompeii, © Werner Forman Archive/ Heritage Image Partnership Ltd/Alamy

LITERATURE AND POLITICS 100 B.C.–A.D. 100

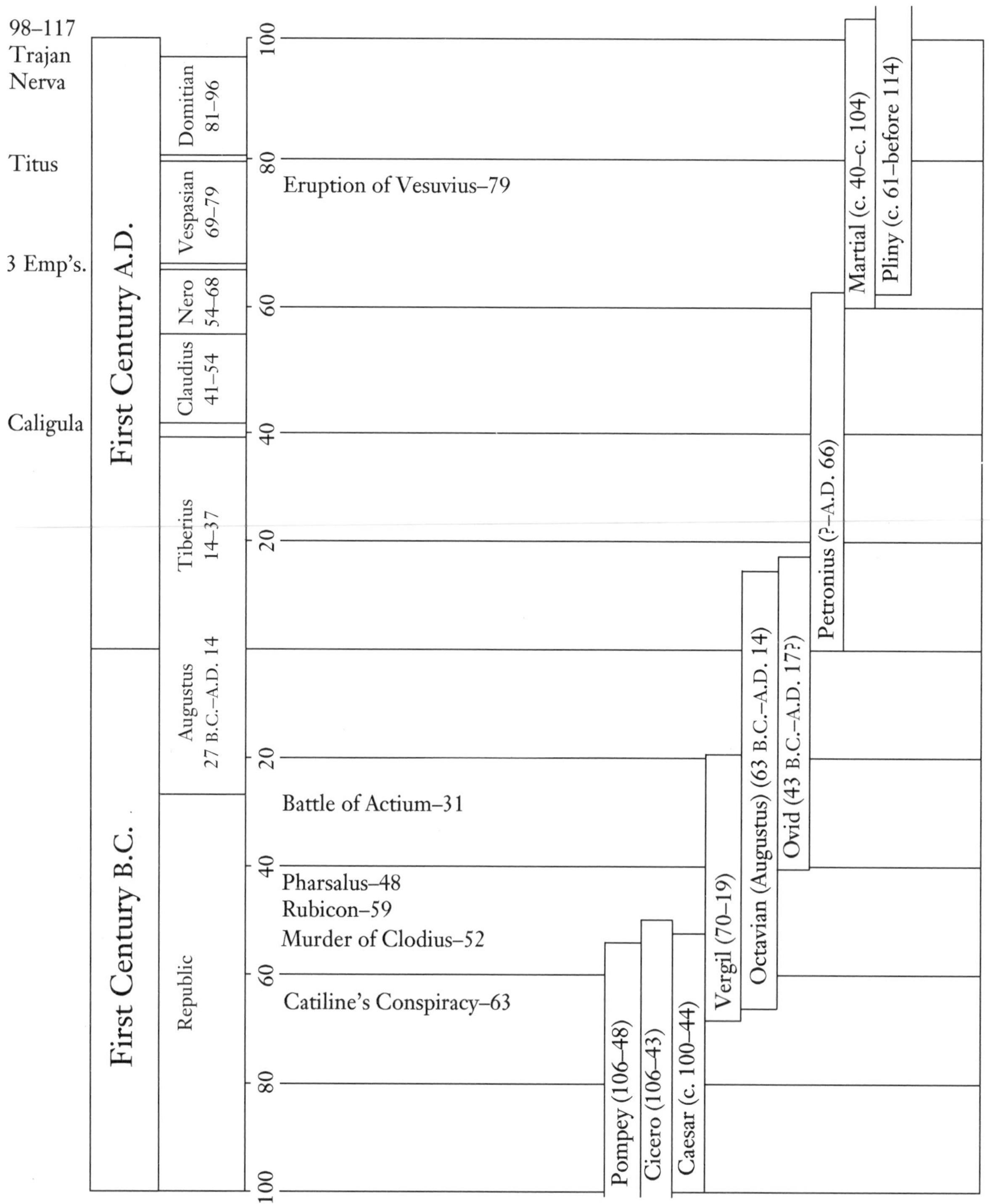

98–117
Trajan
Nerva
Titus
3 Emp's.
Caligula
First Century A.D.
First Century B.C.
Domitian 81–96
Vespasian 69–79
Nero 54–68
Claudius 41–54
Tiberius 14–37
Augustus 27 B.C.–A.D. 14
Republic
100
80
60
40
20
20
40
60
80
100
Eruption of Vesuvius–79
Battle of Actium–31
Pharsalus–48
Rubicon–59
Murder of Clodius–52
Catiline's Conspiracy–63
Martial (c. 40–c. 104)
Pliny (c. 61–before 114)
Petronius (?–A.D. 66)
Octavian (Augustus) (63 B.C.–A.D. 14)
Ovid (43 B.C.–A.D. 17?)
Vergil (70–19)
Pompey (106–48)
Cicero (106–43)
Caesar (c. 100–44)